A SYSTEMS APPROACH TO SMALL GROUP INTERACTION

A SYSTEMS APPROACH TO SMALL GROUP INTERACTION

THIRD EDITION

STEWART L. TUBBS

Dean, College of Business
Eastern Michigan University

McGraw-Hill, Inc.

New York St. Louis San Francisco Auckland Bogotá Caracas
Hamburg Lisbon London Madrid Mexico Milan Montreal
New Delhi Paris San Juan São Paulo Singapore Sydney
Tokyo Toronto

A SYSTEMS APPROACH TO
SMALL GROUP INTERACTION

Third Edition

468975

Library of Congress Cataloging-in-Publication Data

Tubbs, Stewart L., 1943—
    A systems approach to small group interaction.

    Bibliography: p.
    Includes index.
    1. Work groups.   2. Small groups.   3. Organizational
behavior.   I. Title.
HD66.T82   1987   302.3'4   87-23394
ISBN 0-07-555073-3

Cover Design— Lawrence R. Didona
Book Design— Glen M. Edelstein
Cover Photo Credit— Reginald Wickham

To the memory of
my father and mother

PREFACE

A Systems Approach to Small Group Interaction is written as a primary text for theory-based courses in group communication.

In preparing the third edition, I have retained the general systems approach of the earlier editions. This approach views the small group as an open system of simultaneously interacting forces. These forces include (1) relevant background factors of the group members, (2) the internal influences or group processes, and (3) the consequences of the interaction of these factors. This conceptual framework originally evolved out of my desire to organize and synthesize the small group literature for my own teaching. For this edition, new material has been added from over thirty sources, all of which have been published since the last edition of this book.

FEATURES

The book's format continues to be unique for a small group text.

Each chapter begins with a real-life case study that illustrates the principles discussed in the chapter. Three out of the seven cases are new for this edition.

Exercises designed for student involvement and skill development follow each chapter.

Two carefully selected reading selections follow the exercises section of each chapter. The readings elaborate on one or more of the topics discussed in the chapter. Half of all the reading selections are new for this edition.

PLAN OF THE BOOK

Chapter 1, entitled "What Is Small Group Interaction?" offers key definitions and reviews the classic models for analyzing small group behavior. It also explains the conceptual overview of the remainder of the book. New in this edition is extensive material on the use of groups as the mechanism for implementing modern management theory. There is also an expanded section on systems theory.

Chapter 2, "Relevant Background Factors," discusses six group member characteristics that influence groups. They are personality, sex, age, health, attitudes, and values. There is more material on FIRO-B, but less material on other personality theories. There is also a new case study in the exercises section.

Chapter 3, "Internal Influences: Group Circumstances and Structure," discusses the group's physical environment, group size and structure, and different types of groups. This edition has less material on encounter groups and new material on group size as it affects absenteeism.

Chapter 4, "Internal Influences: Leadership and Social Influence Processes," discusses status, power, leadership, group norms, and conformity pressures. This edition has less historical material on leadership and an expanded treatment of contingency theory as it applies to management.

Chapter 5, "Internal Influences: Communication Processes," discusses the unique aspects of communication in the small group setting. It covers language behavior, self-disclosure, and interaction roles. It has a reduced emphasis on psychological theories.

Chapter 6, "Internal Influences: Conflict Resolution and Decision-Making Processes," examines different methods of both problem-solving and conflict resolving. This edition has new material on creativity as well as on decision-making and conflict-resolution.

Chapter 7, "Consequences," is devoted to the outcomes of group activity. It covers solutions to problems, changes in interpersonal relations, improved information flow, increased risk taking, interpersonal growth, and organizational change. This edition has extensive new material on quality circles and on accomplishing organizational change.

Much of the new material shows the applications of group dynamics to business settings, thus strengthening the book's use for students interested in career applications.

INSTRUCTOR'S MANUAL

The Instructor's Manual that accompanies the text has sample syllabi, additional class exercises, suggested films, and multiple-choice test questions that cover each chapter. The goal is to make the book as usable as possible for the instructor.

ACKNOWLEDGMENTS

I would like to thank the reviewers whose valuable suggestions helped guide the revision. They are Robert A. Cocetti, Kearney State College; RoLayne S. DeStaphen, Sinclair College; Gene D. Fowler, University of Colorado; and John W. Wilson, Jr., Corpus Christi State University.

Finally, I would like to especially thank my friend, colleague, and former student, Mrs. Jody Judkins, who served as research assistant on the book. Her valuable contributions will be obvious as you read on.

S.L.T.
Ann Arbor, Michigan

CONTENTS

6   Internal Influences
Conflict Resolution and Decision-Making Processes   257

7   Consequences   324

What Is Small Group Interaction?

CASE STUDY

As always, there is some distance between press releases and reality, and the U.S. Big 3 have the easy part out of the way: They've bombarded the public with rhetoric about their programs to drastically cut manufacturing costs: Saturn at General Motors Corp., Alpha at Ford Motor Co. and Liberty at Chrysler Corp. Now they have to make something.

Exactly what they will make and how they will build and sell it becomes increasingly murky as the weeks roll past and the flamboyant use of the phrase "high-tech" loses some of its sheen. But the target hasn't moved: They still are shooting at a bullseye marked $2,000—the bucks they hope to shave from costs of each car produced domestically to match foreign competitors. What's learned in the process, of course, will spread to their entire vehicle operations to bolster productivity, quality and efficiency.

Surrounding the public-relations assault, with GM leading the charge and expending the most ammo, has been the idea that each is well on the road to fundamentally rethinking and redesigning how to make cars and trucks.

Saturn is clearly the biggest gamble among the three automakers' projects: It alone is a specific, independently measurable entity because it's organized as a GM subsidiary that aims to market a specific car line. What's learned from Saturn Corp. already is filtering throughout GM, but capitalized at $5 billion, Saturn is no penny-ante escapade. Alpha and Liberty in comparison have more to do with ideas than readily identifiable hardware. Neither's project budget is revealed, but it's certain they pale next to Saturn's outlays.

Beginning in early 1984, GM loudly trumpeted Saturn as a grand-scale attempt to build a new, domestic, entry-level small car at a 500,000-unit yearly pace to fight low-cost imports. It soon became clear, however, that Saturn would move upscale where the profits lie. That didn't stop the hype, though, as GM trotted out a Saturn concept car repeatedly for photo "opportunities" (President Reagan was among several famous drivers) and otherwise ballyhooed the project.

And the search for a site to build the car indisputedly became the most publicized plant-location reconnoitering in American history. But in recent months GM is a blabbermouth struck dumb where its Saturn project is concerned.

Saturn's top people aren't saying boo—and won't, says a spokesperson, for at least eight months. There are too many other things to do, she says, suggesting that action now speaks louder than words.

What is known is that Saturn President Richard C. LaFauve broke ground in early April for Saturn's massive new manufacturing complex at Spring Hill, TN, and has begun ordering tooling for what is billed as an eventual investment of more than $3.5 billion at that location; the remaining $1.5 billion goes to development and other costs. Saturn expects to build cars by 1989.

The GM subsidiary now has 550 full-time employes, 200 data-processing experts from GM-owned Electronic Data Systems Corp. and 200 contract employes. Only what is described as a "skeleton staff" is stationed in Tennessee, with remaining personnel assigned to Saturn headquarters in Troy, MI, or the nearby GM Technical Center in Warren, MI.

Interestingly . . . talk at GM has shifted from emphasizing the level of high technology going into the Saturn project and toward more efficient use of people. "People programs will be the real legacy of Saturn," a source says in talking of intensive employe training.

Chrysler Chairman Lee A. Iacocca barked at one point about Saturn: "I don't think WWII got as much ink." The change since then is like night and day: GM declines to give many hints about what the car will look like (offering no comment on reports of styling changes in the works) or how it will be marketed.

GM initially said Saturn cars would be sold through an entirely independent dealer organization in free-standing showrooms, but word on the street in Detroit has even that plan under re-evaluation.

Even such basic questions as where Saturn will fit in the market are left hanging. At one time, GM targeted the $6,000 range (1984 dollars), but now the sticker seems headed upward, and the car may well replace GM's current J-body subcompacts. Analysts doubt GM will duke it out with a domestic Saturn line against the growing tide of South Korean, Taiwanese and Eastern European imports, let alone the Japanese. Besides, GM already is covered well at the lower end with three Japanese-derived lines and another coming from South Korea during the '87 model year.

What largely has gotten lost in the tidal wave of press coverage of the Big 3's advanced projects is that the issue is not so much the cars as it is the way they're manufactured and distributed.

John A. Manoogian, formerly Ford's leading quality executive, was named in May as general manager-advanced manufacturing and engineering with Alpha under his wing. President Harold A. Poling points up Alpha's mission: "The objective of Alpha is to make Ford North American-built cars, particularly small cars, fully competitive with the best in the world. Every aspect of company operations, including design, engineering, manufacturing, component purchasing, marketing, distribution and business systems, is being reexamined through Alpha."

Mr. Manoogian, who turns 65 in August, has delayed his retirement—after 46 years at Ford starting as an apprentice draftsman—because "it's a helluva challenge; I couldn't resist," he says.

The challenge at Ford as well as at GM and Chrysler seems, when the razzle-dazzle is baked out, to involve process more than product. The marketplace, current wisdom suggests, will dictate what customers want. How to deliver that vehicle profitably is the focus of the effort.

"As each decision point comes up, we're going to have to look at all alternatives," says Mr. Manoogian. "Obviously, if we're successful, we'll retain more small car business (in North America)."

Unlike Saturn, Alpha at this point encompasses no solid commitment to open a specific plant or produce a specific car to demonstrate a new manufacturing approach.

But if he had to select a model through which most Alpha elements may fall into place, Mr. Manoogian says it likely will be the replacements for compact Tempo/Topaz lines in the early '90s. "I think that represents the largest opportunities," he says. Ford has "cut the umbilical" on cars smaller than that: Rather than develop them on its own, it will import or build domestically models developed by its Mazda Motor Corp. affiliate. Ford is also known to be weighing a Mazda derivative for its compact replacements, which suggests its success in keeping that-size car under its own umbrella lies with Alpha and Mr. Manoogian.

Given Alpha's present scope, that's a tall order. Mr. Manoogian has only 45 full-time people, most of them corporate staff-level personnel. "We need a lot of cooperation from operating people," he acknowledges. "Historically, we do advanced work in a vacuum without operating people and then it was always changed . . . We're asking how we should build prototypes: Can we get prototype vehicles without needing all the parts off production tooling? Can we reduce product development time by minimizing production changes?"

Like Saturn, Alpha's chief goal is to narrow Ford's development and manufacturing costs to compete more effectively in all of its car and truck operations. One way to do that is to enhance flexibility. "Quality is always the No. 1 target, but we've got to build in flexible machinery to meet changing market demands instead of taking months, for example, to convert from 4's to 6's (engines)," says Mr. Manoogian.

. Chrysler is covering similar turf. Chrysler Vice President-Advance Product Development Erick A. Reickert says there's more hard work than mystery involved in what his company is doing.

His group was established in February to work on new products for 1990 and beyond, and it carries Liberty and a related project, Genesis, under its banner. Although not a separate entity like Saturn, the project is based in "Liberty Center" located near the Pontiac, MI, Silverdome; 300 staffers are stationed there. Liberty dovetails its activities with Chrysler central engineering in Highland Park, MI, and with the automaker's Outer Drive Manufacturing Technical Center in Detroit, "which has day-to-day experience launching plants," Mr. Reickert explains.

"We are trying a separate-company approach to apply all of our brainpower to address specifics at hand not encumbered by existing ways of doing things," he says. Liberty includes a broad cross-section of disciplines: procurement, finance, planning, product engineering, manufacturing engineering and design.

Although Liberty Center isn't working on a designated model per se, "we will be getting into specific car and truck programs," he says. Liberty will focus on "process-driven technology far upstream from the manufacturing processes. Vehicle design will be driven by manufacturing objectives not just styling."

A running subcompact concept car, dubbed Liberty, was built and unveiled a year ago strictly to try out some ideas and give engineers a "real-world" feel for them, he says. Chrysler has no plans to make that car, but much of Liberty's input could well coalesce in a '92 Chrysler model.

That may well also include results from Genesis, which represents Chrysler's push to develop plastic composites. "We're exploring a variety of concepts on how to use this technology, some of them radical," says Mr. Reickert. He concedes Chrysler lags behind in this flourishing new technology. "But we intend to leapfrog our competitors," he declares. An all-plastic body, he adds, "could be" in the works.

Chrysler, like the Big 2, is keeping a few hole cards off the table. The best-case scenario is that these projects enable American car companies to build cars with American parts from the ground up. Liberty Center, says Mr. Reickert, "in general is aimed at domestic production. However, we've got a worldwide procurement effort. Obviously, the good results of that effort will be fed into our cars. We are using sourcing as one of the arrows in our attack (on costs). It's part of our overall effort—cost, quality, and technology."

But key to the Chrysler program is making sure the dive into new technology doesn't become a loose bomb on the plant floor. "We're trying to get Liberty Center upstream so we can consider new equipment with sufficient time so it will work when we get it into the production line," Mr. Reickert says. "We want to make sure factory-of-the-future ideas are tested far in advance."

Mr. Reickert says Liberty eyes a 30% cut in Chrysler production costs, even as Japan's yen moves higher to narrow imports' cost advantage. But it's not that simple to do. "We never expected to get the full amount in one year," he explains.

The worshiped bottom line seems a little out of focus at this point as the U.S. Big 3 face the brave, new, international auto world. Whether projects like Saturn, Alpha and Liberty will produce vehicles made from the ground up in the U.S. or screw together pieces shipped in from around the world becomes a valid question that no one wants to answer right now.

And it's an issue that only people can resolve. Technology can help get you there faster, but somebody has to decide where you're going.

1. What is the most important point of the case study as it relates to the topic of this book?
2. How are these three auto companies typical of many American companies today?

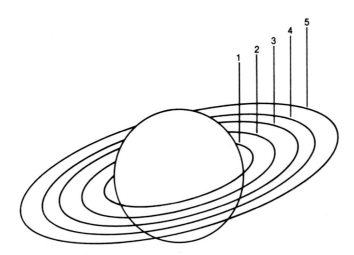

S aturn Corporation, a wholly owned subsidiary of General Motors, was created with a radical new organizational structure which uses teams as the basic supervisory unit. In fact, the name Saturn was chosen to reflect the concentric rings of decision-making groups that run the organization. Tichy and Devanna (1986) describe the various levels of group activity represented by the "rings of Saturn" compared to the traditional role of an individual manager at that level (p. 231):

Traditional GM Plant	The Saturn Plant
Plant Manager	1. Strategic advisory committee. Does long-term planning. Consists of Saturn president and his staff, plus top UAW advisor.
Production Manager	2. Manufacturing advisory comittee. Oversees Saturn Complex. Includes company and elected union representatives, plus specialists in engineering, marketing, and so on.

General Superintendent	3. Business unit. Coordinates plant-level operations. Made up of company representatives and elected union advisor, plus specialists.
Production Superintendent (5 per shift)	4. Work unit module. Groups of three to six work units led by a company "work unit advisor."
General Supervisor (15 per shift)	5. Work units. Teams of 6 to 15 workers led by an elected UAW counselor.
Supervisor/foreman (90 per shift)	

As the opening case study shows, General Motors is not the only company to use new manufacturing procedures. Smith (1985) cites the "Team Taurus" concept at Ford Motor Company in which groups or teams were responsible for bringing out the Ford Taurus and the Mercury Sable, two extremely successful new car lines. He writes: "Some 15,000 workers enrolled in employee-involvement programs are involved in Taurus/Sable. If ten years ago they heard of our repair-rate targets, they would have laughed. Back then, 10 or 15 of every 100 cars built were diverted after assembly for repair. We've cut that back to five, two, and one." (p. 33)

The GM and Ford examples are but two of many that illustrate the important way in which groups are becoming an inherent part of a very different way of managing modern organizations. Bradford and Cohen (1984) have argued persuasively in their best-selling book, *Managing for Excellence,* that the Manager as Hero style which worked well in the past has given way to the Manager as Developer, which is the style for today and for the future. They identify four myths of the heroic management style:

1. The good manager knows at all times what is going on in the department;

2. The good manager should have more technical expertise than any subordinate;

3. The good manager should be able to solve any problem that comes up (or at least solve it before the subordinate can);

4. The good manager should be the primary (if not the only) person responsible for how the department is working. (pp. 10–11)

They go on to say that:

> The solution that worked yesterday is only slightly appropriate today and will be irrelevant tomorrow. Task complexity virtually assures that no one person can have all the necessary knowledge which forces a heightened degree of interdependence among subordinates (and a much greater demand for coordination) if work is to be

successfully accomplished, especially at an excellent level. . . . Heroism may be motivating for the superior but it has the opposite effect on subordinates. . . . Today there are far more subordinates who want to be challenged by work; they place "challenging jobs" and "a chance to grow and develop" ahead of such rewards as pay, status, and job security." (pp. 12, 15)

In this book we will explore the working mechanism of the Manager as Developer—namely, the small group.

See the article by Bradford and Cohen at the end of this chapter.

The effective use of small groups has been found to be essential to management success. After extensive examination of management theory and research, Whetton and Cameron (1984) have identified what they consider nine of the most important skills required for successful management. They are:

> (1) Development of Self Awareness; (2) Managing Personal Stress; (3) Solving Problems Creatively; (4) Establishing Supportive Communication; (5) Gaining Power and Influence; (6) Improving Employee Performance Through Motivation; (7) Delegating and Decision Making; (8) Managing Conflict; and (9) Conducting Effective Group Meetings. (p. 6)

Of the nine, only the second (managing personal stress) is not part of the material covered in this book. In other words, the material in this book is devoted to improving your understanding of the major action skills required for successful management. The important thing to remember, however, is that we are talking about behavioral *skills,* not just knowledge about those skills. Like all skills, development begins with new information and proceeds with practice, practice, and more practice, with continual modification based on feedback from previous performance.

Just in case you are wondering how typical the idea of group decision making is, Goldhaber (1974, p. 214) states:

> Tillman (1960) found that 94 percent of organizations with more than 10,000 employees had formal committees. Kriesberg (1950) reported that executives typically spend an average of 10 hours per week in formal committee meetings. My own research at the University of New Mexico (Goldhaber 1971) showed that the average tenured faculty member served on one college committee, two to three departmental committees, one university standing committee and two to three sub-committees *simultaneously* (in addition to attending departmental, college, and university faculty meetings). The number of hours per week spent in committees and other regularly scheduled meetings (by tenured faculty) was 11. When nonscheduled and informal meetings are added on, it is easy to understand why faculty members reported that they were "tired" of all the committee assignments. One faculty member reported that he barely had time left to prepare for his classes.

Harold Geneen, former chairman of the board of the giant conglomerate ITT, describes the extreme importance meetings had in his company:

> Our normal General Managers meetings ran from ten in the morning to ten at night. In Europe, they often went on past midnight because we could only spend a limited number of days there. . . . Now if you add up the days and weeks spent in those meetings, you will find that we spend three weeks in February and March on our preliminary, rough business plans and budgets for the coming year, and then twelve weeks at the end of the year reviewing and agreeing on those plans. That's fifteen weeks. One General Managers Meeting in Brussels and one in New York, a week each, ten months of the year, and you add another twenty weeks. That's thirty-five weeks of time. (Geneen, 1984, p. 101)

A survey made by Executive Standards, a management consulting firm, and reported by Connecticut General Life Insurance Company (1975) showed that the average executive spends almost 700 hours a year in meetings. That averages out to almost two out of every five working days that are totally consumed in meetings. One Ford Motor Company division improved its meetings by requiring committee members to report in writing to the division general manager any meeting lasting over one hour. In addition, each member was encouraged to indicate whether he or she thought the meeting was worth the time involved. This plan resulted in shorter meetings, better agendas, and an increased sense of responsibility on the part of the committee chairperson.

On the other hand, while meetings may be time-consuming, the potential strength of the group seems to have been borne out by the recent innovations at Trans World Airlines and Sears, Roebuck. In one week, both giant corporations drastically altered their top management structure by eliminating the corporate chief executive's position for one person and replacing it with the so-called office of the chairman. This position is shared by a group of between three and five top corporate officials. This form of team top management has been used for some time by other firms such as General Electric, ITT, Morgan Guaranty Trust Co., Honeywell, Armco Steel, and Associated Dry Goods (*Time* 1976).

The system appears to offer several advantages. It allows for greater continuity in leadership as older executives retire and are replaced one at a time. Greater flexibility is allowed, since the company's top executives can be in more than one place at a time. Finally, company officials tend to become less inhibited in pushing

FRANK AND ERNEST by Bob Thaves

SINCE WE JUST INVENTED MEETINGS, I ASSUME THERE ISN'T ANY OLD BUSINESS. . . .

THAVES 9-16

Reprinted by permission. © 1980 NEA. Inc.

BERRY'S WORLD

"*Let's not get into anything too heavy today. I'm suffering from interpersonal overload!*"

Reprinted by permission. © 1979 NEA, Inc.

for important innovations. (See Chapter 7 for a discussion of the risky-shift phenomenon in groups.)

The extensive use of committees is by no means limited to the United States. Moseley (1974) writes that the Russians have begun to use committees extensively (from the Communist party central committee on down). He states: "A survey of 1,235 heads of large Soviet industrial enterprises showed that many of them spend much of their day in conference. It said the director, chief engineer, and other officials of one plant in the Ukraine hold an average of 71 conferences a month" (better than two a day).

Because discussions and meetings are so prevalent in all aspects of society, it seems well worth the effort to learn more effective ways of interacting in small groups. Several studies by Burke and Bennis (1961), Larson and Gratz (1970), Mosvick (1971), and Weaver (1971) have shown that courses in small group interaction do bring about higher levels of personal competence in small group methods. After reading this book, you should be able to get more out of your small group experiences than you did in the past. However, no one can improve communication skills simply by reading a book. At the end of each chapter you will find a number of small group activities that should help you gain experience as well as intellectual growth.

A DEFINITION

Just what is meant by the term *small group interaction?* This question is more complicated than you might think. For one thing, what is a group? Shaw (1976) has proposed six different ways in which we can identify a group. They are (1) in terms of perceptions (do members make an impression on others?), (2) in terms of motivation (is the group membership rewarding?), (3) in terms of goals (working together for a purpose), (4) in terms of organization (each person has some organized role to play—such as moderator, note taker, etc.), (5) in terms of interdependence (each person is somewhat dependent on the others), and (6) in terms of *interaction* (the group is small enough to allow face-to-face communication among members). To summarize, a *group* is a collection of individuals who influence one another, derive some satisfaction from maintaining membership in the group, interact for some purpose, assume specialized roles, are dependent on one another, and communicate face to face.

Shaw (1976) states that small group communication can be considered virtually synonymous with interaction. Other authors have taken a similar position. Thibaut and Kelley (1986, p. 10) put it this way:

> The essence of any interpersonal relationship is interaction. . . . By interaction it is meant that they emit behavior in each other's presence, they create products for each other, or they communicate with each other.

Berelson and Steiner (1964, p. 326) go into a bit more detail when they write that *interaction*

> is a generic term for the exchange . . . between people. Usually interaction is direct communication—mainly talking and listening—but it can also include gestures, glances, nods or shakes of the head, pats on the back, frowns, caresses or slaps, and any other way in which meanings can be transmitted from one person to another and back again . . . "interaction" refers to communication in its broadest sense.

If we employ the term *group* as defined above, small group interaction may be defined as *the process by which three or more members of a group exchange verbal and nonverbal messages in an attempt to influence one another.* This definition incorporates the views of Thibaut and Kelley (1986), Berelson and Steiner (1964), and Shaw (1976), among others.

CONCEPTUAL ORIENTATIONS

Small group interaction is very complicated and involves a large number of factors that act and interact simultaneously. In addition, these factors are in a continual state of flux. Think of the difficulty of trying to describe and analyze all the behaviors that occur at just one party! We have all been to parties that generate far more reactions than we would have thought. One entire book (Pettinger 1964) was devoted to the *first five minutes* of interaction in one communication situation. This prompted one friend to speculate that, at that rate, a *one-hour* discussion would require a 12-volume series! The point is that any attempt to provide a conceptual orientation for small group interaction or any social process must be highly simplified.

Mills's Models

Mills (1967) identified six models for studying and analyzing small groups. They are (1) the quasi-mechanical model, (2) the organismic model, (3) the conflict model, (4) the equilibrium model, (5) the structural-functional model, and (6) the cybernetic-growth model. Each of these models offers a different perspective from which to view small group processes. Each model is based upon certain assumptions that affect the questions we ask about group behavior, as well as the answers we are likely to obtain.

The *quasi-mechanical model* assumes that a group is like a machine. All behavioral acts in a group are seen as functions that can be categorized. Each functional act (e.g., a question) calls for a reaction (e.g., an answer). All actions and reactions are quantifiable and may be added, subtracted, multiplied, or divided in such a way to represent the dynamics of the group mathematically. Bales's (1950, 1970) work, as described in Chapter 4, is an example of such an approach. Group behavior is considered to follow universal and unchanging laws. This model also assumes that people are merely interchangeable parts in the system, and that all problem-solving groups will exhibit many of the same behaviors. Mills (1967) criticizes the quasi-mechanical model for not telling us much about group discussion and for not being very relevant in its application.

The *organismic model* assumes that groups are like biological organisms. That is, they have a period of formation (birth), a life cycle, and eventually a death. Different people in the group become differentiated in their behaviors (e.g., task leader, recorder, social leader) just as bodily systems carry on different functions (e.g., digestive, respiratory, muscular). The emphasis is upon the group's *natural* evolution and development. Thus natural, ongoing, real-life groups are more often the object of study than artificial, zero-history groups created for the purpose of a laboratory study.

The *conflict model* assumes that the small group is a context for an endless series of conflicts. All members of groups have to face the conflict of being truly independent versus conforming to some extent to the group norms and expectations. Also, since there are many groups to affiliate with, individuals feel conflict in deciding which group to join. The person with several bids from fraternities is a classic example—the choice is difficult to make. Within the group, differences of opinion are a continual source of potential conflict. Conflicts arise between groups as well. Mills (1967) argues that this model is too limited in that it tends to overlook all the socially binding (cohesive) factors in favor of the socially divisive factors. It is too one-sided.

The *equilibrium model* assumes that groups and group members have a need to maintain some sort of balance or equilibrium—for example, that conflicts between group members tend to be followed by attempts to smooth over hard feelings and return to a state of interpersonal harmony. Several equilibrium models have been developed. The first was Heider's balance theory, which is described in Chapter 2.

Although the equilibrium models give us insight on a relatively simple level of analysis, when all the important elements are considered, the model is too limited to be able to explain much. For example, if I have an attitude toward a friend (positive) and he says something I don't like (negative), I can resolve this by agreeing with him or disliking him. But what if I forgive his comment, even though I still disagree with him on that issue, and continue to like him and agree with him on lots of other issues?

The *structural-functional model* assumes that the group is a goal-seeking system that is constantly adapting to meet new demands. It assumes that goal attainment is the primary source of satisfaction to its members. It also assumes that some members will take on the function of keeping the group functioning. These so-called group-maintenance functions serve to keep interpersonal relations from breaking down so that the group ceases to function. The model is one of the better ones available because it includes the role of learning, by which groups survive by adapting to the demand for new behaviors.

The *cybernetic-growth model* shifts the emphasis from group survival to group growth. This model assumes the existence of agents that help the group adapt to new information (or feedback). Thus growth and development are attained by the group's responding to feedback from its earlier performance. Three types of feedback, (1) goal seeking, (2) group restructuring, and (3) self-awareness, are required to help the group grow and develop. Mills (1967, p. 20) uses the example of the quarterback of a football team to illustrate the three types of feedback:

> He reads the weakness in other teams' defenses and tries to capitalize on them (goal seeking); due to unforeseen circumstances, he may have to revise the pre-game strategy, trying out one modification after the other (internal re-arrangement); and on each play he assesses the developing weaknesses or strengths in his team, and, in general, the present state and condition of his team (consciousness). Since he can act on his ideas—observe the effects of his action and therefore test them—he is in a position to learn to direct his team. Through self-monitoring, self-steering, and testing these processes, he is able to increase his capabilities for self-determination.

Mills argues convincingly that this model is strong in that it helps us identify the important factors or variables that lead to growth on the part of the group as well as on the part of the individual members. A partial list of potential end results of group growth for individual members includes the following (Mills 1967, p. 22):

Indicators of a Person's Capacity to Grow

1. *Adaptation*

   a. Receptivity to a wider range of information about himself, others, his groups, his and other societies, and the physical environment

   b. Receptivity to new freedoms, responsibilities, and obligations—to new roles

   c. Flexibility in modifying his ideas, beliefs, personal norms, and emotional attachments without loss of intellectual or moral integrity

2. *Goal-attainment*

   a. Capacity to postpone immediate gratification, and to conceive of and evaluate an increasing number of avenues for gratification

   b. Capacity to decommit himself from one goal, and to recommit himself to new and additional goals, and to learn how to attain them

3. *Integration*

   a. Capacity to perform in an expanded repertoire of roles and variety of social relations without suffering diffusion of his identity

4. *Pattern-maintenance and extension*

   a. Capacity for deeper emotional involvement with others without surrendering his self

   b. Increasing ability to convey his experience, learning, and capabilities to others

THE SYSTEMS PERSPECTIVE

Although the six models described here have a number of worthwhile characteristics, a seventh model that synthesizes elements of the first six seems to be even more appropriate for conceptualizing small group interaction. The remainder of this book is organized around the idea that small group interaction can most adequately be thought of as occurring in a system of interdependent forces, each of which can be analyzed and set in the perspective of other forces. This idea represents a so-called general systems theory of thinking about small groups.

The general systems theory originated with Ludwig Von Bertelanffy, a theoretical biologist, as a way to think about and study the constant, dynamic adjustments of living phenomena. An open system such as a group is defined as an organized set of interrelated and interacting parts that attempts to maintain its own balance amid the influences from its surrounding environment. Seiler (1967, p. 4) describes the systems method of analysis as emphasizing "the notions of multiple causation and the complex interrelation of forces." In other words, it is a way of thinking about behavior that avoids the idea that complex behaviors in groups result from a single cause.

According to most strategic management literature, an organization is an open system that exists within an environment. The objective environment may be accurately or inaccurately perceived, but in either case the task of strategic managers is to maintain congruence between environmental constraints and organizational needs (Tosi *et al.* 1986). Camp et al. (1986) also argue that the open systems model is the best way to "sort out the various factors . . . in organizations" (p. 10).

With this in mind, let us turn to a general systems model of small group interaction that should help clarify some of these conceptual problems. The model (Figure 1.1) is meant to suggest the relationships among a number of the variables frequently discussed in the small group literature.

FIGURE 1.1   THE TUBBS MODEL OF SMALL GROUP INTERACTION.

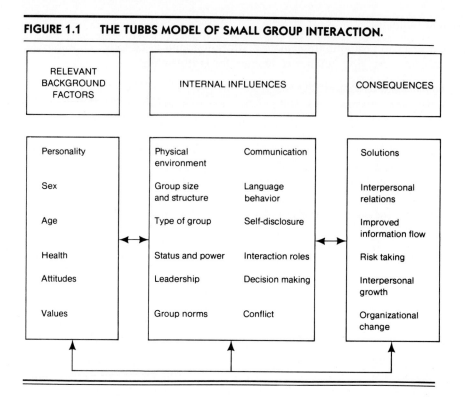

Because Chapters 2 through 7 discuss the elements in the model in greater detail, the analysis at this point will be relatively brief. The model identifies three categories of variables. First, *relevant background factors* refers to attributes within the individual participants that existed prior to the group's formation and that will endure in some modified form after the group no longer exists. These background factors, such as personality, attitudes, and values, influence the group's functioning: in turn, the group process modifies the background factors.

The second set of variables in the model is referred to as *internal influences*. These influences include (among others) the type of group, the style of leadership used, and the language behavior, interaction roles, and decision style employed by the group. Each of these factors may be varied to change the nature and functioning of the group.

The third set of variables in the systems model is the *consequences* of small group interaction. Consequences will obviously vary with the background of the participants, as well as with the nature of the internal influences. Consequences may include solutions to problems, interpersonal relations among group members, the amount and quality of information sharing, the level of risk taking, the amount of interpersonal growth of participants, and possibly the amount of change in any larger organization of which the group may be a part. The consequences are the outputs of the group's activities. They are the raison d'être of a group, the reason the group is formed in the first place.

Finally, as suggested by the open systems model, the consequences or outputs of the group are fed back into the system through the feedback loop. Katz and Kahn (1978, p. 17) describe an open system this way: "Activities can be examined in relation to the *energic input* into the system, the *transformation of energies within the system,* and the *resulting product or energic output."* (Italics added.) They also say (p. 16) that "our theoretical model for the understanding of [social] organizations is that of an input-output system in which the energic return from the output reactivates the system."

Let's look at it in less theoretical terms. A highly successful baseball team develops a renewed sense of energy from having a winning season. This energy is reinvested in the team by new attitudes of becoming even more successful, admiring each other more, and so forth. This new energy and motivation level may allow team members to enjoy a higher level of status, a new and more democratic style of leadership, and a more luxurious physical environment within which to work or live. This entire process of multiple causation is indicated by the two-headed arrows in the model (Figure 1.1). Keep in mind that the model appears to be static, like a photograph. But in reality, small group behaviors should be modeled by a movie with each of the parts *moving* in relation to the others.

Different levels of systems analysis and the type of system studied include:

- Astronomy—universal systems

- Ecology—planetary systems

- Political science—political systems

- Sociology—social systems

- Psychology—human systems

- Physiology—organ systems

- Molecular biology—microscopic systems

General systems theory has been applied to many different fields of study, including biology, engineering, mathematics, and psychiatry. Systems analysis has become a particularly popular way of analyzing human behavior in organizations and has been written about in several sources (Katz and Kahn 1978; Seiler 1967; Kast and Rosenzweig 1970; Huse and Bowditch 1973). Communication scholars have paid relatively little attention to the application of systems theory to the communication field. Ruben (1972, p. 135) states: "Of the growing number of basic human communication books, I am familiar with only two, *Communication and Communication Systems* [Thayer 1968] and *Pragmatics of Human Communication* [Watzlawick *et al.* 1967] which utilize an integrated system framework as an approach to human communication." In addition to these, a third book now applies systems theory concepts to human communication (Ruben and Kim 1975). However, no other book currently available applies a systems theory analysis to small group communication.

With some of this background in mind, let us look briefly at ten general systems concepts that apply to small group communication and are suggested by our general systems model (Katz and Kahn, 1978, pp. 23–30).

INPUT   Input refers to the raw material of small group interaction. It includes all six of the relevant background factors depicted in the model. It also includes information the group receives from outside the group. For example, problem-solving group members in the midst of a discussion may notice that they are running short on time. This new information will probably influence the group to change procedures (e.g., stop talking about side issues) and focus more directly or efficiently on solving the problem at hand.

A system that has inputs from outside is called an *open system.* An open system is said to interact with its environment, in contrast to remaining isolated. Gross (1964, p. 113) identifies four phenomena characteristic of open systems:

1. Entries and exits, which transform outsiders into members and members into outsiders.

2. Multiple membership, which results in members' loyalties to outside groups.

3. Resource exchange, which involves the absorption of inputs in the production process and in the delivery of output produced.

4. Mutual or reciprocal influence on the part of both members and outsiders.

Anyone who has ever felt torn between two different groups will be able to understand the relevance of Gross's four points.

THROUGHPUT   Throughput refers to the internal influences depicted in our model. It means all of the actual verbal and nonverbal behaviors that occur in the course of a group discussion. It includes the process of creating and modifying ideas in the course of a discussion. Throughput is the heart and in some cases the entirety of what most small group communication books discuss. Chapters 3 through 6 will discuss these variables in detail.

OUTPUT   Output is referred to in the consequences section of our model. These are sometimes called the end results of group interaction. However, as we shall soon see, end results imply a beginning and an end, which is somewhat misleading, because groups often have an ongoing life history during which these outputs or consequences are continually being modified on the basis of continuing interaction. Chapter 7 is devoted to discussing the consequences or outputs of small group interaction.

CYCLES   Often the outputs of group interaction are fed back to the group and become inputs for future interactions. For example, a severe personality conflict in

one meeting (of a group) may reduce the level of cohesiveness or interpersonal closeness of group members. As a result some members may refuse to attend future meetings, some may attend but will not participate as openly, or some may try harder the
next time to be more diplomatic in their remarks in order to avoid a recurrence of
the conflict. The arrows at the bottom of our model (Figure 1.1) indicate what is
commonly called a feedback loop. This loop represents the cyclical and ongoing
nature of group processes and also implies that the process does not begin and end
anew with each group meeting, but rather builds on all the past experiences of each
group member.

NEGATIVE ENTROPY   The entropic process is a universal law of nature in which all
systems eventually move toward disorganization or death. Recently, we have seen the
entropic process overtake Frontier Airlines, several hundred banks, Osborn Comput-
ers, Addressograph-Multigraph, and many others. To combat the process of disorganization and/or death, a system must employ negative entropy. If you have ever been
in a meeting that seemed to be completely out of control and was a total waste of
time, you know how easily entropy can overtake a group.

FEEDBACK   All systems must receive feedback to modify themselves. Think of a
bowling game in which you saw the ball go down the lane and through a black cover
and you never saw which pins you hit and never heard the sound of the ball striking
the pins. You would never play a second game. Or imagine going to school year after
year and never getting an assignment back and never getting any grades or comments
from an instructor. We all want feedback on our performance. In a rather funny
example of feedback modifying a group's behavior, the City Council of Boise, Idaho,
decided to change its meetings from Monday night to Tuesday night because of Monday night football. The council had been meeting on Monday nights since 1929.
However, since the public turnout was so poor, the council decided to modify its
meeting time in response to the feedback that the televised football games were just
too much competition (Popkey, 1986).

DYNAMIC EQUILIBRIUM   Management and labor have reached an unspoken agreement in virtually every organization of what constitutes "a fair day's work for a fair
day's pay." This is an example of an equilibrium. Similarly, students and teachers
often negotiate throughout the course of a term. However, should students fail to
read their assignments, teachers will often react by throwing "pop" quizzes, thus
upsetting the equilibrium. Once the students change their performance, equilibrium
returns. Similarly, when an organization finds itself losing market share or profit mar-
gins, it often has to upset the fair day's work for a fair day's pay equilibrium. In 1985
General Motors decided to eliminate the Cost of Living Allowance (COLA) for its
salaried workers. This seemed to change the "fair day's pay" side of the equation.
Salaried employees decided not to work so hard, thus restoring their feeling of equilibrium. In groups, we each decide if membership is worth what we are putting into

it. If not, we slack off and may even eventually quit the group to find one that more nearly meets our sense of equilibrium.

DIFFERENTIATION   Ever since the Industrial Revolution began, organizations have become increasingly more specialized. It is no longer adequate to have generalists; organizations must now have specialists in production, inspection, materials handling, transportation, legal affairs, accounting, payroll, sales, engineering, plant layout, maintenance, management information systems, distribution, service, real estate, finance, public relations, and labor relations, for example. In groups we also see different people gravitating toward certain roles. In addition, it is a rare group in which each member's attitudes are the same toward any topic.

INTEGRATION   As groups and organizations become more complex and differentiated, the need for integration and coordination of the various parts increases. Without integration, the group or organization becomes chaotic. Imagine being in a hospital in which the lab results or X rays couldn't be communicated to the physician for interpretation, or the pharmacy couldn't get your prescription in order to obtain your medication. Or worse yet, the emergency room wasn't accessible because the driveways were blocked for repair. In groups, if too many subgroups talk at once, coordination soon breaks down, as it does if each person is trying to follow a different agenda (or no agenda). Integration, then, is synonymous with organizing.

EQUIFINALITY   You have undoubtedly heard the expression, "There is more than one way to skin a cat." This expression captures part of what is meant by the term *equifinality.* This concept means that, although two groups may have different members, leadership styles, decision-making methods, and so on, they may still arrive at the same solution to a given problem. There is an incredibly large number of combinations of all the variables in our small group model. These combinations may in some cases interact in such a way as to produce the same group consequences, but from dramatically different processes. Conversely, two groups may attempt to use the same procedures but end up with different outcomes. Thus equifinality refers to the unpredictability and potential for adaptation groups possess.

For readers who are familiar with small group literature, a synthesis of different small group models is offered in Figure 1.2. You will note the considerable similarity of conceptual approaches that span more than thirty years of writing. Note, however, that the present model is the only one that explicitly emphasizes the dynamic and simultaneous interaction of all the component parts.

SUMMARY

This chapter began with a real-life example of managing with small groups. From there we noted that groups are a pervasive part of modern management. Next, we

FIGURE 1.2   SYNTHESIS OF GROUP MODELS.

Homans (1950)	External system		Internal system	
Stogdill (1959)	Member inputs	Mediating variables	Resultant variables	
Thibaut and Kelley (1959)	Exogenous variables	Endogenous variables	Resultant variables	
McGrath and Altman (1966)	Properties of group members	Conditions imposed on group	Interaction process	Performance
Kibler and Barker (1969)	Antecedents	Messages	Consequences	
Fisher (1971)	Inputs	Mediating variables	Outputs	
Gouran (1973)	Context of communication	Communication behaviors	Group outcomes	
Tubbs (1988)	Relevant background factors	Internal influences	Consequences	

discussed some key definitions, along with six theoretical models for small group analysis. Finally, a general systems model was offered as an organizing framework for the analysis of small group interaction. This framework also serves as an outline for the remainder of this book. In the next six chapters and the accompanying readings, each part of the model will be discussed in greater detail: Chapter 2 covers *relevant background factors,* Chapters 3 through 6 are devoted to *internal influences,* and Chapter 7 deals with the *consequences* of small group interaction.

EXERCISES

1. First Impressions

Each person in the class should introduce himself or herself. Class members should feel free to ask each person questions to get a more complete impression. After the introductions, each person should write down some first impressions of the other class members (if you each display a large name card this is much easier). Those who want to may share their first impressions with the class. Then reactions to those impressions may also be shared and discussed.

2. Interpersonal Perceptions

Separate into groups of five and fill out the Preliminary Scale of Interpersonal Perceptions on each of the other four group members. Pass the completed scales to each person in the group. Examine the feedback you get and discuss these with the others in the group. You may want to share with one another the behaviors that led to these perceptions.

PRELIMINARY SCALE OF INTERPERSONAL PERCEPTIONS

Group Member's Name _____

On the scale below each question, circle the number that best describes the way you see this person's participation in group discussion. Try to distinguish between those areas where the person rates high and those where he/she rates less well.

1. How well does this person understand himself/herself in relation to this group? (Circle one numeral)

5	4	3	2	1
He/she has a very good understanding				He/she has very little understanding

2. How effective do you think this person is in contributing ideas, insights, and suggestions that help the group solve problems and achieve its goals? (Circle one numeral)

5	4	3	2	1
He/she is exceptionally effective				He/she is very ineffective

3. How effective do you think this person is in performing functions that build the group and keep it working well? (Circle one numeral)

5	4	3	2	1
He/she is exceptionally effective				He/she is very ineffective

4. In your opinion, how able is this person to express himself/herself freely and comfortably in the group? (Circle one numeral)

5	4	3	2	1
He/she is exceptionally free and comfortable				He/she is very restricted and tense

5. To what extent do you feel that this person really understands your ideas and feelings? (Circle one numeral)

5	4	3	2	1
He/she has a very good understanding				He/she has very little understanding

3. Group Consensus Activity

Form into groups of five, and then read and discuss the following article on cloning. As an agenda, try to answer the questions that follow the article.

SCIENTISTS REPORT CLONING OF MOUSE—A FIRST FOR MAMMALS*
By WALTER SULLIVAN, The New York Times

NEW YORK—Scientists in Switzerland have reported the first authenticated cloning of a mammal. Using cells from mouse embryos, they say they have produced three mice that are genetically identical to the original embryos.

Cloning is the production of a plant or animal identical with one from which a cell or cell nucleus has been taken and activated to become a complete organism. In plants, the procedure, using a cutting, is relatively routine. Cloning has been performed to a limited extent in frogs and other amphibians, but the possibility of cloning mammals had not previously been demonstrated.

The mice were cloned by taking nuclei from embryonic rather than adult cells, the scientists reported. Whether it will be possible to produce clones from adult mice or other adult mammals, including man, remains uncertain.

Some researchers hope to mass-produce prize livestock in this manner. Others believe such experiments can provide an understanding of the development of individuals from embryos to adults, including the origin of birth defects.

In the mouse experiments, each clone was produced by taking a nucleus obtained from a mouse embryo at an early stage of development and inserting it into a fertilized egg from another mouse. The original nuclear material in that egg was then extracted, leaving only the inserted nucleus.

The egg, after being cultured about four days, was placed in the womb of a mouse that then gave birth to an offspring with all the genetic features of the embryo from which the nucleus had been taken. The offspring bore no relationship to the mouse whose egg had been used or to the mother that bore it.

Two of the three mouse clones later produced seemingly normal offspring. The third died after seven weeks, but an autopsy revealed no abnormalities related to the cloning.

Earlier reports that mammals, and even a human being, had been cloned have never been authenticated or taken seriously by biologists.

The achievement shows that cloning, because it has been successfully performed in amphibians, is also possible with embryonic mammals, presumably including humans. It also suggests that the ability of amphibians to regenerate body parts may not be entirely beyond reach in mammals. Regeneration would be possible if genetic information within the nuclei of cells of an adult could be reactivated to perform roles, such as producing a new limb or new individual, other than those assigned to that specialized cell.

The transplants of the nuclei were performed at the University of Geneva by Dr. Karl Illmensee and Dr. Peter C. Hoppe, who is from the Jackson Laboratory in Bar Harbor, Maine. Their work has been reported at several scientific meetings and will be described later this month in the journal Cell, published by the Massachusetts Institute of Technology in Cambridge, Mass.

As in earlier nuclear transplants, the nucleus was extracted by a glass tube, or pipette, honed to hairlike sharpness. Under observation with a microscope, the pipette, controlled by a mechanical micromanipulator, was inserted into a cell taken from a mouse embryo at an early stage of development (the spherical, or blastocyst, stage, reached a few days after fertilization).

The pipette was then inserted into an egg from another mouse so recently fertilized that the sperm nucleus had not yet joined with the egg nucleus. The pipette was then used to extract the two original nuclei.

Altogether, 542 transplants were performed. Of these, 363, including the three that produced live mice, were of nuclei derived from the inner cell mass of an embryo at the blastocyst stage. It is the inner cell mass that evolves into the fetus.

The remaining nuclei were from cells forming the outer part of the blastocyst sphere, or the trophectoderm. These cells normally evolve into such structures as the uterus and umbilical cord. Their nuclei were apparently incapable of being sufficiently activated within the egg to produce an individual.

Of the 363 transplants of nuclei from the inner cell mass, 142 survived the micromanipulation and were cultured in glass vessels. Of these, 96 subdivided at least once, and within four days 48 had developed into many-celled blastocysts.

Of these embryos, 16 that appeared normal were transferred into the wombs of five white mice prepared for pregnancy by hormone treatment. The embryos had developed from eggs taken from black mice, but the nuclei inserted into them were from mice colored either grey or agouti (the color of wild mice).

Specially prepared mice also received 44 embryos taken from white mice and not subject to nuclear transplants. The added embryos enabled the prepared mice to produce litters of normal size. They all become pregnant and gave birth to a total of 35 mice. All but the three mice recognized as clones were white. None had the black fur of the strain that provided the egg cells.

The three clones had the color of the strains from which the transplanted nuclei were derived. Two, a male and female, were gray. The third was an agouti female. Tiny samples of tissue were taken from the ear, tail and skin of these mice to be cultured for genetic screening. Enzymes from the mice were also analyzed as genetic markers.

In all respects the mice resembled the embryos from which the nuclei had been taken, rather than the egg donor or the mouse prepared for pregnancy.

What are the implications of this case for the cloning of humans? Would clones be human? Would they have souls? What rights should they have? Is it desirable to clone humans? What should be U.S. policy toward the cloning of humans?

4. Ice-Breaking Exercises

Fill out the two forms that follow, and then get into groups of five or so and share answers. Later, you can discuss what you as a group experience from these exercises.

1. The person in the group I would like to get to know better is

    _____

2. The person in the group who seems to be most like myself is

    _____

3. The person in the group whom I would like to know, that I care and am concerned about, is

    _____

4. The person who has been the most helpful is

    _____

5. A person I would like to hitchhike around the country with is

    _____

6. A person I would trust to fold my parachute before jumping from an airplane is

    _____

7. A person I would like to have a deep discussion with is

    _____

8. A person I would like most to keep in touch with is

    _____

9. A person I would trust with my secrets is

    _____

10. A person whom I feel I know least well is

    _____

What other things would you like to say to someone in this group? Take a risk (be constructive).

_____

_____

What person in this group:

_____   1. Has the darkest eyes?

_____   2. Has the longest name?

———————————— 3. Could hide in the smallest place?

———————————— 4. Has the biggest hands?

———————————— 5. Has the oldest brother or sister?

———————————— 6. Can give the biggest smile?

———————————— 7. Can make the scariest face?

———————————— 8. Has the most brothers and sisters?

———————————— 9. Has the fewest brothers and sisters?

———————————— 10. Has the lightest hair?

———————————— 11. Has the most freckles?

———————————— 12. Can make the highest mark on the wall without jumping?

———————————— 13. Is wearing the most colors?

———————————— 14. Has the longest hair?

———————————— 15. Has the shortest name?

———————————— 16. Has lived in the most places?

———————————— 17. Has had the most pets?

———————————— 18. Can hum the lowest note?

———————————— 19. Has the smallest waist?

———————————— 20. Can stand on one foot for the longest time without holding on to something?

5. Group Decision Making

Separate into groups of five or so. Choose one of the cases described below, and decide as a group what you would do in the situation. Then discuss your group processes.

*WHAT WOULD YOU DO?**

Every day, doctors, nurses, patients and patients' families face life-and-death decisions. There is rarely an obvious "right" choice; each of them is, in some way, bad. Here are some real cases that present painful alternatives. The choices made by those responsible—and the results of their actions—appear below.

1. Doctors at a university hospital examined a 10-year-old boy whose bone cancer of the upper arm had recurred in spite of radiation treatments. The

physicians advised amputation of the limb and warned that without the operation, the child would almost certainly die. But the boy, an enthusiastic Little Leaguer, begged his parents and the doctors to let him keep his arm so that he could continue to play baseball.

2. A 7-year-old girl was suffering from a progressive neurological disease that had made her totally dependent on a respirator. She could talk and think normally, but the rest of her body functions were deteriorating rapidly and she was obviously in pain. Attempts to "wean" her from the respirator were unsuccessful, and doctors eventually realized it was unlikely she would ever recover. The parents, who were deeply religious, agonized over a decision about whether to turn off the machine.

3. A young woman, who was dying of multiple sclerosis, finally lapsed into an irreversible coma. She remained totally unresponsive for about a week, and her doctors agreed there was nothing more they could do to help her. One evening the patient, still comatose, began to gasp for breath. Her parents, who were sitting by the bedside, summoned the nurse and asked her to call a doctor.

4. A 6-year-old boy had severe renal failure in both kidneys; his best chance of survival would be a transplant from a sibling. Each of his two older sisters, 8 and 12, was willing to donate a kidney in an effort to save the boy. The risk to either girl—from the operation or from living with one kidney— was quite small. But common medical practice dictated that young donors should not be used, except in the case of a twin.

5. At the student-health service of a major university, a young man told his psychotherapist that he wanted to kill a young woman who lived nearby but who was then on a trip abroad. The therapist conferred with two colleagues, and, in a limited breach of professional confidentiality, informed the campus police; they picked up the student and detained him for questioning. Concluding that the youth was harmless, the police decided to release him after extracting a promise that he would not bother the woman he had spoken of murdering. The health service thought it unnecessary to take any further action.

1. The family decided against surgery. Now, nearly a year later, the boy is receiving radiation and chemotherapy—and playing baseball. Physicians say it is too soon to estimate his chances of recovery.

2. The physician asked the parents if they wanted to discover whether God wished the child to breathe on her own. The distraught couple agreed and, as they sat vigil, the respirator was removed; the child died about four hours later.

3. The nurse requested that the parents leave the room. Instead of summoning the doctor immediately, she waited until the patient had stopped breathing. Then she went, with a physician, to tell the parents that their daughter had died. "It was the hardest thing I ever did in my life," the nurse admits.

4. The doctors refused the sisters as donors, on the ground that they were too young to make a major medical decision that could affect their whole lives. The brother has survived for four years on dialysis.

5. Two months later, shortly after the woman's return, the student went to her home and killed her. Her parents sued the university—and won. The state supreme court ruled that the health service and the university had a "duty" to warn the girl of the threat on her life.

READINGS: OVERVIEW

The systems model presented in Figure 1.1 represented an attempt to show the interrelated nature of 24 variables relevant to the study of small group interaction (6 variables in each of the 4 columns in the model). Dorwin Cartwright's article shows how three variables fit together as he discusses the tremendous influence groups can have in changing people. The eight principles in the article are as relevant today as when he presented them over thirty years ago. This fact helps to emphasize both the predictability and the importance of knowing group dynamics principles. It is also interesting to note that these principles fit quite comfortably within the systems approach to studying small group interaction, which is the conceptual model around which this book is structured.

The second article by Bradford and Cohen shows the complexity and power of management's effective use of small groups.

Achieving Change in People: Some Applications of Group Dynamics Theory

Dorwin Cartwright

What principles of achieving change in people can we see emerging? To begin with the most general proposition, we may state that the behavior, attitudes, beliefs, and values of the individual are all firmly grounded in the groups to which he belongs. How aggressive or cooperative a person is, how much self-respect and self-confidence he has, how energetic and productive his work is, what he aspires to, what he believes to be true and good, whom he loves or hates, and what beliefs and prejudices he holds—all these characteristics are highly determined by the individual's group memberships. In a real sense, they are properties of groups and of the relationships between people. Whether they change or resist change will, therefore, be greatly influenced by the nature of these groups. Attempts to change them must be concerned with the dynamics of groups.

In examining more specifically how groups enter into the process of change, we find it useful to view groups in at least three different ways. In the first view, the group is seen as a source of influence over its members. Efforts to change behavior can be supported or blocked by pressures on members stemming from the group. To make constructive use of these pressures the group must be used as a *medium of change*. In the second view, the group itself becomes the *target of change*. To change the behavior of individuals it may be necessary to change the standards of the group, its style of leadership, its emotional atmosphere, or its stratification into cliques and hierarchies. Even though the goal may be to change the behavior of *individuals*, the target of change becomes the group. In the third view, it is recognized that many changes of behavior can be brought about only by the organized efforts of groups as *agents of change*. A committee to combat intolerance, a labor union, an employers association, a citizens group to increase the pay of teachers—any action group will be more or less effective depending upon the way it is organized, the satisfactions it provides to its members, the degree to which its goals are clear, and a host of other properties of the group.

Dorwin Cartwright, "Achieving Change in People: Some Applications of Group Dynamics Theory" from Human Relations, *Vol. 4, 1951. Reprinted by permission of Plenum Publishing Corporation.*

An adequate social technology of change, then, requires at the very least a scientific understanding of groups viewed in each of these ways. We shall consider here only the first two aspects of the problem: the group as a medium of change and as a target of change.

The Group as a Medium of Change

Principle No. 1   If the group is to be used effectively as a medium of change, those people who are to be changed and those who are to exert influence for change must have a strong sense of belonging to the same group.

Kurt Lewin described this principle well. "The normal gap between teacher and student, doctor and patient, social worker and public, can . . . be a real obstacle to acceptance of the advocated conduct." In other words, in spite of whatever status differences there might be between them, the teacher and the student have to feel as members of one group in matters involving their sense of values. The chances for reeducation seem to be increased whenever a strong we-feeling is created (5). Recent experiments by Preston and Heintz have demonstrated greater changes of opinions among members of discussion groups operating with participatory leadership than among those with supervisory leadership (12). The implications of this principle for classroom teaching are far-reaching. The same may be said of supervision in the factory, army, or hospital.

Principle No. 2   The more attractive the group is to its members the greater is the influence that the group can exert on its members.

This principle has been extensively documented by Festinger and his co-workers (4). They have been able to show in a variety of settings that in more cohesive groups there is a greater readiness of members to attempt to influence others, a greater readiness to be influenced by others, and stronger pressures toward conformity when conformity is a relevant matter for the group. Important for the practitioner wanting to make use of this principle is, of course, the question of how to increase the attractiveness of groups. This is a question with many answers. Suffice it to say that a group is more attractive the more it satisfies the needs of its members. We have been able to demonstrate experimentally an increase in group cohesiveness by increasing the liking of members for each other as persons, by increasing the perceived importance of the group goal, and by increasing the prestige of the group among other groups. Experienced group workers could add many other ways to this list.

Principle No. 3   In attempts to change attitudes, values, or behavior, the more relevant they are to the basis of attraction to the group, the greater will be the influence that the group can exert upon them.

I believe this principle gives a clue to some otherwise puzzling phenomena.

How does it happen that a group, like a labor union, seems to be able to exert such strong discipline over its members in some matters (let us say in dealings with management), while it seems unable to exert nearly the same influence in other matters (let us say in political action)? If we examine why it is that members are attracted to the group, I believe we will find that a particular reason for belonging seems more related to some of the group's activities than to others. If a man joins a union mainly to keep his job and to improve his working conditions, he may be largely uninfluenced by the union's attempt to modify his attitudes toward national and international affairs. Groups differ tremendously in the range of matters that are relevant to them and hence over which they have influence. Much of the inefficiency of adult education could be reduced if more attention were paid to the need that influence attempts be appropriate to the groups in which they are made.

Principle No. 4   The greater the prestige of a group member in the eyes of the other members, the greater the influence he can exert.

Polansky, Lippitt, and Redl (11) have demonstrated this principle with great care and methodological ingenuity in a series of studies in children's summer camps. From a practical point of view it must be emphasized that the things giving prestige to a member may not be those characteristics most prized by the official management of the group. The most prestige-carrying member of a Sunday school class may not possess the characteristics most similar to the minister of the church. The teacher's pet may be a poor source of influence within a class. This principle is the basis for the common observation that the official leader and the actual leader of a group are often not the same individual.

Principle No. 5   Efforts to change individuals or subparts of a group which, if successful, would have the result of making them deviate from the norms of the group will encounter strong resistance.

During the past years a great deal of evidence has been accumulated showing the tremendous pressures which groups can exert upon members to conform to the group's norms. The price of deviation in most groups is rejection or even expulsion. If the member really wants to belong and be accepted, he cannot withstand this type of pressure. It is for this reason that efforts to change people by taking them from the group and giving them special training so often have disappointing results. This principle also accounts for the finding that people thus trained sometimes display increased tension, aggressiveness toward the group, or a tendency to form cults or cliques with others who have shared their training.

These five principles concerning the group as a medium of change would appear to have readiest application to groups created for the purpose of producing changes in people. They provide certain specifications for building effective training or therapy groups. They also point, however, to a difficulty in producing change in people in that they show how resistant an individual is to changing in any way contrary to group pressures and expectations. In order to achieve many kinds of changes in people, therefore, it is necessary to deal with the group as a target of change.

The Group as a Target of Change

Principle No. 6   Strong pressure for changes in the group can be established by creating a shared perception by members of the need for change, thus making the source of pressure for change lie within the group.

Marrow and French (9) reports a dramatic case-study which illustrates this principle quite well. A manufacturing concern had a policy against hiring women over 30 because it was believed that they were slower, more difficult to train, and more likely to be absent. The staff psychologist was able to present to management evidence that this belief was clearly unwarranted at least within their own company. The psychologist's facts, however, were rejected and ignored as a basis for action because they violated accepted beliefs. It was claimed that they went against the direct experience of the foremen. Then the psychologist hit upon a plan for achieving change which differed drastically from the usual one of argument, persuasion, and pressure. He proposed that management conduct its own analysis of the situation. With his help management collected all the facts which they believed were relevant to the problem. When the results were in they were now their own facts rather than those of some "outside" expert. Policy was immediately changed without further resistance. The important point here is that facts are not enough. The facts must be the accepted property of the group if they are to become an effective basis for change. There seems to be all the difference in the world in changes actually carried out between those cases in which a consulting firm is hired to do a study and present a report and those in which technical experts are asked to collaborate with the group in doing its own study.

Principle No. 7   Information relating to the need for change, plans for change, and consequences of change must be shared by all relevant people in the group.

Another way of stating this principle is to say that change of a group ordinarily requires the opening of communication channels. Newcomb (10) has shown how one of the first consequences of mistrust and hostility is the avoidance of communicating openly and freely about the things producing the tension. If you look closely at a pathological group (that is, one that has trouble making decisions or effecting coordinated efforts of its members), you will certainly find strong restraints in that group against communicating vital information among its members. Until these restraints are removed there can be little hope for any real and lasting changes in the group's functioning. In passing it should be pointed out that the removal of barriers to communication will ordinarily be accompanied by a sudden increase in the communication of hostility. The group may appear to be falling apart, and it will certainly be a painful experience to many of the members. This pain and the fear that things are getting out of hand often stop the process of change once begun.

Principle No. 8   Changes in one part of a group produce strain in other related parts which can be reduced only by eliminating the change or by bringing about readjustments in the related parts.

It is a common practice to undertake improvements in group functioning by providing training programs for certain classes of people in the organization. A training program for foremen, for nurses, for teachers, or for group workers is established. If the content of the training is relevant for organizational change, it must of necessity deal with the relationships these people have with other subgroups. If nurses in a hospital change their behavior significantly, it will affect their relations both with the patients and with the doctors. It is unrealistic to assume that both these groups will remain indifferent to any significant changes in this respect. In hierarchical structures this process is most clear. Lippitt has proposed on the basis of research and experience that in such organizations attempts at change should always involve three levels, one being the major target of change and the other two being the one above and the one below.

These eight principles represent a few of the basic propositions emerging from research in group dynamics. Since research is constantly going on and since it is the very nature of research to revise and reformulate our conceptions, we may be sure that these principles will have to be modified and improved as time goes by. In the meantime they may serve as guides in our endeavors to develop a scientifically based technology of social management.

In social technology, just as in physical technology, invention plays a crucial role. In both fields progress consists of the creation of new mechanisms for the accomplishment of certain goals. In both fields inventions arise in response to practical needs and are to be evaluated by how effectively they satisfy these needs. The relation of invention to scientific development is indirect but important. Inventions cannot proceed too far ahead of basic scientific development, nor should they be allowed to fall too far behind. They will be more effective the more they make good use of known principles of science, and they often make new developments in science possible. On the other hand, they are in no sense logical derivations from scientific principles.

I have taken this brief excursion into the theory of invention in order to make a final point. To many people "group dynamics" is known only for the social inventions which have developed in recent years in work with groups. Group dynamics is often thought of as certain techniques to be used with groups. Role playing, buzz groups, process observers, post-meeting reaction sheets, and feedback of group observations are devices popularly associated with the phrase "group dynamics." I trust that I have been able to show that group dynamics is more than a collection of gadgets. It certainly aspires to be a science as well as a technology.

This is not to underplay the importance of these inventions nor of the function of inventing. As inventions they are all mechanisms designed to help accomplish important goals. How effective they are will depend upon how skill-fully they are used and how appropriate they are to the purposes to which they are put. Careful evaluative research must be the ultimate judge of their useful-ness in comparison with alternative inventions. I believe that the principles enu-merated in this paper indicate some of the specifications that social inventions in this field must meet.

References

1. Cartwright, D. Some principles of mass persuasion: Selected findings of research on the sale of United States war bonds. *Human Relations,* 1949, 2(3), 253–67.
2. Cartwright, D. *The research center for group dynamics: A report of five years' activity and a view of future needs.* Ann Arbor: Institute for Social Research, 1950.
3. Coch, L. and French, J. T. P., Jr. Overcoming resistance to change. *Human Relations,* 1948, 1(4), 512–32.
4. Festinger, L., *et al. Theory and experiment in social communication:* Collected papers. Ann Arbor: Institute for Social Research, 1950.
5. Lewin, K. *Resolving social conflicts,* p. 67. New York: Harper & Bros., 1951.
6. Lewin, K. *Field theory in social science,* pp. 229–36. New York: Harper & Bros., 1951.
7. Lewin, K., Lippitt, R., and White, R. K. Patterns of aggressive behavior in experi-mentally created "social climates." *Journal of Social Psychology,* 1939, 10, 271–99.
8. Lippitt, R. *Training in Community Relations.* New York: Harper & Bros., 1949.
9. Marrow, A. J. and French, J. T. P., Jr. Changing a stereotype in industry. *Journal of Social Issues,* 1945, 1(3), 33–37.
10. Newcomb, T. M. Autistic hostility and social reality. *Human Relations,* 1947, 1(1), 69–86.
11. Polansky, N., Lippitt, R., and Redl, F. An investigation of behavioral contagion in groups. *Human Relations,* 1950, 3(4), 319–48.
12. Preston, M. G. and Heintz, R. K. Effects of participatory vs. supervisory leadership on group judgment. *Journal of Abnormal and Social Psychology,* 1949, 44, 345–55.

Managing for Excellence

David L. Bradford and Allan R. Cohen

I. Dealing with Subordinates: Only One-third of the Manager's Job

In writing a book about how to create excellence, we have told only part of the story. In order to do justice to the complexity of how to deal with subordinates, we have had to limit our discussion of dealing with peers and superiors to how the manager can gain the autonomy to use a Developer approach. But this emphasis is not meant to downplay the importance of these other key managerial issues. Departments and leaders do not exist in splendid isolation; it is the rare manager whose success isn't highly dependent on successful interactions with colleagues and superiors. In most cases it is impossible to create excellence without considerable skills in managing laterally and upwards, as well as down. These other players can have a major impact in terms of their willingness to share information, deliver resources, provide support, and cooperate in implementing decisions.

Furthermore, these three aspects of managing interact with each other so that success in one area influences outcomes in the others. Having clout with your boss gains respect from subordinates and peers; being influential with colleagues lets you deliver what your boss wants and your subordinates need; and high-performing subordinates increase your power sideways and upwards because you can deliver on your obligations and promises.

Although a full exploration of how to be more effective with these other two aspects of the manager's job is the subject for another book, it is worth noting that:

> Many of the skills needed to get the most from subordinates are useful in dealing with boss and peers. For example, the ability to build common vision and compatible goals is important laterally and upwards. Skills in negotiation, confrontation, and joint problem-solving also apply to all three directions. You as a manager not only lead and have to develop your own team but are a member of your boss's team; group development skills are crucial in the latter situation as well.
>
> The Developer model, once it is reasonably in place, frees you from many of the burdens of managing downward. If subordinates are genuinely sharing responsibility so that you do not have to carry all the weight on your shoulders, consid-

From: David L. Bradford and Allan R. Cohen, Managing for Excellence. *New York: Wiley, 1984, pp. 280–289. Copyright © 1984, John Wiley & Sons, Inc. Reprinted by permission of John Wiley & Sons, Inc.*

erable time and energy are released for the work needed outside your unit. What we have seen with managers who operate under heroic assumptions is the extent to which their time and energy are consumed in putting out the constant internal brush fires that prevent them from adequately dealing with these external functions.

These points speak to a concern frequently raised by many of the managers who are considering the Developer approach. When we have taught the model, the response is often one of worry: "If I share my managerial responsibility with subordinates, won't that take away my job? Won't subordinates see me as superfluous?" With unemployment among middle managers an increasing phenomenon, many fear that the best way to justify their existence is to manage (downwards) in a more visible fashion.

However, the opposite is true. Creating a team that is committed to departmental success frees the manager to spend more time on those functions which often only the leader can do. This includes not only interfacing with other units in the organization but dealing with the powers-that-be. In an increasingly turbulent world, the leader has to manage the core processes of innovation and change. As Kanter (1983) has demonstrated in *The Change Masters,* leaders have to sense opportunities from above and outside, formulate new possibilities, build coalitions with peers to support cross-departmental change, and sell higher-ups on the ways these innovations will help achieve corporate goals. These are the ways in which effective middle and upper-middle managers get things done— and make themselves more valuable in the process.

All of that not only takes time but is difficult to deliver without a strong department and willing subordinates. The Developer model is useful insofar as it can ultimately free you to spend most of the time where your skills are ultimately needed and where the largest payoffs are.

II. Manager-as-Developer: Making the Most of Your Imperfect World

We began this guide to achieving excellence by declaring that something is wrong with leadership in American organizations. In that initial chapter we reported some of the experiences of managers who did operate at an excellent level. In our consulting and training work, we frequently have posed the question, "What does it take to get excellence." We have raised this question in several ways and, to come full cycle from that first chapter, we want to describe a conversation we had with a group of savvy middle managers from some of America's leading companies.

We raised the following hypothetical issue: "How would you respond if the president of your organization came to you and said, 'I want you to take over Department X and make it perform at an excellent level. What would it take for you to do that?'" The managers in this session quickly agreed that they could deliver on the president's request if the following three conditions were met:

> First, "Let me pick my own staff so that I can have highly competent people who will work well together."
> Second, "Give me an exciting assignment that is important to this organization."
> Third, "Give me a boss who doesn't interfere or tell me exactly what to do."

We then asked this group of managers how frequently those conditions are given to them; they laughed. If you can by skill, luck, or magic acquire these loaded-for-success conditions, life would be considerably easier than it is now. But one way to think about the message of this book is that it tells you how to build these conditions when they are not so fortuitously given to you. Few managers can completely pick their own staff—what we have shown is how you can develop high performers and a mature team with the individuals you presently have. Few leaders in any organization are anointed by the president with just the perfect, crucial mission—what we have illustrated is how you can take the department's function and reconceptualize it into a challenging and exciting goal. Finally, few of us are blessed with the perfect superior—but we have given some hints about ways you can negotiate with your boss so that you can have the necessary autonomy and support.

III. Some Concluding Paradoxes

Rather than being dependent on those fortuitous but rare events when the perfect conditions are laid in your lap, this book is about how you can take control of what happens to you. By now, you should have a clear idea of how to go about countering the tendencies of organizational units to perform at levels far below what is possible. With determination, careful planning, and a willingness to risk doing things differently, you can produce excellence in the department you manage. You can make it a place where all the members are committed to the unit's goals, feel personal responsibility for its success, take initiative rather than wait passively for directions, and share a dedication to quality.

The experiences of managers who have begun using the Developer model show that it can work in a variety of conditions. Extra effort is needed when subordinates, superiors, or peers are resistant or unprepared, but these obstacles can be overcome. The key is to set up a process where you and your subordinates, working jointly, can discover the approach that best fits your specific situation. The act of sharing the responsibility for finding your ways to the shared-responsibility team is itself more important than following the model to a T.

Keep that paradoxical admonition in mind as you turn to our final words of wisdom, which we have formulated as a series of six paradoxes for postheroic managing.

PARADOX 1.

The Manager-as-Developer has to be both less active and more active than the heroic manager.

On the one hand, the postheroic manager has to back away from feeling solely responsible for solving all problems and managing the department. That obligation can be paralyzing at first, especially if you are used to achieving daily satisfactions from carrying the world on your shoulders. Although it is by no means appropriate to withdraw and go passive, you may not be able to see what else to do when you are trying to let go of heroic riding to the rescue. You might perceive heroism's apparent opposite as standing by while the damsel is run over by the onrushing locomotive.

Nevertheless, this dichotomy is false. We are not advocating management-by-absence; excellence can't be achieved by leader abdication. The Manager-as-Developer has to be quite active, but in a very different way from conventional heroics. While the traditional leader focused activity almost exclusively on solving task issues, Developers have to be active in managing procedural issues. Except when they have clearly greater expertise than their subordinates on that topic, Developers concentrate on managing the process so that full use is made of subordinate ability. The Developer's hard work and initiative are directed at seeing that the real issues are raised, arguments are joined, and commitments are made. Great activity is required of the Developer—to develop individuals and groups so that they can perform well in solving the problems and in sharing in the management of the unit.

Once a department is reasonably developed, there are fewer managerial demands on the Developers, but that hardly means that they have created their own unemployment. "Development" is not an end state in which the manager withers away. Improved performance just surfaces a new set of problems—redefined tasks, increased responsibilities, more complex issues. There will always be new people coming into the department who have to be integrated or changes in external conditions that require adjustments. And, as pointed out earlier, any time saved by the manager's not having to deal with internal issues can well be spent with the other crucial aspects of the leader's job: dealing sideways with other departments, upward with the boss, or outside the organization. The problem of having nothing to do or being reduced to watching the action from outside while longing to get into the game is not a problem in this postheroic world.

PARADOX 2.

The Manager-as-Developer must give greater autonomy to subordinates while establishing more controls.

To allow subordinates to share responsibility requires that the leader be willing to give up some of the conventional controls. The Developer must loosen the reins on problem solving, task assignment, and meeting agendas. Yet this loss of manager-based control is balanced by the increased controls that evolve when all subordinates are personally committed to departmental success. Collective acceptance of the same central overarching goal is a form of control. If members feel responsible for managing the unit, they will be more willing to pressure (exert control over) peers who are not coming through. If they accept the team as theirs, they will believe it is right for them to influence each other. All of this activity produces far more control than could be exerted by even the most watchful manager. Of course, these controls affect you as well as your subordinates; you become accountable to subordinates for commitments made, and they are more likely to push you to perform.

PARADOX 3.

Managers-as-Developers increase their own power by giving subordinates greater power.

Power and influence are not a fixed sum. In most organizations, there is too little power to produce excellence. Leaders who sense they are in low-power situations are hesitant about giving their subordinates increased influence in the decision-making process—in determining how the department is to be run and in deciding how best to carry out their assignments. Yet giving power begets power; subordinates who feel empowered and committed to the departmental goal are not only more motivated but are also more willing to be influenced by their peers and by you. People with low power most resist the power of others. The best way for you to increase your influence with subordinates is to increase their power with each other, with you, and with others outside the unit. This procedure is better defined as power-enhancement, rather than power-sharing.

PARADOX 4.

The Manager-as-Developer builds a team as a way to support member individuality.

Groups can be dangerous forces toward conformity in thought and behavior. Too many people experience their organizations as constraining. But groups can also support individuality. As a team develops, it moves from a collection of individuals who are suspicious of each other (and therefore want to limit differences among themselves) into a cohesive but consensual group where individual differences are valued and supported. A genuinely collaborative team can allow more diversity and autonomy than one that clings together for mutually distrustful motives.

In this vein, the Manager-as-Developer needs to hold meetings so that the team can develop to a point where fewer meetings are needed! So many present-day organizations support far more meetings than are necessary. The majority of unnecessary meetings are held because people don't trust each other or the manager is afraid that people will all march to their separate drummers. When the team has developed so that trust has developed and everybody is committed to the same goals, members know what to do and can usually act on their own in ways that are close to what the group and manager would have directed.

PARADOX 5.
The Manager-as-Developer model requires an optimistic faith in subordinate possibilities but tough implementation to work.

The Manager-as-Developer model is optimistic in several ways. First, the model is based on the premise that virtually everyone wants to do well—that no reason exists for basic incompatibility between what the organization needs (in its search for excellence) and what individuals want to produce (in terms of performing competently). Second, the model optimistically posits that most people basically do not seek to empire-build, play politics, and do each other in unless the organizational situation makes it difficult to accomplish anything otherwise. Nasty behavior arises mostly when members feel blocked from legitimate methods for getting their work done, not as a result of an innate component of personal nastiness. Finally, the model's optimism is revealed in its tenet that most people can change—their behaviors, not personalities. Under the proper conditions, which include a manager who functions as a Developer, a relatively high percentage of subordinates can learn and grow.

Many managers resist this optimism. There is a kind of comfort taken in cynicism—in hanging onto the beliefs that people are not to be trusted, are out for their own self-interest, and can't change. The developmental approach cannot be utilized without giving up this cynicism.

At the same time, the Manager-as-Developer model is basically a tough approach. It is tough in setting high standards (and holding people to them). It is tough in requiring that the manager hold subordinates' feet to the fire when they may want to avoid the difficult issues. It is tough in pushing for conflicts to be identified and worked through rather than smoothed over. It is tough in requiring that people be confronted (rather than shunted aside, or ignored) when they don't come through. And it is tough in demanding that the manager be willing to be open to confrontation as well.

Many managers avoid this toughness. Some are so concerned about being liked that they do not even raise the important issues. But even many of the managers who think themselves hard-boiled are not very tough in important dimensions. There is a difference between hardness and toughness. The manager can be hard by not listening to subordinate complaints, exploiting others for the sake of short-term productivity, or by showing a hard exterior to prevent subordinates from broaching difficult issues. Such hardness is not toughness. Being tough is fully listening to subordinates, acknowledging validity in their complaints, and still being able to take the difficult actions when appropriate. Toughness is not dropping bombs on distant, impersonal targets; insisting on performance despite closeness and caring is far tougher.

PARADOX 6.
Although the Developer model requires new behavior, the best way to improve your performance as a manager is to focus on the needs of others, rather than on yourself.

It is easy to become frozen by self-help books. Although we have tried to avoid detailed, step-by-step advice, we have drawn your attention to a lot of things at once, many of them involving changes in your attitudes, skills, and even behavior. This multi-faceted process can be like trying to learn how to play tennis by memorizing each motion in microscopic, sequential detail. By the time you remember how to hold the racket, where to plant your feet, how to line up parallel to the net, what to look at, and the angle of your arm, the ball is long since dead. At some point in your playing progress, you might benefit from minute examination of some aspect of your game, but only after you have the basic idea and rhythm of tennis to depend on. To build the idea and rhythm, you need to use the Zen tennis approach: Focus on the ball going back over the net and where you want it to land. Your swing and positioning will follow naturally.

Managing by a new style requires something similar to this attitude. You need to maintain your focus outward, on your subordinates and their needs, the nature of the tasks you all face, and the kind of results you desire. Too close attention to how you're doing—where your feet are planted (or how precisely you are executing the model)—only causes ungainly awkwardness.

Learning anything new requires a period of awkwardness, so don't let the prospect be discouraging. More important, even while checking once in a while to see how you are doing, don't become so self-conscious that you come to the fate of the centipede who was asked how he coordinated 100 legs: You can't move at all.

Remember, a long journey starts with small steps, even while your eye is on the guiding star. You have to do both at once. Happy trip.

Relevant Background Factors

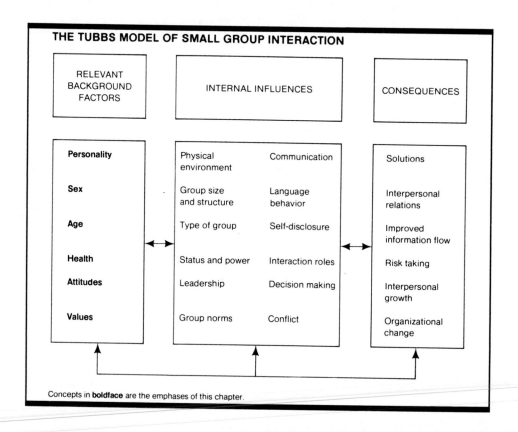

THE TUBBS MODEL OF SMALL GROUP INTERACTION

| RELEVANT BACKGROUND FACTORS | INTERNAL INFLUENCES | | CONSEQUENCES |

Personality	Physical environment	Communication	Solutions
Sex	Group size and structure	Language behavior	Interpersonal relations
Age	Type of group	Self-disclosure	Improved information flow
Health	Status and power	Interaction roles	Risk taking
Attitudes	Leadership	Decision making	Interpersonal growth
Values	Group norms	Conflict	Organizational change

Concepts in **boldface** are the emphases of this chapter.

CASE STUDY

When our supervisor, Bud Thomas, retired after 37 years of service, the men in the department threw one of the biggest retirement parties that Engineering had ever seen. Bud was well liked by everyone and we were sorry to see him go. As far as the engineers he supervised were concerned, he was the ideal boss. Bud was the type of supervisor who provided support when an employee needed it, while managing to supervise not so closely that his employees felt that they had someone constantly looking over their shoulders. He was the type of supervisor who always made sure that we received credit for jobs well done.

After Bud's retirement, everyone was speculating as to who would be promoted to his vacancy. The majority of the engineers felt that one of our department's older men who had been on the job for years would be promoted. We were wrong.

Upper management decided to promote one of the younger engineers who had 7 years seniority in another engineering section. His name was John Simpson. John was 29 years old and a competent engineer. He came to our Division as a low level College Graduate in Training Employee in 1981. By 1986, he had worked his way up to engineer, and now with Bud's retirement, to a supervisory position over our section.

All went well the first few months. The older employees with more seniority were a bit resentful at first, but after a couple of weeks the initial "grumbling" faded away and the department resumed its business-as-usual atmosphere.

After John had been our supervisor for about three weeks, he called a meeting of the 11 people he supervised to announce some changes. First of all, John announced that he thought we should have a group meeting every day at 7 A.M. He thought that this would enable him to get a better picture of "what is going on" on a daily basis. John also stated that he felt that since he was working 6:30 A.M. to 3:30 P.M. each day that all of us should be on the same schedule. When some of the employees complained that this violated the current flex-time policy on working hours and also conflicted with what was being allowed in other engineering groups in our division, John asserted that flex-time was his prerogative and that he could set working hours as he is our supervisor.

Some of the engineers were so mad that they took their case for flex-time to the head engineer. He told them that flex-time could be waived at the discretion of the supervisor. So we had to start at 6:30 each morning.

Therefore, at the first 7 A.M. meeting, John did all the talking with the engineers talking only when spoken to. The engineers managed to limit the amount of information about the jobs they were working on. So John never had a clear picture of "what is going on."

The only change John achieved by the elimination of flex-time and the mandatory attendance at morning meetings was the alienation of himself from other engineers. This became more evident as each day passed.

When John asked for volunteers to attend a conference and give a brief presentation about a topic in engineering, everyone turned him down. The same was true on the issue of overtime; John always had a hard time convincing anyone to stay over a couple of hours.

John furthered his alienation from the department when he announced that the company car we used to go from building to building (our plant complex is 2 miles long) and run errands with would be eliminated. He said that this was an upper management decision over which we had no control.

Our productivity sagged so much after this that we started missing deadlines. For the first time, our group started to have morale problems.

At this point, John decided that the best way to solve our problems would be to have a Quality of Work Life meeting at which we could air our problems. When the meeting was held, John asked what our main problem was and we replied that he was our problem. Three days later, John transferred to another division.

1. What issues or problems can you identify in this case?

2. How would have you have handled this situation if you had been John Simpson?

This case clearly illustrates the very complex systems nature of group dynamics. The attitudes of John Simpson were at the heart of the problem. Yet, the attitudes, age, work values, and seniority of the work group interacted with John's attitudes, age, values, and behaviors. If John had not been so young, their attitudes might have been more receptive. If he had been female, it would have added still another dimension which might have influenced their attitudes. The short-term result was a decrease in productivity. The longer-term result was that John was relieved of his supervisory position. Although the case doesn't go into it, probably the groups' attitudes will be strengthened, cohesiveness will be increased, and the new supervisor will face an even more close-knit group as a result of this incident.

In this chapter we will examine six factors which we refer to as relevant background factors. They are personality, sex, age, health, attitudes, and values. Several of these are illustrated in the case of Simpson versus Engineering. One of the basic premises of systems theory is that all these factors are interrelated, so that a change in one part of the system creates changes in other parts of the system.

EXPLAINING WHY WE DO WHAT WE DO

Perhaps you may have wondered why John or the rest of the group acted the way they did. Or more generally, why does anyone behave the way they do? This question has intrigued humans for centuries. Behaving in specific ways is usually seen as an attempt by the individual to meet certain needs. For example, have you ever been in a group situation and wondered why you were there? Suppose you look out a classroom window and see a beautiful sky—it is a great day for being outside. You begin to experience competing needs: the need to go outside and have fun and the need to accomplish whatever the group's purpose is (such as studying for an upcoming exam). Whichever need is more intense will most probably determine the behavior you pursue.

Probably one of the best-known models for explaining people's needs is Maslow's (1970) hierarchy of needs (see Figure 2.1).

Physiological needs must be met in order to survive. Some groups formed in the

FIGURE 2.1   MASLOW'S NEED HIERARCHY.

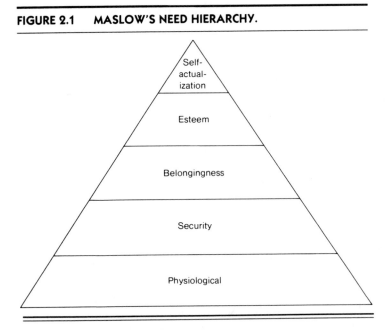

days of the cave dwellers to fight off saber-toothed tigers, as well as other unfriendly cave people, and to help gather food.

Security needs often motivate the formation of groups by individuals who lack sufficient power on their own. This is demonstrated by the union movement, which resulted from the fact that there were far more workers than jobs. With ten people waiting to fill each job, workers were somewhat hesitant to make demands of bosses. Thus unions helped workers gain power and eventually job security.

Belongingness needs are easy for most people to identify with. Think about what you felt like during your first week as a college freshman. One student member of a freshman discussion group wrote about this belongingness need not being fulfilled: "During our discussion, I felt like I wasn't even supposed to be in my group. The others seemed like they were all very familiar with each other and discussed almost entirely among themselves. They took over the discussion basically by looking only at each other and asking a lot of questions of each other (and cracking a lot of really funny jokes). I tried to contribute but felt ignored. It was very uncomfortable and I became quiet after a few more attempts to contribute. I'm glad I didn't receive a grade on that discussion because I was annoyed at how little I participated." Eventually, the feelings of aloneness begin to subside as people develop their own circles of friends (social groups).

Esteem needs may also be met by groups. Often people are attracted to certain fraternities or sororities because of the prestige of membership, which adds to their feeling of self-esteem. All people need to feel that they are important, and being a part of a good group or organization is one very good way to accomplish that goal.

Self-actualization needs are the highest-level needs Maslow identified. A person

Reprinted with special permission of King Features Syndicate, Inc.

may be attracted to a group because of the need for self-development. Encounter groups are one particular type of group devoted to the growth and development of members. Educational groups or work groups may also help individuals achieve a higher level of human potential.

Maslow argued that the needs lowest on the hierarchy must be satisfied before the higher-level needs are activated. For example, we worry less about self-actualization in a job when we are unemployed and the bills haven't been paid.

Probably one of the reasons Maslow's theory has been so popular is because it seems intuitively valid. It is important to have an understanding of what motivates people (including ourselves). When we are in a group and one person talks a lot, it may be that he or she is trying to meet a belongingness need. If they brag, they are probably trying to satisfy an esteem need. If they consistently offer creative ideas that seem quite unusual, they may be trying to meet a self-actualization need.

PERSONALITY

Since each of us is a member of numerous groups throughout our lives, have you ever wondered what motivates us to join groups in the first place? Although there are many personality theories, one seems particularly relevant to small group behavior. Schutz (1958, 1967, 1971) hypothesized that most people share three needs that groups help fulfill: needs for inclusion, control, and affection. You will find Schutz's theory explained in detail at the end of this chapter. It is called the FIRO—B theory. FIRO—B stands for Fundamental Interpersonal Relations Orientation—Behavior. It means that everyone relates or orients themselves to others in ways that can be identified, measured, and predicted. If you are trying to lead a work group, it is very useful to be able to understand what motivates you and your group members, in order to get a task accomplished.

Schutz's work began at the Naval Research Laboratory in Washington, D.C., nearly forty years ago. The FIRO—B test has been used to select submarine crews as well as astronaut teams who would have personality styles that would help them work more efficiently together under high stress conditions. The major premise of Schutz's theory is that people need people, and that we join groups to help fill this need. Each person from childhood on develops a fundamental interpersonal relations orientation with differing levels of needed inclusion, control, and affection.

All of us have felt the need for inclusion. If you have ever been in a physical education class in which teams were chosen, you know this feeling. Do you remember waiting to be chosen and fearing not being chosen? Some people have also experienced the need for control. If you are trying to lead a group and several conversations are going on simultaneously, it brings out the need to control the discussion. Finally, if a group pays a lot of attention to certain members, it can make us feel the need to have some attention and affection directed our way too. These are important needs in all people, but obviously they vary in intensity from person to person.

Inclusion

Inclusion refers to our need for belonging, feeling a part of, and being together with others. Have you ever been in a group in which you felt ignored? Perhaps you have felt this way in this very class, especially on the first or second day. This is because you were not being responded to as much as your need for inclusion required. Other people may not necessarily disagree with what you are saying, they just may not be responding. Such behavior violates our need to be included in the group. On a more basic level, it also makes us doubt our self-worth. If this exclusion happens over and over, most of us would begin to doubt our intrinsic worth as a person.

On the job, if people go to lunch and don't invite us, our need for inclusion may not be met. On the other hand, if we prefer to do things on our own and people are constantly around us, this too violates our low need for inclusion. Most of us want to be included in some groups and prefer to avoid others. If we are ignored by the attractive groups and sought after by the unattractive groups, this also violates our need for inclusion.

Several years ago I conducted a three-hour evening class. Bob, one of the class members, brought his fiancee Lisa. Since she was visiting from another city, she felt pretty left out of the group. Others felt awkward because she was watching, and it made them feel self-conscious. I suggested an exercise in which we all formed a circle and held hands. One by one, each person was asked to step outside our circle and to try to break into it by running through the tightly held hands. Then it was Lisa's turn; she tried several times and couldn't break into the circle. Finally, she tried to get in by running through where I was standing. I willingly let her in. It was a symbolic way of including her in the group. After that, we went on with our activities and the group seemed to accept her. A footnote to the incident is that Lisa and Bob, now happily married, told me several years after that class that they still remembered the incident vividly. This indicates that feelings about inclusion may be quite strong. Bob had been unaware of her feelings of exclusion since the classmates were all friends of his. She, on the other hand, was really experiencing the need for inclusion or acceptance into his group of close-knit friends.

The inclusion issue raises its head over and over throughout our lives. Each time we take a new job, join a new work group, or meet a new group socially, we feel it. Problems occur when we are not sensitive to another person who is new in the group. They, like Lisa, are experiencing the feeling, but we may not be tuned into their needs. Often, when a person comes in late for a meeting, the others do not make any attempt to orient that person or bring him or her up to date. All of us have a need for inclusion which must be met before we are able to function fully in a group. Keep in mind that this need recurs, much like our need to eat.

Control

Control refers to our need to influence, lead, and develop power over others; or to be influenced, led, or have others exert power over us. If you have ever been in a group with no appointed leader, you know how uncomfortable it is to break the ice and get the discussion started. Those who attempt to get the group organized are trying to exert control over the others. At first, this may be welcomed, but often people begin to resent the control takers and will eventually ask them to stop being so pushy with comments like "Who died and left you boss?" The issue of who is in control remains alive throughout the life of any group. Especially as membership changes, the pecking order is reshuffled and has to be reestablished. Here is an account of an MBA class exercise in which resentment of a control-taker is very obvious:

> The group consisted of seven people. The purpose of the class exercise was to form a manufacturing company and produce products. One individual chose himself as General Manager and also appointed an Assistant General Manager. The remaining members formed the assembly line workers. . . . The General Manager was a very forceful, energetic individual. He chose his own Assistant and appointed himself almost before we had formed the group. He is a very impatient individual. His entire manner left everyone in doubt as to the final outcome of the exercise. . . . The practice run was a complete disaster. We didn't know what the product was, let alone how to build it. Step by step instructions were available for everyone to read, but we weren't given time to read them. The General Manager didn't pay attention to his duties. He was more interested in production line speed than he was in purchasing materials or financial matters. He couldn't get quality products because of the haphazard organization of the work force. We had to start over again and again. The third time through, we got fairly decent quality. By that time it was too late. Dissension in the ranks of the group was rampant. . . . We were not motivated to do a good job, the only challenge was to beat the opposition (i.e., management).

A laboratory study comparing need for control with success of group performance found that members of a leaderless discussion group who scored high on need for control were more often seen by their peers as leaders in groups. However, the quality of solutions derived from these groups was relatively low. The researchers write: "A [high control] leaders had poorer solutions than B [low control] leaders. . . . We had predicted the [solution] quality results by reasoning that A leaders would be so busy gaining and exerting control that they would gain relatively few ideas from the discussion" (Sanders and Malkis, 1982, p. 84).

Control, power, and leadership are closely related subjects. Why do you suppose so much has been written about them? Who is in control seems to be one of life's basic issues. Some studies have shown that whenever two people meet for the first time, a dominant-submissive relationship is established within the first 60 seconds. The perceptions of who is dominant between two people have been found to correlate over 90 percent with carefully constructed personality tests measuring the same phenomenon. Some books on power and control go to extreme lengths to help people gain control over others. Korda (1975) suggests that in order to gain and hold control over others, you should position your desk with your back to a window so that the other person has to look into the sunlight, thus putting him or her at a disadvantage.

The control issue is relevant to every organization on a daily basis, from the formal organization and the so-called span of control, to who talks the most in meetings. Supervisors typically talk more than subordinates. They also usually control the topic of conversation as well. Control is often demonstrated in rather subtle ways too. I once saw an office worker throw a report on a secretary's desk. He said: "Sandy, I need to have this typed for the three o'clock meeting today." You could tell by her expression that she did not like the way he talked to her. Later that day, he came to pick up the finished report. She said: "Gee Dave, I'm really sorry. I just didn't have time to get it done. Mr. Jenkins [the top boss] had me on another project all day." She was giving Dave a lesson in organizational control. Any experienced supervisor knows how much control his or her subordinates have if they choose to use it.

Affection

Affection refers to the friendship and closeness between people. Often our best friends are co-workers. Why is it that when we have time off from the job we will organize bowling leagues, golf outings, and baseball leagues with co-workers? Some of these activities, like the company picnic or Christmas party, may be more or less required. But for the most part we socialize off the job as well as on because we want to—picture the many winning-team locker-room scenes with the champagne pouring over people's heads and players hugging each other as extreme examples of this affection.

Schutz (1967) compares inclusion, control, and affection in the following way:

> A difference in inclusion behavior, control behavior, and affection behavior is illustrated by the different feelings a man has in being turned down by a fraternity, failed in a course by a professor, and rejected by his girl. . . . Inclusion is concerned with the problem if in or out, control is concerned with top or bottom, and affection with close or far."

In each of these areas we have both the need to receive these behaviors from others and the need to express such needs toward others. Wanted inclusion would be hoping to be asked to go to lunch or coffee or to have a beer with the group; expressed inclusion would be inviting someone else to go. A compatible need level would exist when a person's wanted and expressed needs are at about the same level of intensity. Compatibility between individuals seems to occur when their needs are similar on the inclusion and affection dimensions and complementary or different on the control dimension. Otherwise a group may suffer from too many power struggles if members are all high in need to control. Compatibility on these three dimensions tends to reduce conflict and increase group cohesiveness and satisfaction.

A carefully controlled laboratory study found that Schutz's predictions were substantiated. Liddel and Slocum (1976) constructed groups that were neutral, compatible, or incompatible based on FIRO—B scores. When the groups were allowed to work on a problem-solving task, the compatible groups completed their tasks significantly faster than the neutral groups, which were significantly more efficient than the incompatible groups.

FIRO—B has also been found to be useful in organizational development. Varney and Hunady (1978) conducted a study in a fifty-year-old heavy metal production plant with 900 employees and 95 managers. They used the FIRO—B test as a tool to give feedback to the work groups regarding their own individual needs and to give them insight into each other. The plant manager originally described the organization's needs in the following summary:

> . . . There is a considerable amount of disagreement and disharmony among members of the management staff, resulting in a failure on the part of individuals as well as the team as a whole to accomplish set tasks. The performance indicators for the plant are in almost all cases below the normal, and we ranked among a total of six plants in our division as the lowest performer. The basic problem seems to be that people cannot work together when it comes to sorting out problems, and they spend a lot of time blaming each other for the failures that occur. (p. 445)

As a result of the study, the researchers reported numerous changes in the behavior of the employees involved in the study. They concluded: "FIRO—B is a powerful stimulus to change. In the research reported here, we have demonstrated the value of the use of a "high energizer" such as the FIRO—B in team-building interventions" (p. 445).

Although personality is one of the most important background factors in small group communication, other factors are also involved. *Organismic* factors or variables are those that are part of the organism. These include a number of characteristics, but three seem to be especially pertinent to small group interaction: sex, age, and health.

SEX

Perhaps the most obvious thing about groups that include both sexes is that they are most interesting! Schutz (1971, p. 226) writes:

> Usually, if there's a girl in the group who attracts me I find more interest in the group as a whole, and must watch myself because I tend to find everything she says and does somehow much more fascinating than I do anyone else's contribution.

Women emphatically point out that the increased arousal brought about by a member of the opposite sex is every bit as much a part of the feminine response pattern as it is the masculine.

Sex does seem to play an increasing role in work groups. Blotnick (1986) surveyed 1,800 professional women between the ages of 18 and 45. They had a median age of 32 and an average income of $26,000. He found that an astonishing 56 percent reported having had an affair with a co-worker, customer, or client. This compared to only 7 to 9 percent in the 1970s and even lower percentages in the 1950s and 1960s. These statistics would lead to the conclusion that sex is a volatile and extremely relevant background factor to consider in work group settings.

These statistics are even more shocking given that Thomas (1986) reports that 53 percent of all the full-time workers in America are women, and of all the women in the country between ages 25 and 35, fully 66 percent are working full time (p. 26).

Differences in behavior between the sexes have for years been known to be a function of cultural influences and childhood learning experiences. Margaret Mead (1968) found as early as in 1935 that certain behaviors the Western world had assumed were innately masculine or feminine were instead culturally determined. In her studies of New Guinea tribes, she found certain societies in which women dominated. She writes (p. 259): "Among the Tchambuli the woman is the dominant, impersonal, managing partner, the man the less reponsible and the emotionally dependent person." Mead describes the husband, on the other hand, as being catty toward other men but charming toward women. He danced in the tribal ceremonies, spent hours on his personal makeup, and gossiped about the other *men* in the village. Obviously such behaviors cannot be an inherent function of one's sex.

Berg and Bass (1961) report that men tend to be more task-oriented in groups, while women are more concerned with interpersonal harmony. Kibler, Barker, and Cegala (1970) found no differences between sexes in ability to comprehend and retain information from orally communicated messages. Furthermore, in a more recent study Rosenfeld and Christie (1974) found no significant differences in persuasibility between men and women. They cite four other studies between 1968 and 1973 that also failed to find sex differences in persuasibility, while older studies from 1935 to 1968 more often than not found women more persuasible. Rosenfeld and Christie (1974, p. 253) concluded:

> If earlier studies were correct concerning persuasibility . . . women are gradually growing away from the "traditional" dependence upon others and acquiring more confidence in their own judgments. It is futile to attempt to conclude that one sex is more persuasible than another based upon the present study and other available research.

It would seem that the same futility presently exists in attempting to predict *group* communciation behaviors on the basis of sex alone. However, it is important to emphasize that certain stereotypes concerning male and female roles are probably outdated, and new research is needed to establish if any sex differences do exist regarding small group behaviors. For example, review the stereotypes listed below.

How to Tell a Businessman from a Businesswoman
A businessman is aggressive; a businesswoman is pushy.
A businessman is good on details; she's picky.
He loses his temper because he's so involved in his job; she's bitchy.
When he's depressed (or hung over), everyone tiptoes past his office.
She's moody so it must be her time of the month.
He follows through; she doesn't know when to quit.
He's confident; she's conceited.
He stands firm; she's impossible to deal with.

He's firm; she's hard.

His judgments are her prejudices.

He is a man of the world; she's been around.

He drinks because of excessive job pressure; she's a lush.

He isn't afraid to say what he thinks; she's mouthy.

He exercises authority; she's power mad.

He's close-mouthed; she's secretive.

He's a stern taskmaster; she's hard to work for.

It seems reasonable to predict that groups comprised of both sexes will be different from those whose members are all of the same sex. We might expect that sexually heterogeneous groups would have more socially oriented behaviors and fewer task-oriented behaviors, since members would be more interested in promoting social relationships than in homogeneous groups. South (1927) found that a one-sex committee is usually more efficient than a mixed one for this reason. However, much more research is needed to establish the role of sex in group discussion. As women's role in our society changes, more modern research can help to clarify and probably disprove some long-held beliefs.

For a comprehensive discussion of gender and communication, see Eakins and Eakins (1978).

AGE

Obviously communication patterns differ from childhood through adolescence to adulthood and old age. Older group members in college-age groups (for example, married students, veterans, and so forth) tend to be more influential, based on their relatively greater number of years of experience. While this may not always hold true, it tends to be the case. There is some evidence (Bass et al., 1953) that older college women are held in higher esteem than younger college women. It generally takes time to develop leadership qualifications. In fact, one study (Quinn, 1973) indicated that one reason younger people in general have lower job satisfaction is that they tend to have lower-level jobs, which are inherently less satisfying. On the other hand, as they gain in age and experience, they move into more challenging job capacities and gain in satisfaction.

Over two thousand years ago Aristotle made what today seems like a very sound observation regarding the differences in behavior that go along with age differences. As quoted by Roberts (1941, pp. 1404–1406), he wrote:

Younger men have strong passions, and tend to gratify them indiscriminately. Of the bodily desires, it is the sexual by which they are most swayed, in which they show absence of self-control. . . . They are hot-tempered and quick-tempered, and apt to give way of their anger; bad temper often gets the better of them, for . . . they cannot bear being slighted, they are indignant if they imagine themselves unfairly treated. While they love honor, they love victory still more; for youth is eager for superiority over others, and victory is one form of this. . . . They look at the good side rather than the bad. . . . They trust others readily. . . . They would always rather do noble deeds than useful ones. . . . All their mistakes are in the direction of doing things excessively and vehemently. . . . They think they know everything, and are always quite sure about it.

. . . The character of elderly men—men who are past their prime–. . . . is the contrary of all these. . . . They have often been taken in, and often made mistakes; and life on the whole is a bad business. . . . They "think," but they never "know"; and because of their hesitation they always add a "possibly" or a "perhaps." . . . They are cynical. . . . They are small-minded, because they have been humbled by life. . . . They are not generous. . . . They lack confidence in the future. . . . They live by memory rather than by hope.

. . . As for men in their prime . . . they have a character between that of the young and that of the old. . . . They have neither that of excess of confidence which amounts to rashness, not too much timidity, but the right amount of each. They neither trust everybody nor distrust everybody, but judge people correctly.

Finally, Shaw (1981, pp. 181–182), summarizing the literature on age and group behavior, stated:

[T]here is good evidence that chronological age of the group member is related to several aspects of group interaction. With increasing age, the individual has an increasing . . . selectivity of contacts and greater complexity of . . . interaction. . . . Age is related to behavior in groups, it provides the time required for the individual to learn appropriate social responses . . . in most cases it is not the mere fact that the individual has aged that is important, but rather that he has had greater experience in social situations.

It is also interesting to speculate that groups with age heterogeneity would perform differently than those with age homogeneity. A number of studies indicate that some member heterogeneity relates positively to such group outcomes as cohesion (Hare, 1962). It is apparent that age, and the experiences that go along with age, will affect group interaction and subsequent group outcomes. For the time being, however, the exact nature of these relationships is not clear.

HEALTH

Although health may not be a highly significant factor in the study of small groups, it does play a part. Deficiencies in both physical and mental health would seem to impede group performance. A member who fails to attend meetings or who is unable to carry his or her portion of the group workload will sooner or later reduce total group output. Also, physical health frequently affects stamina. Strength and stamina may not be important in relatively short discussions (lasting up to an hour); however, discussions and conferences frequently last for days. Labor-management negotiations may go 20 hours a day for a week or even longer. In one case, a local labor agreement was settled after a prolonged strike, and the week after the agreement was reached the local union president died of a heart attack. So physical health and stamina can play an important part in small group interaction.

Those who are spaced out on drugs or who are hung over from the night before will also harm group performance. In one case a college professor was consistently abusive and aggressive in department meetings. He later admitted that he had been so high on drugs he didn't even remember being at the meetings. Yet his behavior caused severe setbacks in his department, since he argued vociferously against all attempts to cover the items in the group's agenda, and he seriously hurt the feelings of other group members through his verbal assaults. Physical and mental health factors are out of the control of other group members, yet they have an effect on the group's end results.

As each of us develops through childhood and adolescence, a myriad of experiences shape our view of the world. Since we each have different experiences, we would expect our outlooks to differ also. These experiences are called developmental factors, and we will look at three that are related to small group interaction: attitudes, values, and anxieties.

ATTITUDES

Almost fifty years ago, Allport (1935) defined an *attitude* as "a mental and neural state of readiness, organized through experience, exerting a directive or dynamic influence upon the individual's response to all objects and situations with which it is related." According to Triandis (1971), attitudes have three components: (1) a cognitive component, which refers to an idea or a concept, such as "Chevrolets," (2) an affective component or the emotion toward the idea (Chevrolets are good), and (3) a behavioral component, which is the readiness to act (that is, to drive or buy a Chevrolet).

McGrath and Altman (1966) indicate that group members may hold several types of attitudes that are relevant to their participation in small groups. For example, they have attitudes toward the task itself, toward the situation within which the group is operating, toward people inside and outside of the group, and toward other issues that may be related to the one under discussion. All these attitudes will ultimately affect their behavior in the group, which in turn will affect the group's results. How many times have you been a member of a project team or group in which either you or others in the group have found that you just can't seem to get too enthusiastic about accomplishing the task? Or perhaps you would ordinarily be interested in the task, but it comes at a time when you are preoccupied with other things, such as romantic difficulties or financial worries. These illustrations help to indicate the important role that attitudes may play in determining one's actions in the group.

Some of the most intuitive yet provocative theories concerning attitudes are the so-called cognitive consistency theories. These closely related theories are all based on the assumption that human beings have a strong psychological need for consistency. Heider (1958), the first of the consistency theorists, refers to this as a need to maintain *balance*. He reasons that if we hold an attitude X and another person holds the same value, then we are likely to feel positively toward that person. For example, if Lance likes motorcycles and Brad also likes motorcycles, Lance is likely to have positive feelings toward Brad. This can be illustrated as shown in Figure 2.2. If, on the other hand, Brad does not like motorcycles, Lance would feel some imbalance and would

FIGURE 2.2

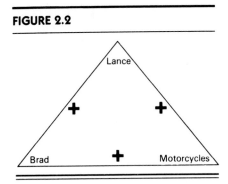

be motivated to resolve it in one of several ways. First, he could try to change Brad's evaluation of motorcycles. Second, he could change his feeling toward Brad. Finally, he could change his own evaluation of motorcycles. The specific alternative Lance chooses would depend on the relative strength of his attitudes toward Brad and toward motorcycles.

Heider predicts that balanced triads are rewarding, or pleasant to experience, while imbalanced triads result in pressure to restore balance. An easy rule of thumb for differentiating between balanced and imbalanced triads is that if the algebraic product of the three elements in the triad is positive, the triad is balanced. If the algebraic product is negative, the triad is imbalanced. Which of the triads in Figure 2.3 is imbalanced, thus creating pressure to restore balance? How could balance be restored?

A related consistency theory is called *cognitive dissonance theory* (Festinger 1957). In this theory, *consonance* is the same as Heider's concept of balance, and *dissonance* is equivalent to imbalance in that it serves to motivate a change back to consonance. One of the interesting finds of research in this area is that a severe initiation for attaining group membership creates a high level of dissonance, which is usually resolved by the person valuing membership in the group more than if the initiation was less severe (Aronson and Mills 1959).

Fraternities and sororities have used pledging as a device to increase the severity

FIGURE 2.3

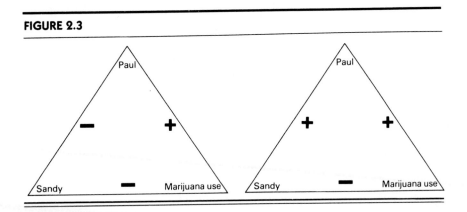

of initiation into membership. The result is usually that one who endures these experiences reduces the dissonance caused by them and begins to believe they are necessary and even desirable for the new pledge class to endure. The traditional pride in being a United States Marine has also resulted largely from the severity of initiation experienced in Marine Corps boot camp.

Group interaction may also create dissonance. If you are confronted in a discussion with an opinion contrary to your own, some degree of dissonance will result. The dissonance will increase if you value the other person and if the issue over which you disagree is one of high relevance. According to Festinger and Aronson (1968) you may reduce the dissonance in these five ways (starting with the most likely and going to the least likely approach): (1) Devalue the importance of the issue; (2) derogate the disagreeing person; (3) attempt to change his or her attitude; (4) seek additional social support for your view; and (5) change your attitude. Aronson (1973) posits that although people like to think of themselves as rational animals, they are more likely than not a "rationalizing animal." It is important to point out that we all use these methods of dissonance reduction, and we need to have them. Although rationalizing may sound like something we should avoid, it can be a helpful tool if we are consciously aware of using it.

Organ and Bateman (1986) remind us of the difficulty of attempting to change a person's attitude when they write:

> We would expect people to be jealous of their freedom with respect to attitudes that are central to their self-concepts. Attempts to change such attitudes represent, in essence, attempts to change their identities. Consider the workers who like to use certain materials and procedures because they are so closely linked to their self-images as meticulous artisans. A supervisor trying to alter their sentiments toward those methods is, perhaps unwittingly, striking at the core of their vocational self images. It would not be surprising if they defended their freedom to hold such attitudes by valuing their procedures and materials all the more, in response to influence attempts. (p. 218)

On the other hand, actual research evidence has shown that successful attitude change can be accomplished. For example, Miller and Monge (1985) studied the impact of communication regarding organizational change on employee attitudes and anxiety level. From their research, they conclude:

> The results of this study have several implications for organizational managers interested in improving employees' attitudes toward work or the organization or helping them adjust to organizational change . . . managers should also be aware of employee interaction and consider information a means of reducing anxiety and stress, improving worker satisfaction, or influencing other job attitudes.
>
>   Second, this research indicates that any information is better than no information, so managers facing change should try to provide employees with as much information as possible. Third . . . managers should attempt to isolate needs relevant to the change and see that the needs are being met in the new situation and help employees to know that their needs are being considered. (p. 382)

VALUES

Although an overwhelming amount of research has been conducted on attitudes and attitude change, Rokeach (1968, 1971, 1973) has argued that people's *values* are also important as a predictor of behavior. His rationale is that we have thousands of different attitudes, but we have only several dozen values. Values, then, are seen as more fundamental than attitudes and are more stable and long-lasting. For an exercise concerning your own values and how they relate to the values of others, see the exercises at the end of this chapter.

Value differences may significantly influence the course of any given group discussion. Suppose you are in a group attempting to determine a policy regarding pregnancy leaves of absence for employees of a company. Suppose also that your committee consists of six women, three who have been to college and three who have not. Based on the study data in Figure 2.4, how likely do you think it would be that the committee might achieve consensus on this issue?

This research indicates that educational differences would generate severe value

FIGURE 2.4
Bar graph from the *Flint Journal*,
November 13, 1974

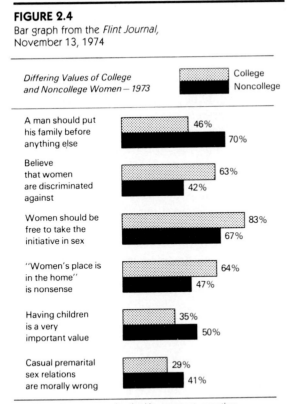

Differing Values of College and Noncollege Women — 1973

College
Noncollege

A man should put his family before anything else — 46% / 70%

Believe that women are discriminated against — 63% / 42%

Women should be free to take the initiative in sex — 83% / 67%

"Women's place is in the home" is nonsense — 64% / 47%

Having children is a very important value — 35% / 50%

Casual premarital sex relations are morally wrong — 29% / 41%

Women's movement has had its warmest reception on America's campuses. The recent Yankelovich "Study of American Youth" reports that the values of Women's Lib have created a wide schism between women in college and women who do not have a college education.

differences between the two subgroups on the committee. If one group, the noncollege women, basically valued motherhood and devalued careers for women, it would probably be difficult for them to agree with the others on a leave-of-absence policy decision. Similar difficulties arise in discussions dealing with sexual behaviors, obscenity, abortion, religion, and politics, for example. Any discussion on a topic on which people have strong value differences is likely to be complicated by such differences.

With the graduating class of 1986, there were two nationally publicized examples of values influencing graduation committees' decisions. At Rice University in Houston, Texas, two graduates who were vegetarians asked administrators to allow them to have diplomas printed on paper rather than on sheepskin. One of the graduates said: "I don't participate in eating meat. If I draw the line there; why not draw it one step further?" (AP, May 10, 1986). At Tufts University in Boston, the medical school students no longer wanted to take the 2,000-year-old Hippocratic oath because they no longer believed in the values it upheld. Instead, they vowed to "stress prevention over cure, tend to their patients' psychological needs, seek help from others, and, above all, 'not play God'" (AP, May 18, 1986).

At every university, committees decide such policies. It is conceivable that the values of the administrators on those committees played a part in determining the decisions described above. In fact, Naisbitt (1982) argues that these are simply examples of one "megatrend" which he calls "From either/or to Multiple Option." As other examples, he cites the number of television channels that used to be available (3 networks) compared to cable television's 36. If you have a satellite dish, you may be able to get over 100. An organizational example would be the so-called cafeteria of compensation and benefits approach in which employees can select from a wide variety of company benefits to suit their own particular needs (e.g., tuition refund, versus optional life insurance, versus tax sheltered employee investment programs, versus increased retirement contributions). These are all current examples of changing values influencing our behaviors.

Earlier we discussed the influence of age on values and behaviors. As it turns out, modern research corroborates Aristotle's intuitive observations (Payne, Summers, and Stewart 1973, pp. 24–25. Subjects from three generations (college students, their parents, and their grandparents) were asked to respond on a seven-point scale (1) "not at all bad" to (7) "extremely bad" to each of 85 items. Sample items were:

- Becoming involved in unusual sex practices with persons of the opposite sex
- Being unpatriotic
- Cheating on your income tax
- Cheating on an exam and getting caught
- Going to a party in casual clothes and finding that everyone is dressed up
- Having to go on welfare to feed or clothe your children adequately

The researchers found that college students were significantly less severe in their judgments than were their parents, who were in turn less severe than the grandparents.

Although differences exist between generations, it is also likely that major differences exist between individuals in the same age group. A question arises as to the degree of value differences that can be tolerated in a group before these differences become a major obstacle to group functioning. Fortunately, some related research sheds light on this question. Rogers and Shoemaker (1971) discussed this issue with regard to homophily and heterophily of relationships. *Homophily* is defined as "the degree to which pairs of individuals who interact are similar in certain attributes (beliefs, values, education, social status)" (McCroskey 1971, p. 174). Rogers and Bhowmik (1971, p. 213) state that "heterophilic interaction is likely to cause message distortion, delayed transmission, restriction of communication channels, and may cause cognitive dissonance, as the receiver is exposed to messages that may be inconsistent with his existing beliefs and attitudes, an uncomfortable psychological state." In other words, two students would probably communicate more easily than a student and a professor. While considerable research has been conducted on the effect of homophily-heterophily on the diffusion of innovations, more research is needed to determine the effects these factors have on group functioning and group outcomes.

THE SYSTEMS PERSPECTIVE

As we pointed out in Chapter 1, small group interactions are the result of influences that can be labeled inputs, throughputs, and outputs. These factors are in a constant state of simultaneous and reciprocal influence. This chapter has focused on some of the inputs—namely, the relevant background factors of the group members. Through the discussion of personality we tried to illustrate the role personality plays in shaping individual behavior. For example, those high on inclusion will probably be more inclined to join groups in the first place (if we assume that membership is voluntary). Those high on affection are very likely to smile more, express more feelings both verbally and nonverbally than low affiliators, give more direct eye contact to more members of the group, and agree more than low affiliators. We would expect that high affection members would have higher satisfaction resulting from harmonious group experiences, and greater dissatisfaction with groups that experience a high degree of conflict and disagreement. The person low on need for inclusion would tend to avoid meetings and group memberships whenever possible and would avoid talking in the groups he or she was forced to be in. Group interaction would generally be viewed by the introvert as threatening and therefore less satisfying than engaging in the same activity alone. However, if the group were conducted by a supportive and nonthreatening leader, the introvert's satisfaction level would increase dramatically (Giffin and Bradley 1969).

High control members tend to enjoy working on task-oriented projects, since they are more task-oriented than most others and find that the group tends to slow down their progress. The exception, of course, would be a group composed of a lot of high controllers. In this case, high cohesion or high conflict might result, depending on the way the members decided to reward their efforts. Thus group norms, leadership style, and communication patterns all tend to influence the satisfaction level of group members. In the example at the beginning of this chapter, the group including John Simpson provided an illustration of a controller that resulted in a low level of satisfaction. John was seen by the rest of the group as too domineering. He got into one argument after another with other members. In this case, his high degree of dominance and dogmatism seemed to overshadow most of his expertise.

The three organismic factors discussed in this chapter were sex, age, and health. A group with both sexes tends to have more socially oriented communication patterns and fewer task-oriented comments resulting. A clever study by Rosenfeld and Fowler (1976) found that sex and personality combined to influence an individual's leadership style. The most interesting finding of this study seems to be that men and women who act similarly are perceived differently. According to Rosenfeld and Fowler (1976, p. 324):

> Whereas democratic males were characterized as forceful, analytical, and as valuing the love of people . . . democratic females were characterized as open-minded and nurturing. The democratic male may appear to group members as analytical and thereby aloof, while the democratic female may appear to be warm and affectionate.

This study illustrates what is meant by the systems aspects of small group interaction. Personality, sex, style of leadership behavior, and the resulting perception of the person behaving are all interrelated.

This chapter also dealt with age as an organismic variable. Age seems to be somewhat similar to attitudes and values in that the more similar group members are (in age, attitudes, and values), the easier it is for them to communicate in a way that leads to higher satisfaction. It stands to reason that it is more comfortable to be in groups with people like ourselves (in terms of age, attitudes, and values) than it is to be in groups in which we feel we "don't fit in" as well. However, some of the most interesting experiences occur when we meet someone of a drastically different age group who shares our attitudes and values. Conversely, even people of one's own age may differ so much in attitude or personality that hard feelings result.

In the readings at the end of this chapter. William Schutz shows the importance of the need for inclusion, control, and affection in relation to several aspects of group behavior. The second selection by Widgery and Tubbs applies attitude change theory to supervision.

EXERCISES

1. Employee Selection Problem

You are a member of a personnel selection committee. You need to hire two people as first-line supervisors in an industrial foundry. The supervisors would be in charge of 30-person (mostly male) work groups who do machining processes (grinding, drilling, polishing) on metal castings made from molten metal in a different part of the foundry. Examine all five information sheets, which describe the candidates who have passed the physical examination and are available for immediate employment.

1

NAME: Sally A. Peterson   AGE: 23

MARITAL STATUS: Married   NUMBER OF CHILDREN: 0

NUMBER OF DEPENDENTS OTHER THAN SELF (explain relation):   1—husband

EDUCATION:

	Years	Degree or Diploma	Major (where applicable)
Elementary	8	Yes	
High School	4	Yes	College prep.
College	4	Yes (B.A.)	Sociology

CURRENT EDUCATIONAL OR VOCATIONAL SITUATION: Has been management trainee for four months with XYZ Aircraft Company. Began with XYZ immediately after serving two years with Peace Corps.

VOCATIONAL SKILLS OR EXPERIENCE: None other than a few elementary skills learned while in Peace Corps.

POLICE RECORD: None

ADDITIONAL COMMENTS: Currently active in volunteer community social work. Has taken over Junior Achievement group in underprivileged neighborhood.

2

NAME: Thomas Browne   AGE: 26

MARITAL STATUS: Married   NUMBER OF CHILDREN: 0

NUMBER OF DEPENDENTS OTHER THAN SELF (explain relation):   1—wife

EDUCATION:

	Years	Degree or Diploma	Major (where applicable)
Elementary	8	Yes	
High School	4	Yes	College prep.
College	4	Yes (B.A.)	Economics
	½	(toward M.A.)	Economics

CURRENT EDUCATIONAL OR VOCATIONAL SITUATION: Is completing first year in graduate school working toward M.A. in economics which should be completed in one more semester. Is classified in top third of his graduate school class. Is currently a research assistant to leading economist in graduate school of business.

VOCATIONAL SKILLS OR EXPERIENCE: None

POLICE RECORD: Arrested with a number of other students involved in campus disturbance—released without charges being made.

ADDITIONAL COMMENTS: None

3

NAME: William Cross   AGE: 20

MARITAL STATUS: Married   NUMBER OF CHILDREN: 0
                                       (expecting first child in 6 months)

NUMBER OF DEPENDENTS OTHER THAN SELF (explain relation):   1—wife

EDUCATION:

	Year	Degree or Diploma	Major (where applicable)
Elementary	8	Yes	
High School	4	Yes	Vocational
College			

CURRENT EDUCATIONAL OR VOCATIONAL SITUATION: Plumber's apprentice completing second year of apprenticeship. Employed by large building contractor.

VOCATIONAL SKILLS OR EXPERIENCE: Plumbing, some automotive repair skills, welding. General construction work.

POLICE RECORD: Two arrests, no convictions.
First arrest while in high school—no details because of juvenile status. Second arrest for disorderly conduct—charges dismissed.

ADDITIONAL COMMENTS: None

4

NAME: Jane Williams   AGE: 24

MARITAL STATUS: Single   NUMBER OF CHILDREN:

NUMBER OF DEPENDENTS OTHER THAN SELF (explain relation):   0

EDUCATION:

	Years	Degree or Diploma	Major (where applicable)
Elementary	8	Yes	
High School	4	Yes	College prep.
College	4	Yes (B.A.)	Sociology
	1½	Yes (M.B.A.)	Production Management

CURRENT EDUCATIONAL OR VOCATIONAL SITUATION: Completing second year of graduate school. Has B.A. in sociology, working toward Ph.D. which should be completed in 3 to 4 semesters. Ranks in middle third of graduate class. Working one-half time as a teaching assistant. Doing volunteer work and beginning research on urban sociology project.

VOCATIONAL SKILLS OR EXPERIENCE: None

POLICE RECORD: None

ADDITIONAL COMMENTS: None

5

NAME: Robert Smith   AGE: 21

MARITAL STATUS: Single   NUMBER OF CHILDREN:

NUMBER OF DEPENDENTS OTHER THAN SELF (explain relation): 0

EDUCATION:

	Years	Degree or Diploma	Major (where applicable)
Elementary	8	Yes	
High School	4	Yes	College prep.
College	3½	B.S. expected at end of semester	Business Administration

CURRENT EDUCATIONAL OR VOCATIONAL SITUATION: College senior expecting degree at end of current (spring) semester. "A−" student.

VOCATIONAL SKILLS OR EXPERIENCE: Typing. Has also worked part time in selling, construction work, and on farms.

POLICE RECORD: None

ADDITIONAL COMMENTS: Father unemployed for medical reasons. Mother works to support family. It is known that he has worked his way through college and has incurred a small debt in the form of a student loan.

Group Task   After reviewing all five information sheets, meet as a group for 30 minutes to decide which two candidates should get the jobs. Each of you in the group will be assigned to argue in favor of one of the five candidates. After each of you presents the best "case" for your candidate, you must work together collectively to determine in the best interest of everyone concerned who should be hired. Your company is an equal opportunity/affirmative action employer.

2. Self-Esteem Exercise

Rate yourself on the following list of terms. First put an *I* in the appropriate blank indicating how you would like to be *ideally*. After completing all the items, begin the list again. This time put an *R* in the appropriate blank indicating how you think you *really* are. After you have rated your ideal self and your real self, compare the two. You may want to talk to others to see how their ratings compare.

1. Attractive   ___:___:___:___:___:___ Unattractive

2. Intelligent   ___:___:___:___:___:___ Unintelligent

3. Weak   ___:___:___:___:___:___ Strong

4. Passive   ___:___:___:___:___:___ Active

5. Fair	___:___:___:___:___:___	Unfair
6. Kind	___:___:___:___:___:___	Unkind
7. Quiet	___:___:___:___:___:___	Loud
8. Introverted	___:___:___:___:___:___	Extroverted
9. Nervous	___:___:___:___:___:___	Relaxed
10. Liberal	___:___:___:___:___:___	Conservative
11. Happy	___:___:___:___:___:___	Sad
12. Boastful	___:___:___:___:___:___	Humble
13. Controlled	___:___:___:___:___:___	Uncontrolled
14. Vulnerable	___:___:___:___:___:___	Invulnerable
15. Excited	___:___:___:___:___:___	Calm
16. Sexy	___:___:___:___:___:___	Unsexy
17. Trusting	___:___:___:___:___:___	Untrusting
18. Powerful	___:___:___:___:___:___	Weak
19. Conforming	___:___:___:___:___:___	Independent
20. Sensitive	___:___:___:___:___:___	Insensitive

3. Personal Styles Exercise

Read the descriptions of the tough battler, friendly helper, and objective thinker that follow. Then anonymously rate volunteer class members on these three dimensions by placing an *X* inside a triangle as illustrated.

After this has been done, distribute them to the person who is rated. Class members may ask questions to get more feedback on what behaviors create these impressions on fellow students.

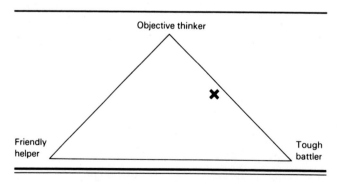

PERSONAL STYLES IN GROUPS AND ORGANIZATIONS*

Listed below are three characteristic types that may be found in any group or organization.

	Tough Battler	Friendly Helper	Objective Thinker
Emotions	Accepts aggression, rejects affection	Accepts affection, rejects aggression	Rejects both affection and interpersonal aggression
Goal	Dominance	Acceptance	Correctness
Influences others by	Direction, intimidation, control of rewards	Offering understanding, praise, favors, friendship	Factual data, logical arguments
Value in organization	Initiates, demands, disciplines	Supports, harmonizes, relieves tension	Defines, clarifies, gets information, criticizes, tests
Overuses	Fighting	Kindness	Analysis
Becomes	Pugnacious	Sloppy, sentimental	Pedantic
Fears	Being "soft" or dependent	Desertion, conflict	Emotions, irrational acts
Needs	Warmth, consideration, objectivity, humility	Strength, integrity, firmness, self-assertion	Awareness of feeling, ability to love and to fight

Above are shown characteristic emotions, goals, standards of evaluation, techniques of influence of each type, and his/her service to the organization.

Each can be overdone and distorted. The *Tough Battler* would be a better manager, a better parent, a better neighbor, and a more satisfied person if he/she could learn some sensitivity, accept his/her inevitable dependence on others, and come to enjoy consideration for them. The Tough Battler would be more successful if he/she recognized that some facts will not yield to pugnacity.

The *Friendly Helper* would be a better manager, parent, citizen, and person if he/she could stand up for his/her own interests and for what is right, even against the pleas of others. This type needs firmness and strength and courage not to evade or smooth over conflicts. He/she must face facts.

The *Objective Thinker* would be a better human being and a better business leader is he/she could become more aware of his/her own feelings and the feelings of others. The Objective Thinker needs to learn that there are times when it is all right to fight and times when it is desirable to love.

*This material is adapted from the *Reading Book* of the NTL Institute for Applied Behavioral Science, associated with the National Education Association. The papers were originally prepared for theory sessions at the Institute's laboratories.

4. Gender Conditioning and the Stress It Produces

In groups of five or so, discuss your feelings about the following statements on the topics of sex roles and gender conditioning. The outline that follows this list may help you get started.

1. I am moving away from the idea that there is one role for men and one role for women, but I feel guilty when the man or woman in my life does something I have traditionally felt responsible for.

2. I know that society's view of a man's showing emotion, or its traditional rules of what he may eat or wear, is no measure of the man, but openly breaking these rules is just asking for people to question his sexuality and not worth the hassle.

3. Women's liberation, carried to the extreme, is responsible for the high rate of male impotency and homosexuality we find today.

4. Right or wrong, a man's sexuality is measured by his status and ability to make money. By many people's standards, all a woman needs to be successful is to find a man who will take care of her.

5. The thing a man should be most proud of is his success in his work. Mainly, he works to provide the "good life" for his wife and family. Not having a job is the worst thing that can happen to him.

6. I think I (my husband) work(s) too hard, but not maintaining our present lifestyle would cause more problems and be even harder to deal with than my (his) overwork.

For Men:

1. Since adulthood I have found it difficult to become close friends with another male. It really doesn't matter though, since, once I become involved with a woman, I find I really don't need any other close friends.

2. I understand that the woman in my life has a need to be liberated, but I am still doing everything that I always did and constantly she wants more from me. Her liberation is costing me mine.

For Women:

1. The man in my life finds activities he can do without me that bring him satisfaction, partly because we agree that everyone is responsible for his own happiness. I don't enjoy going out without him. Social events seem to be designed for couples and I feel out of place when I am alone or with women.

2. For the first time the man in my life feels that it is important for me to know who I am and what I want out of life. I am so accustomed to "not wanting anything" that I can't answer those two questions. I jump from one idea to another and it is driving us both crazy.

I. Gender conditioning distorts one's "world consciousness"

    A. His vision of the world situation

    B. Her vision of the world situation

II. Gender conditioning distorts one's body consciousness

    A. View of pain: Male denies pain—e.g., drops dead at 54. Female affirms pain—e.g., lives in Palm Springs till age 90.

    B. View of dependency: Male denies dependency—e.g., won't go to doctor. Female affirms dependency—e.g., likes doctors.

    C. View of passivity: Male feels need to be aggressive. Female feels need to be dependent/passive.

    D. View of diet: Male equates food with masculinity: the more food, the more masculine. Female is obsessed with diet.

    E. View of touching: Male gets touched only as prelude to sex. Female desires to be touched often.

    F. View of emotions: Male denies emotions. Female affirms emotions.

Summary: The process (gender conditioning) undermines the content (feelings) of a relationship.

III. What holds traditional relationships together

    A. Role: Male knows what society expects of his role and so does female.

    B. Ritual: Life is programmed by events.

    C. Religion: Sanctifies traditional relationship.

IV. Actor/reactor: The roles created by society over the centuries

    A. Actor = Male = Mr. Macho: Is aggressive, emotionless, does not have needs, is a sexual performer and initiator and feels like a machine

    B. Reactor = Female = Earthmother: Is passive, indirect aggressor, gives up autonomy, is sexually submissive, is emotional, sees self as a child who is controlled and used

C. Result can be withdrawing, passive men and raging women who destroy one another

---

5. A Fable

Read the following fable and rank the characters on the basis of how much you like each person. Your number-one rank will be the person you like best; number five, the person you like the least. This information will be shared.

Once upon a time, four people lived on a river. On one side of the river lived Ann and Jack. On the other side of the river, Ralph and Mike lived. None of the people could cross the river because they had no boats and there were no bridges or safe places to swim across. The river was infested with crocodiles and piranhas. It was possible to talk across the river, and over a period of time Ann and Ralph fell in love and spent a great deal of time looking at and talking to each other. They became engaged but had no way of getting together.

Ann and Jack were friends and Jack was Ann's confidant. On the other side of the river, Mike and Ralph were also friends.

One day a sailor, Sinbad, came down the river on his boat. He was hailed by Ann, who asked him to take her across the river so that she could be with Ralph,

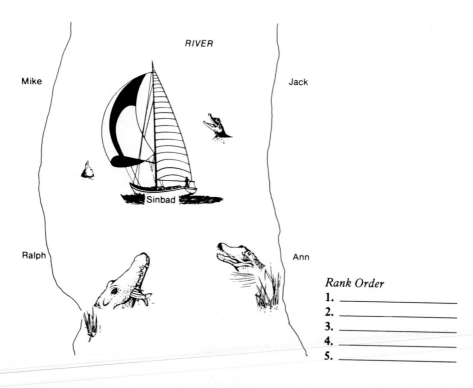

Mike

Jack

RIVER

Sinbad

Ralph

Ann

Rank Order

1. _____
2. _____
3. _____
4. _____
5. _____

her betrothed. Sinbad agreed to do this on one condition—that she let him sleep with her.

Ann was placed in a deep conflict by this offer and she sought help from Jack, her friend and confidant. Jack spent several hours talking with Ann. He was most sympathetic to her plight, but essentially communicated that he had confidence that Ann could make up her own mind about this decision.

Ann decided to take up Sinbad's offer. She spent the night with Sinbad on his boat, and the next day Sinbad deposited her on the opposite shore. Ralph was awaiting her landing and they embraced at once.

After a while, Ralph asked her how she had managed to convince Sinbad to take her across and Ann told him the whole story.

Upon hearing the story, Ralph pushed Ann away and said he would have nothing more to do with her.

Just at this time, Mike came by. He had overheard what happened, and as soon as he saw Ralph pushing Ann away, he moved in and beat up Ralph thoroughly.

6. The New Hire Case

Andrea Turner was a new faculty member at a small private college (150 faculty members). This was her first teaching job after receiving her Ph.D. from one of the most prestigious graduate schools in the country. She worked in the psychology department, which employed twenty-five faculty and three secretaries. Andrea commuted from a city 50 miles away. Therefore, she came to work only on the three days she taught classes and on other days did her other work at home.

When she was at work, she always kept her office door closed. Most others in the department left theirs open. Occasionally faculty members would go to the student center for coffee breaks in groups of three or four. Andrea was invited, but almost never went. After a while, the others stopped asking her to join them. She was busy writing her first book for a prestigious publishing house.

Andrea was an effective teacher and participated on several faculty committees. She was a prolific writer and scholar. Over the course of three years, Andrea performed well above average for a new faculty member.

When it came time for her review for promotion, a great divison was apparent among the other faculty members in their attitudes toward Andrea. A few felt that her work was very strong and that she deserved to be promoted. About two-thirds of the professors on the committee felt that she was too much of a loner and did not contribute to the overall needs of the department, only to her own personal success. After much heated discussion, the decision was made not to promote her.

Within three months, Andrea resigned and took a new teaching job at an excellent university. She left without the usual farewell party for departing colleagues. She apparently cleared out her office one night after everyone had left work. Nobody remembered saying goodbye to her.

Postscript: Several other women faculty members had been promoted in this department, and there was a favorable attitude toward affirmative action among the group. So it can be assumed that sex discrimination was not a factor in this case.

Discussion Questions

1. How would you analyze this case in light of Schutz's theory?

2. How would you analyze it from Andrea's viewpoint?

3. From the department's viewpoint?

4. Would you have done anything about this situation if you had been Andrea's department head?

5. Would you have done anything if you had been one of her colleagues in the department?

6. How typical do you think this case is?

7. What implications does this case (and Schutz's theory) have for you?

READINGS: OVERVIEW

William Schutz has been studying the influence of personality needs on interpersonal and small group interaction for over forty years. During this time he has identified the three basic needs described in this chapter of *inclusion, control,* and *affection.* In this article he elaborates on the manner in which these needs consistently influence our interaction patterns with others.

The second article examines some practical applications of attitude change theory for the supervisor.

The Interpersonal

William Schutz

Our self-concept is largely derived from our relations with other people. In our dealings we exchange various commodities with these people and must make adjustments. In order to understand this interpersonal level I will use a framework first introduced in my book *FIRO*.

Each person has three basic interpersonal needs that are manifested in behavior and feelings toward other people. But this activity is rooted in a person's feelings about himself, his self-concept. The three basic need areas are posited to be *inclusion, control,* and *affection.*

Inclusion refers to feelings about being important or significant, of having some worth so that people will care. The aspect of the self-concept related to *control* is the feeling of competence, including intelligence, appearance, practicality, and general ability to cope with the world. The area of *affection* revolves around feelings of being lovable, of feeling that if one's personal core is revealed in its entirety it will be seen as a lovely thing.

Inclusion behavior refers to associations between people, being excluded or included, belonging, togetherness. The need to be included manifests itself as wanting to be attended to, and to attract attention and interaction. The college militant is often objecting mostly to the lack of attention paid him, the automated student. Even if he is given negative attention he is partially satisfied.

Being a distinct person—that is, having a particular identity—is an essential aspect of inclusion. An integral part of being recognized and paid attention to is that the individual be distinguishable from other people. The height of being identifiable is to be understood, since it implies that someone is interested enough to discover a person's unique characteristics.

An issue that arises frequently at the outset of group relations is that of commitment, the decision to become involved in a given relationship. Usually, in the initial testing of a relationship, individuals try to present themselves to one another partly to find out what facet of themselves others will be interested in. Frequently a member is silent at first because he is not sure that people are interested in him.

Inclusion is unlike affection in that it does not involve strong emotional attachments to individual persons. It is unlike control in that the preoccupation is with prominence, not dominance. Since inclusion involves the process of for-

From William Schutz, Here Comes Everybody *(New York: Harper & Row, 1971), 17–30.*
Copyright © 1971 by William Schutz, reprinted by permission of The Sterling Lord Agency, Inc.

mation, it usually occurs first in the life of a group. People must decide whether they do or don't want to form a group.

A person who has too little inclusion, the undersocial, tends to be introverted and withdrawn. He consciously wants to maintain this distance between himself and others, and insists that he doesn't want to get enmeshed with people and lose his privacy. Unconsciously, however, he definitely wants others to pay attention to him. His biggest fears are that people will ignore him and would just as soon leave him behind. His unconscious attitude may be summarized by, "No one is interested in me, so I'm not going to risk being ignored. I'll stay away from people and get along by myself." He has a strong drive toward self-sufficiency as a technique for existence without others. Behind his withdrawal is the private feeling that others don't understand him. His deepest anxiety, that referring to the self-concept, is that he is worthless. He thinks that if no one ever considered him important enough to receive attention, he must be of no value whatsoever.

The oversocial person tends toward extroversion. He seeks people incessantly and wants them to seek him out. He is also afraid that they will ignore him. His unconscious feelings are the same as those of the withdrawn person, but his overt behavior is the opposite. His unconscious attitude is summarized by, "Although no one is interested in me, I'll make people pay attention to me in any way I can." His inclination is always to seek companionship, for he is the type who can't stand to be alone. All of his activities will be designed to be done in a group.

The interpersonal behavior of the oversocial type of person is designed to focus attention on himself, to make people notice him, to be prominent. The direct method is to be an intensive, exhibitive participator. By simply forcing himself on the group, he forces the group to focus attention on him. A more subtle technique is to try to acquire power (control) or to be well-liked (affection), but it is still for the primary purpose of gaining attention.

To the individual for whom inclusion was resolved in childhood, interaction with people presents no problem. He is comfortable with or without people. He can be a high or low participant in a group without anxiety. He is capable of strong commitment to and involvement with certain groups, but can also withhold commitment if he feels it is appropriate. Unconsciously, he feels that he is a worthwhile, significant person.

On the physical level, inclusion has to do with penetration of the boundaries between the self and the rest of the world, and therefore deals primarily with the periphery of the body, the skin and sense organs, the eyes, ears, nose, and mouth. Attitudes toward these organs may be related to attitudes toward being included with people. If contact with people is a fearsome thing, then the eyes keep people from intruding by not seeing others clearly, and then in order to see them clearly, it is permitted to put up a barrier—a barrier called glasses. When eyes are in the active process of seeing, and don't really want to see, they become dull and seem to retire toward the back of the head. Ears which don't want inclusion hear people who are close as if they were far away. Closeness is not accepted and people are kept at a distance. The mouth and lips become tight and impenetrable. The skin shies away from being touched; it is easily tickled, gets rashes and hives easily so that people will not come near. The muscles of the skin may also become tightened so that feeling is minimized, resulting in a leathery touch feeling.

All of these devices need not be used by one individual. There are probably special circumstances that bring about the preeminence of one over the other. The rock opera *Tommy* describes a boy who sees his mother in bed with another man and becomes blind, who hears them talking and becomes deaf, and who is told never to tell anyone what he saw and heard and becomes mute. In a dramatic form this is probably a good example for the reason for specifying which sense organ is the preferred one for avoiding inclusion.

On a recent trip that involved discussing work with a large number of people, my voice started getting hoarse, which I took to mean that I didn't want to talk any more. But then I noticed my hearing becoming erratic. Of course it was psychological; I simply didn't want to listen to all these people anymore. I began to understand how desirable and possible it would be to become deaf, at least in that situation.

If being included is important, the body may reflect it by having these peripheral organs perform in the opposite way. The eyes become vigilant, looking for people in order to see them clearly. They try to see people who are far away as actually being closer. Possible outcomes of this are especially good vision and perhaps vertical lines between the eyebrows reflecting the effort put into seeing clearly. You can try this right now by looking at some object, preferably a person, in two ways. First look at him dully, as if your eyes were open but actually way back in your head and seeing as little as possible while appearing to give attention. Then look at the same object and feel your eyes leap out and grab him, taking in every aspect of him. The difference in the two feelings is usually very marked and gives some sense of how voluntary such a common phenomenon as looking can be.

The person with a high need for inclusion will have acute senses of smell and hearing, bringing far things near. The skin is receptive to touch and probably is open and soft. This is the pure inclusion pattern. Very quickly complications arise. The person open to inclusion can be sensitive to rejection and develop a barrier. Or he may allow touch and then be afraid.

An interesting body difference occurred in a class in Rolfing. One man, who was learning to be a Rolfer, reacted to the assaults of the teacher Ida Rolf—who uses assault as a teaching method—by immediately responding with a defense, a self-justification, a counterattack, a lengthy explanation. I on the other hand responded to her attacks with utter coolness and calm, allowing her to continue unabated, sometimes agreeing with her point, possibly joking away some of her steam, while underneath, quietly knowing that I was right.

When it came to Rolfing each of us, a startling difference appeared in the way we responded at the periphery of our bodies, the skin. When my friend was physically penetrated he would scream and holler, ask for time out, complain, cry, and reassess the competence of the Rolf practitioner. I would feel most of those things, too, but be very stoic and allow the practitioner to penetrate quite far. But then he would be disconcerted by two things. When he took his hand out my skin would spring back to where it was like rubber, apparently unaffected by his push. Also, if he pushed deeply enough into the flesh, he met a barrier that felt like steel. In other words, he and I represented in our bodies almost the identical reactions we made psychologically, his immediate response, my apparent acceptance but deeper resistance.

Another possibility in exploring the physical correlates of inclusion comes from a comment about sexual intercourse, and brings up physical function to add to the structural physical considerations I have been talking about. In the sexual act, various phases can be distinguished that parallel inclusion, control, and affection. Inclusion problems refer to the initial phases of the act, the feelings about penetration. A male with problems of inclusion will probably have erection problems. His conflict over whether or not to penetrate would be reflected in the nervous enervation of the penis and its willingness or not to be ready to enter. A similar situation arises for a woman where inclusion problems are reflected in the readiness of her vagina to receive the penis, whether she's loose enough and moist enough. Also, the pelvic muscles for both that should be relaxed for maximum pleasure may be tightened if conflict still exists.

Breathing is also primarily an inclusion phenomenon. It's the way of entering or leaving any situation. If no commitment is desired the breath is cut off along with a tightening of the muscles. This cuts down virtually all vital functions. A full commitment of a person's time and energy involves full breathing, a charged-up body. The Indians and yogis have recognized the importance of breathing control, pranayama, for centuries. It is the key to someone's involvement. Routinely, when I'm giving a lecture or demonstration to a large group, I will begin by doing some activity that requires them to breathe deeply, either screaming, pounding, deep breathing, or anything that gets them pumped up. I find it makes a big difference in the audience's attention and presence.

The same holds for an encounter group. Whenever a member shows a lack of involvement, getting him into some activity requiring deep breathing almost inevitably brings him in. Breathing patterns become ingrained early in life, and a person is usually not aware of his lack of full breathing. Improving the breathing pattern is probably one of the fastest ways to change the feeling of the entire organism. In bioenergetic therapy, the "air or breath is equivalent to the spirit, the pneuma of ancient religions, a symbol of the divine power residing in God, the father figure. Breathing is an aggressive act in that inspiration is an active process. The body sucks in the air. The way one breathes manifests one's feeling about his right to get what he wants from life."

In terms of the body systems, not only are the sense organs and respiration related to inclusion, but so are the digestive and excretory systems, which focus on exchange with the environment and which deal with whether an object will be in or out of the body. These systems express the body's desire to incorporate or reject outside objects. A person with a desire to exclude will reject food and/ or excrete readily and, in the extreme, develop vomiting and diarrhea. One who is anxious to include will go in the other direction, namely, overeating and constipation. A well-resolved relation in the inclusion area should result in good digestion and elimination.

If we consider the interaction between a person and his body, the inclusion problem is one of energy. A body excludes itself in the world by being energy-less. The difference between living and not living is the difference between having the flows of energy, nerve impulses, blood circulation, breathing, and so on, and not having them. When a body includes itself, it is filled with energy and feeling.

Hence the problem of inclusion is in or out; the interaction centers on encounter, and the physical aspect is that of energy.

Control behavior refers to the decision-making process between people and areas of power, influence, and authority. The need for control varies along a continuum from the desire for authority over others (and therefore over one's future) to the need to be controlled and have responsibility lifted from oneself.

An argument provides the setting for distinguishing the inclusion-seeker from the control-seeker. The one seeking inclusion or prominence wants very much to be one of the participants in the argument, while the control-seeker wants to be the winner, or, if not the winner, on the same side as the winner. If forced to choose, the prominence-seeker would prefer to be the losing participant, while the dominance-seeker would prefer to be a winning nonparticipant.

Control is also manifested in behavior directed toward people who try to control. Expressions of independence and rebellion exemplify lack of willingness to be controlled, while compliance, submission, and taking orders indicate various degrees of accepting control. There is no necessary relation between an individual's behavior toward controlling others and his behavior toward being controlled. The sergeant may domineer his men, for example, and also accept orders from his lieutenant with pleasure and gratefulness, while the neighborhood bully may dominate his peers and also rebel against his parents.

Control behavior differs from inclusion behavior in that it does not require prominence. The power behind the throne is an excellent example of a role that would fill a high-control need and a low need for inclusion. The joker exemplifies a high-inclusion and low need for control. Control behavior differs from affection behavior in that it has to do with power relations rather than emotional closeness. The frequent difficulties between those who want to get down to business and those who want to get to know one another better illustrate a situation in which control behavior is more important for some and affection behavior for others.

Concern about one's competence, especially in the area of masculinity, leads to overmasculine responses. This is often seen in politics, where concern about one's assertiveness often leads to absurd overreaction to physical threats, especially when a government official has police or soldiers at his disposal.

Control problems usually follow those of inclusion in the development of a group or of an interpersonal relationship. Once the group has formed, it begins to differentiate; different people take or seek different roles, and often power struggles, competition, and influence become central issues. In terms of inter-action, these issues are matters of confrontation, to use a term now in vogue.

The extreme person who is too low on control, called an abdicrat, is one who tends toward submission and abdication of power and responsibility in his inter-personal behavior. He gravitates toward a subordinate position where he will not have to take responsibility for making decisions, where someone else takes charge. He consciously wants people to relieve him of his obligations. He does not control others even when he should; for example, he would not take charge even during a fire in a children's schoolhouse in which he was the only adult. He never makes a decision if he can refer it to someone else.

For the individual who has successfully resolved his relations in the control area in childhood, power and control present no problem. He feels comfortable giving or not giving orders, taking or not taking orders, whatever is appropriate to the situation. Unlike the abdicrat and autocrat, he is not preoccupied with fears of his own helplessness, stupidity, and incompetence. He feels that other people respect his competence and will be realistic with respect to trusting him with decision-making.

Speculation on the physical concomitants of control behavior begins with control of the muscles through tightening and through intellectual or nervous system activity. The central nervous system, along with the endocrine system, is generally credited with controlling the anatomy.

Ida Rolf has a fascinating concept of the relation of the core of the body, by which she means the head and spinal column, to the envelope, which includes the two girdles, the pelvic and shoulder girdles with attached appendages, legs and arms. Her idea is that the core represents *being* and the envelope *doing*. Some people develop one and not the other, both, or neither.

For a male, a great deal of control is usually expressed in the formation of the upper arms, shoulders, and neck. Attaining masculinity is frequently related to having hulking, heavily developed shoulders and neck and back muscles. Wrestlers and football linemen typify this formation in the extreme, as the large muscle that goes from the middle of the back up into the neck, the trapezius, is so overdeveloped that it appears that they have no necks.

The feeling of being out of control, and thereby vulnerable, was brought home to me personally when a Rolfer working on my neck freed the trapezius muscle that I had held chronically tight so that my head and neck began to rise up out of my shoulders. As I stood there with my head elevated to a place where it felt both unfamiliar and wonderfully free, I felt frightened. The image that came to mind was of the boy in the circus who sticks his head through the bullseye of a target for people to throw balls at. I felt very exposed, very much in plain sight for everyone to see, with no place to hide. You may capture some of that feeling by standing up straight, putting your chin in and letting your head rise up as if it had a string through the crown, and let your shoulders relax down. When you get as high as you can, look around. When this happened to me I had a clear feeling of why my head had sunk into my shoulders. It was safer, more protected, and less vulnerable.

In general, the pattern of muscle tensions represents the defense pattern of a person. It is the way in which he controls himself so that he can cope with the world. A pattern of no chronic muscle tensions—as opposed to muscle tone—would then represent a nondefensive state, perhaps something like the egolessness of the Eastern mystics.

Intellectual control involves voluntary shaping of the body propensities. Control is exercised over the body's desires by moral codes and in line with parental upbringing so that thought is used to govern action.

In the interaction between a person and his body, the control problem is one of centering. A body undercontrolled is disorganized; a body overcontrolled is rigid. A well-controlled body functions with integration among its parts so that they flow easily and appropriately. Inappropriate movement and coordination result when the body is uncertain of what it is doing. Centering means placing everything in its appropriate place so that one is "hooked-up." Being off center makes all movement slightly disconnected.

In the sexual act, control has to do with the occasion and timing of the orgasms and the direction of movement. Withholding an orgasm is an act of personal control that often has a hostile motive, "you can't satisfy me." Sexual control problems would include difficulty of orgasm, premature ejaculation, and the lack of ability to let go.

Thus the problem of control is top or bottom; the primary interaction is confrontation, and the physical aspect is that of centering.

Affection behavior refers to close personal emotional feelings between two people, especially love and hate in their various degrees. Affection is a dyadic relation, that is, it can occur only between pairs of people at any one time, whereas both inclusion and control relations may occur either in dyads or between one person and a group of persons.

Since affection is based on building emotional ties, it is usually the last phase to emerge in the development of a human relation. In the inclusion phase, people must *encounter* each other and decide to continue their relation; control issues require them to *confront* one another and work out how they will be related. To continue the relation, affection ties must form and people must embrace each other to form a lasting bond, and also to say goodbye.

The person with too little affection, the underpersonal type, tends to avoid close ties with others. He maintains his one-to-one relations on a superficial, distant level and is most comfortable when others do the same with him. He consciously wishes to maintain this emotional distance, and frequently expresses a desire not to get emotionally involved, while unconsciously he seeks a satisfactory affectional relation. His fear is that no one loves him, and in a group situation he is afraid he won't be liked. He has great difficulty in genuinely liking people, and distrusts their feelings toward him.

His attitude could be summarized by, "I find the affection area very painful since I have been rejected, therefore I shall avoid close personal relations in the future." The direct technique of the underpersonal is to avoid emotional closeness or involvement, even to the point of being antagonistic. The subtle technique is to be superficially friendly to everyone. This behavior acts as a safeguard against having to get close to, or become personal with, any one person.

In his self-concept, the underpersonal believes that if people knew him well, they would discover traits that make him unlovable. As opposed to the inclusion anxiety that the self is worthless and empty, and the control anxiety that the self is stupid and irresponsible, the affection anxiety is that the self is nasty and unlovable.

The overpersonal type attempts to become extremely close to others. He definitely wants others to treat him in a very close way. The unconscious feeling on which he operates is, "My first experiences with affection were painful, but perhaps if I try again they will turn out to be better." Being liked is extremely important to him in his attempt to relieve his anxiety about being always rejected and unloved. The direct technique for being liked is an overt attempt to gain approval, be extremely personal, ingratiating, intimate, and confiding. The subtle technique is more manipulative and possessive, to devour friends and subtly punish any attempts by them to establish other friendships.

The basic feelings for the overpersonal are the same as those for the underpersonal. Both responses are extreme, both are motivated by a strong need for affection, both are accompanied by a strong anxiety about ever being loved and basically about being unlovable, and both have considerable hostility behind them stemming from the anticipation of rejection.

For the individual who successfully resolved his affectional relations in childhood, close emotional interaction with another person presents no problem. He is comfortable in such a personal relation as well as in a situation requiring emotional distance. It is important for him to be liked, but if not he can accept the fact that the dislike is the result of the relation between himself and one other person; in other words, the dislike does not mean that he is a totally unlovable person. And he is capable of giving genuine affection.

The primary interaction of the affection area is that of embrace, either literal or symbolic. The expression of appropriate deeper feelings is the major issue, particularly in group situations, where a paradox arises. At the beginning of the group there are many expressions as to how difficult it is to express hostility to people. It often later develops that there is only one thing more difficult—expressing warm, positive feelings.

A difference between inclusion, control, and affection behavior is illustrated by the different feelings a man has in being turned down by a fraternity, failed in a course by a professor, and rejected by his girl. The fraternity excludes him, telling him that as a group they don't have sufficient interest in him. The professor fails him and says, in effect, that he finds him incompetent in his field. His girl rejects him, implying that she doesn't find him lovable.

The affectional aspect of the sexual act is the feeling that follows its completion. This can be anything from a flood of warm, affectionate, loving feelings to a revulsion and thoughts of "what am I doing here?" It depends partly on how well the heart and genitals are connected. The circulatory (heart) and reproductive (genital) systems are most directly related to the area of affection.

In the interaction between a person and his body, the affectional problem is one of *acceptance.* The body may be charged up with energy and coordinated through centering, but the problem of body acceptance remains. An accepted body can allow feeling to flow through it without avoiding any part. Sensation is not blocked. An unaccepted body works against itself, trying to become sickly or dissociated. Thus, the ideal body feels energetic, centered, and acceptable.

With respect to an interpersonal relation, inclusion is concerned primarily with the formation of a relation, whereas control and affection are concerned with relations already formed. Within existent relations, control is the area concerned with who gives orders and makes decisions, whereas affection is concerned with how emotionally close or distant the relation becomes.

In summary, the problem of affection is close or far; the interaction is embrace, and the physical aspect is acceptance.

Attitude Change Theory: Applications for Managers

Robin N. Widgery and Stewart L. Tubbs

One can hardly pick up a book today which is written by a successful manager (Geneen, 1984; Iacocca, 1984; McCormack, 1984) or in some cases even an academician (Bradford and Cohen, 1984; Ruch and Goodman, 1983) without encountering criticism of management education as being severely out of touch with the real world of managing. Perhaps many scholars would find shortcomings in these books; however, it should be of major concern to management educators that there is such an abundance of criticism from such highly respected sources. Therefore, this paper attempts to address one possible solution to these criticisms.

Attitude change theory is but one example of a theoretical body of knowledge which has great promise for application in the real world. For several decades, numerous scholars have found this area of study to be a relevant part of the Organizational Communication literature (Pigors, 1949; Thayer, 1961; Scholtz, 1962; Redding and Sanborn, 1964; Zelko and Dance, 1965; Bormann, et al., 1969; Huseman, et al., 1969; Rogers and Shoemaker, 1971; Lesikar, 1972; Redding, 1972; Goldhaber, 1974; Schneider, et al., 1975; Conley, et al., 1976; Sanford, et al., 1976; Allen, 1977; Downs et al., 1977; Farace, et al., 1977; Wilcox, 1977; Tortoriello, et al., 1978; Goldhaber, et al., 1979; Haney, 1979; Sussman and Krivonos, 1979; Hunt, 1980; Tacey, 1980; Fisher, 1981; Hawkins and Preston, 1981; Seiler, et al., 1982; Timm and Peterson, 1982; Pace, 1983; and Zima, 1983).

One specific subset of attitude change theory is consistency theory. Although different researchers have proposed consistency theories (Newcomb, 1953; Festinger, 1957; Osgood, Suci, and Tannenbaum, 1957; and Heider, 1958), the first to record a theory of cognitive consistency was Heider (1946). He developed the now famous "Balance Theory." The basic premise of the theory is that people prefer to have psychological or cognitive comfort and avoid situations which involve an inconsistency or imbalance. For example, an employee (E) who feels negatively toward performance of a task (T), but who receives a directive from a liked superior (S) would suffer some pressure to change his cognitive system. The important elements demonstrating this relationship can be diagrammed in the model below.

The basic principle of Heider's theory is that if the algebraic product of the signs in the triad is positive, the cognitive system is balanced. If it is negative, the system is imbalanced. The practical implication of this is that when a system

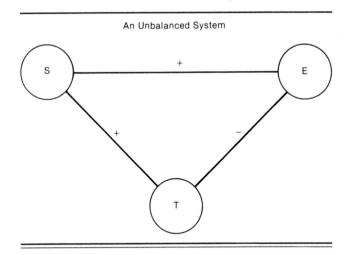

An Unbalanced System

is imbalanced, the person is motivated to change the system to restore balance. When the system is balanced, no pressure exists to change an attitude. Below are the eight permutations of Heider's theory.

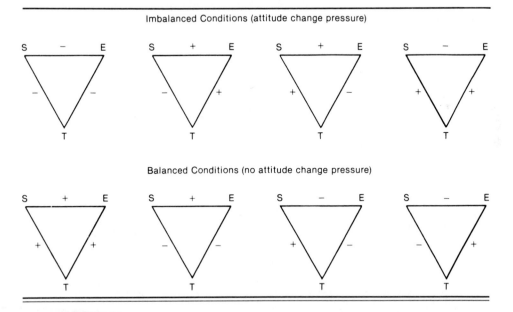

Imbalanced Conditions (attitude change pressure)

Balanced Conditions (no attitude change pressure)

If there is an imbalanced condition, there is pressure for the person to restore balance. Summarizing considerable research on this issue, Festinger and Aronson (1968) indicate that there are three predictable ways for that to occur. First, the employees' attitude toward the supervisor may change. In fact, this is the most likely part of the system to change. If a person tries to get us to do something we don't want to, we tend to discredit that person rather than to believe that it is a good thing to do. This change is diagrammed below.

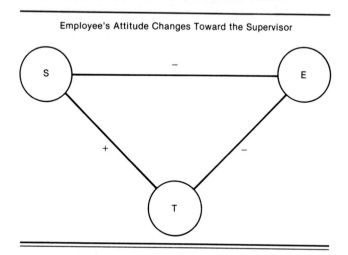

Employee's Attitude Changes Toward the Supervisor

A second possibility is for the employee's perception of the supervisor's attitude toward the task to change. In this instance, the employee can rationalize the supervisor's attitude toward the task instead of actually changing his own attitude toward the task. This situation is diagrammed below.

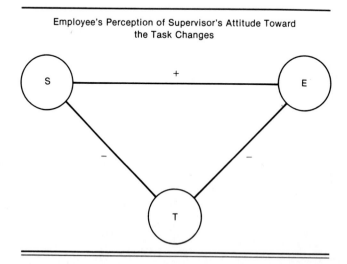

Employee's Perception of Supervisor's Attitude Toward the Task Changes

A third and least likely way for the employee to restore balance is to change his attitude toward the task itself. This is the outcome preferred by the supervisor. However, as we have seen, it is the least likely to occur given the other two alternatives. This possibility is diagrammed below.

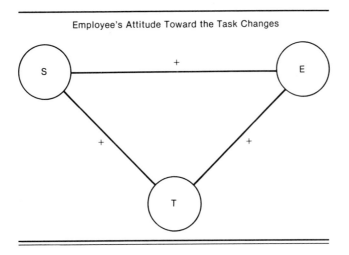

Employee's Attitude Toward the Task Changes

Implications for Supervisors

Supervisors and theorists alike are interested in how attitude change can be made to occur. In this section we will explore some methods for accomplishing attitude change. First, if we know that in an imbalanced condition the most likely relationship to change is the supervisor-employee link, then the first thing that can be done is to bolster that link. If the supervisor wants to increase her credibility with the employee, she must demonstrate that she has certain key values which most employees associate with an effective supervisor. For example, Hellriegel, Slocum and Woodman (1983) argue that the overwhelming bulk of leadership research would support the conclusion that most employees value competence, consistency, fairness, concern, clarity of directions, honesty, and sensitivity to the feelings of the employee. If the supervisor can bear this in mind, she can try to emphasize these aspects of her behavior toward her subordinates. If this is done, then it becomes more difficult for the employee to change this part of the triad in order to restore balance in the system. This is illustrated below by adding a secondary triad to the primary triad in Heider's model.

As stated above, the second most likely change used to restore balance in the system is for the employee to change (distort) his perception of the supervisor's attitude toward the task. This is a form of rationalization which allows the employee's system to restore balance without having to actually change his attitude toward the task itself. The supervisor can try to keep this rationalization from occurring by demonstrating sincerity, commitment, enthusiasm, excitement, and unambiguous support for the task (O'Donel and Kable, 1982; Smith,

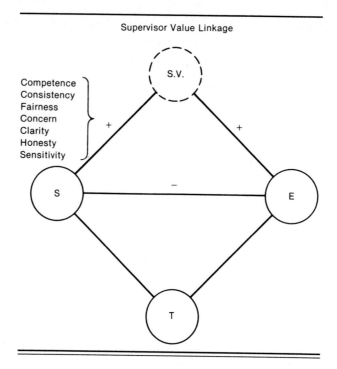

Supervisor Value Linkage

1982). By demonstrating these behaviors, it will be harder for the employee to rationalize that the supervisor doesn't really believe in what she is saying about the task. This situation is diagrammed below.

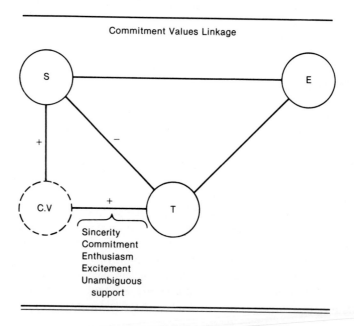

Commitment Values Linkage

The third alternative for restoring balance to the system is for the employee to actually change his attitude toward the task. In order for this to happen, he has to see what needs of his own will be met by changing. Each of us wants to have our actions result in positive outcomes for us. Extending Maslow and Herzberg's theories, Durbin (1982) lists twenty-two outcomes which most employees would consider as meeting their needs. They are:

Feedback on desired behavior

Praise, encouragement, and related rewards

Approval

Recognition

Comradeship

Job security

Money

Favorable performance appraisal

Privy to confidential information

Challenging work assignments

Freedom to choose one's own work activity

Opportunity to see oneself become more important, more useful

Seeing results of one's work

Chance to use one's mind

Power to influence co-workers and management

Promotion

Improved working conditions

Capable and congenial co-workers

Business luncheon

Time off from work

Attendance at trade show or convention

Status symbols (p. 18).

The superior is more likely to be successful in creating attitude change if she can relate one or more employee needs to the task. This approach is diagrammed below.

If we put together the primary triad and the three secondary triads we can see how the entire system looks.

Finally, if we put in the signs, we can see how the system looks with all parts balanced.

As you can see from the above rationale, balance theory offers a potent model for creating attitude change by using the individual's own need for psychological consistency as a driving force for attitude change. In order to allow that, however, other more tempting alternatives must be changed so that the person changes the one element in the system that is the one we want to change.

This has been a very brief example of the way our field can be more in touch with the world of managers. Our two decades of experience both as university professors and as consultants to FORTUNE 500 companies has been that the approach discussed [here] results in enthusiastic acceptance from both students and managers alike. We encourage others to examine methods for applying additional theoretical models to real-world applications.

Needs Values Linkage

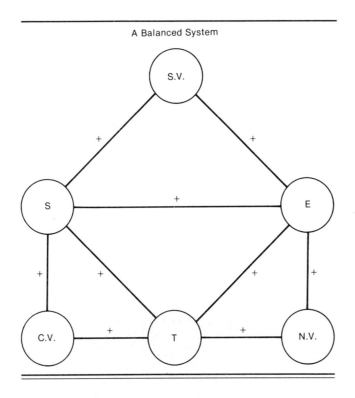

A Balanced System

References

Allen, Richard K. *Organizational Management Through Communication.* (New York: Harper & Row, 1977).

Bormann, Ernest G., William S. Howell, Ralph Nichols, and George L. Shapiro. *Interpersonal Communication in the Modern Organization.* (Englewood Cliffs, N.J.: Prentice-Hall, 1969).

Bradford, David L. and Allan R. Cohen. *Managing for Excellence: The Guide to Developing High Performance in Contemporary Organizations.* (New York: John Wiley, 1984).

Conley, James H., Jon H. Huegli, and Robert L. Minter. *Perspectives on Administrative Communication.* (Dubuque, Iowa: Kendall/Hunt, 1976).

Downs, Cal W., David M. Berg, and Wil A. Linkugel. *The Organizational Communicator.* (New York: Harper & Row, 1977).

Dubrin, Andrew J. *Contemporary Applied Management.* (Plano, Texas: Business Publications, Inc., 1982).

Farace, R. Vince, Peter R. Monge, and H. M. Russell. *Communicating and Organizing.* (Reading, Mass.: Addison-Wesley, 1977).

Festinger, Leon. *A Theory of Cognitive Dissonance.* (Evanston, Ill.: Row, Peterson, 1957).

Festinger, Leon, and Elliot Aronson, "Arousal and Reduction of Dissonance in Social Contexts," In Dorwin Cartwright and Alvin Zander (eds.), *Group Dynamics: Research and Theory.* 3rd ed. (New York: Harper & Row, 1968, 125–136).

Fisher, Dalmar. *Communication in Organizations.* (St. Paul: West, 1981).

Geneen, Harold. *Managing.* (New York: Doubleday, 1984).

Goldhaber, Gerald M. *Organizational Communication.* (Dubuque, Iowa: Wm. C. Brown, 1974).

Goldhaber, Gerald M., Harry S. Dennis, Gary M. Richetto, and Osmo Wiio. *Information Strategies: New Pathways to Corporate Power.* (Englewood Cliffs, N.J.: Prentice-Hall, 1979).

Haney, William V. *Communication and Interpersonal Relations: Text and Cases.* 4th ed. (Homewood, Ill.: Irwin, 1979).

Hawkins, Brian L., and Paul Preston. *Managerial Communication.* (Santa Monica: Goodyear, 1981).

Heider, Fritz, "Attitudes and Cognitive Organization," *Journal of Psychology,* 1946, 21, 107–112.

Heider, Fritz. *The Psychology of Interpersonal Relations.* (New York: John Wiley, 1958).

Hellriegel, Don, John W. Slocum, and Richard W. Woodman. *Organizational Behavior.* 3rd ed. (St. Paul: West, 1983), Ch. 13.

Huseman, Richard C., Cal M. Logue, and Dwight L. Freshley. *Readings in Interpersonal and Organizational Communication.* (Boston: Holbrook Press, 1969).

Hunt, Gary T. *Communication Skills in the Organization.* (Englewood Cliffs, N.J.: Prentice-Hall, 1980).

Iacocca, Lee. *Iacocca.* (New York: Bantam Books, 1984).

Lesikar, Raymond. *Business Communication: Theory and Application.* 2nd ed. (Homewood, Ill.: Irwin, 1972).

McCormack, Mark. *What They Don't Teach You at the Harvard Business School.* (New York: Bantam Books, 1984).

Newcomb, Theodore. "An Approach to the Study of Communicative Acts," *Psychological Review,* 1953, 60, 393–404.

O'Donnel, Victoria, and June Kable. *Persuasion: An Interactive-Dependency Approach.* (New York: Random House, 1982), Ch. 6.

Osgood, Charles, George J. Suci, and Percy H. Tannenbaum. *The Measurement of Meaning.* (Urbana: University of Illinois Press, 1957).

Pace, R. Wayne. *Organizational Communication: Foundations for Human Resource Development.* (Englewood Cliffs, N.J.: Prentice-Hall, 1983).

Pigors, Paul. *Effective Communication in Industry.* (New York: National Association of Manufacturers, 1949).

Rogers, Everett M., and F. Floyd Shoemaker. *Communication of Innovations.* (New York: The Free Press, 1971).

Redding, W. Charles, and George A. Sanborn. *Business and Industrial Communication: A Sourcebook.* (New York: Harper & Row, 1964).

Ruch, Richard, and Ronald Goodman. *Image at the Top.* (New York: The Free Press, 1983).

Sanford, Aubrey C., Gary T. Hunt, and Hyler J. Bracey. *Communication Behavior in Organizations.* (Columbus, Ohio: Merrill, 1976).

Schneider, Arnold, William C. Donaghy, and Pamela Jane Newman. *Organizational Communication.* (New York: McGraw-Hill, 1975).

Scholtz, William. *Communication in the Business Organization.* (Englewood Cliffs, N.J.: Prentice-Hall, 1962).

Seiler, William J., E. Scott Bauduin, and L. David Scheulke. *Communication in Business and Professional Organizations.* (Reading, Mass.: Addison-Wesley, 1982).

Smith, Mary John. *Persuasion and Human Action: A Review and Critique of Social Influence Theories.* (Belmont, Cal.: Wadsworth, 1982), Ch. 9.

Sussman, Lyle, and Paul D. Krivonos. *Communication for Supervisors and Managers.* (Sherman Oaks, Cal.: Alfred, 1979).

Tacey, William S. *Business and Professional Speaking.* 3rd ed. (Dubuque, Iowa: Wm. C. Brown, 1980).

Thayer, Lee. *Administrative Communication.* (Homewood, Ill.: Irwin, 1961).

Timm, Paul R., and Brent D. Peterson. *People at Work.* (St. Paul: West, 1982).

Tortoriello, Thomas R., Stephen J. Blatt, and Sue DeWine. *Communication in the Organization: An Applied Approach.* (New York: McGraw-Hill, 1978).

Wilcox, Roger P. *Communication at Work.* (Boston: Houghton Mifflin, 1977).

Zelko, Karold, and Frank E. X. Dance. *Business and Professional Speech Communication.* (New York: Holt, Rinehart and Winston, 1965).

Zima, Joseph P. *Interviewing: Key to Effective Management.* (Palo Alto: Science Research Associates, 1983).

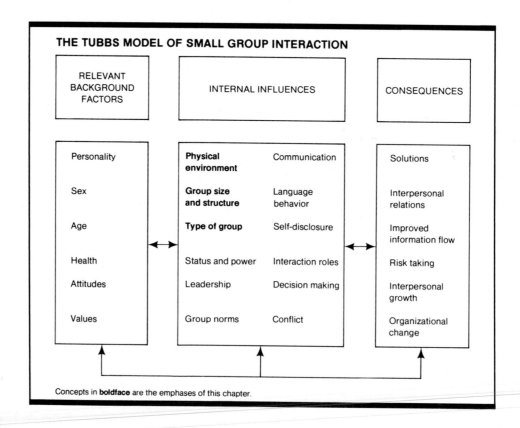

Internal Influences

Group Circumstances and Structure

THE TUBBS MODEL OF SMALL GROUP INTERACTION

RELEVANT BACKGROUND FACTORS	INTERNAL INFLUENCES		CONSEQUENCES
Personality	**Physical environment**	Communication	Solutions
Sex	**Group size and structure**	Language behavior	Interpersonal relations
Age	**Type of group**	Self-disclosure	Improved information flow
Health	Status and power	Interaction roles	Risk taking
Attitudes	Leadership	Decision making	Interpersonal growth
Values	Group norms	Conflict	Organizational change

Concepts in **boldface** are the emphases of this chapter.

CASE STUDY

Management consultant Scott Myers tells a story that shows how simple yet complex the communication function is. He was called in by a client to suggest ways management might communicate better with its work force. The company, always run along traditional lines, was trying to update itself and its communication practices. Before retaining Myers, management had decided to stress the traditional media methods—more articles in the company paper on corporate objectives and employee benefits, improvement of bulletin board displays, and a new monthly letter from the president.

In his initial talk with the president, Myers learned that the company was about to spend almost $300,000 to install what it saw as the most effective and up-to-date way to transmit messages to employees: closed-circuit television monitors scattered throughout the premises. Myers, dismayed by this news, asked for a short delay of the order until he could size up the situation and make some recommendations. The president reluctantly agreed.

In the course of examining the organization's communication efforts, Myers discovered an interesting practice. For some years employees had had a common coffee break during which all coffee machines were programmed to dispense the beverage free. At the same time, a cart carrying free pastries for everyone was wheeled into each area.

Watching the proceedings one morning, Myers recognized an opportunity. At his next meeting with the president, Myers suggested that he join his people out in the corridor at a coffee bar. The president smiled patiently and said that he couldn't do that. Asked why not, he replied that "it simply wasn't done." Top officers all had their coffee in their own offices dispensed from a mahogany cart. They never mingled with other employees during breaks. It would have been bad form and might even constitute an intrusion.

Myers persisted, however, and reluctantly the president agreed to try the radical idea. His first attempt was an abysmal failure. He didn't even know how to work the coffee machine. A bystander, seeing him fumble with coins, walked over and told him the coffee was free. Red-faced, he took the cup in hand and looked for someone to begin a conversation with. No one approached him; employees were clustered in little groups quietly discussing their various concerns and glancing curiously at him. He drank his coffee and walked back into his office.

To Myers he pronounced the experiment a flop—they wouldn't talk to him. Myers told him that the problem was twofold. He made his appearance too formal; instead of wearing his suit coat, he should have gone out in his shirt sleeves. Moreover, the workers weren't used to seeing him in their area. To make this a fair test, Myers urged, he must go back tomorrow. At first the president was emphatic in his refusal to subject himself again to such humiliation. Eventually he agreed to try it one more time, but with his coat off.

This time he got his coffee without incident and screwed up the courage to break into the perimeter of a small gathering. After some conversation about the weather, he asked how things were going and heard some pleasantries from the group indicating that everything was fine.

The following morning, after doing some homework on a current concern of the work force (the opening of a plant in Europe), he raised the subject with a coffee-break group and explained the logic behind the decision. He was surprised to find himself in the middle of an animated discussion about the plant.

The next day and the next the president went out to the corridor for his morning coffee. In time he found himself holding forth on all kinds of company issues with employees, who now felt comfortable enough to air their concerns. The kaffee-klatsches were working so well that he asked his senior staff to begin mingling with their people at coffee time. He also canceled the TV equipment in favor of the simpler and more effective technique of firsthand, face-to-face communication.

1. What factors in this case caused the communication gap between the top officers and the employees?

2. What principles in this case can be generalized to virtually any organization?

From Roger D'Aprix, "The Oldest (And Best) Way to Communicate with Employees," *Harvard Business Review* (September–October 1982), 31–32. Reproduced by permission of the Harvard Business Review. Copyright © 1982 by the President and Fellows of Harvard College; all rights reserved.

The case study beautifully illustrates an informal work group. In this chapter we will be looking at several very different types of groups ranging from the family or primary group to street gangs, encounter groups, and problem-solving groups. Although each type of group differs from the others, some common conceptual links connect all types of groups. The first factor that is relevant to all groups is the so-called ecology of the group.

The dispute over the size and shape of the negotiating table at the Paris peace talks in 1968 represents one of the most significant examples in our nation's history of ecology in group discussion. The disagreement lasted eight months and was typical of the many political implications of each issue under negotiation. McCroskey, Larson, and Knapp (1971, p. 97) explain the reasons for the dispute:

> The United States (US) and South Viet Nam (SVN) wanted a seating arrangement in which only two sides were identified. They did not want to recognize the National Liberation Front (NLF) as an "equal" party in the negotiations. North Viet Nam (NVN) and the NLF wanted "equal" status given to all parties—represented by a four-sided table. The final arrangement was such that both parties could claim victory. The round table minus the dividing lines allowed North Viet Nam and the NLF to claim all four delegations were equal. The existence of the two secretarial tables (interpreted as dividers), the lack of identifying symbols on the table, and an AA, BB speaking rotation permitted the United States and South Viet Nam to claim victory for the two-sided approach. Considering the lives lost during the eight months needed to arrive at the seating arrangement, we can certainly conclude that territorial space has extremely high priority in some interpersonal settings.

In this chapter we will look more closely at small group ecology as well as other internal influences in small group interaction.

Chapter 1 defined *internal influences* on a group as factors that are influenced by the individual characteristics of group members and that in turn influence a group's functioning and its ultimate end results. Internal influences are somewhat under the control of group members (that is, members are able to change them). In this chapter we will examine three major types of internal influence: (1) physical environment, (2) group structure, and (3) type of group.

PHYSICAL ENVIRONMENT

For many years writers have hypothesized that a room's environment influences the interaction within it. Supposedly, "warm" colors, hues of orange, red, and brown, facilitate interaction, while "cool" hues of blue and green tend to encourage reserved, formal conversation. A series of studies conducted to test these assumptions (Maslow and Mintz 1956; Wong and Brown 1923; Bilodeau and Schlosberg 1959) found that people consistently associated an ugly room with monotony, fatigue, irritability, headache, discontent, and hostility. A beautiful room evoked such reactions as pleasure, enjoyment, importance, comfort, and a desire to remain in the room. The ugly room was stark, gray, and disheveled, while the beautiful room had carpeting, drapes, and warm beige walls. These studies also showed that mental functioning was better in beautiful rooms. Both memory and ability to solve problems were found to be better in the beautiful room. Along this same line, Barnlund (1968, p. 514) writes: "A colleague after attending a meeting in a conference room created by [Frank Lloyd] Wright was similarly impressed, confessing that he believed interpersonal antagonism could not be provoked in such a setting." Although it is doubtful that we could ever design a room that would eliminate all antagonism, it seems plausible that rooms can be designed that at least do not act as a source of irritation. It is also interesting to speculate that inadequate ventilation, heating, lighting, and roominess might serve to detract from the overall effectiveness of groups.

Territoriality

Edward Hall (1959) coined the term *territoriality* to describe the tendency for humans and other animals to lay claim to and defend a particular area or territory. We are all familiar with this behavior among dogs, birds, and gorillas, but we may be less aware of our own attempts to defend our territories. It has been estimated that college students begin to identify a particular seat in the class as "their chair" by as early as the second class period. Although we probably would not ask a person to give up the chair, we would feel some annoyance at having to move to another one. This is reminiscent of the home court advantage in basketball: Teams traditionally play better on the home court than they do at "away" games.

In addition to identifying certain places as our territory, we also move about in a portable space bubble of about 18 inches in each direction that we let only certain people violate. This is referred to as our *personal space.* Sommer (1959, p. 248) distinguishes personal space from territory in the following way:

> The most important difference is that personal space is carried around while territory is relatively stationary. The animal or man will usually mark the boundaries of his territory so that they are visible to others, but the boundaries of his personal space are invisible. Personal space has the body at its center, while territory does not.

Kinzel (1969) conducted a study of inmates at the United States Medical Center for Federal Prisoners. He found that men who had committed violent crimes had a personal space or "body buffer zone" twice as large as that of prisoners classified as nonviolent. The violent group stated that they felt threatened when a person came close to them, as if the person were an intruder who was "looming up" or "rushing in" at them.

Hall (1959) describes the humorous situation in which people with different-sized space bubbles try to communicate. Arabs or South Americans will try to step closer, reducing the distance between them and their listeners. North American or German listeners will then step backward to reestablish what they feel is a comfortable distance for conversation. And so it continues as one individual ends up backing the other all the way around the room. Rosenfeld (1965) found that personality factors influenced the size of one's personal space. Those high in need for affiliation (see Chapter 2) sat an average of 57 inches away from a target person, while those low in affiliation averaged 94 inches in distance.

Hall (1959) refers to the study of personal space and distance as *proxemics.* He has identified four zones that seem to influence interaction in North American culture. He points, out, however, that these distances do not apply to other cultures that have different zones. The four types of distances are intimate, personal, social, and public.

Intimate distance extends from touching to about 18 inches. This distance encourages soft whispers about very confidential matters. It also allows us to use more of our senses in communicating (for example, touching, smelling, and even tasting). *Personal distance* ranges from 18 inches to about 4 feet. Conversation is usually soft and topics are usually personal. *Social distance* refers to the distance between 4 and 12 feet. At this distance voices are usually raised and the topics are nonpersonal public information for anyone to hear. *Public distance* refers to 12 feet and beyond. This requires a loud voice and impersonal topics. As we shall see later in this chapter, different groups may at one time or another involve the use of all of these four distances. Encounter groups frequently include physical touching, while large committees may be seated around tables more than 25 feet in diameter. Figure 3.1 gives more examples of various distances and kinds of communication.

FIGURE 3.1

Adapted from Hall 1959, p. 163–164. Chart from *The Silent Language* by Edward T. Hall. Copyright © 1959 by Edward T. Hall. Reprinted with permission of Doubleday & Company, Inc.

Distance	Content	Vocal Shifts
3–6 inches	Top secret	Soft whisper
8–12 inches	Very confidential topics	Audible whisper
12–20 inches	Confidential topics	Soft voice
20–36 inches	Personal topics	Soft voice
4½–5 feet	Nonpersonal topics	Full voice
5½–8 feet	Public information	Loud voice
8–20 feet	Public Information to a group	Very loud voice
20–100 feet	Hailing and departing comments	Very loud voice

FIGURE 3.2   SEATING PATTERN.

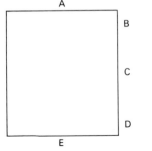

Seating Patterns

Have you ever noticed the difference in interaction between a group sitting on the grass or the floor and one whose members are seated indoors around a rectangular table? One difference is that sitting on the floor or grass allows greater informality and tends to facilitate interaction. However, research has shown that even the seating patterns around rectangular tables have a major impact on interaction as well. Strodbeck and Hook (1961) found that in jury deliberations, members from professional and managerial classes took positions at the head of the table significantly more often than people from other classes. Paper-and-pencil tests revealed that those seated at the head position were chosen significantly more often as the leader. Hare and Bales (1963) found that those seated in positions marked A, C, and E in Figure 3.2 were frequent talkers and frequently scored high on dominance in personality tests.

Sommer (1969) also studied several possible seating patterns (see Figure 3.3). The corner-to-corner or face-to-face arrangements were most often preferred for casual conversation, while cooperating pairs (studying together) preferred the side-by-side arrangement. Competing pairs chose the face-to-face or the distant-opposite arrangements about equally often. Coacting pairs (those doing simultaneous but unrelated activities) preferred the distant-opposite positions, which maximized distance without the potential eye contact that might result from the end-to-end arrangement. Russo (1967) found that people seated in the more distant positions (when all positions around the rectangular table were occupied) were perceived to be less friendly, less well acquainted, and less talkative than those seated closer to the person filling out the questionnaire.

Hearn (1957) verified a phenomenon known as the "Steinzor effect" (Steinzor 1950), in which members of groups with minimal leadership directed many more comments to those facing opposite them than to those sitting on either side. However, with a dominant, assertive leader, the behaviors were reversed and significantly more conversation was directed to those sitting next to them.

Sommer (1965) also studied the seating preferences at round tables (Figure 3.4). He found that conversing or cooperating pairs preferred to sit side by side, while competing pairs preferred to sit at distant-opposite points, and coacting pairs preferred the so-called side-to-end arrangement. These findings have been more recently

FIGURE 3.3   SEATING PATTERNS AT RECTANGULAR TABLES: (A) CORNER-TO-CORNER, (B) FACE-TO-FACE, (C) DISTANT-OPPOSITE, (D) CORNER-TO-END, (E) SIDE-BY-SIDE, AND (F) END-TO-END.

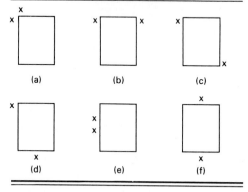

corroborated by Batchelor and Goethals (1972), who found much the same result with groups who had no tables at all, but simply were allowed to move their chairs to positions they preferred.

All this research taken collectively indicates that groups with differing personalities and tasks will exhibit predictable seating patterns. Also, dominant seating positions at the ends of rectangular tables will tend to give some members a leadership advantage and will result in some frustration and disenchantment for those in the "blind spots" on the sides of the tables.

GROUP SIZE AND STRUCTURE

The concept of group structure refers to the idea that groups are made up of people who are related to one another in a number of ways. Although group structure may

FIGURE 3.4   SEATING PREFERENCES AT ROUND TABLES: (A) SIDE-BY-SIDE, (B) DISTANT-OPPOSITE, AND (C) SIDE-TO-END.

(a)   (b)   (c)

include a number of interrelated topics, we will be concerned with only two: (1) communication networks and (2) group size.

Communication Networks

The research on communication networks commonly employs five different networks, which are illustrated in Figure 3.5. Leavitt (1951) found that the central person in a network such as the wheel usually becomes the leader and enjoys the position more than those on the periphery, whose communication is much more restricted. That is, the central person can communicate to any of them, but they must direct *all* of their comments through the center. Both the chain and the Y networks have characteristics similar to the wheel. On the other hand, the circle and the all-channel patterns are much less centralized and are sometimes leaderless.

A person who dominates the discussion will sometimes create a network similar to the wheel. While this may be more centralized and efficient, it results in dependence on the leader and lower group satisfaction for everyone but the leader. The chain or the Y network allows members to communicate with one or two other persons, but not with all others in the group. This produces subgroups, decreased satisfaction, and a relatively poor amount of idea sharing.

The all-channel network may be relatively slow, but it is superior in terms of idea-sharing and member satisfaction. Feedback is more immediate and, as a result, accuracy of communication is better. Shaw (1964) summarized the findings of 18 group

FIGURE 3.5   COMMUNICATION NETWORKS: (A) WHEEL, (B) CHAIN, (C) Y, (D) CIRCLE, AND (E) ALL-CHANNEL.
By permission of News America Syndicate.

(d)   (e)

(a)   (b)   (c)

network studies by concluding that *centralized networks* such as the chain and the wheel are better for solving simple problems, such as identifying colors or picturelike symbols. However, when the problem is complex (as most real-life problems are) the *decentralized networks* such as the circle and the all-channel are faster and more accurate and result in higher member satisfaction. It seems clear that the all-channel network is the most desirable for most problem-solving situations a group would be likely to encounter.

Group Size

Perhaps one of the questions most frequently asked by students of small group interaction is this: What is the best size of group to work with? On one hand, it seems that a relatively small group would be more efficient; on the other hand, larger groups would have more resources. A great deal of research has been conducted on this question, and some fairly clear results emerge.

Groups of only two people may find themselves deadlocked in statements on many questions. They also suffer the disadvantage of having too few members to contribute ideas. Groups of three are still too small, and tend to result in two-against-one coalitions that leave one person out. Groups of four begin to be effective, but due to their even number of members may end up with tie votes on decisions. Bales (1954) found that the optimum group size appeared to be five. This size seems to be small enough for meaningful interaction, yet large enough to generate an adequate number of ideas.

As groups grow larger than five, members complain that the group is too large and that they are not able to participate as often as they would like. Also, as size gets larger, there is an increasing tendency for subgroups to form, which may carry on side conversations that annoy the rest of the group and detract from group progress. Groups of ten or more tend to spend an inordinate amount of time simply organizing themselves, so that more attention is diverted away from the task and toward simply maintaining the group's functioning.

The influence of the number of members within a group is mixed with other variables such as the function of the group and its membership composition. Luft (1984) concludes that "Cohesion tends to be weaker and morale tends to be lower in larger groups than in comparable smaller ones. How often groups meet varies inversely with size and duration and directly with closeness of feelings" (p. 23).

As the group's size increases arithmetically (linearly), the potential number of interactions increases geometrically (exponentially). Bostrom (1970, p. 257) shows how rapidly these interaction patterns multiply. In a dyad (two people) only two relationships are possible, A to B and B to A, but in a triad (three people) there are nine possibilities:

A to B	B to C	A to B and C
A to C	C to B	B to A and C
B to A	C to A	C to A and B

The calculations from group sizes 2–8 are (Bostrom 1970, p. 258):

Number in Group	Interactions Possible
2	2
3	9
4	28
5	75
6	186
7	441
8	1056

Bostrom (p. 263) concludes from his study:

> The data here seem to indicate that the individual who sends more than he receives is not only more often chosen as a good discussant but is also more satisfied with the discussion than the member who receives more than he sends . . . satisfaction apparently comes from talking, not listening.

Markham, Dansereau, and Alutto (1982) have suggested that there can be a positive relationship between size and absenteeism when within-group overtime is applied. This could be explained by a number of possibilities. Perhaps greater strain is placed on the supervisor of that unit as the quality of supervision declines. Or members' perceptions of the new situation might help them rationalize a few extra days' absence when more labor is available to the work group.

The term *free rider* refers to a group member who obtains benefits from group membership but does not uphold a proportional share of the costs involved.

This concept can be useful in that it alerts managers to a probable negative influence on group productivity, and provides a rationale for analyzing the effect of group size on group productivity and the design of organizational units. The studies made to date provide no clear conclusions. However, these guidelines are suggested (Albanese and Van Fleet, 1985, p. 253):

> 1. To the extent that group members act rationally in their decision to contribute to a group's public good, a free-riding tendency will operate in groups.
> 2. As group size increases, the average contribution of group members to the group's public good may decrease, even though the total public good provided by the group may increase.
> 3. The basic strategy for countering the free-riding tendency is to build various private goods that are contingent on the provision of the group's public good into the group member's incentive system.

Actually management is most concerned with point 3. Through effective use of power, design of organizations (size of organizational units included) as well as control of rewards and punishment, management influences the incentive system of group members. As a result of these findings, it would seem desirable to keep the group size to about five *whenever possible,* unless some other objective such as increased widespread participation seems to be worth increasing group size. Even when increasing participation (for example, to include all members of a fraternity or sorority) is the goal, subcommittees of about five would allow the widespread participation *as well as* the efficiency and satisfaction of working in a small group. This optimal size, however, depends on the type of group. Five is the recommended size for a problem-solving group. Obviously, a work group, family group, or even some problem-solving groups may require a different number of members, depending on the particular situation.

TYPE OF GROUP

One of the confounding problems in the study of small groups is the variety in types of groups that have been studied. It is obvious that certain critical differences will emerge when the term *group* is applied to studies of primitive tribes, street gangs, factory work groups, and artificially formed laboratory groups. Although there may be some important similarities among these groups, we would also expect to find some real confusion resulting from attempts to compare different groups across the board. In addition, it seems likely that differing group types will have an effect on subsequent interaction and group outcomes or end results. For example, social groups will interact differently from work groups, and the outcomes of their separate group interactions will be different. In this section we will look at six commonly recognized types of groups.

Primary Groups

Primary groups usually include one's family and closest friends. Certainly the vast majority of attitudes and values people hold are a result of the influences of their primary groups. Primary groups influence self-concept, as well as personality from childhood to adulthood (for example, see Faris 1932, and Shils 1951). The members of our primary groups are sometimes referred to as our "significant others," since they are probably the most important people in our lives. Although we may sometimes develop deep friendships from other associations on the job, in school, and so forth, family members usually remain our most significant others throughout our lives.

Casual and Social Groups

Casual and social groups include neighborhood groups, fraternities, bowling partners, golf partners, and in some cases, fellow members of street gangs. While these relationships may be relatively short-lived, their impact on behavior can be quite profound.

Whyte (1943) conducted an in-depth study of a street group—the Norton Street Gang—from a slum district in a large eastern city. The gang had a status hierarchy with the toughest member (Doc) at the top. The group norms dictated that each

FRANK AND ERNEST   by Bob Thaves

Reprinted by permission. © 1977 NEA, Inc.

member steal and "make it" with a woman if he could, but only a "sucker" got married. Some gangs require their members to commit murder as an initiation. According to one source, Los Angeles alone has nearly 200 gangs, and in 1973 New York had 27 gang-related murders, while in Philadelphia (the City of Brotherly Love) 191 youths were killed in gang wars and assassinations in a five-year period. A large percentage of gangs include mostly blacks and Chicanos. Here is a description (from *Time,* July 23, 1973, p. 32) of one black gang in Philadelphia, the Norris Avenue corner gang:

> Each Norris [gang member] is reputed to have two or three "bodies" under his belt . . . shooting someone in another gang is the surest way a younger member has of "getting a rep" and climbing in the corner hierarchy. . . . Serving a term in jail also boosts a member's reputation.

While these behaviors may seem unbelievable, they are quite real to the group members (especially the victims).

Newcomb (1943, 1963) conducted an in-depth study of the influence of college friendships on political attitudes at Bennington College. Data were collected from all of the 250 students and 50 faculty members at the school at that time. The girls had relatively conservative political views upon entering as freshmen and became progressively more liberal over the course of their four years. Newcomb found that even 30 years later these women had maintained a relatively liberal set of political attitudes. He concluded that although the college women had begun adopting liberal ideas and practices to gain acceptance with their peers, the changes remained for a lifetime. It might be interesting to stop for a moment and think about what changes you are undergoing as a result of the college experience. It is likely that these changes will differentiate you for the rest of your life from your high school friends who did not go to college.

Another systematic study of social groups was conducted by Gardner and Thompson (1956). The subjects were members of the nine fraternities at Syracuse University. Several questionnaire measures were constructed to measure the degree to which members of the fraternity reciprocally respected and liked one another. As we might expect, an individual might choose four different fraternity brothers to meet the four different psychological needs measured in the study. The four needs were (1) affiliation—simply a friendship choice; (2) playmirth—someone to go on a double date or to go have a beer with; (3) succorance—someone to tell your troubles to; and (4) achievement-recognition—someone to help you make a good impression somewhere. There was also considerable overlap in choices (that is, one friend may be chosen to meet two or more of these social needs).

Once Gardner and Thompson had conducted their measurements, they were able to determine which fraternities had the highest levels of morale or esprit de corps. In addition, independent judges (deans, housemothers, and so on) ranked the nine fraternities from best to worst based on number of honors, members, average grade point, number of trophies, and the like. On the basis of this analysis, the researchers concluded that the more a fraternity developed a high level of reciprocal liking and respect among its members, the more successful the fraternity was (that is, the higher its rank in comparison with the other fraternities). Gardner and Thompson (1956, p. 257) concluded that "cooperative group action is favored by mutually satisfying interactions between all possible pairs within the membership." In other words, compatible individual personalities tended to develop more effective groups. They also found a negative relationship between the number of other extracurricular activities of members and the success of the fraternity. It appears that a group with members who accept leadership positions in other groups suffers from that diversification of member commitment. A person who gets overextended simply doesn't have enough time for each of his or her commitments.

These studies of street gangs, college friendships, and fraternities show the profound influences that social groups have on each of us. It may very well be that we profoundly influence the social groups as well. It is worth keeping in mind that we are all creatures of experience and that these experiences help shape us for a lifetime.

Educational Groups

Educational groups may also be called learning groups or enlightenment groups. They get together for the primary purpose of study or instruction. These may include, for example, management training seminars, orientation meetings, or quarterback clubs. These groups may discuss recent books, movies, childrearing, meditation, Kung Fu, or many other topics centering around personal development. Brilhart (1984) refers to an enlightenment discussion as one in which members may attempt to solve problems without having authority to implement their decisions. Small group interaction classes frequently conduct problem-solving discussions concerning national or international issues. Unfortunately, although these groups may develop worthwhile answers to important real world problems, they are not usually in a position to implement their decisions. The experience of attempting to improve problem-solving skills, however, is a worthwhile result even if the group's decision does not always affect reality. It is interesing to note that even when we *do* have the authority to implement, the results are sometimes not as dramatic or satisfying as we might like. For example, one group determined an excellent solution to a campus parking problem. The solution was accepted by the university administration. However, due to a major construction program, the parking lot was torn up and replaced by a new classroom building before the new plan could be implemented.

At Harvard Business School, each class may include up to 100 people. But since group dynamics literature has shown that this number is too large for effective group discussion, the classes are broken up into smaller discussion groups of ten people each. This discussion group then becomes the class's working unit and is small enough for members to relate effectively to. Students learn from each other in discussion groups. Over the course of the term, the discussion groups often become social groups and, for some, surrogate families as well.

In 1985, *The Organizational Behavior Teaching Review Journal* devoted an entire issue to the use of groups in teaching. The editor (1985) explained it this way:

> This special issue is devoted to promoting an increased understanding of why groups should be used in teaching and how they can be used effectively. These issues are becoming increasingly important to everyone in higher education, in part because there is a growing recognition that learning groups provide a potential solution of some of our most difficult pedagogical problems. (p. 1; see also Tubbs, 1985)

Work Groups

Some of the most influential small group research ever to be conducted has occurred in work groups. The now-classic studies conducted by Harvard Business School in the Western Electric Hawthorne plant in Chicago are a case in point. This company was a subsidiary of AT&T and manufactured telephone equipment for the Bell System. The studies lasted from 1927 to 1932 and are described in detail by Mayo (1933) and Roethlisberger and Dickson (1939).

The studies were originally designed to determine the influence of illumination on industrial productivity. It was hypothesized that improved lighting would improve productivity. The first study showed that productivity increased whether lighting levels were increased or *decreased* to a level darker than moonlight (three footcandles). This of course puzzled the researchers.

A second study was conducted to determine the effect of periodic rest breaks on productivity. Once again it was found that productivity kept increasing whether a rest break was added or taken out of the work schedule. The researchers hypothesized that the productivity increases resulted from the workers' changed social situation, increased satisfaction, and new patterns of social interaction brought about by the creating of an experimental condition and paying of special attention to the workers. This productivity increase resulting from special attention has since been labeled the *Hawthorne effect.*

In order to more carefully determine the influence of these social factors on productivity, a second set of studies was designed and labeled the Bank Wiring Observation Room experiment. Workers were observed as they wired, soldered, and inspected switchboards or "banks" of switches. Workers were on an economic incentive system that allowed them to earn more pay if they produced more. The experiment showed that workers were producing far below what they were capable of producing, due to the group's social norm enforced by the co-workers. The researchers referred to this as artificial restriction of output.

The group norm or unwritten rule was to set a relatively low level of work, which was called a fair day's work for a fair day's pay. Anyone who produced much more was branded a "rate buster" or a "speed king." Those who underproduced were called "chiselers," and those who might tell anything to a supervisor that would get them in trouble were called "squealers." In each case, the person who violated the group's norm was punched hard in the arm or shoulder, a punishment affectionately referred to as "binging." These social practices did indeed influence the workers' output more than the opportunity to earn more money for more work. The major findings of the Hawthorne studies were summarized by Etzioni (1964, pp. 34–35):

1. The level of productivity is set by social norms, not by physiological capacities.

2. Noneconomic rewards and sanctions significantly affect the behavior of the workers and largely limit the effect of economic incentive plans.

3. Often workers do not act or react as individuals but as members of groups.

See the reading by Hatvany and Pucik at the end of this chapter for an example of the effective use of work groups.

It was also found that the informally chosen group leader was the best liked, and most represented the values of the group. This leader was often more influential than the appointed leader (the supervisor). On the basis of these studies, management theorists began to stress the importance of (1) communication within the work group, (2) the importance of participation in the decision-making process, and (3) the potential values of democratic leadership. The emphasis on these three factors was later to be referred to as the *human relations* approach to management.

Andrew S. Grove is president of Intel Corporation, a computer chip and microprocessor company in Silicone Valley. In his best-selling book, *High Output Management* (1983), Grove discusses the importance of groups to his company:

> . . . a big part of a middle manager's work is to supply information and know-how, and to impart a sense of the preferred method of handling things to the groups under his control and influence. A manager also makes and helps make decisions. Both kinds of managerial tasks can occur during face-to-face encounters, and therefore only during meetings. Thus I will assert again that a meeting is nothing less than the MEDIUM through which managerial work is performed. That means we should not be fighting their very existence, but rather using the time spent in them as efficiently as possible. (p. 71)

Problem Solving Groups

Although we have looked at other types of groups, by far the greatest emphasis in group discussion textbooks has been on improving problem-solving and decision-making abilities (Barnlund and Haiman, 1959; Collins and Guetzkow, 1964; Harnack and Fest, 1964; Gulley, 1968; Sattler and Miller, 1968; Bormann, 1969; Patton and Giffin, 1973; Applbaum et al, 1974; Brilhart, 1984; Gouran, 1974; and Goldberg and Larson, 1975).

The terms *task-oriented, problem-solving,* and *decision-making* groups have been used interchangeably to stress the emphasis on the cognitive end products of group discussion. Although interpersonal relations are often discussed, they are considered not as important and merely a means to an end (that is, to solve a problem).

Among the many kinds of decision-making groups in organizations, Quality Circles have become a highly successful mechanism for increasing employee involvement and solving company problems. Mohr and Mohr (1983) illustrate the value of problem-solving groups in the following instances:

- A study done at B. F. Goodrich of vendors' invoices showed that the top 11 percent accounted for 68 percent of the dollars recovered.

- At Westinghouse, a purchasing department quality circle discovered that 78 percent of their vendor overshipment problems was caused by 12.5 percent of the causes identified by the circle members.

- In a machine and sheet metal shop at Sunnyvale, California, 77 percent of the rejected parts resulted from 15 percent of the causes.

As these examples suggest, most organizations find that a few key issues typically cause most of the problems demanding attention. This idea originated with the nineteenth-century Italian economist Vilfredo Pareto, whose studies showed that a small percentage of the population held a high percentage of the wealth, while the great majority lived in poverty. Many authors since Pareto have confirmed his principle that some issues (a vital few) result in the largest percentage of problems, while most issues (the trivial many) result in relatively few problems. Another name for the Pareto principle is the 80–20 rule: 80 percent of the problems are caused by 20 percent of the issues (pp. 131–132).

Kanter (1983) states that groups are the cornerstone of participative decision making in American organizations. She writes:

> It is hard to mention "teams" or "participation" anymore without someone's labeling them "Japanese-style management." In the first place this is faintly ridiculous. . . . Innovating companies emphasize teamwork, but they also reward individuals, and they give internal entrepreneurs free rein to pioneer—as long as they can also work with the team. So "American-style" participation does not and should not mean the dominance of committees over individuals, the submergence of the individual in the group, or the swallowing of the person by the team, but rather the mechanism for giving more people at more levels a piece of the entrepreneurial action. (p. 364)

Types of Discussion Questions

Problem-solving groups must spend a great deal of time and energy in careful deliberation. Generally, the group will be attempting to provide some answer or answers to the discussion question. Sample discussion questions include these:

1. How can we keep from eliminating the earth's ozone shield?

2. What can be done about the problem of cheating in our school?

3. How do we determine local obscenity and pornography standards?

4. What are the long-term effects of marijuana use?

5. How do we achieve equal opportunity for women and minorities?

6. How can we reduce energy consumption?

7. Should abortion or contraception be made mandatory for families that already have two children?

8. What is an acceptable level of unemployment?

9. Should marijuana be legalized?

10. Should handguns be outlawed?

11. Has the decline of civilization begun in this country?

12. How can we curb drug abuse in industry?

An effective problem-solving discussion begins with an effectively structured discussion question. First, a topic should be limited to one issue. Notice that question 7 includes both abortion and contraception. These two issues may require different answers, so only one should be included in the discussion question. An improved version of number 7 would be, "How can we help curb population growth?"

QUESTIONS OF FACT   Questions of fact deal with truth and falsity. Is it or is it not so? "What are the long-term effects of marijuana use?" is a question of fact. "Can the disease AIDS (Acquired Immune Deficiency Syndrome) be transmitted by casual contact in a school classroom?" is another.

Discussions involving questions of fact require evidence and documentation to establish whether or not the phenomenon exists. For example, "Does the Bermuda Triangle really pose a major threat to ships and planes traveling in the area?" or "Does intelligent life exist in outer space?" Frequently, such questions remain somewhat unresolvable, but they are interesting to discuss anyway.

QUESTIONS OF DEFINITION   Questions of definition are fairly narrow, but are often quite difficult to answer. The problem of defining obscenity and pornography has been with us for decades. The emotionalism experienced in numerous states over textbook wording is but one of many examples of disagreement over what is obscene. Several years ago the Supreme Court ruled that no one definition could be made for all communities, so each local community had to define obscenity and pornography for itself.

In the medical arena, lawsuits are arising over differences in the medical definition of death. If accident victims become organ transplant donors, what signs do doctors use to determine if the donor is dead? Cessation of the heartbeat is certainly not a reliable sign, since numerous people walking around today have had their hearts stop temporarily. What about cessation of brain activity? The point is that the definition is important and is not as easily determined as it might first appear.

QUESTIONS OF VALUE   Questions of value invoke an evaluation of the issues once the facts and the definitions have been determined. Whereas facts can be verified by others, values are personal and often differ drastically from one individual to another. Perhaps we can agree on a definition of affirmative action as *unequal* opportunity for women and minorities to undo the wrongs that have existed for decades. Yet can we agree that *unequal* opportunity of any kind is desirable? Some judges have ruled that this is still another form of discrimination (against white males) and is inconsistent with the ideals of the Equal Employment Opportunity Commission. Yet others feel strongly that reverse discrimination is required to tip the scales of justice to where they should have been a long time ago.

Differences in values are at the base of the controversies over abortion and contraception as well. Those who believe in the right of the unborn child see abortion and even contraception as unthinkable. Those on the other side feel that the individual woman should have the right to decide whether she wants a child and that these decisions should not be dictated by others. Here is another case in which the "right" answer will definitely vary depending on one's own personal and very individual value system.

QUESTIONS OF POLICY   Questions of policy involve establishing the facts, determining of definitions, a discussion of values, and the determination of the ways and means of solving a problem. "What can be done to solve the problems of drug abuse?" "What should our state's policy be toward abortions?" "Should the United States provide more public service jobs for the unemployed?" "How can the misuse of handguns be reduced?" All these are examples of policy questions. Discussions regarding questions of policy are often the most complicated, since they encompass some of the other three types of discussion questions (fact, definition, and value). Let us look at one topic (equal rights for women) as it might be discussed in each of the four ways.

1. *Fact:* "Do women have equal rights in this country?"

2. *Definition:* "What do we mean by the term *equal rights for women?*"

3. *Value:* "Is it desirable to change women's role in our society?"

4. *Policy:* "How can we achieve equal rights for women in this country?"

As you can see, the policy question assumes, to some extent, that (1) equal rights do not presently exist, (2) agreement on a definition of equal rights can be reached, (3) equal rights for women are desirable, and (4) something ought to be done to bring about equal rights for women. It is important to remember that policy discussions may bog down on these earlier questions if all group members do not agree on these assumptions.

GRIN AND BEAR IT   by Lichty & Wagner

By permission of News America Syndicate

"We're an ad hoc committee from our room, and we demand to know what ad hoc means."

In addition to trying to find a solution to the problem, policy questions frequently must deal with the question of how to implement the solution. Should equal rights be dictated by law? Should they evolve through generations of attitude change produced by the mass media and word of mouth? Should they be implemented at the local level, like obscenity laws, or at the national level, like crimes against the government? All these questions deal with the specifics of how the solution actually gets enacted.

Figure 3.6 summarizes the elements involved in various types of discussion questions.

Discussion Group Formats

Discussion questions may be approached in a variety of different small group formats. The selection of an appropriate format largely depends upon group members' own needs and circumstances. Although there are any number of possible formats, these five are representative of most problem-solving discussions:

Dialogue: The dialogue is simply a discussion or conversation between two people. It may be conducted privately or in front of an audience.

Panel: The panel discussion usually involves a small number of people (up to five or six) conducting an informal discussion on a topic they have all thought about and possibly researched beforehand.

FIGURE 3.6   ELEMENTS INVOLVED IN DISCUSSION QUESTIONS.

Elements Included	Type of discussion			
	Fact	Definition	Value	Policy
Facts	X	X	X	X
Definitions		X	X	X
Values			X	X
Policies				X
Implementation				X

One person is appointed moderator to help move the group along its planned agenda. Conversation is mostly spontaneous, and participants may interrupt one another.

Symposium: The symposium includes several participants, each of whom gives a short formal presentation on a prepared topic usually built around a central theme. Participants do not interrupt each other during the formal presentations, but a less formal discussion usually follows.

Forum: A forum is a question-and-answer period designed to allow audience members to interact with the discussion group. A forum period often follows a panel discussion or a symposium. It is customary for the chairperson to introduce the panel or symposium members and to serve as a moderator for the forum period.

Colloquy: A colloquy may take a number of forms, but each involves the questioning of experts by the other experts on the panel, laypersons on a second panel, or laypersons in the audience. This format is very similar to the panel discussion except that experts are involved and a second panel of laypersons may also be involved.

Discussion Group Techniques

In addition to the major formats discussed above, there are a number of subformats or techniques that may be employed in discussion groups. These techniques are often used for short periods of time as *part* of a discussion group format.

Phillips 66: Phillips 66 is a specific technique developed by J. D. Phillips (1948). It simply allows all the members of an audience to form groups of about six people to discuss a specific topic for about six minutes and then report the group's conclusion through a spokesman. Realistically, this technique is more useful if longer time limits are allowed (up to an hour or so). The general term for this, when time and group size are not limited to six, is a *buzz group* or *buzz session.* The technique offers the advantage of allowing a lot of people to participate in a fairly efficient manner. The results from all groups are compiled and used to solve the problem faced by the entire assembly.

Case Discussion: A case discussion is an educational discussion centered on a real or hypothetical event. The case problem is presented to the group, and members attempt to solve it as best they can. A case problem is included at the beginning of each chapter in this book to illustrate the way in which small group theory and research apply to real-life problems.

Role Playing: Role playing simply allows participants to adopt a new "role" or set of behaviors other than their own. For example, quiet individuals may be assigned the role of leader, or argumentative members may be assigned the role of harmonizer or compromiser. Meek members may be asked to play the role of the "devil's advocate." In each case the individual gets an opportunity to practice a role in an attempt to build his or her group skills. This helps develop role flexibility so that participants can adopt new and different role behaviors as the need arises. Role playing also may be used to demonstrate to the rest of the group what a given role may do to a group discussion. The chronic nonconformist role can be secretly given to one member to demonstrate how the others will react. The typical reaction is that that person gets a lot of attention from the rest of the group for a while, but will be ignored after a time if he or she continues to deviate (see Chapter 4 for more on deviation).

Another version of role playing is the role reversal. In this case, participants try to take the part of another person (usually one with whom they have a conflict). Biracial groups, labor-management groups, and others frequently use this technique to develop empathy for the other person's point of view. It often results in funny situations, which also help relieve some of the tension. Try some of the role-playing exercises in this book to help get a feel for what role playing is like—for example, Exercise 1 at the end of Chapter 2.

Fishbowl: The fishbowl technique has one small group attempt to solve a problem for a specified period of time (often 30 minutes), while a second group, seated around the outside of the first group, observes the process. After the discussion, the observer group gives feedback to the first group as to what behaviors they were able to identify as helpful or harmful to the group's progress. Then the two groups reverse positions and roles: The observers become the observed, and vice versa. This technique may be aided by the use of videotape equipment.

Conference: A conference is a series of meetings on topics of common interest between and among people who represent different groups. For example, representatives from different colleges and universities may gather at a conference to discuss problems of finance, curriculum, community service, and others. Conferences often involve hundreds of people and may last several days. For the past several years, different countries have hosted world food conferences in an attempt to plan for the feeding of the world's population. Conferences may also be quite small and last a short period of time. The critical element is that different groups are represented. An example of the latter type of conference is the plant manager's weekly conference in a manufacturing plant where representatives from production, engineering, maintenance, inspection, personnel, and other departments get together to organize their efforts and to solve common problems.

THE SYSTEMS PERSPECTIVE

In this chapter we have looked at some of the elements that constitute the internal influences section of our model. In systems theory these elements would be called part of the *throughput* of small groups. Early in the chapter we examined territoriality, physical environment, and seating behavior in groups. As suggested by the Vietnam negotiations, different cultures have drastically differing perceptions of how to position furniture or whether to have furniture at all. This illustrates the way in which relevant background factors influence such internal influences as territoriality, physical environment, and seating behavior. For example, in Western culture we typically place furniture along the walls with open space in the middle of the room. The Japanese tend to cluster furniture in the center of the room, leaving the space along the walls open. Also, imagine conducting a group discussion while seated barefoot on the floor around very low tables. This should help you picture the importance of background factors in relation to seating behaviors.

Probably the most important internal influence in the model is the type of group. Obviously the procedures, norms, expectations, and outcomes of a work group will be radically different from those in a social group. For example, a norm of openness in both self-disclosure and candid feedback to others exists in many social groups. However, you might find that to tell your boss or friend exactly what you do *not* like about them is certainly inappropriate. The type of group has an enormous impact on the way in which that group functions.

In this chapter we also looked at the literature on communication networks. We saw that the all-channel network was best for group member satisfaction, while the wheel produced the fastest results. As our systems perspective leads us to believe, determining the "best" network depends, among other things, on the demands of the situation.

When we discussed the issue of group size, we began to see the connection between the type of group and the appropriate group size. All other things being equal, five seems to be the optimum size for a problem-solving group. However, the optimum size for a group discussion in a classroom may be radically different from that of a work group on an assembly line or in a large office. Even the idea of the "right" size of family group depends on each of our relevant background factors. Typically people have quite strong feelings about what is the "right" sized family. These feelings usually result from a lifetime of attitude formation influenced by parents, friends, and perhaps religious affiliation.

Group size is also related to the idea of communication networks. As the size increases, the all-channel network begins to bog down in the confusion and a more controlled network tends to be more appropriate. Group size is also related to the consequences of group interaction. Larger groups tend to produce lower levels of satisfaction and interpersonal relations among participants. Bostrom's research, cited in this chapter, is very revealing. It showed that most people like to talk far more than they like to listen in groups.

In the preceding section of this chapter we looked at different group formats and techniques (for example, panel, symposium, role playing, fishbowl, conference). Obviously there is a connection between type of group and appropriate format. Can you imagine the U.S. president's cabinet engaging in role-playing and fishbowl simulations? Certainly educational groups use these formats and techniques with a great deal of success, but work groups would be more likely to use panels, symposiums, and conferences.

The type of group format is also related to the desired group outcome. If personal growth is the goal, then role playing or fishbowls are helpful. On the other hand, if the group goal is to solve a task-oriented problem, such as how to cut energy consumption by 10 percent, the panel discussion is probably more appropriate. As usual, it all depends . . .

EXERCISES

1. Discussion of Case Studies

Divide into five-person groups. Each group can discuss *one* of the cases below.* Each of these cases describes real-life psychological studies involving naive human subjects. Ask yourself, "How do I feel about the use of this procedure

---

*These cases were used in a study on ethics in social research practices conducted by Edwin A. Rugg (personal correspondence, May 20, 1975).

in social research?" Then, within each group try to agree on one of the six reactions listed below.

(a) I am totally unopposed to its use.

(b) I am basically unopposed to its use.

(c) I am slightly more unopposed to its use.

(d) I am slightly more opposed than unopposed to its use.

(e) I am basically opposed to its use.

(f) I am opposed to its use under any circumstances

After you have arrived at group agreement on one of the six reactions above, each group should share its reaction and the reasoning behind it. Discuss the different reactions among the groups.

Case 1—Homosexual Attitudes   Men are recruited to participate in an experiment on sexual attitudes, although they are not told that it is actually a study of attitudes toward homosexuality. Participants are led to believe that a "psycho-galvanometer" used in the experiment is capable of detecting sexual arousal. They are also told that if the galvanometer registers when an individual looks at slides of nude males, the individual is probably a latent homosexual. The galvanometer is rigged so that all participants are led to believe they are latent homosexuals. Following the experiment, the researcher informs the participants that the galvanometer was rigged and gives detailed information about the study and its true purpose.

Case 2—Obedience   Individuals are recruited to participate in an experiment on memory and learning, although the actual purpose of the experiment is to study obedience. Participants are given the role of "teacher" and told to administer increasingly strong electric shocks to the "learner" whenever the learner makes an error in the memory task. The learner is actually an assistant to the researcher and receives no actual shocks. He only pretends to experience pain as the shock level becomes more and more severe. The psychological dilemma for the participant involves deciding whether to obey the experimenter, who insists that the participant continue to shock the learner, or to side with the learner, who begs the participant to stop administering shocks. When the participant refuses to continue or when the highest shock level is reached, the experiment is over. At that point, the participant is told that the shocks and cries of pain were faked. The true purpose and details of the study are explained.

Case 3—Reactions to Fear and Anxiety   Students, participating in a series of experiments for course credit, are told when they arrive at one of the research laboratories that they will receive an electric shock as part of the experiment. The researcher is interested in the reactions of groups under conditions of fear and anxiety. In order to facilitate anxiety arousal, the researcher describes in detail the pain and uncomfortable side effects that usually accompany the electric shock. Actually, no shocks are ever administered. Following the experiment, the researcher informs the participants that they will not be shocked after all. He then explains the actual experiment that took place and why they were purposefully misled.

Case 4—Self-concept and Achievement   Students at a teacher's college complete a series of placement tests but are not told that the tests are actually part of a psychological experiment. The experiment involves giving half of the students false test results that indicate that they are unfit for a teaching career. The researcher is interested in studying the effects of lowered self-concept on subsequent achievement. Two weeks later the study is completed, and the researcher tells the students that the test results were falsified and explains the details of the research project.

Case 5—Reward and Performance   Individuals are promised $2 if they participate in an experiment that involves performing a simple but boring task. Some of the participants are later led to believe that they may receive up to $20 for their participation, even though the researcher has no intention of paying participants more than $2 for their time. The researcher is interested in the effects of different anticipated rewards on attitudes toward the task and the quality of task performance. At the end of the experiment, the researcher explains why he/she cannot pay participants more than the $2 initially agreed upon and discusses the purpose and nature of the research.

READINGS: OVERVIEW

In the first article, Sommer discusses the research on small group ecology. This article illustrates the interesting combinations between seating patterns and people's interaction.

In the second article, Hatvany and Pucik describe the important role groups play in the Japanese method for achieving high productivity in their society. To what extent to you think these group methods could be used in the Western world?

Studies of Small Group Ecology

Robert Sommer

The study of ecology covers both the distribution and the density of organisms. Within the social sciences the major ecological studies have taken place at the societal rather than at the small group level (e.g., demography) although it has been known for a long time that the arrangement of individuals in face-to-face groups is not accidental. In American society, leaders tend to occupy the head positions at a table with their lieutenants at their sides, while opposition factions frequently are found at the other end of the table.[1] Numerous accounts of these phenomena are found in observational studies such as those by Whyte[2] and Wilmer.[3] Considering the number of studies concerned with small discussion groups, relatively few have made the arrangement of people a variable. The early studies by Steinzor[4] and Bass and Klubeck[5] were primarily concerned with other factors (e.g., leadership) and only afterwards was the physical arrangement of individuals examined for its effects upon interaction. This is also the procedure followed by Strodtbeck and Hook[6] who reanalyzed their jury trial data to learn the effects of table position on contribution to the discussion, and more recently Hare and Bales[7] who reexamined group discussion data for positional effects.

One of the oldest problems in social psychology concerns the classification of face-to-face groups.[8] A heuristic taxonomy of groups resolved some of the contradictory findings of experiments concerned with "social facilitation," some of whose results indicated a social increment while others showed a social decrement. It was Allport[9] who made the distinction between cooperating, competing, and co-acting groups. Since most of the small group research of the last decades has concerned itself with discussion groups, this distinction has been largely neglected. The goal of the present study is to learn how people in different types of face-to-face groups arrange themselves. . . .

Observational Studies

The Situation Where People Desire to Interact

Over a fourteen-month period, observations were made during non-eating hours in the student union cafeteria at a California university. During these hours the cafeteria is used by students for casual conversation and studying (and to a lesser extent by faculty and nonteaching staff for coffee breaks). The observations were made irregularly and there was some bias in these times in that the writer's schedule led him to pass this way at certain times rather than others but most of the daylight non-eating hours were covered. Records were kept of the seating of pairs of people. In the first series of observations, no distinction was made whether the people were conversing, studying together, or studying separately. The only category specifically excluded from the study was a pair where one or both people were eating. These criteria contained two different table sizes: single pedestal square tables (36 inches per side) each surrounded by four chairs, one to a side; double pedestal rectangular tables (36 × 54 inches) each surrounded by six chairs, two on the long sides and one at each end.

The 50 pairs seated at the small square tables showed a preference for corner rather than opposite seating (35 pairs sat corner to corner while 15 sat across from one another).[10] The double pedestal tables permit side-by-side and distant seating as well as corner and opposite seating. During the course of the observations, 60 pairs were observed at double tables. Table 1 shows clearly that side-by-side and distant seating were infrequent. The vast majority of pairs chose to occupy the corners or sit across from one another.

It was planned to continue these observations for another six months, but in February 1965 the furniture of the cafeteria was changed. In order to accommodate more people the management moved in new tables and rearranged others. Rather than combine these new observations with the previous ones, it seemed preferable to look upon them as a new series in which additional information could be gained. In the next four months 52 additional observations were made in which the *major activity* of the people as well as their seating arrangement was recorded. A distinction was made between those pairs who were interacting (conversing, studying together) and those who were co-acting (occupying the same table but studying separately). In order to keep the data comparable to the previous observations, the present analysis focused upon the square tables (36″ × 36″) observed previously, as well as rectangular tables (36″ × 72″) which were made by pushing two of the small square tables together. The situation at the other rectangular tables (36″ × 54″) was confused since

TABLE 1　ARRANGEMENT OF PAIRS AT RECTANGULAR TABLES (IN PERCENT)

Seating Arrangement	Series 1 (N = 50)	Series 2	
		Conversing (N = 74)	Co-acting (N = 18)
Corner	40	54	0
Across	43	35	32
Side	8	6	0
Distant	10	4	68
Total	100	100	100

these tables now accommodated anywhere from four to eight people, sometimes with end chairs and sometimes without, so these are excluded from the analysis.

Of the 124 pairs seated at the small square tables, 106 were conversing or otherwise interacting while 18 were co-acting. The interacting pairs showed a definite preference for corner seating, with 70 seated corner-to-corner compared to 36 seated across from one another. However, co-acting pairs chose a very different arrangement, with only two pairs sitting corner-to-corner and 18 sitting opposite one another. These results support the previous studies in which corner seating was preferred over opposite and side-by-side seating in a variety of conditions where individuals interact. It suggests that corner seating preserves the closeness between individuals and also enables people to avoid eye contact since they do not sit face to face. The co-acting pairs use the distance across the table for books, handbags, and other belongings, and can avoid visual contact by looking down rather than across the table.

Seating at the rectangular tables is shown in the second and third columns of Table 1. The interacting groups prefer corner-to-corner seating, and to a lesser extent opposite seating, with little use made of side-by-side or distant seating. On the other hand, more than two-thirds of the co-acting groups chose a distant seating arrangement which separated the people geographically and visually.

The Situation Where Interaction Is Discouraged

One set of observations took place in the reading area adjacent to the reserve room of a university library. This is a large room (29′ × 83′) containing 33 rectangular tables (48″ × 64″) in the main area. Each table has a capacity of four persons, two sitting on opposite sides with the ends free. The room was generally quiet even when filled to capacity. This made it a good place to study how people arranged themselves when they did *not* want to interact. All observations took place when the room was relatively uncrowded since this provided some choice as to seating. Due to the size of the room, it was not possible to record the arrangements at all the tables in the room without appearing conspicuous. Thus the observer randomly selected some location in the room and diagrammed the seating arrangements within the visible portion of the room on a prepared chart.

A pilot study[11] had shown that the majority of people who came alone sat alone if there was an empty table. This trend was more marked for the males (70%) than for the females (55%). The next largest group arranged themselves diagonally across from whoever already occupied the table. Only 10% of the students sat opposite or beside another student (i.e., in either of the two near positions) when there were empty seats available elsewhere.

Following this, there were 19 occasions when the seating patterns of those individuals presently in the reserve room were recorded, including people who came alone as well as those who came with friends. The sample consisted of 193 males and 304 women. Again it was found that a higher percentage of males (34%) than females (25%) sat alone. However, the major focus of the study was on those students who sat two at a table (since there is only one possible way that people can arrange themselves three or four to a table). The results showed that 30% of the pairs sat across from one another, 15% sat side-by-side, while 56% used the diagonal or distant arrangement. Although the observations were cross-sectional and spanned only several minutes each, a record was made of any conversations at the table. Conversations were observed among 8% of the pairs sitting across from one another, 3% of those pairs sitting in a diagonal or distant arrangement, and 37% of those sitting side-by-side.

A second set of observations was made independently in the Periodical Room of the same library. The same general technique was followed in that the arrangement of all pairs was diagrammed on 14 occasions over a two month period. This room, excluding the magazine and transit areas, was 36' × 74' and contained two types of rectangular tables, one (48" × 64") with two chairs on each side and the ends free, and the other (48" × 90") with three chairs on each side and the ends free. The arrangements of pairs at the two types of tables were similar; and the pooled data show that of the 74 pairs, 19% sat across from one another, 13% sat side-by-side, and 68% sat in a distant arrangement. Conversations were noted between 14% of the people sitting opposite one another, 6% of those people sitting in a distant relationship, and 60% of those pairs sitting side-by-side.

Questionnaire Studies

Rectangular Table Ecology

To learn something of the way that group task influences the way people arrange themselves, a paper-and-pencil test was administered to 151 students in an introductory psychology class. Each student was asked to imagine how he and a friend of the same sex would seat themselves under four differernt conditions: a. To chat for a few minutes before class; b. To study together for the same exam; c. To study for different exams; and d. To compete in order to see which would be the first to solve a series of puzzles. Each time the student was asked to indicate his own seating and that of his friend on a diagram showing a table and six chairs (see Figure 1). There was one chair at the head and one at the foot and two chairs on each of the sides. In order to maximize the realism of the test, the hypothetical activity was located in the student union cafeteria during *non*-eating hours (which is, as has been noted, actively used for casual conversation, studying, etc., and has similar rectangular tables). The tasks set for the students included cooperating, co-acting, and competing activity. In addition, a distinction was made between casual interaction such as conversation and structured cooperative activity (joint studying for an exam). The different tasks were presented in random order in the test booklet.

There were no significant differences between the sexes in seating arrangements under any of the conditions. This was unexpected, since previous studies

FIGURE 1   SEATING PREFERENCES AT RECTANGULAR TABLES.

Percentage of Ss Choosing This Arrangement

Seating Arrangement	Condition 1 (conversing)	Condition 2 (cooperating)	Condition 3 (co-acting)	Condition 4 (competing)
X on top side	42	19	3	7
X on both sides (middle)	46	25	31	41
X top-left and bottom-right	1	5	43	20
X top-left and bottom	0	0	3	5
X both on left side	11	51	7	8
X top and bottom	0	0	13	18
TOTAL	100	100	100	99

have shown that females make greater use of side-by-side seating while males prefer to sit across from other people.

Figure 1 shows the seating preferences for the total group of 151 students. If we take "near seating" to include side-by-side, corner and opposite arrangements, and let "distant seating" refer to all other patterns, Figure 1 shows that distant seating was rarely used by casual or cooperating groups. People who want to converse or work together use the near arrangements. On the other hand distant seating is the dominant pattern in co-acting groups. The most common distant pattern shows people sitting on opposite sides of the table but not directly facing one another rather than the more physically distant head-foot arrangement. This suggests that it is the visual contact between people rather than bodily presence that is the major source of distraction in co-acting groups. Distant seating is important in competing groups although the dominant arrangement here is opposite seating.

People conversing overwhelmingly chose a corner-to-corner or opposite arrangement. On the other hand, those studying together strongly prefer to sit side-by-side. In no other condition is side seating used anywhere near this frequency. There is a metaphorical quality to these arrangements with people competing sitting "in opposition," people cooperating sitting "on the same side," people conversing sitting "in a corner" and people co-acting choosing a "distant" arrangement.

The identical questionnaire was given to 26 students in a social psychology class. After the students completed the questionnaire in the usual way, each was asked to go through his responses and explain why he chose this particular arrangement.

For the *casual group,* the dominant preference was for corner seating, and the students' explanations were: "We would be sitting close to each other and yet be able to see each person." "It's nice to be close when chatting but you should face each other instead of side-by-side." "You would be closer with only a corner than *across* the table, you'd have to turn less than side-by-side." "The corner arrangement is the most intimate. You wouldn't have to shout *across* the table, but, sitting adjacent you could still face the person. Sitting beside the person it is hard to look at them when you're talking." Those people who chose to sit across from one another emphasized the desirability of a direct face-to-face arrangement.

In the *cooperating group,* those people who liked the corner arrangement mentioned the ease of conversing in corner chairs ("Because we could look at each other's notes with the least change of place and effort.") while those people who chose the side arrangement emphasized the ease of sharing things in this position.

For the *co-acting group,* the dominant arrangement was a distant one and those students emphasized the need to be apart yet feel together ("This would allow for sitting far enough apart so we wouldn't interfere with each other, but if we wanted to pass comments we were close enough." "Effectively divides table into two halves yet allows brief remarks without having to raise voice. Also allows staring into space and not at neighbor's face.")

As in the previous study, opposite, distant-opposite, and distant seating were preferred by *competing groups.* The way that a face-to-face arrangement stimulates competition was frequently mentioned: e.g., "Able to see how friend is doing but there's enough room"; or, "In this situation the friend can be watched to determine his progress." The reason given most frequently by people preferring the distant-opposite arrangement was that it reduced the temptation to look at the other person's answers while the long distance aided concentration. Those people electing a distant arrangement explained that this would minimize distraction. Two of the three people preferring a side arrangement mentioned that it was easier to concentrate when not looking directly at the other person.

Round Table Ecology

In order to learn how the group task would affect the arrangement of people at a round table, 116 students in another introductory psychology class were asked to fill out a questionnaire similar to that of the preceding study except that the diagram showed a *round* table surrounded by six chairs. The same four situations were described (i.e., conversing with a friend, studying for the same exam, for different exams, or competing). Since the results showed no significant difference between the 65 females and 51 males, the composite totals are presented in Figure 2. People can sit in only three possible arrangements under these conditions (see Figure 2), these three arrangements comprising a rank order of physical distance.

Figure 2 shows that casual and cooperating groups made greatest use of adjacent chairs. This trend was most marked among the cooperating groups where 83% chose adjacent chairs. Although the co-acting group makes heavy use of an arrangement where one empty chair is left between the people, the majority of co-acting groups places a gap of two seats between them (i.e., sit directly opposite one another). The trend for opposite seating is most pronounced in the competing group.

FIGURE 2   SEATING PREFERENCES AT ROUND TABLES.

Percentage of Ss Choosing This Arrangement

Seating Arrangement	Condition 1 (conversing)	Condition 2 (cooperating)	Condition 3 (co-acting)	Condition 4 (competing)
	63	83	13	12
	17	7	36	25
	20	10	51	63
TOTAL	100	100	100	100

If we make certain assumptions on the basis of our previous study with rectangular tables, it is possible to formulate hypotheses as to how positions at a round table compare with those at a rectangular table. Adjacent seating at a round table seems somewhere between side and corner seating. Physically, it places people side-by-side at a lesser angle than in a corner arrangement. Sitting one seat away from another person at a round table does not seem to be as "distant" an arrangement as leaving the same gap at a rectangular table. This suggests that people at a round table are psychologically closer than at a corresponding position at a rectangular table. Opposite seating in the round table arrangement used here seems to serve some of the functions of both distant and opposite seating at a rectangular table.

The same questionnaire was given to 18 students who, after filling out the questionnaire in the usual way, explained why they arranged themselves as they did. Most of the students in the *converging condition* selected adjacent seats: "I want to chat with my friend, not the whole cafeteria, so I sit next to her"; "More intimate, no physical barriers between each other." In the *cooperating group,* the vast majority chose to sit in adjacent chairs. Their explanations stressed the advantages of this arrangement for comparing notes and sharing materials. Most students in the co-acting condition chose to sit two seats away from one another, the greatest physical distance permitted in this diagram. Of those who chose to sit one seat away, several mentioned that this "Doesn't put us directly opposite each other . . . keep looking at each other if we look up from studying," and "Not directly across from each other because we'd have more of a tendency to talk then." In the *competing condition,* most students chose to leave two seats between them which placed them directly opposite one another. The explanations emphasized the need to keep separate in order to avoid seeing each other's material. Several mentioned that opposite seating permitted them to see how the other person was doing and enhanced feelings of cooperation.

Discussion

These results indicate that different tasks are associated with different spatial arrangements; the ecology of interaction differs from the ecology of co-action and competition. Exactly why these particular arrangements are chosen we do not know for certain. On the basis of what our subjects report, eye contact seems an important factor in spatial arrangements. Under certain conditions direct visual contact represents a challenge to the other, a play at dominance. Among chickens and turkeys in confinement, McBride[12] has shown that the dominant bird in the flock has the most eye space. When he looks at a submissive bird, the latter looks away. When birds are crowded together, they stand at the wire of the coop facing outward to avoid the stress that would be generated by extended visual contact. We may only speculate as to the extent to which eye contact regulates spatial arrangements, though it is interesting to note that the only questionnaire condition in which opposite seating was chosen over other distant alternatives was in the competitive task where the subject indicated a desire to "keep an eye on what the other person was doing." It is hypothesized that gestures of threat (antagonistic displays) are more appropriate in competitive conditions than cooperative or strictly social tasks. On the other hand, antagonistic displays are stressful to both parties, and in the animal kingdom are generally terminated by ritualized submissive behavior rather than actual combat. In a previous pilot study,[13] people were asked how they would seat themselves at a table already occupied by someone they disliked. It was found that people chose to sit at some distance from the disliked person, but *not* directly opposite him, i.e., in a distant-side position. In this way they were removed visually as well as geographically from the source of stress. The relationship between distance and aggressive behavior among chaffinches has been studied nicely by Marler.[14] Placing the cages of chaffinches various distances apart, he found the point at which aggressive displays began. Female chaffinches tolerated closer presence than males, while females whose breasts were dyed to resemble males were kept at the typical male distance by other birds.

Most stressful encounters are avoided through spatial segregation. The orbits in which people travel tend to remove them from contact with those with whom they disagree or dislike. Avoidance is the first line of defense against interpersonal stress but when this is not possible or effective, an individual develops alternate methods. Limiting the range of visual contact through social conventions or actual physical barriers are other possibilities. The present studies all took place in settings whose furnishings consisted solely of tables and chairs. No attempt was made to explore the role of physical barriers such as posts, partitions, tables, etc., in regulating interaction. The ways in which people gain privacy in public areas warrants further exploration in a society in which more and more people share a finite amount of space. In settings such as libraries, study rooms, and large open offices, it is exceedingly important to develop methods whereby unwanted or stressful interpersonal contact is avoided.

Chapin,[15] in his discussion of housing factors related to mental hygiene, indicated the importance of ease of circulation as well as areas that can be closed off from the main traffic flow. Just as people moving about a house require resting places for solitude or individual concentration, people rooted to a given spot in a public area require places where their eyes can rest without stress. There is the apocryphal story of the stress produced by the newspaper strike in New York City where the seated men were unable to "retreat into" newspapers and had to look at the other occupants, particularly women standing above them. Subway officials believe that the advertisements on the wall provide safe resting places for the patron's eyes.

Since the topological similarities between different arrangements of people make it necessary to experiment with every conceivable physical arrangement, it seems most fruitful to isolate the socially and psychologically genotypic arrangements. The two most obvious ones are near and distant seating. In ordinary social intercourse, near seating is the rule. In American society it is only among strangers, co-acting individuals or schizophrenic mental patients that one finds distant seating patterns in any frequency.

One can divide seating patterns into several important subclasses. One possible category involves arrangements which maximize direct visual contact between individuals. According to Goffman,[16] Hall,[17] and Birdwhistell,[18] direct visual contact can be exceedingly uncomfortable and disconcerting under ordinary conditions, producing feelings of anxiety in the person upon whom the eyes are directly centered.

References

1. Edward T. Hall, *The Silent Language* (Garden City: Doubleday, 1959); Robert Sommer, "Leadership and Group Geography," *Sociometry,* 24 (March, 1961), pp. 99–110; Fred L. Strodtbeck and L. Harmon Hook, "The Social Dimensions of a Twelve-Man Jury Table," *Sociometry,* 24 (December, 1961), pp. 397–415.
2. William H. Whyte, *The Organization Man* (New York: Simon and Schuster, 1956).
3. Harry A. Wilmer, "Graphic Ways of Representing Some Aspects of a Therapeutic Community," *Symposium on Preventive and Social Psychiatry* (Washington: Government Printing Office, 1957).
4. Bernard Steinzor, "The Spatial Factor in Face-to-Face Discussion Groups," *Journal of Abnormal and Social Psychology,* 45 (July, 1950), pp. 552–555.
5. Bernard M. Bass and S. Klubeck, "Effects of Seating Arrangements in Leaderless Group Discussions," *Journal of Abnormal and Social Psychology,* 47 (July, 1952) pp. 724–727.
6. Strodtbeck and Hook, *op. cit.*
7. A. Paul Hare and Robert F. Bales, "Seating Position and Small Group Interaction," *Sociometry,* 26 (December, 1963), pp. 480–486.
8. F. H. Allport, *Social Psychology* (Boston: Houghton Mifflin, 1924); W. Moede, *Experimentelle Massenpsychologie* (Liepzig: S. Hirzel, 1920).
9. Floyd Allport, *Social Psychology.*
10. A similar preference for corner seating was found in subsequent study of eating pairs in a hospital cafeteria. Of the 41 pairs, 29 sat corner-to-corner while 12 pairs sat across from one another.
11. This study was carried out by David Addicott.
12. Glen McBride, *A General Theory of Social Organization and Behavior* (St. Lucia: University of Queensland Press, 1964).
13. This study was conducted by Vera Stevens and Corinne Sundberg.
14. Peter Marler, "Studies of Fighting Chaffinches: Proximity as a Cause of Aggression," *British Journal of Animal Behavior,* 4 (1956), pp. 23–30.
15. F. S. Chapin, "Some Housing Factors Related to Mental Hygiene," *Journal of Social Issues,* 7 (1951), pp. 164–171.
16. Erving Goffman, *Behavior in Public Places* (Glencoe: Free Press, 1963).
17. Edward T. Hall, "Silent Assumptions in Social Communication," in *Disorders of Communication,* 42 (1964), pp. 41–55.
18. Ray Birdwhistell, "Field Methods and Techniques," *Human Organization,* 11 (Spring, 1952), pp. 37–38.

Japanese Management Practices and Productivity

Nina Hatvany
Vladimir Pucik

The [United States] is the most technically advanced country and the most affluent one. But capital investment alone will not make the difference. In any country the quality of products and the productivity of workers depend on management. When Detroit changes its management system we'll see more powerful American competitors.

—Hideo Suguira, Executive Vice-President, Honda Motor Co.

Productivity—or output per worker—is a key measure of economic health. When it increases, the economy grows in real terms and so do standards of living. When it declines, real economic growth slows or stagnates. Productivity is the result of many factors, including investment in capital goods, technological innovation, and workers' motivation.

After a number of years of sluggish productivity growth, the United States now trails most other major industrial nations in the rise in output per worker, although it still enjoys the best overall rate. This state of affairs is increasingly bemoaned by many critics in both academic and business circles. Some reasons suggested to "explain" the U.S. decline in productivity rankings include excessive government regulation, tax policies discouraging investment, increases in energy costs, uncooperative unions, and various other factors in the business environment.

Some observers, however—among them Harvard professors Robert Hayes and William J. Abernathy—put the blame squarely on American managers. They argue that U.S. firms prefer to service existing markets rather than create new ones, imitate rather than innovate, acquire existing companies rather than develop a superior product or process technology and, perhaps most important, focus on short-run returns on investment rather than long-term growth and research and development strategy. Too many managers are setting and meeting short-term, market-driven objectives instead of adopting the appropriate time-horizon needed to plan and execute the successful product innovations needed to sustain worldwide competitiveness.

Reprinted by permission of the publisher, from Organizational Dynamics, *Spring 1981.* © *1981 by American Management Association, New York. All rights reserved.*

The performance of the American manufacturing sector is often contrasted with progress achieved by other industrialized countries—particularly Japan. Japan's productivity growth in manufacturing has been nearly three times the U.S. rate over the past two decades—the average annual growth rate between 1960 and 1978 was 7.8 percent. In the last five years alone, the productivity index has increased by more than 40 percent and most economists forecast similar rates for the 1980s. Such impressive results deserve careful examination.

Students of the Japanese economy generally point out that Japanese investment outlays as a proportion of gross national product are nearly twice as large as those in the United States, and this factor is backed by a high personal savings ratio and the availability of relatively cheap investment funds. Also, a massive infusion of imported technology contributed significantly to the growth of productivity in Japan. Among noneconomic factors, the Japanese political environment seems to support business needs, especially those of advanced industries. In addition, the "unique" psychological and cultural characteristics of the Japanese people is frequently cited as the key reason for Japan's success.

It is indeed a well-known fact that absenteeism in most Japanese companies is low; turnover rates are about half the U.S. figures, and employee commitment to the company is generally high. But although cultural factors are important in any context, we doubt that any pecularities of Japanese people (if they exist) have much impact on their commitment or productivity. In fact, several recent research studies indicate that Japanese and American workers show little or no difference in the personality attributes related to performance. Rather, we join Robert Hayes and William Abernathy in believing that, in this context, productivity stems from the superior management systems of many Japanese firms. But the focus of our analysis is not on such areas as corporate marketing and production strategies. Instead, we will examine management practices in Japan as they affect one key company asset: human resources.

Our analysis is guided by our experience with subsidiaries of Japanese firms in the United States. Typically, these companies are staffed by a small group of Japanese managers with varying levels of autonomy relative to the company's parent. The rest of the employees are American. Although they operate in an alien culture, many of these subsidiaries are surprisingly successful. While it is often very difficult to measure the performance of newly established operations, it is no secret that production lines in several Japanese subsidiaries operate at the same productivity rate as those in Japan (for example, the Sony plant in San Diego).

This example—as well as others—serves to demonstrate that what works in Japan can often work in the United States. The techniques used by the management of Japanese subsidiaries to motivate their American workers seem to play an important part in the effort to increase productivity. Therefore, a careful examination of management practices in Japan is useful not only for a specialist interested in cross-cultural organization development, but also for the management practitioner who is losing to foreign competition even on his or her home ground. What is it that the Japanese do better?

Our discussion attempts to answer this question by presenting a model of the

Japanese management system that rests on a few elements that can be examined in different cultural settings. The model will be used to highlight the relationship between the management strategies and techniques observed in Japan and positive work outcomes, such as commitment and productivity. Our review is not intended to be exhaustive, but rather to suggest the feasibility of integrating findings from Japan with more general concepts and theories. We will therefore focus on relationships that may be verified by observations of behavior in non-Japanese, especially U.S., settings.

We propose that positive work outcomes emanate from a complex set of behavioral patterns that are not limited to any specific culture. The emphasis is on management practices as a system and on the integration of various strategies and techniques to achieve desired results. We hope thus to provide an alternative to statements—often cited but never empirically supported—that the high commitment and productivity of Japanese employees is primarily traceable to their cultural characteristics.

A Management System Focused on Human Resources

Most managers will probably agree that management's key concern is the optimal utilization of a firm's various assets. These assets may vary—financial, technological, human, and so on. Tradeoffs are necessary because utilization of any one asset may result in underutilization of another. We propose that in most Japanese companies, *human assets are considered to be the firm's most important and profitable assets in the long run.* Although the phrase itself sounds familiar, even hollow, to many American managers and OD consultants, it is important to recognize that this management orientation is backed up by a well-integrated system of strategies and techniques that translate this abstract concept into reality.

First, long-term and secure employment is provided, which attracts employees of the desired quality and induces them to remain with the firm. Second, a company philosophy is articulated that shows concern for employee needs and stresses cooperation and teamwork in a unique environment. Third, close attention is given both to hiring people who will fit well with the particular company's values and to integrating employees into the company at all stages of their working life. These general strategies are expressed in specific management techniques. Emphasis is placed on continuous development of employee skills; formal promotion is of secondary importance, at least during the early career stages. Employees are evaluated on a multitude of criteria—often including group performance results—rather than on individual bottom-line contribution. The work is structured in such a way that it may be carried out by groups operating with a great deal of autonomy. Open communication is encouraged, supported, and rewarded. Information about pending decisions is circulated to all concerned before the decisions are actually made. Active observable concern for each and every employee is expressed by supervisory personnel (Figure 1).

Each of these management practices, either alone or in combination with the others, is known to have a positive influence on commitment to the organization and its effectiveness.

We will discuss these practices as we have observed them in large and medium-size firms in Japan and in several of their subsidiaries in the United States. Although similar practices are often also in evidence in small Japanese companies, the long-term employment policies in these firms are more vulnerable to drops in economic activity and the system's impact is necessarily limited.

Strategies

Once management adopts the view that utilizing human assets is what matters most in the organization's success, several strategies have to be pursued to secure these assets in the desired quality and quantity. These strategies involve the following:

Provide Secure Employment   Although Japanese companies typically provide stable and long-term employment, many smaller firms find it difficult to do so in times of recession. The policy calls for hiring relatively unskilled

FIGURE 1   JAPANESE MANAGEMENT PARADIGM.

employees (often directly from high schools or universities), training them on the job, promoting from within, and recognizing seniority.

The implicit guarantee of the employee's job, under all but the most severe economic circumstances, is a marked departure from conventional managerial thinking about the need to retain flexibility in workforce size in order to respond efficiently to cyclical variations in demand. However, this employment system, at least as practiced in large corporations in Japan, is far from being inflexible. Several techniques can be applied to ride out recession with a minimum burden of labor cost while keeping a maximum number of regular workers on their jobs—a freeze on new hiring, solicitation of voluntary retirement sweetened by extra benefits, use of core employees to replace temporaries and subcontractors doing nonessential work, and so forth. Thus a labor force cut of approximately 10–15 percent in a short time period is not an unusual phenomenon. In addition, across-the-board salary and bonus cuts for all employees, including management, would follow if necessary.

Japanese managers believe that job security has a positive impact on morale and productivity, limits turnover and training costs, and increases the organization's cohesiveness. For that reason, they are willing to accept its temporary negative effect in a period of reduced demand. Long-term employment security is also characteristic of all the U.S. subsidiaries that we have visited. Layoffs and terminations occur extremely rarely. For example, the Kikkoman Company instituted across-the-board wage cuts in an attempt to preserve employment during the last recession. Murata instituted a four-day workweek, and at Matsushita's Quasar plant, a number of employees were shifted from their regular work to functions such as repairs, maintenance, and service. It should be noted that there are several well-known U.S. corporations—for example, IBM and Hewlett-Packard—that follow similar practices when the alternative would be layoff.

In Japanese companies, even poor performers are either retrained or transferred, instead of simply being dismissed. The plant manager in an electronics component factory explained how the company copes with personal failures: "We give a chance to improve even if there has been a big mistake. For example, the quality control manager didn't fit, so we transferred him to sales engineering and now he is doing fine."

Research on behavior in organizations suggests that the assumptions of Japanese managers and some of their U.S. colleagues about the positive impact of job security are, at least to some degree, justified. It has been shown that long tenure is positively associated with commitment to the organization, which in turn reduces turnover. High commitment in conjunction with a binding choice (employees of large firms in Japan have difficulty finding jobs of the same quality elsewhere, given the relatively stable labor market) also leads to high satisfaction, but whether this contributes to high productivity still remains to be proved. It is, however, necessary to view the policy of secure employment as a key condition for the implementation of other management strategies and techniques that have a more immediate impact on the organization's effectiveness.

Articulate a Unique Company Philosophy   A philosophy that is both articulated and carried through presents a clear picture of the organization's objectives, norms, and values—and thus helps transform commitment into productive
effort. Familiarity with organizational goals gives direction to employees'
actions, sets constraints on their behavior, and enhances their motivation. The
understanding of shared meanings and beliefs expressed in the company philosophy binds the individual to the organization and, at the same time, stimulates the emergence of goals shared with others, as well as the stories, myths,
and symbols that form the fabric of a company philosophy. William Ouchi and
Raymond Price suggest that an organizational philosophy is an elegant infor-
mational device that provides a form of control at once pervasive and effective;
at the same time it provides guidance for managers by presenting a basic theory
of how the firm should be managed.

An explicit management philosophy of how work should be done can be
found in many successful corporations in both Japan and the United States;
examples in the United States include IBM, Texas Instruments, and U.S.
Homes. Nevertheless, it is fair to say that the typical Japanese firm's management philosophy has a distinct flavor. It usually puts a heavy emphasis on cooperation and teamwork within a corporate "family" that is unique and distinct
from that of any other firm. In return for an employee's effort, the family's
commitment to the employee is translated into company determination to avoid
layoffs and to provide a whole range of supplementary welfare benefits for the
employee and his or her family. Naturally, without reasonable employment
security, the fostering of team spirit and cooperation would be impossible. The
ideal is thus to reconcile two objectives: pursuit of profits and perpetuation of
the company as a group.

In a number of cases, a particular management philosophy that originated
within the parent company in Japan is also being actively disseminated in its
U.S. subsidiaries. Typically, claims of uniqueness range from the extent of the
company's concern for employees' worklives to the quality of service to the customer. We quote from the in-house literature issued by one of the fastest growing Japanese-owned electronics component makers in California:

> *Management Philosophy*
> Our goal is to strive toward both the material and the spiritual fulfillment of all
> employees in the Company, and through this successful fulfillment, serve man-
> kind in its progress and prosperity.

> *Management Policy*
> [. . .] Our purpose is to fully satisfy the needs of our customers and in return gain
> a just profit for ourselves. We are a family united in common bonds and singular
> goals. One of these bonds is the respect and support we feel for our fellow family
> co-workers.

Integrate Employees into the Company   The benefits of an articulated company philosophy are lost, however, if it's not visibly supported by management's
behavior. A primary function of the company's socialization effort, therefore, is

to ensure that employees have understood the philosophy and seen it in action. Close attention is given to hiring people who are willing to endorse the values of the particular company and to the employees' integration into the organization at all stages of their working life. The development of cohesiveness within the firm, based on the acceptance of goals and values, is a major focus of personnel policies in many Japanese firms.

Because employees are expected to remain in the company for a major part of their careers, careful selection is necessary to ensure that they fit well into the company climate. In many U.S.-based Japanese firms also, new hires at all levels are carefully screened with this aspect in mind. As in Japan, basic criteria for hiring are moderate views and a harmonious personality, and for that reason a large proportion of new hires come from employee referrals. In general, "virgin" workforces are preferred, since they can readily be assimilated into each company's unique environment as a community.

The intensive socialization process starts with the hiring decision and the initial training program and continues in various forms thereafter. Over time, the employee internalizes the various values and objectives of the firm, becomes increasingly committed to them, and learns the formal and informal rules and procedures, particularly through job rotation. That process usually includes two related types of job transfers. First, employees are transferred to new positions to learn additional skills in on-the-job training programs. These job changes are planned well in advance for all regular employees, including blue-collar workers. Second, transfers are part of a long-range experience-building program through which the organization develops its future managers; such programs involve movement across departmental boundaries at any stage of an employee's career.

While employees rotate semilaterally from job to job, they become increasingly socialized into the organization, immersed in the company philosophy and culture, and bound to a set of shared goals. Even in the absence of specific internal regulations that might be too constraining in a rapidly changing environment, a well-socialized manager who has held positions in various functions and locations within the firm has a feel for the organization's needs.

Techniques

The basic management orientation and strategies that we have just discussed are closely interrelated with specific management techniques used in Japanese firms and in their subsidiaries in the United States. The whole system is composed of a set of interdependent employment practices in which the presence of one technique complements as well as influences the effectiveness of others. This interdependence, rather than a simple cause-effect relationship, is the key factor that helps maintain the organization's stability and effectiveness. Additional environmental variables may determine which of the strategies or techniques will require most attention from top management, but in their impact on the organization no single technique listed below is of prime importance.

Slow Promotion, Job Rotation, and Internal Training   All Japanese subsidiaries that we have visited have seniority-based promotion systems. At one of them, a medium-size motorcycle plant, a seniority-based promotion system has been reinstituted after an experiment with a merit-based system proved highly unpopular with employees. Training is conducted, as expected, mostly on the job, and as one textile company executive noted, career paths are flexible: "You can get involved in what you want to do." Hiring from outside into upper-level positions is rare. According to another Japanese plant manager: "We want someone who understands the management system of the company. We want to keep the employees with us; we want to keep them happy."

Although promotion is slow, early informal identification of the elite is not unusual and carefully planned lateral job transfers add substantial flexibility to job assignments. Not all jobs are equally central to the workflow in an organization, so employees—even those with the same status and salary—can be rewarded or punished by providing or withholding positions in which they could acquire the skills needed for future promotions.

Job-rotation in U.S.-based Japanese firms seems less planned or structured than in Japan and more an ad-hoc reaction to oganizational needs—but in general, the emphasis on slow promotion and job rotation creates an environment in which an employee becomes a generalist rather than a specialist in a particular functional area. For the most part, however, these general skills are unique to the organization. Several of the Japanese manufacturers that invested in the United States were forced to simplify their product technology because they were not able to recruit qualified operators versatile enough to meet their needs, and there was not enough time to train them internally.

In Japan, well-planned job rotation is the key to the success of an in-company training program that generally encompasses all the firm's employees. For some categories of highly skilled blue-collar workers training plans for a period of up to ten years are not unusual. Off-the-job training is often included, again for managers and nonmanagers alike. However, whether such an extensive training system will be transferred to U.S. subsidiaries remains to be seen.

In addition to its impact on promotion and training, job rotation also promotes the development of informal communication networks that help in coordinating work activities across functional areas and in resolving problems speedily. This aspect of job rotation is especially important for managerial personnel. Finally, timely job rotation relieves an employee who has become unresponsive to, or bored with, the demands of his or her job.

Some observers argue that deferred promotion may frustrate highly promising, ambitious employees. However, the personnel director of a major trading company has commented: "The secret of Japanese management, if there is any, is to make everybody feel as long as possible that he is slated for the top position in the firm—thereby increasing his motivation during the most productive period of his employment." The public identification of "losers," who of course far outnumber "winners" in any hierarchical organization, is postponed in the belief that the increased output of the losers, who are striving hard to do well and still hoping to beat the odds, more than compensates for any lags in the motivation of the impatient winners. By contrast, top management in many American organizations is preoccupied with identifying rising stars as soon as possible and is less concerned about the impact on the losers' morale.

Complex Appraisal System   In addition to emphasizing the long-term perspective, Japanese companies often establish a complex appraisal system that includes not only individual performance measures tied to the bottom line, but also measures of various desirable personality traits and behaviors—such as creativity, emotional maturity, and cooperation with others as well as team performance results. In most such companies, potential, personality, and behavior, rather than current output, are the key criteria, yet the difference is often merely symbolic. Output measures may easily be "translated" into such attributes as leadership skills, technical competence, relations with others, and judgment. This approach avoids making the employee feel that the bottom line, which may be beyond his or her control, in part or in whole, is the key dimension of evaluation. Occasional mistakes, particularly those made by lower-level employees, are considered part of the learning process.

At the same time, evaluations do clearly discriminate among employees because each employee is compared with other members of an appropriate group (in age and status) and ranked accordingly. The ranking within the cohort is generally not disclosed to the employees, but of course it can be partially inferred from small salary differentials and a comparison of job assignments. At least in theory, the slow promotion system should allow for careful judgments to be made even on such subjective criteria as the personality traits of honesty and seriousness. However, the authors' observations suggest that ranking within the cohort is usually established rather early in one's career and is generally not very flexible thereafter.

Employees are not formally separated according to their ability until later in their tenure; ambitious workers who seek immediate recognition must engage in activities that will get them noticed. Bottom-line performance is not an adequate criterion because, as noted, it is not the only focus of managerial evaluation. This situation encourages easily observable behavior, such as voluntary overtime, that appears to demonstrate willingness to exert substantial effort on the organization's behalf. The evaluation process becomes to a large degree self-selective.

Several other facets of this kind of appraisal system deserve our attention. Because evaluations are based on managerial observations during frequent, regular interactions with subordinates, the cost of such an evaluation system is relatively low. When behavior rather than bottom-line performance is the focus of evaluation, means as well as ends may be assessed. This very likely leads to a better match between the direction of employee efforts and company objectives, and it encourages a long-term perspective. Finally, since group performance is also a focus of evaluation, peer pressure on an employee to contribute his or her share to the group's performance becomes an important mechanism of performance control. Long tenure, friendship ties, and informal communication networks enable both superiors and peers to get a very clear sense of the employee's performance and potential relative to others.

Among the management techniques characteristic of large Japanese enterprises, the introduction of a complex appraisal system is probably the least visible in their U.S. subsidiaries. Most of their U.S.-based affiliates are relatively young; thus long-term evaluation of employees, the key point in personnel appraisal as practiced in Japan, is not yet practicable. Furthermore, the different expectations of American workers and managers about what constitutes a fair and equitable appraisal system might hinder acceptance of the parent company's evaluation system.

Emphasis on Work Groups   Acknowledging the enormous impact of groups on their members—both directly, through the enforcement of norms, and indirectly, by affecting the beliefs and values of members—Japanese organizations devote far greater attention to structural factors that enhance group motivation and cooperation than to the motivation of individual employees. Tasks are assigned to groups, not to individual employees, and group cohesion is stimulated by delegating responsibility to the group not only for getting the tasks performed but also for designing the way in which they get performed. The group-based performance evaluation has already been discussed.

Similarly, in the U.S.-based Japanese firms that we have visited, the group rather than an individual forms the basic work unit for all practical purposes. Quality of work and speed of job execution are key concerns in group production meetings that are held at least monthly, and even daily in some companies. The design function, however, is not yet very well developed; many workers are still relative newcomers unfamiliar with all aspects of the advanced technology. Intergroup rivalry is also encouraged. In one capacitor company, a group on a shift that performs well consistently is rewarded regularly. Sometimes news of a highly productive group from another shift or even from the Japanese parent is passed around the shop floor to stimulate the competition.

In Japan, group autonomy is encouraged by avoiding any reliance on experts to solve operational problems. One widely used group-based technique for dealing with such problems is quality control (QC) circles. A QC circle's major task is to pinpoint and solve a particular workshop's problem. Outside experts are called in only to educate group members in the analytical tools for problem solving or to provide a specialized technical service. Otherwise, the team working on the problem operates autonomously, with additional emphasis on self-improvement activities that will help achieve group goals. Fostering motivation through direct employee participation in the work process design is a major consideration in the introduction of QC circles and similar activities to the factory floor.

Nevertheless, work-group autonomy in most work settings is bound by clearly defined limits, with the company carefully coordinating team activities by controlling the training and evaluation of members, the size of the team, and the scope and amount of production. Yet within these limits, teamwork is not only part of a company's articulated philosophy, it actually forms the basic fabric of the work process. Job rotation is encouraged both to develop each employee's skills and to fit the work group's needs.

From another perspective, the group can also assist in developing job-relevant knowledge by direct instruction and by serving as a model of appropriate behavior. The results of empirical studies suggest that structuring tasks around work groups not only may improve performance, but also may contribute to increased esteem and a sense of identity among group members. Furthermore, this process of translating organizational membership into membership in a small group seems, in general, to result in higher job satisfaction, lower absenteeism, lower turnover rates, and fewer labor disputes.

Open and Extensive Communication   Even in the Japanese-owned U.S. companies, plant managers typically spend at least two hours a day on the shop floor and are readily available for the rest of the day. Often, foremen are deliberately deprived of offices so they can be with their subordinates on the floor throughout the whole day, instructing and helping whenever necessary. The same policy applies to personnel specialists. The American personnel manager of a Japanese motorcycle plant, for example, spends between two and four hours a day on the shop floor discussing issues that concern employees. The large number of employees he is able to greet by their first name testifies to the amount of time he spends on the floor. "We have an open-door policy—but it's their door, not management's" was his explanation of the company's emphasis on the quality of face-to-face vertical communication.

Open communication is also inherent in the Japanese work setting. Open work spaces are crowded with individuals at different hierarchical levels. Even high-ranking office managers seldom have separate private offices. Partitions, cubicles, and small side rooms are used to set off special areas for conferences with visitors or small discussions among the staff. In one Japanese-owned TV plant on the West Coast, the top manager's office is next to the receptionist— open and visible to everybody who walks into the building, whether employee, supplier, or customer.

Open communication is not limited to vertical exchanges. Both the emphasis on team spirit in work groups and the network of friendships that employees develop during their long tenure in the organization encourage the extensive face-to-face communication so often reported in studies involving Japanese companies. Moreover, job rotation is instrumental in building informal lateral networks across departmental boundaries. Without these networks, the transfer of much job-related information would be impossible. These informal networks are not included in written work manuals, thus they are invisible to a newcomer; but their use as a legitimate tool to get things done is implicitly authorized by the formal control system. Communication skills and related behavior are often the focus of yearly evaluations. Frequently, foreign observers put too much emphasis on vertical ties and other hierarchical aspects of Japanese organizations. In fact, the ability to manage lateral communication is perhaps even more important to effective performance, particularly at the middle-management level.

Consultative Decision Making   Few Japanese management practices are so misunderstood by outsiders as is the decision-making process. The image is quite entrenched in Western literature on Japanese organizations: Scores of managers huddle together in endless discussion until consensus on every detail is reached, after which a symbolic document, "ringi," is passed around so they can affix their seals of approval on it. This image negates the considerable degree of decentralization for most types of decisions that is characteristic in most subsidiaries we have visited. In fact, when time is short, decisions are routinely made by the manager in charge.

Under the usual procedure for top-management decision making, a proposal is initiated by a middle manager (but often under the directive of top management). This middle manager engages in informal discussion and consultation with peers and supervisors. When all are familiar with the proposal, a formal request for a decision is made and, because of earlier discussions, is almost inevitably ratified—often in a ceremonial group meeting or through the "ringi" procedure. This implies not unanimous approval, but the unanimous consent to its implementation.

This kind of decision making is not participative in the Western sense of the word, which encompasses negotiation and bargaining between a manager and subordinates. In the Japanese context, negotiations are primarily lateral between the departments concerned with the decision. Within the work group, the emphasis is on including all group members in the process of decision making, not on achieving consensus on the alternatives. Opposing parties are willing to go along, with the consolation that their viewpoint may carry the day the next time around.

However, the manager will usually not implement his or her decision "until others who will be affected have had sufficient time to offer their views, feel that they have been fairly heard, and are willing to support the decision even though they may not feel that it is the best one," according to Thomas P. Rohlen. Those outside the core of the decision-making group merely express their acknowledgement of the proposed course of action. They do not participate; they do not feel ownership of the decision. On the other hand, the early communication of the proposed changes helps reduce uncertainty in the organization. In addition, prior information on upcoming decisions gives employees an opportunity to rationalize and accept the outcomes.

Japanese managers we have interviewed often expressed the opinion that it is their American partners who insist on examining every aspect and contingency of proposed alternatives, while they themselves prefer a relatively general agreement on the direction to follow, leaving the details to be solved on the run. Accordingly, the refinement of a proposal occurs during its early implementation stage.

Although the level of face-to-face communication in Japanese organizations is relatively high, it should not be confused with participation in decision making. Most communication concerns routine tasks; thus it is not surprising that research on Japanese companies indicates no relationship between the extent of face-to-face communication and employees' perceptions of how much they participate in decision making.

Moreover, consultation with lower-ranking employees does not automatically imply that the decision process is "bottom up," as suggested by Peter Drucker and others. Especially in the case of long-term planning and strategy, the initiative comes mostly from the top. Furthermore, consultative decision making does not diminish top management's responsibility for a decision's consequences. Although the ambiguities of status and centrality may make it difficult for outsiders to pinpoint responsibility, it is actually quite clear within the organization. Heads still roll to pay for mistakes, albeit in a somewhat more subtle manner than is customary in Western organizations: Departure to the second- or third-ranking subsidiary is the most common punishment.

Concern for the Employee   It is established practice for managers to spend a lot of time talking to employees about everyday matters. Thus they develop a feeling for employees' personal needs and problems, as well as for their performance. Obviously, gaining this intimate knowledge of each employee is easier when an employee has long tenure, but managers do consciously attempt to get to know their employees, and they place a premium on providing time to talk. The quality of relationships developed with subordinates is also an important factor on which a manager is evaluated.

Various company-sponsored cultural, athletic, and other recreational activities further deepen involvement in employees' lives. This heavy schedule of company social affairs is ostensibly voluntary, but virtually all employees participate. Typically, an annual calendar of office events might include two overnight trips, monthly Saturday afternoon recreation, and an average of six office parties—all at company expense. A great deal of drinking goes on at these events and much good fellowship is expressed among the employees.

Finally, in Japan the company allocates substantial financial resources to pay for benefits for all employees, such as a family allowance and various commuting and housing allowances. In addition, many firms provide a whole range of welfare services ranging from subsidized company housing for families and dormitories for unmarried employees, through company nurseries and company scholarships for employees' children, to mortgage loans, credit facilities, savings plans, and insurance. Thus employees often perceive a close relationship between their own welfare and the company's financial welfare. Accordingly, behavior for the company's benefit that may appear self-sacrificing is not at all so; rather, it is in the employee's own interest.

Managers in the U.S.-based companies generally also voiced a desire to make life in the company a pleasant experience for their subordinates. As in Japan, managers at all levels show concern for employees by sponsoring various recreational activities or even taking them out to dinner to talk problems over.

Again, continuous open communication gets special emphasis. However, company benefits are not as extensive as in Japan because of a feeling that American employees prefer rewards in the form of salary rather than the "golden handcuff" of benefits. Furthermore, the comprehensive government welfare system in the United States apparently renders such extensive company benefits superfluous.

In summary, what we observed in many Japanese companies is an integrated system of management strategies and techniques that reinforce one another because of systemic management orientation to the quality of human resources. In addition to this system's behavioral consequences, which we have already discussed, a number of other positive outcomes have also been reported in research studies on Japanese organizations.

For example, when the company offers desirable employment conditions designed to provide job security and reduce voluntary turnover, the company benefits not only from the increased loyalty of the workforce, but also from a reduction in hiring, training, and other costs associated with turnover and replacement. Because employees enjoy job security, they do not fear technical innovation and may, in fact, welcome it—especially if it relieves them of tedious or exhausting manual tasks. In such an atmosphere, concern for long-term growth, rather than a focus on immediate profits, is also expected to flourish.

An articulated philosophy that expresses the company's family atmosphere as well as its uniqueness enables the employee to justify loyalty to the company and stimulates healthy competition with other companies. The management goals symbolized in company philosophy can give clear guidance to the employee who's trying to make the best decision in a situation that is uncertain.

Careful attention to selection and the employee's fit into the company results in a homogeneous workforce, easily able to develop the friendship ties that form the basis of information networks. The lack of conflict among functional divisions and the ability to communicate informally across divisions allow for rapid interdivisional coordination and the rapid implementation of various company goals and policies.

The other techniques we've outlined reinforce these positive outcomes. Slow promotion reinforces a long-range perspective. High earnings in this quarter need not earn an employee an immediate promotion. Less reliance on the bottom line means that an employee's capabilities and behaviors over the long term become more important in their evaluations. Groups are another vehicle by which the company's goals, norms, and values are communicated to each employee. Open communication is the most visible vehicle for demonstrating concern for employees and willingness to benefit from their experience, regardless of rank. Open communication is thus a key technique that supports consultative decision making and affects the quality of any implementation process. Finally, caring about employees' social needs encourages identification with the firm and limits the impact of personal troubles on performance.

What we have described is a system based on the understanding that in return for the employee's contribution to company growth and well-being, the profitable firm will provide a stable and secure work environment and protect the individual employee's welfare even during a period of economic slowdown.

The Transferability of Japanese Management Practices

As in Japan, a key managerial concern in all U.S.-based Japanese companies we have investigated was the quality of human resources. As one executive put it, "We adapt the organization to the people because you can't adapt people to the organization." A number of specific instances of how Japanese management techniques are being applied in the United States were previously cited. Most personnel policies we've observed were similar to those in Japan, although evaluation systems and job-rotation planning are still somewhat different, probably because of the youth of the subsidiary companies. Less institutionalized concern for employee welfare was also pointed out.

The experience of many Japanese firms that have established U.S. subsidiaries suggests that the U.S. workers are receptive to many management practices introduced by Japanese managers. During our interviews, many Japanese executives pointed out that the productivity level in their U.S. plants is on a level similar to that in Japan—and occasionally even higher. Other research data indicate that American workers in Japanese-owned plants are even more satisfied with their work conditions than are their Japanese or Japanese-American colleagues.

The relative success of U.S.-based Japanese companies in transferring their employment and management practices to cover the great majority of their U.S. workers is not surprising when we consider that a number of large U.S. corporations have created management systems that use some typical Japanese techniques. Several of these firms have an outstanding record of innovation and rapid growth. A few examples are Procter & Gamble, Hewlett-Packard, and Cummins Engine.

William Ouchi and his colleagues call these firms Theory Z organizations. Seven key characteristics of Theory Z organizations are the following:

1. Long-term employment.

2. Slow evaluation and promotion.

3. Moderately specialized careers.

4. Consensual decision making.

5. Individual responsibility.

6. Implicit, informal control (but with explicit measures).

7. Wholistic concern for the employee.

The Theory Z organization shares several features with the Japanese organization, but there are differences: In the former, responsibility is definitely individual, measures of performance are explicit, and careers are actually moderately specialized. However, Ouchi tells us little about communication patterns in these organizations, the role of the work group, and some other features important in Japanese settings.

Here's an example of a standard practice in the Theory Z organization that Ouchi studied in depth:

> [The Theory Z organization] calculated the profitability of each of its divisions, but it did not operate a strict profit center or other marketlike mechanism. Rather, decisions were frequently made by division managers who were guided by broader corporate concerns, even though their own divisional earnings may have suffered as a result.

A survey by Ouchi and Jerry Johnson showed that within the electronics industry perceived corporate prestige, managerial ability, and reported corporate earnings were all strongly positively correlated with the "Z-ness" of the organization.

It is also significant that examples of successful implementation of the Japanese system can be found even in Britain, a country notorious for labor-management conflict. In our interpretation, good labor-management relations—even the emergence of a so-called company union—is an effect, rather than a cause, of the mutually beneficial, reciprocal relationship enjoyed by the employees and the firm. Thus we see the coexistence of our management paradigm with productivity in companies in Japan, in Japanese companies in the United States and Europe, and in a number of indigenous U.S. companies. Although correlation does not imply cause, such a causal connection would be well supported by psychological theories. Douglas McGregor summarizes a great deal of research in saying: "Effective performance results when conditions are created such that the members of the organization can achieve their own goals best by directing their efforts toward the success of the enterprise."

Conclusion

Many cultural differences exist, of course, between people in Japan and those in Western countries. However, this should not distract our attention from the fact that human beings in all countries also have a great deal in common. In the workplace, all people value decent treatment, security, and an opportunity for emotional fulfillment. It is to the credit of Japanese managers that they have developed organizational systems that, even though far from perfect, do respond to these needs to a great extent. Also to their credit is the fact that high motivation and productivity result at the same time.

The strategies and techniques we have reviewed constitute a remarkably well-integrated system. The management practices are highly congruent with the way in which tasks are structured, with individual members' goals, and with the organization's climate. Such a fit is expected to result in a high degree of organizational effectiveness or productivity. We believe that the management paradigm of concern for human resources blends the hopes of humanistic thinkers with the pragmatism of those who need to show a return on investment. The evidence strongly suggests that this paradigm is both desirable and feasible in Western countries and that the key elements of Japanese management practices are not unique to Japan and can be successfully transplanted to other cultures. The linkage between human needs and productivity is nothing new in Western management theory. It required the Japanese, however, to translate the idea into a successful reality.

Acknowledgments

The authors would like to thank Mitsuyo Hanada, Blair McDonald, William Newman, William Ouchi, Thomas Roehl, Michael Tushman, and others for their helpful comments on earlier drafts of this paper. We are grateful to Citibank, New York, and the Japan Foundation, Tokyo, for their financial support of the work in the preparation of this paper.

Selected Bibliography

Robert Hayes and William Abernathy brought the lack of U.S. innovation to public attention in their article, "Managing Our Way to Economic Decline" (*Harvard Business Review,* July–August 1980).

Thomas P. Rohlen's book, *For Harmony and Strength: Japanese White-Collar Organization in Anthropological Perspective* (University of California Press, 1974), is a captivating description of the Japanese management system as seen in a regional bank. Peter Drucker has written several articles on the system, including "What We Can Learn from Japanese Management" (*Harvard Business Review,* March–April 1971). His thoughts are extended to the United States by the empirical work of Richard Pascale, "Employment Practices and Employee Attitudes: A Study of Japanese and American Managed Firms in the U.S." (*Human Relations,* July 1978).

For further information on the Theory Z organization see "Type Z Organization: Stability in the Midst of Mobility" by William Ouchi and Alfred Jaeger (*Academy of Management Review,* April 1978), "Types of Organizational Control and Their Relationship to Emotional Well-Being" by William Ouchi and Jerry Johnson (*Administrative Science Quarterly,* Spring 1978), and "Hierarchies, Clans, and Theory Z: A New Perspective on Organization Development" by William Ouchi and Raymond Price (*Organizational Dynamics,* Autumn 1978).

Douglas McGregor explains the importance of a fit between employee and organizational goals in *The Human Side of Enterprise* (McGraw-Hill, 1960).

Internal Influences

Leadership and Social Influence Processes

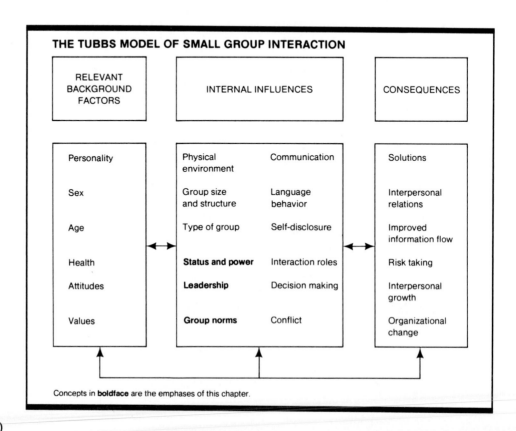

THE TUBBS MODEL OF SMALL GROUP INTERACTION

RELEVANT BACKGROUND FACTORS	INTERNAL INFLUENCES		CONSEQUENCES
Personality	Physical environment	Communication	Solutions
Sex	Group size and structure	Language behavior	Interpersonal relations
Age	Type of group	Self-disclosure	Improved information flow
Health	**Status and power**	Interaction roles	Risk taking
Attitudes	**Leadership**	Decision making	Interpersonal growth
Values	**Group norms**	Conflict	Organizational change

Concepts in **boldface** are the emphases of this chapter.

CASE STUDY

Mayhall House is an independent men's dormitory on the campus of a large midwestern university. The grade average of the dorm was one of the lowest of any house on campus. This was mainly because almost all of our 65 residents were majoring in either engineering or commerce—generally acknowledged as the most difficult schools in the university. And, of course, we had our share of "goof-offs"—five or six fellows who had ability but had never been able to apply themselves to their studies. We chalked them up as immature and hoped they would "see the light" before their academic probation ran out. But as long as they didn't disturb anyone we felt we would get along with them.

As a matter of fact, there was very little "horsing around" in the house. I had visited a number of the other dorms and was surprised to see college men, or rather "boys," running up and down the halls yelling and chasing one another and playing silly pranks on one another. As I said, I had always considered our house remarkably calm and dignified—until this year. Now, you wouldn't know it. Everyone's calling it "Mayhem House."

When we started school in September, two important events (at least to me) occurred. I was elected president of Mayhall House, and a new counselor moved in. His name was John Morrison, 23, a graduate student in theology. John seemed to be very pleasant but made it clear in his first meeting with the residents of the house that he had heard our grade average was low and hoped we could raise it. He gave quite a pep talk and said if we would all pull together, we might put Mayhall near the top of the list.

I agreed with this, but I didn't see how there could be much improvement, in view of the fact that most of us were in the toughest schools.

The first evidence that John meant what he said occurred when he established his "closed-door policy." The fellows had the custom of leaving the doors of their rooms open and occasionally talking across the corridor to one another. If John happened to be passing by, he would simply close the doors without saying a word. I suppose he thought the fellows would take the hint, but they only got sore about the situation and started doing more transcorridor communicating. It got to be quite a joke. John would start at one end of the corridor and close ten sets of doors as he walked to the other end. Two minutes after John was gone, all the doors would be open, and the talking would start in again—only louder and more of it. On one occasion, a student yelled, "Go to hell, John!" after John had closed his door. John opened the door again and put the student on formal warning.

Next was the radio episode. About the middle of November, John posted a notice: "In order to provide proper study conditions, no radios will be turned on after 7 p.m.; effective this date."

This seemed high-handed and unnecessary to me. Radios had never been a problem in the house before. A few students like to study with some soft music in the background. But if anyone objected, they would turn their radios off.

The fellows seemed to accept this as a challenge. The night the notice was posted, about seven or eight men turned on their radios to get them warmed up but not loud enough for anyone to hear.

Then one radio blared up full blast for a second and was quickly snapped off. John came bolting down the corridor to find the radio. When he got near the room, another radio blared up for a moment at the opposite end of the hall. John wheeled and streaked back. At this moment two other radios opened up, and John started twirling around in circles! It was the most ridiculous thing you ever saw, and the fellows couldn't help bursting out laughing.

John was furious. "All right, children! If you can't take proper care of your toys, someone will have to take care of them for you!"

He then started moving from one room to the next, confiscating the radios. It took him about two hours, but he picked up every radio in the house, put them in a storeroom, and locked the door. Maybe the seven or eight pranksters deserved this, but he took *all* the radios—mine included!

Well, that was the sign for open warfare. What happened then was one continuous nightmare. The next night, somebody brought some firecrackers into the house, and the mayhem started! Someone tied a firecracker to a burning cigarette and laid it in front of John's door. A few minutes later, the cigarette burned down and ignited the firecracker. John threw open his door, and not a soul was to be seen. He was fit to be tied. That was a night to be remembered. All night long, about every ten minutes, a firecracker went off somewhere—outside the dorm, in the corridor, in somebody's room, or outside John's door! John didn't even come out.

The next day it snowed, and that night it was snowballs. I won't go into the gory details, but the end result was the damage of various property, including five broken windows!

This, of course, brought in the Dean of Men. I was surprised that he didn't come in before. I guess John never mentioned our situation. . . . The rest is history. John has been transferred to another house, and we are on social probation for the rest of the semester.

1. What mistakes do you think John made as a leader in this case?

2. What, specifically, would you have done differently if you had been John?

3. What would you do if you were a new counselor coming in after John?

From William V. Haney, *Communication and Interpersonal Relations,* 5th ed. (Homewood, Ill.: Richard D. Irwin, Inc., 1986). Reprinted with permission.

I n this case study we see a problem that is not unique to college dormitories. The problem has to do with being able to develop effective leadership behaviors. Each of us from time to time will be called upon to act in the role of a group leader. For some, the role may seem comfortable; others will have to work hard to grow into it. In any case, leadership is a topic that seems to capture the interest of most students of small group interaction.

An indication of the times is revealed in the story that if a Martian spaceman were to land on Earth and demand, "Take me to your leader," we would not know where to take him. No subject in the small group literature has received more attention than leadership. As an achievement-oriented society, Americans are almost obsessed with the topic of leadership. We build and destroy heroes like so many clay pigeons. Charles Lindbergh was reportedly so worshipped that it was even newsworthy when one reporter caught him off guard, picking his nose. Compare this orientation to that of the Japanese, whose ancient proverbs include the saying, "A nail that protrudes is hammered down," and among whom the idea of standing out above one's peers is considered in poor taste. This chapter will examine the process of personal influence and its various ramifications. We begin with a discussion of power and status, then move to the ever-popular topic of leadership, and conclude with an analysis of the uses and abuses of social influence.

STATUS AND POWER

Most farmers who have raised poultry are familiar with the chickens' pecking at one another in an attempt to determine which animal dominates. The eventual result is that one chicken rises to the dominant position, a second chicken dominates all others but the top chicken, the third chicken dominates all but the top two, and so on down the line. This order of dominance is generally referred to as the *pecking order,* and when a new chicken is introduced to the barnyard, it must fight all the others to establish its position in the pecking order.

Pecking orders are also found in human interaction. Most often they are informal and adhered to almost unconsciously. They may also be formalized, as in an organization chart. An example of such a pecking order in the United States government is referred to as the "order of precedence"; it formally designates who precedes whom in the pecking order (or in order of importance as they might be officially introduced to a visiting dignitary or head of state). James Symington (1971, pp. 94–95) remarked that, as Chief of Protocol, "It was always a humbling reminder to read over this list" (since he was at the bottom).

Table of Precedence

The President of the United States
The Vice-President of the United States
The Speaker of the House of Representatives
The Chief Justice of the United States
Former Presidents of the United States
The Secretary of State
The Secretary-General of the United Nations
Ambassadors of Foreign Powers—individually ranked by order of date of presentation of credentials
Widows of former Presidents of the United States
United States Representative to the United Nations
Ministers of Foreign Powers (Chiefs of Diplomatic Missions)
Associate Justices of the Supreme Court of the United States and Retired Associate Justices
The Cabinet
    The Secretary of the Treasury

The Secretary of Defense
The Attorney General
The Postmaster General
The Secretary of the Interior
The Secretary of Agriculture
The Secretary of Commerce
The Secretary of Labor
The Secretary of Health, Education and Welfare
The Secretary of Housing and Urban Development
The Secretary of Transportation
The Senate
Governors of States (unless the function in question occurs in a Governor's own State, in which he ranks after the Vice President)
Former Vice-Presidents of the United States
The House of Representatives
Charges d'affaires of Foreign Powers
The Under Secretaries of the Executive Departments and the Deputy Secretaries
Administrator, Agency for International Development
Director, United States Arms Control and Disarmament Agency
Secretaries of the Army, the Navy, and the Air Force
Director, Office of Management and Budget
Chairman, Council of Economic Advisers
Chairman, Board of Governors, Federal Reserve
Chairman, Joint Chiefs of Staff
Chiefs of Staff of the Army, the Navy, and the Air Force (ranked according to date of appointment)
Commandant of the Marine Corps
(5-Star) Generals of the Army and Fleet Admirals
The Secretary-General, Organization of American States
Representatives to the Organization of American States
Director, Central Intelligence Agency
Administrator, General Services Administration
Director, United States Information Agency
Administrator, National Aeronautics and Space Administration
Administrator, Federal Aviation Administration
Chairman, Civil Service Commission
Chairman, the Atomic Energy Commission
Director, Defense Research and Engineering
Director, Office of Emergency Planning
Director, the Peace Corps
Director, Office of Economic Opportunity
Special Assistants to the President
Deputy Under Secretaries
Assistant Secretaries of the Executive Departments
United States Chief of Protocol

Types of Status

Status is defined as one's position or rank relative to the others in a group. High status tends to result in greater personal power or ability to influence others. Increased power, in turn, tends to elevate an individual's status level. Power and status tend to go hand in hand, reciprocally influencing one another.

Think of the many ongoing groups you have joined. They often have an established pecking order into which you must insert yourself. How does this pecking order come about in the first place? *Ascribed status* refers to the prestige that goes to a person by virtue of some characteristic such as his or her family wealth, good looks, or age. One man who attended an Ivy League school remarked that it was a bit awesome to be in classes with the children of *the* Rockfellers, *the* Firestones, *the* Kennedys. Those born into such families are likely to have high status even though as individuals they have done nothing to earn it.

But what about the many occasions in which a new group forms and there is no established pecking order? How does one get established? What are the effects once it has been set up? Those who rise to positions of status based on the merits of their own individual accomplishments acquire what is called *attained status*. The United States is known as one country in which the Horatio Alger story can still occur—where the person from humble origins can still rise from one socioeconomic class to a higher one more easily than in many other countries.

What kinds of behaviors enable a person to acquire a position of attained status? Goldhamer and Shils (1939) hypothesized that power and status is a function of the ratio of the number of successful power acts to the number of attempts to influence:

$$\frac{Number\ of\ successful\ power\ acts}{Number\ of\ attempts\ made} = power\ and\ status$$

One student stated: "The impact of this ratio dawned on me during our fraternity's officer elections. One brother tried many times, all unsuccessful, for a variety of positions. He is a good worker, so that was not his problem. His problem was that within the fraternity he did not have any status. The number of attempts made was many, but the number of successful acts was zero. His status fell further with each new failure."

Obviously the success rate and relative status of any individual will vary from group to group. Most of us find that we have a relatively higher status level in high school than we achieve when we attend college. This is usually because colleges and universities draw from a much larger population than most high schools and the competition gets tougher as the size of the population increases.

Types of Power

Although each of us has encountered situations in which people have power over one another, we may not have been very systematic in identifying the types of sources of that power. French and Raven (1959) identified five different types of power that can be brought to bear in groups. They classify them as (1) reward power, (2) coercive power, (3) legitimate power, (4) referent power, and (5) expert power.

Reward power refers to the ability an individual has to give or withhold rewards. A company executive obviously has this type of power, which can take the form of financial rewards through raises and promotions, as well as of social rewards such as recognition and compliments or praise. *Coercive power* is the opposite of reward power in that it utilizes punishment rather than reward. A supervisor can reprimand, discipline, and even fire an employee who does not live up to certain behavioral standards. An IBM employee was once sent home when he showed up for work without a tie. Most companies reserve the right to set what they believe to be appropriate standards for employees' dress. Coercive power is sometimes used to enforce these standards.

Legitimate power is defined as the influence we allow others to have over us based on the value we place on certain of their characteristics. For example, we feel that it is legitimate for a judge to determine a sentence in a court case, or for a supervisor to determine work schedules or assignments. A person who is elected to office is felt to have a legitimate right to exercise the power of that office. Of course, this right may be abused and the official may be removed from office.

Referent power is extremely potent, since it is based on the person's identification with the source of power. If you had a teacher you really admired, you would do many things (such as studying hard, or putting off social activities) to accomplish things that would bring approval or praise from that teacher. Ringwald et al. (1971, p. 47) studied different types of college students and found that one type (which they called cluster four students) was especially prone to identify with the professor and to be the "model student" in the eyes of the professor. These students were described as "self-confident, interested, involved; tend to identify with [the] teacher and see him as a colleague. Older than average [mostly upperclassmen]." Although Ringwald et al. studied only undergraduates, this description would also apply to a large segment of graduate students.

Expert power refers to our acceptance of influence from those whose expertise we respect. We accept the advice of lawyers in legal matters, of physicians in medical matters, or of others whom we perceive as having credibility on a given topic. In a group discussion concerning the dangers of heroin addiction, the speakers who had the most expert power of persuasion were the former addicts who told tragic stories of how heroin had destroyed parts of their lives.

Yates (1985) makes an interesting point about power when he writes:

> Thus, a fundamental shortcoming of organizational behaviorists . . . is that they tend to ignore or underemphasize the importance of power relationships and differing authority roles in the group process. If a decision making group is, in reality, a small representative body comprising a variety of broader interests and institutional claims and statuses, it will function as a group, as a microcosm of larger forces and conflicts, in the organization. To that extent, to treat individual relations in the group as the essential stuff of decision making risks missing the forest for the trees. (p. 123)

In other words, we not only need to be aware of the power relationships which exist within a group context, but also those which grow out of the group and which act as an entity in the larger organizational context.

Kotter (1985) offers some practical advice on how to build a power base for those starting out in their careers. He writes:

> [You could ask yourself,] over the past twelve months, how much have I really learned about the products or services, the markets, the technologies, and the people with whom I deal?
>
> In the past year, how many people have I gotten to know at work? How many people have I strengthened or improved my relationship with? Have I alienated anyone?
>
> Is my reputation as good or better than it was a year ago? If not, why not? (p. 129)

As we think in terms of status and power, we might want to keep in mind that the different types of power usually overlap. A person may be in a position to use reward power as well as coercive power, but may prefer to rely on referent power, legitimate power, or expert power. In any event, there are different types of power that can be used (and abused).

Assuming that different group members have different levels of status and power, what effect does this fact have on the interaction in the group? Cartwright and Zander (1968, p. 415) state that if you were to observe a company board meeting, you would be able to differentiate between a lower status person (the junior executive) and the vice-president by the following differences in their behavior:

> The man whom you believe to be the junior executive addresses the majority of his remarks to the man you believe to be the vice-president. Moreover, he chooses his words with care in order that he not seem to imply any criticism of the other man or appear inadequate. He listens carefully to what the vice-president has to say and is usually ready to see the reasonableness of the arguments made by him. He is friendly toward the boss, ready to tell a joke or talk about his family, and to copy some of the older man's mannerisms.
>
> In contrast, the vice-president talks pretty much to the entire group. He freely offers information, advice, and even criticism to others. He seldom makes critical remarks about himself. Nor is he nearly so ready as the younger man to listen to statements made by the rest of the group. He is more likely to defend his own position than to see the value in the points made by the staff. And on the whole he is less inclined to idle talk than is the junior executive.
>
> You may come away from the meeting feeling that the two men acted the way they did because they had quite different personalities, and you would undoubtedly be correct—in part. If, however, you were to see the junior executive in a meeting with *his* staff in which he is now the boss, you would probably be surprised to see how differently he behaves. Now it is likely that you would find the young man acting toward others in a way very similar to that shown by the vice-president in the earlier meeting.

The scene described above is one example of the *results* of differences in status or power. We also know that information directed toward high-status persons tends to be "whitewashed" in that it is more often positive than negative. One company plant manager told a friend of mine that he appreciated having a consultant who was independent enough of his operation to give him the honest truth. My friend told the manager that if he worked in that company he wouldn't tell the manager the truth either. The manager demanded so much success from his subordinates that they were afraid to tell him of the failures (he acted as if he did not want to hear about them). This was a little like the old custom of killing the messenger when he delivered bad news to a king; pretty soon all the king ever got was good news.

Another application of power in groups is the use of the group itself by a higher authority to develop support for decisions. Pfeffer (1981, pp. 175–176) writes:

> Given that committees are established to legitimate decisions and provide outlets for the expression of various interest, the important aspect of committees in organizational politics is not their function as much as their very existence. It is the process of cooptation, the process of interest representation, and the process of meeting and conferring which is critical in providing acceptance and legitimacy of decisions. These processual aspects may be as important as the substance of the decisions actually reached.

Thus the very process of involving groups in making decisions may increase the boss's power to have those decisions implemented.

It has also been found that comments in small groups tend to be directed more often (by direction of eye contact) to higher-status group members than to those of lower status. If you want quickly to determine the high-status members of any group, just notice to whom people direct their comments. Thibaut and Kelley (1986) found this phenomenon in an experimental study and hypothesized that this type of upward communication acts as a substitute for a member's own upward mobility in the group's pecking order. Thus if we can't be football stars or sorority presidents, we can at least try to become friends with them.

Finally, high status results in a group's being willing to tolerate deviation on the part of a group member. Highly successful people are notoriously idiosyncratic. It has been suggested that a person who is idiosyncratic but not successful is simply considered weird. Albert Einstein and Thomas Edison both were considered eccentric, yet their eccentricities were tolerated because of the magnitude of their contributions. Most groups will tolerate deviations from those who are highly valued in the group. One rule of thumb is that new members are not allowed to deviate nearly as much as those who are oldtimers. This is true among college faculty members, in companies, in government agencies, and even in prisons. We discuss deviation and conformity pressure further later in this chapter.

LEADERSHIP

Definitions of leadership are numerous, but we like that of Tannenbaum, Wechsler, and Massarik (1961), who define leadership as:

> Interpersonal influence, exercised in [a certain] situation and directed, through a communication process, toward the attainment of a specified goal or goals. Leadership always involves attempts on the part of a leader (influencer) to affect (influence) the behavior of a follower (influencee) or followers in [a certain] situation.

This straightforward definition includes three of the most important factors of leadership: (1) successful or real influence (as opposed to the attempt to influence exemplified by the military leader who charged up the hill with no soldiers willing to follow), (2) the recognition that the situation involved may make a big difference, and (3) acknowledgment that the influence occurs through both verbal and nonverbal communication (see Chapter 5). With these three factors in mind, let us examine what people have historically thought about leadership.

Historic Trends

During the eighteenth and nineteenth centuries, philosophers argued the relative merits of two viewpoints regarding leadership. These were the trait or "great man" theory and the circumstances theory. Although we have come a long way in our study of leadership, it is still interesting to go back and examine the evolution of the different approaches.

Trait Theory

Trait theory grew out of the idea that leaders are born, not made. Examples from history could include Alexander the Great, Madam Chiang Kai-shek, John F. Kennedy, and Ronald Reagan. The assumption was that certain physical traits or personality traits enable a person to be a leader.

The physical traits associated with leadership were height, weight, and physical attractiveness and body shape. In our culture, taller people are sometimes associated with higher status and vice versa. In one study (Wilson 1968) a speaker named Mr. England was introduced to each of five different college classes by a different title:

- Class 1—a student from Cambridge

- Class 2—a demonstrator in psychology from Cambridge

- Class 3—a lecturer in psychology from Cambridge

- Class 4—Dr. England, senior lecturer from Cambridge

- Class 5—Professor England from Cambridge

When students were asked to estimate the speaker's height, the average estimate increased from class 1 to class 5. In other words, the more prestigious England's title, the taller the students thought he was. A study at the University of Pennsylvania showed that height in inches correlated more closely with a graduate's starting salary after graduation than any other index (such as grade-point average, number of extracurricular activities, parents' education level). Although correlation does not prove causality, it is still interesting to see the anecdotal evidence supporting the belief that height is viewed positively. As one student aptly put it, "I would define a leader as someone I can look up to, both figuratively and literally."

What relationship might there be between weight and leadership? The heavier the better? No, actually the predicted relationship is curvilinear (see Figure 4.1). Thus

FIGURE 4.1   HYPOTHETICAL RELATIONSHIP BETWEEN WEIGHT AND LEADERSHIP.

© 1971 Henry R. Martin. Reprinted with permission of Meredith Corporation and Henry Martin.

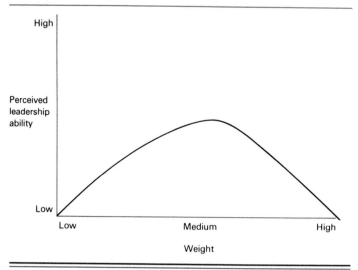

people who are too thin or too heavy would be considered either too weak and fragile or too self-indulgent and undisciplined to be good leaders. In one unpublished study conducted in a large company, employees were divided into groups, one whose members weighed within 10 percent of their "desirable" weight (based on a doctor's chart of height and weight), and one whose members deviated more than 10 percent above or below their charted body weight. The percentage of promotions was tabulated for the two groups, and it was found that the medium-weight group had more promotions.

In a study conducted by a Madison Avenue employment agency with branches in 43 American cities, it was found that overweight persons may be losing as much as $1,000 a year for every pound of fat. According to the agency's president, Robert Hall (1974), the survey showed that among executives in the $25,000–50,000 salary group only 9 percent were more than 10 pounds overweight. In the $10,000–20,000 group only 39 percent were more than 10 pounds overweight (according to the standards established by life insurance companies). Hall said that the overweight "are unfairly stereotyped as slow, sloppy, inefficient, and overindulgent. When important, high-paying jobs are at stake and candidates are under close scrutiny, the overweight are less likely to be hired or promoted into them." Hall also stated that companies frequently specify their preference for slim candidates, but only once in 25 years did a company request a plump executive; the company was a manufacturer of oversized clothing.

Closely related to body weight is body type. Sheldon (1940, 1942, 1954) identified three different body types or *somatotypes*. The very thin person is called an *ectomorph*, the very heavy and soft person an *endomorph*, and the medium weight, muscular type is the *mesomorph*. Intuitively, we might expect leaders to come from the meso-morphic body type. Although there are no studies to support or refute this prediction, it is a provocative theory that might someday be tested. For example, those who are successful in political campaigns and in movie careers seem to be more often than not mesomorphic. We also know from several research studies that more attractive people are perceived as having higher credibility (for example, higher expertise and better character) on the basis of their looks alone (Mills and Aronson 1965; Widgery and Webster 1969; Widgery, 1974).

In addition to physical traits, certain personality traits were thought to be associated with leadership. A list of some of these traits includes self-confidence, dominance, enthusiasm, assertiveness, responsibility, creativity, originality, dependability, critical thinking ability, intelligence, and ability to communicate effectively. Although all these traits have some commonsense appeal, Bird (1940) and Stogdill (1948) surveyed over 200 leadership studies and found that out of all the identified traits, only 5 per-cent were common to four or more of the studies surveyed. In a recent update, how-ever, Stogdill (1974, p. 93) has had somewhat greater success in securing a level of agreement among leadership trait studies. His results appear in Figure 4.2.

In summarizing his latest thoughts on the trait theory, Stogdill (1974, p. 413) states:

> Although leaders differ from followers with respect to various aspects of personality, abil-ity, and social skills, tests of such traits have been of limited value for selection of leaders. Traits do not act singly but in combination. . . . The leader who acquires leadership status in one group tends to emerge as leader when placed in other groups. Thus, perhaps the best prediction of future leadership is prior success in this role.

On the other side of the coin, Geier (1967) was able to identify five negative traits that consistently prevented group members from emerging as leaders. Such members were (1) uninformed about the problem being discussed, (2) nonparticipative, (3) extremely rigid in holding to pet ideas, (4) authoritarian in bossing others around, and (5) offensive and abusive in language style. Although the trait theory has not held as many answers as early philosophers and theorists had hoped, it has provided us with some helpful information and insight.

Bennis and Nanus (1985) interviewed 90 contemporary American leaders, from Ray Kroc, founder of McDonalds, to John H. Johnson, publisher of *Ebony,* to John Robinson, coach of the Los Angeles Rams. They concluded:

> Myth 3. Leaders are Charismatic. Some are, most aren't. Among the ninety there were a few—but damned few—who probably correspond to our fantasies of some "divine inspi-ration," that "grace under stress" we associated with J.F.K. or the beguiling capacity to spellbind for which we remember Churchill. Our leaders were all "too human"; they were short and tall, articulate and inarticulate, dressed for success and dressed for failure, and there was virtually nothing in terms of physical appearance, personality, or style that set them apart from their followers. Our guess is that it operates in the other direction; that is, charisma is the result of effective leadership, not the other way around, and that those who are good at it are granted a certain amount of respect and even awe by their followers, which increases the bond of attraction between them. (pp. 223–224)

FIGURE 4.2   FACTORS APPEARING IN THREE OR MORE STUDIES.
Reprinted with permission of The Free Press, a Division of Macmillan, Inc. from *Stodgill's Handbook of Leadership*, rev. ed., by Bernard M. Bass. Copyright © 1974, 1981 by The Free Press.

Factor No.	Factor Name	Frequency
1	Social and interpersonal skills	16
2	Technical skills	18
3	Administrative skills	12
4	Leadership effectiveness and achievement	15
5	Social nearness, friendliness	18
6	Intellectual skills	11
7	Maintaining cohesive work group	9
8	Maintaining coordination and teamwork	7
9	Task motivation and application	17
10	General impression (halo)	12
11	Group task supportiveness	17
12	Maintaining standards of performance	5
13	Willingness to assume responsibility	10
14	Emotional balance and control	15
15	Informal group control	4
16	Nurturant behavior	4
17	Ethical conduct, personal integrity	10
18	Communication, verbality	6
19	Ascendance, dominance, decisiveness	11
20	Physical energy	6
21	Experience and activity	4
22	Mature, cultured	3
23	Courage, daring	4
24	Aloof, distant	3
25	Creative, independent	5
26	Conforming	5

They summarize their research this way: "Managers do things right, leaders do the right thing."

Circumstances Theory

Ira Hayes was an American Indian who became famous for having been one of the United States Marines who lifted the American flag after the battle of Iwo Jima in the South Pacific during World War II. Ira Hayes just happened to be standing nearby when the photographer solicited a group to pose for the picture that later became world famous. Ira instantly became a national hero and was sent on cross-country United States Savings Bond drives to raise money for the American war effort. Ira's pride made him feel so guilty for being a "counterfeit hero" that he began to drink. He eventually died an alcoholic.

Ira Hayes is the classic example of a person being at the right place at the right (or wrong) time. This is sometimes called the circumstances theory of leadership. Another facet of this theory is that a person may be an effective leader in one circumstance, but perform poorly in a different circumstance. Therefore some theorists would argue that the circumstances make the leader. A good example of this is the student/faculty softball, football, or basketball teams that are found on some campuses. While the professors are usually the leaders in the classroom (due to a relatively higher level of expertise in the subject), the students are usually the leaders on the athletic field, where they often know more about the game and are almost always in better physical shape than the professors.

Like trait theory, circumstances theory too seems to have some validity. However, there are many exceptions to the rule. Charles Percy was president of Bell and Howell Corporation at age 30 and has also functioned effectively as a United States senator. Robert McNamara functioned well as president of Ford Motor Company, United States Secretary of Defense, and head of the World Bank organization. Ronald Reagan and John Glenn are two more individuals who have succeeded in numerous capacities in and out of government. Circumstances theory, while somewhat valid, leaves something to be desired in explaining the complex phenomenon of leadership.

Function Theory

A theory that deviates rather dramatically from the first two is function theory. Underlying this theory is the notion that leaders are made, not born. That is, leadership consists of certain behaviors or *functions* that groups must have performed. These functions are identifiable behaviors that can be learned by anybody. We can all improve our potential as leaders by learning to perform these key functions more effectively. While trait and circumstance theories assume there is little we can do to become leaders if we aren't a certain height, or if we never seem to be in the right place at the right time, function theory offers hope for those of us who may not have been born Kennedys or Rockefellers or who are not asked to be in famous photographs.

The two important functions that have been consistently identified are referred to by a variety of terms, but are basically the same concepts. They are (1) task orientation and (2) people orientation. The terms used to describe these concepts are summarized in Figure 4.3.

Wood, Phillips and Pedersen (1986) summarize the literature on this point by writing:

> Designated leaders perform a variety of important functions. They provide liaison with groups or other individuals in the surrounding environment, they furnish a central point

FIGURE 4.3   SUMMARY OF COMPARABLE TERMS FOR LEADERSHIP FUNCTIONS.

	Task Orientation	People Orientation
Bales 1950	Task	Social-emotional
Halpin and Winer 1957	Initiating structure	Consideration
Cartwright and Zander 1968	Goal achievement	Group achievement

of responsibility, which is especially significant in organizational settings that demand clear lines of accountability; they represent a central point when there are problems, changes in plans, complications, and so on. Without one person who assumes responsibility for these functions, a group may factionalize, become chaotic, or operate inadequately. (p. 80)

Penley and Hawkins (1985, p. 82) measured interpersonal communication between supervisors and subordinates. They conclude:

The results emphasize the need to focus attention on leaders' communication, including their relational messages.

Much of the research concerning communication and leadership has focused primarily upon the communication behavior of the effective supervisor (Jablin, 1979) rather than upon communication as the observable behavior of leadership. Earlier, Redding (1972) summarized this research. He stated that effective supervisors (1) were more communication-oriented than the ineffective leader and enjoyed speaking up, (2) tended to be receptive and responsive to subordinate inquiries, (3) tended to ask or persuade rather than to tell and (4) gave advance notice of changes and explained the why of things—that is, were more open.

This study contributes one description of supervisor-subordinate communications that is characteristic of attributed leadership qualities. Subordinates perceive that supervisors who show consideration communicate more task and career messages and are more responsive in their communication.

A negative example is provided by Bennis and Nanus (1985), who write about Jimmy Carter's leadership style. They quote one of his loyal cabinet officers, who said: "Working for him was like looking at the wrong side of a tapestry—blurry and indistinct" (pp. 36–37).

With function theory, the emphasis has shifted away from the leader as a person and toward the specific behavioral acts that facilitate group success. Leadership may be "possessed" by any group member who performs these leadership functions. The task-oriented behaviors are those directed toward the group's accomplishing its goal. The people-oriented behaviors are directed toward the maintenance of the interpersonal relationships in the group. It is assumed that people-oriented activities ought to have an indirect effect on helping accomplish the group's task. An analogy would be that of a machine. The machine operates to accomplish a task (producing parts). However, if the machine is not cleaned and lubricated, it will break down sooner or later, thus halting its productivity. Similarly, although task-oriented groups may require a leader who can help them accomplish their goal, they may cease functioning if they become too bogged down in personality conflicts or counterproductive interpersonal friction. Both task-oriented and people-oriented behaviors are required to enable a group to progress. Bales in Figure 4.4 offers a summary of the 12 types of specific behavioral acts (6 task-oriented, 6 people-oriented) and the average percentage of the interaction in any given group discussion that would probably fall into each category. Ross summarizes the work of Bales and others in an extended model of the twelve Bales Interaction Process Analysis (IPA) categories (Figure 4.5).

The function theory of leadership seems to hold the most promise for teaching most of us how to improve our own leadership abilities. For example, many students

FIGURE 4.4
Adapted from *Personality and Interpersonal Behavior* by Robert F. Bales. Copyright © 1970 by Holt, Rinehart & Winston, Inc. Reprinted by permission of Holt, Rinehart & Winston, Inc.

	Category	Percentage	Estimated Norms
People-oriented (positive)	1. Seems friendly	3.5	2.6– 4.8
	2. Dramatizes	7.0	5.7– 7.4
	3. Agrees	18.5	8.0–13.6
Task-oriented	4. Gives suggestions	3.8	3.0– 7.0
	5. Gives opinions	24.5	15.0–22.7
	6. Gives information	8.3	20.7–31.2
	7. Asks for information	10.3	4.0– 7.2
	8. Asks for opinions	12.5	2.0– 3.9
	9. Asks for suggestions	2.3	0.6– 1.4
People-oriented (negative)	10. Disagrees	1.0	3.1– 5.3
	11. Shows tension	7.8	3.4– 6.0
	12. Seems unfriendly	0.5	2.4– 4.4
	Total:	100.0	

hesitate to participate in discussions for fear of "saying something stupid." Yet several research studies indicate that simply participating at all is one primary requirement of becoming more of a leader (Morris and Hackman 1969; Hayes and Meltzer 1972; Regula and Julian 1973). Other studies show that individuals who are able to perform both task- and people-oriented functions in groups are likely to get better results from their groups than those who are less effective in performing these two functions (Likert 1961; Stogdill 1974).

The final important implication to grow out of the function theory of leadership is that these functions need not be performed by the one person designated as group leader. In fact, the implication is the reverse. To the extent that all group members learn to perform these two functions, overall group leadership will be improved. This is often referred to as *shared* or *democratic* leadership, which we will examine in the next section.

Leadership Styles

A great deal of attention has been paid to the different types of available leadership styles since the early studies conducted by Kurt Lewin and his associates (Lewin, Lippitt, and White 1939; White and Lippitt 1968). The early studies identified three different styles: autocratic, democratic, and laissez-faire.

The issue in these three leadership styles is the degree and location of control. The authoritarian or autocratic leader has a high need to maintain control of the group himself or herself. Some might even say that the autocratic leader has an obsession for control. When this obsession reaches the extreme, it is manifested in the following types of behaviors (Sattler and Miller 1968, pp. 250–251):

1. The authoritarian leader usually plans to get to the conference room when everyone else is assembled. He fears getting to the meeting early, for he has

FIGURE 4.5 INTERACTION PROCESS ANALYSIS, CATEGORIES OF COMMUNICATIVE ACTS.

Based on Robert F Bales, *Interaction Process Analysis*, Reading, Mass: Addison-Wesley, 1950, p. 9; A. Paul Hare, *Handbook of Small Group Research*, New York: Free Press of Glencoe, 1962, p. 66; and Clovis R. Shepherd, *Small Groups: Some Sociological Perspectives*, San Francisco: Chandler, 1964, p. 30.

Major Categories		Subcategories	Illustrative Statements or Behavior
Social emotional area	Positive reactions	1. Shows solidarity	Jokes, gives help, rewards others, is friendly
		2. Show tension release	Laughs, shows satisfaction, is relieved
		3. Shows agreement	Passively accepts, understands, concurs, complies
Task area	Attempted answers	4. Gives suggestion	Directs, suggests, implies autonomy for others
		5. Gives opinion	Evaluates, analyzes, expresses feeling or wish
		6. Gives information	Orients, repeats, clarifies, confirms
	Questions	7. Asks for information	Requests orientation, repetition, confirmation
		8. Asks for opinion	Requests evaluation, analysis, expression of feeling
		9. Asks for suggestion	Requests direction, possible ways of action
Social emotional area	Negative reactions	10. Shows disagreement	Passively rejects, resorts to formality, withholds help
		11. Shows tension	Asks for help, withdraws, daydreams
		12. Shows antagonism	Deflates other's status, defends or asserts self, hostile

Key: a. Problems of communication   b. Problems of evaluation   c. Problems of control
d. Problems of decision   e. Problems of tension reduction   f. Problems of reintegration

no interest in carrying on nontask-related conversation. This does not mean that the leader is a latecomer—he isn't; if the meeting is scheduled to start at 3:10 p.m., you will be sure that the leader will be present and the meeting will start on the proper split second.

2. Often the leader will present an extended introduction to start a meeting, in part because he wishes others to know how well informed he is.

3. Sometimes the authoritarian will outline precise procedures on how the discussion is to be conducted. Thus, he might tell the group that Mr. A will comment on Item 1, B and C on Item 2, and D on Item 3. Such advice on procedure is not given in order to be helpful to others; largely, it seems, the authoritarian uses rules of order to make his own task easier.

4. Authoritarians, more than other leaders, specialize in questions directed to specific persons such as, "Jones, what are your facts . . . ?" . . . "Now I want to hear from Smith. . . ." Such leaders do not frequently use open or "overhead" questions that any person in the group may answer.

5. Authoritarians appear to be unable to withstand pauses in discussion—if such leaders cannot get rapid verbalization from others, they will themselves supply verbal noises.

6. The leader almost invariably maintains strict control over the order and sequence of topics; he appears to love placing group members in a "straitjacket" of restrictions.

7. The authoritarian leader interrupts others often, for at least three reasons: to correct errors whether major or insignificant, to keep persons talking about what he desires, and in general to show who is in command.

8. Clever authoritarians at times encourage group members to discuss irrelevant matters at considerable length. This is true, of course, only when to discuss the irrelevant is in keeping with the leader's designs.

9. When the leader clarifies contributions he is sometimes guilty of changing the intent of statements to make them more acceptable to himself. (Here, of course, we have both procedural and content control.)

The laissez-faire style of leadership goes to the opposite extreme. Not only is there no concern for control, but there is no direction, concern for task accomplishment, or concern for interpersonal relationships. The laissez-faire style is not really a style of leadership at all; it is nonleadership.

The democratic leadership style represents an attempt to find a reasonable compromise between the other two extremes. The leader does attempt to provide direction and both task and social leadership functions, but at the same time tries to avoid dominating the group with one person's views. Some would argue that no matter how hard an individual tries, some domination cannot be avoided, as the cartoon shows.

Which leadership style is best? In order to answer this question we must determine the criteria for judging effectiveness. Some criteria would include (1) the quality of the group output, (2) the time taken to accomplish the task, (3) the satisfaction of the group members, (4) the absenteeism of group members, and (5) the independence developed in group members. White and Lippitt (1968) reported (1) that the quality of group output in their study was better under democratic leadership, (2) that democratic leadership took more time than autocratic, (3) that member satisfaction was higher under democratic leadership (in fact, hostility was 30 times as great in the autocratic groups, and 19 out of 20 preferred the democratic group to the autocratic), (4) that the democratic group had the lowest absenteeism, and (5) that the democratic group fostered more independence, while the autocratic style bred dependence and submissiveness among group members.

The democratic style got better results in each case except in time taken to accomplish the task. However, subsequent studies (Likert 1967) have shown that the autocratic leader gets fast results in the short run, but that these results may be of poor quality or may be resisted by others. The net effect is that the solution may not be enacted and the problem will have to be dealt with again on future occasions. Since this amounts to less efficiency, the democratic style may even prove to be less time-consuming in the long run (see Chapter 7 for more on this). In addition, the hostility bred by autocratic leadership produces counterproductive results. For example, in industrial groups, absenteeism, grievances, work stoppages, and sabotage are all ways in which employees attempt to "get back" at what they consider to be harsh leadership. "Goldbricking" in the military is another typical example. An autocratic leadership style fosters group norms that say, "Do as little as possible to get by and look busy when the boss is around. However, when the cat's away . . ."

"Now, the round table symbolizes our equality while my fancy chair and golden crown signify that I, perhaps, am just a smack more equal."

Group-centered leadership or nondirective leadership is a method that has grown out of the desire to develop more effective forms of democratic leadership. Haiman (1951, p. 40) wrote:

> Probably the most important single concept that has emerged in the last twenty years from the ever growing wealth of psycho-therapeutic experience is the realization that the most effective way to direct the behavior of human beings is simply to help them direct themselves.

Thirty-five years later we can see that, if anything, Haiman's conclusion is even more relevant than it was when written.

Gordon (1955) outlined the philosophy of group-centered leadership in further detail. He criticized the long-held assumption that leadership involves functions that should be carried out by one person. We have already encountered this fallacy in the section on the functional theory. In addition, we have seen that the autocratic leadership style breeds dependence and submissiveness. The group-centered approach would be to allow each member to grow and develop whatever leadership skills he or she possesses.

The group-centered or nondirective approach lends itself more to the social group or the unstructured encounter group than the work group or the task-oriented discussion group. However, certain aspects of the group-centered approach may be applied to any group situation. Figure 4.6 gives a detailed description of the group-centered approach and the more traditional leader-guided (or leader-centered) approach.

The group-centered leadership philosophy is well summarized in the famous words of Lao-tzu:

A leader is best
When people barely know that he exists,
Not so good when people obey and acclaim him,
Worse when they despise him.
"Fail to honor people,
They fail to honor you";
But of a good leader who talks little,
When his work is done, his aim fulfilled,
They will say, "We did it ourselves."

FOLLOWERSHIP

While leadership is written about more than most topics relating to small group interaction, followership is much less frequently discussed. Since leadership is defined as successful attempts to influence, followers are required to make leaders. In fact, leadership and followership go hand in hand. Earlier we saw that one style of leadership (democratic) in many cases seems to be best. What style of followership is best? Let us first look at three alternative followership styles.

FIGURE 4.6 TWO CONTRASTING APPROACHES TO LEADERSHIP IN SMALL GROUPS.

Based on Thomas Gordon, *Group-Centered Leadership* (Boston: Houghton Mifflin, 1955), pp. 197–200.

Group-Centered	Leader-Guided

Principal Behaviors

Group-Centered	Leader-Guided
1. Allows group to diagnose its needs. Tries to facilitate communication in group during this process.	1. Finds out as much as possible about group's needs, in order to provide group with situation where it can get what it needs.
2. Allows group to plan its own experiences. Tries to facilitate communication during this process.	2. Plans specific learning situations and/or group experiences from which group may draw insights.
3. Avoids making decisions for group, except those which facilitate bringing members together initially.	3. Makes decisions for group when group seems too immature to make correct decisions.
4. Preparation involves doing things that will improve his own contributions to group.	4. Preparation involves doing things that will improve his own contribution and things that he feels group needs.
5. Tries to lose his special status position so that he can participate in decision making without having his contributions given special consideration by group.	5. Uses influence of his special status position in group to bring about decisions or to guide group in certain directions.
6. Leaves responsibility with each member for participating. Tries to facilitate group's developing a permissive and accepting atmosphere by being as permissive and accepting as he can.	6. Facilitates participation by subtle or direct methods of involving each member in group activities.
7. Sets limits in terms of his own ability to be accepting of group action.	7. Sets limits more in terms of what will be best for group.
8. Wants to contribute resources just like any other member of group. Tries to avoid being used by group as *only* or *chief* resource person.	8. Wants group members to use him as the special resource person, and generally lets himself be used by group in this way.
9. Tries to understand members' expressed wishes for him to behave in some particular role, but does not always feel compelled to do so.	9. Usually accedes to members' wishes that he play some particular role or else tries to convince them that another role is best.
10. Tries not to influence others to play some particular role.	10. Often influences or directly manipulates members to play some particular role.
11. Tries not to think beyond the level of expressed understanding of group members, feeling that only meaningful insights will be those arrived at by members themselves.	11. Often interprets group's behavior in order to give members understandings they might not acquire themselves.
12. Tries not to be perceived as "the leader," believing that, as long as he is so perceived, group members will not be completely free to be themselves and often will react to his contributions either submissively and uncritically or with hostility and resistance.	12. Tries to be perceived as "the leader," believing that he will thus be better able to control the situation to meet group's needs.
13. Takes no special responsibility for seeing that group evaluates its achievement or its progress.	13. Takes special responsibility to ensure that evaluative function is carried out in group.
14. Tries to lose his "official role" in order to be free to resist group's needs for dependence and to reduce his own anxiety about the outcome of group action.	14. Tries to reinforce his "official role" in order to have more influence on the group action.
15. Takes no special responsibility to reduce anxiety, to resolve tension, etc. Feels such elements are inevitable consequence of group interaction.	15. Takes special responsibility to reduce anxiety and to resolve tension. Feels such elements hinder group purposes and should be avoided.

Followership Styles

Milgram (1974) summarizes almost 15 years of research on this topic in his book *Obedience to Authority*. In Milgram's experiments, subjects were told to administer electric shocks to other subjects as a part of an experiment in learning associations between word pairs. The victim was strapped in a chair and was unable to escape the shocks. The control panel on the shock generator indicted voltage up to 450 volts, which level was labeled, "Danger: Severe Shock," As the voltage was increased, the victim screamed, "Get me out of here; I can't stand the pain: please, I have a heart condition." These protests were continued for any and all shocks administered above 150 volts. (No actual shocks were given, but the subjects really thought they were shocking the victims.)

A group of psychiatrists was asked to predict how much shock the subject would administer to the victim. They predicted that almost every subject would refuse to obey the experimenter, that those who administered any shocks at all would stop at 150 volts, and that only about one in a thousand would go all the way to 450 volts (the end of the control panel). Out of Milgram's original 40 subjects, however, 26 (65 percent) obeyed the experimenter's orders and administered the shocks right up to the 450-volt limit. However, Milgram found that as situations were changed (for example, if the victim was brought into the same room with the subject), the subject was less willing to shock the victim.

The behavior found in Milgram's experiments illustrates what might be termed a *dependent* style of followership. Two other situations involving *dependent* followership were the My Lai massacre and the Watergate scandal. Accounts of the My Lai incident included the following description by one participant as he was interviewed on CBS by Mike Wallace.

A: ... Lieutenant Calley told me, he said, "Soldier we got another job to do." And so he walked over to the people, and he started pushing them off and started shooting. ...

Q: Again—men, women, and children?

A: Men, women, and children.

Q: And babies?

A: And babies. And so we started shooting them and somebody told us to switch off to single shot so that we could save ammo. ...

Q: Why did you do it?

A: Why did I do it? Because I felt like I was ordered to do it, and it seemed like that, at the time I felt I was doing the right thing, because like I said, I lost buddies. I lost a damn good buddy, Bobby Wilson, and it was on my conscience. So after I done it, I felt good, but later on that day, it was getting to me.

Obviously, more than personality factors are operating in situations such as the one described above. The situation (during a war) and the role (being in the military) also have a great deal to do with producing this type of behavior. Large organizations such as the military, organized religions, and government and industrial organizations frequently produce a higher level of dependence in people. James McCord, one of the convicted Watergate burglars, was described by Woodward and Bernstein (1974, p. 22) as " . . . deeply religious, . . . ex-FBI agent, . . . military reservist, . . . [and] as the consummate 'government man'—reluctant to act on his own initiative, respectful of the chain of command, unquestioning in following orders." As we saw earlier, autocratic leadership produces a higher level of dependent followership. As the cartoon indicates, most of us are caught up to some degree in the obedience syndrome, but with much less harmful or dramatic results.

A second type of follower is the *counterdependent* person. Counterdependence is a type of behavior that is rebellious and anti-authoritarian. While the dependent personality is thought to result from overly punitive parents, the counterdependent personality is thought to result from overly permissive parents. People who are used to doing things more or less their own way resent a leader or any authority figure who intervenes. This type of person would be dissatisfied with almost any style of leadership. It may not be too much of an exaggeration to say that this group consists of misfits who are pretty much chronic problems. In the industrial work force they create major problems for leaders wherever they go. Steinmetz (1969, pp. 10–11) quoted Edward Cole, former president of General Motors, as stating:

> A research study found that a relatively few employees—28%—filed 100% of the grievances and accounted for 37% of the occupational hospital visits; 38% of the insurance claims, 40% of the sick leaves, 52% of the garnishments, and 38% of the absenteeism experienced at a certain factory. Thus not only are there a comparatively small proportion of people who are absentee-oriented, but these same people tend also to be the ones who create a significant number of all the other problems generated within the organization.

This type of follower would be hard for any leader to lead. We saw earlier that a democratic leadership style tends to produce higher levels of member satisfaction. However, Runyon (1973) found in an industrial chemical plant that some hourly employees (primarily young workers) did not have high job satisfaction regardless of type of supervisory style. Even a participative (democratic) style did not produce a high level of satisfaction. Perhaps it is fair to say that some people are simply difficult

Reprinted with special permission of King Features Syndicate, Inc.

to lead, and that in dealing with them one leadership style would be about as good (or bad) as any other. The problem then would be to try to bring the followers to a point where they could accept legitimate leadership from others.

The third followership style is the *independent*. The independent is one who can either take over and lead when the situation demands, or follow the lead of others when that role is more appropriate. Benjamin Franklin once said, "He that cannot obey cannot command." This implies the role flexibility required of both an effective leader and an effective follower. Note, for example, these comments at the beginning of one college group discussion. Randy was the group's appointed leader and John was one of the group participants.

Randy: Today our discussion topic is, "What can be done to improve the grading system at GMI?" Let's begin with a look at some facets of the causes, I mean criteria for solutions, I mean . . . *Help!*

John: You mean facets of the problem.

Randy: Yes—thanks.

Although Randy was the appointed leader and John the follower, John helped Randy assume the leadership role in getting the discussion started. Anyone who has ever had a case of "nerves" when speaking in front of a class can understand how Randy could get so tongue-tied and confused.

Interestingly enough, in a totally different context, Milgram (1974) found that when he asked subjects to shock the victims in his studies, psychiatrists (professional group) predicted that they would disobey rather quickly, while middle-class adults (nonprofessional group) predicted that they would obey somewhat longer and give more intense shocks. It appears that to some extent education and perhaps the subsequent self-confidence tends to correlate with independence of followership and decision making.

To illustrate the contingency aspects of leadership, one student wrote:

As a second grade instructional aide, I led dependent followers. For these students, who were highly motivated, "gifted" children, I found that a group-centered approach was best, because it forced the students to make decisions which affected them. This improved their academics and matured their thinking processes. As a resident adviser, I led counterdependent followers. The beginning of the year was handled democratically but after about six weeks the autocratic method proved more effective. Those students who became dissatisfied changed their followership style, so that they would be treated more democratically; those students who did not change at least accomplished the basic tasks—to establish a community conducive to study and to obey the rules of the school and the laws of Michigan and the U.S., which they were not doing under a democratic style of leadership. Finally, as the vice-president of a fraternity, I found a democratic style to be most effective. This provides for personal development and satisfaction, while still accomplishing the tasks which are outlined. However, becoming too group-centered can be a detriment because of the physical size of the membership, and the nature of the tasks which are accomplished.

This is an excellent example of the systems aspect of small group interaction. In each of the situations described above, several factors were acting in combination to influence and determine the most effective leadership style.

In this section we have looked at three styles of followership. We have labeled them the dependent, the counterdependent, and the independent types. They have also been referred to as the slave, the rebel, and the responsible individual (Zaleznik and Moment 1964, pp. 278–279), and, in a different context, the nonassertive person, the aggressive person, and the assertive person, respectively (Jakubowski-Spector 1973, pp. 1–6). Based on this discussion, which followership style seems to describe your predominant style? How does your style change in response to different leaders and different situations? Note the trends shown in Figure 4.7.

CONTINGENCY THEORY

Building on the previous theories, two approaches have been offered that are highly consistent with the systems approach taken in this book. Fiedler (1967) has developed a *situational* or *contingency* theory of leadership. Hersey and Blanchard (1982) have developed a somewhat different theory. Although these models are both referred to as situational theories, the term *contingency theories* also seems appropriate, since the leader's effectiveness is contingent or dependent upon the combination of his or her behaviors and the situation.

Fiedler and Chemers (1974) argue that a combination of three separate factors determine a leader's effectiveness: (1) leader-member relations, (2) task structure, and (3) position power. For example, leader-member relations are roughly equivalent to what we have come to know as a person's interpersonal skills or people orientation. If a leader is people oriented, the leader-member relations are likely to be good. If, on the other hand, his or her orientation is that people are a necessary evil in getting something done, then the leader-member relations are likely to be poor.

Task structure is the second variable in Fiedler's theory. If a group's task is highly structured and the leader has a manual of procedures to be followed, it would be harder for group members to challenge the leader's approach. On the other hand, if the task is highly ambiguous, such as trying to determine policy by predicting future events, then the group members might have quite a bit of legitimate input that could be as good or better than the leader's idea alone.

FIGURE 4.7   LEADERSHIP AND FOLLOWERSHIP STYLES.

Leadership Styles	Followership Styles		
Autocratic	Dependent	Slave	Nonassertive
Democratic	Independent	Responsible individual	Assertive
Laissez faire	Counterdependent	Rebel	Aggressive

The third variable is position power. This can be either strong or weak. If the leader heading a work group has the power to hire and fire, to promote or not, and to determine raises or punishment, then the leader has strong position power. If, on the other hand, the group is comprised of volunteers working for a church committee or a student organization, the leader has weak position power to get people to do the task. In the model shown in Figure 4.8, we see the results of Fiedler's research. This model clearly shows that these three variables have a strong influence on the leader's effectiveness; in other words, leadership effectiveness is congruent upon these three variables. If we take the example described above in which a leader is working with a group of volunteers for a student organization and the task is fairly unstructured (without clear guidelines on how to proceed), then the person who is not people-oriented will be very ineffective. In fact, the group members will simply not come back to the next meeting. This theory is fascinating in its implications for leadership, since the same leader acting in the same way would likely be very successful in leading a military group where the operations manual supported "going by the book," and where followers who didn't obey would end up in the guardhouse.

Over two decades ago Barnlund (1962, p. 52) wrote: "Leadership [effectiveness] is dependent upon situational variables, at least two of which seem to be changes in group task and membership." More recently, Hersey and Blanchard's 1982 model very clearly pointed out the role of these variables on leadership effectiveness.

Building on the ideas we presented earlier in the functions theory section, these authors also stress the two leadership functions of (1) task-oriented behavior, and (2) people-oriented or relationship behavior. To these they add a third important variable, (3) the maturity of the followers. Maturity level could be defined in various ways, but Hersey and Blanchard define it in terms of three components. The first is the ability of the group members. If their ability is quite low, the leader has to be more

FIGURE 4.8   FIEDLER'S CONTINGENCY LEADERSHIP MODEL.
From Fiedler and Chemers, *Leadership and Effective Management* (Glenview, Ill.: Scott, Foresman, 1974), p. 80. Copyright 1974 Scott, Foresman & Co. Reprinted by permission of the author.

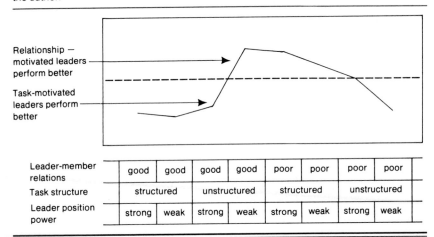

Leader-member relations	good	good	good	good	poor	poor	poor	poor
Task structure	structured		unstructured		structured		unstructured	
Leader position power	strong	weak	strong	weak	strong	weak	strong	weak

directive than if the group members have high ability. Second, if the followers have high levels of motivation to achieve, they need less direction than followers who are not "self-starters." In fact, one professor gave a motivation test to a group so low in motivation that they would not even fill out the test! They simply didn't care about it.

The third component of follower maturity is the level of education or experience with that particular task. If a follower is totally inexperienced with fixing a malfunctioning car engine, a high level of ability and motivation may not be enough.

For more on determining the maturity level of the followers, see the article by Hersey and Blanchard at the end of this chapter.

As we see in Figure 4.9, when the maturity of followers is lowest (M1), the leadership style most likely to be effective is S1, or *telling.* With an M2 level, the S2 style, *selling,* is best. *Participating* goes best with a higher level of follower maturity, and *delegating* is the recommended supervisory style for the highest level of follower maturity.

While it is important to develop some flexibility in our approaches to leadership in different situations, it is also important to realize that we all have limitations. As one colleague remarked, "We can't be a chameleon changing drastically for each situation." Hersey and Blanchard recognize that each of us tends to prefer one or two of these leadership patterns (that is, telling, selling, participating, and delegating). In most situations we gravitate toward whichever of these patterns has worked well for us in the past. The difficulty comes when the leadership that is *required* is different from the one we feel comfortable choosing. For example, George Steinbrenner, the owner of the New York Yankees, uses a *telling* leadership pattern. However, since he has had severely unhappy players and managers, maybe a different pattern (for example, delegating to his manager) would be more appropriate. Yet it is probably quite hard for Mr. Steinbrenner to move to this other style because of his strong personality. Another factor to keep in mind is that if he were not the owner of the team and a millionaire, his behavior pattern would probably be even less tolerated by others in the organization.

In spite of their limitations, contingency models seem to offer the most promising theories to help guide us in determining the most effective leadership behaviors. They also fit well into the systems approach taken in this book.

GROUP NORMS: SOCIAL INFLUENCE AND CONFORMITY

This entire chapter deals with the process of social influence. In earlier sections we have seen that some people tend more to be the influencers and others the influencees. In this section we will explore some of the results of social influence—namely, conformity pressure.

Like individuals, groups form habits. When people have been together for a time, they develop standardized ways of managing tasks, procedures, and the environment. Wood, Phillips, and Pedersen (1986) define *norms* as "standardized patterns of belief, attitude, communication and behavior within groups. They grow out of member interaction. Then, in systematic fashion, they influence future interaction" (p. 40).

Every one of us has undoubtedly felt the pressure to conform at one time or another. We notice pressure from the childhood challenges where we are "chicken" if we don't go along with the group, to the high school or college scene where we are labeled a "brown-nose" if we appear to be spending more time in the teacher's office than our classmates think is normal. Note the following letter (Courtesy Ann Landers, Field Newspaper Syndicate).

FIGURE 4.9   HERSEY AND BLANCHARD'S (1982) CONTINGENCY MODEL OF LEADERSHIP.

Four Words That Can Ruin Teenagers*
June 14, 1975

Dear Ann . . . I just read some remarks made by Dr. Chester Ewing, a physician in Chester County, Pa. He identified the four most terrible words in the English language. Please print this letter. Many a teenager's life might be changed by it.

The most terrible words are: 1. "Chicken." 2. "Square." 3. "Yellow." 4. "Brown-nosing."

Ewing said he knew of three instances where kids had been hounded by the word "yellow" until they tried dope.

He listed some conversations he had had with young people—in hospitals. They admitted the reason they were drag-racing (which leads to accidents) was because they were called "chicken."

Being called "square" has made young people ashamed of dressing decently, being courteous to adults, and showing respect for authority. All young people want to be considered with it. A "square" is out of it. That name encourages kids to prove they are gutty and up front.

"Brown-nosing" is a slang term for trying to curry favor. It is especially applied to teacher-student relationships. Students who raise their hands in class to ask questions are called "brown-nosers" because they give the teacher the impression they are interested. This stands the students in good stead with the teacher—but not with their peers.

I hope the teens who read your column will pay attention to this letter. It could change their entire outlook and lengthen their lives.

Pa. Reader

Dear Reader: Amen.

Although norms can be described in terms of their functional value to the group, this does not imply that members of the group deliberately develop norms with the conscious intention of achieving positive group benefits. According to Thibaut and Kelley (1986):

> The developmental process underlying the emergence of norms are likely to yield rules that have positive functional values for the relationship. As norms are decided upon, imported from other relationships, and tried out, only the more useful ones are likely to be retained. This is not to say that the norms found in any group will be the best solutions to various problems of control, coordination, and synchronization. (p. 141)

Actually, the term *norms* refers to the written or unwritten laws or codes that identify acceptable behavior. Obviously norms will vary drastically from one group to another. Ouchi (1981) writes:

> The influence of cultural assumptions is clearly reflected in the contrast between Japanese and American styles of decision making. Typically, the Japanese devote extensive time to defining and analyzing problems, but move with great speed in making final

---

*Reprinted by permission.

decisions. Americans follow an opposite path in which minimum time is devoted to analysis, while making the final decision consumes substantial time. No wonder international negotiations are often so frustrating for all parties. (p. 28)

The Japanese norms for group productivity have been widely admired and written about in our country. Perhaps the most fascinating spinoff is where Japanese companies have started firms in the United States and have brought their norms here. Hatvany and Pucik (1981, p. 14), in their comprehensive analysis of successful Japanese management policies, write:

> Acknowledging the enormous impact of groups on their members—both directly, through the enforcement of norms, and indirectly, by affecting the beliefs and values of members—Japanese organizations devote far greater attention to structural factors that enhance group motivation and cooperation than to the motivation of individual employees. Tasks are assigned to groups, not to individual employees, and group cohesion is stimulated by delegating responsibility to the group not only for getting the tasks performed, but also for designing the way in which they get performed.

In our society it is customary for people to engage in some degree of "one-upmanship," in which they drop names and in many ways try to impress each other with their accomplishments. (For example, What? You haven't been to Paris?). In one commune a concerted effort was made to reduce this type of social game playing. Some of the norms for this commune included the following (Kinkade, 1973):

- We don't use titles. All members are "Equal" in the sense that all are entitled to the same privileges, advantages, and respect.

- We don't discuss the personal affairs of other members, nor speak negatively of other members when they are not present, or in the presence of a third party.

- Seniority is not discussed among us. This is because we wish to avoid prestige groups of any kind.

- We try to exercise consideration and tolerance of each other's individual habits.

- We don't boast of individual accomplishments. We are trying to create a society without heroes. We are all expected to do our best, so making a big fuss over some accomplishment is out of place.

This commune, called Twin Oaks, was described more extensively by Kinkade (1973).

By now you may have asked yourself, "Why do we even need to have norms?" Actually, norms often serve to reduce ambiguity and to help us feel more at ease. We often feel uncomfortable when we don't know what behaviors are acceptable in a given situation—for example, in moving from elementary school to junior high or middle school; or going from junior high to high school; then graduating from high school and going to college. Remember the uneasiness you felt during your first day in each of these new situations. Only after we have learned some of the common practices or norms can we begin to relax and "be ourselves." One student who went

Reprinted by permission. © 1977 NEA. Inc.

to Harvard a few years ago learned that the norm was to buy expensive sweaters and then take scissors to fray the elbows so that the sweaters didn't look like new. A reverse attitude is prevalent today toward designer jeans. Nobody would be caught dead in what looked like old baggy jeans.

The norms in our society regarding clothing are quite strong. It is interesting to note that even going without clothes involves certain norms. On a nude beach, wearing clothes or even a bathing suit is frowned upon. Jones (1981) writes that at Black's Beach in San Diego forty to fifty thousand nude bathers gather on a given day. He describes the norms there as follows:

> Nude beaches usually are pretty remote. Gawkers aren't interested in walking very far. . . .
>
> If someone is obnoxious, if some guy keeps his clothes on and stares at the women, it's a matter of peer pressure telling him, hey buddy, what's your problem? Why don't you move on now? This isn't a peep show.

Thirty years ago, a psychologist named Leon Festinger hypothesized a theory of social comparison (1954). This theory pointed out the need each of us has to check out our own ideas with those of others. The more ambiguous the situation, the greater is this need. In addition, when we find ourselves at odds with others, we feel pressure to reduce the discrepancies one way or another. The more we are attracted to the group, the more pressure we will feel to change toward the group norms.

On the hunch that this theory might have some relevance in predicting attitude influence on pot smoking, one student (Unger 1974) conducted a modest study in which he asked, "What has been the most significant source of influence on your views toward pot smoking?" The largest source of influence (43 percent) was from peers; the second largest (37 percent) was from authoritative written documents; the next (8 percent) was from lectures; and 12 percent said from other sources. These data would seem to confirm Festinger's thesis that we are inclined to look to others to help us determine the guidelines for our own opinions and behaviors. It is also significant to note that, as we saw from the study at Bennington College discussed in Chapter 3, the value changes we undergo in college are likely to last for a lifetime (Newcomb 1943).

Conformity: Research and Applications

One of the earliest conformity studies was conducted by Muzafer Sherif (1936) in the late 1930s. He showed subjects a pinpoint of light projected onto a wall in a completely darkened room. The light appeared to move even when the subjects knew that it was stationary. This optical illusion is called the *autokinetic effect*. Subjects were tested alone and in groups. Subjects were told to report when the light appeared to move and to judge about how far it moved. When tested individually, subjects estimated the light's range of movement at 3.6 inches. After they had discussed their experiences in groups of two and three, the average range of estimated movement had reduced to 0.4 inches. Clearly, the group discussion provided an influence on each person's judgment of the amount of the light's movement. In Festinger's words, the subjects had a need to compare their judgment with that of others in the group. Where the judgments were discrepant, there was a felt pressure to reduce the discrepancy. This resulted in the reduced range of estimates of the light's movement. This clearly fits Kiesler and Kiesler's (1969, p. 2) definition of conformity as "a change in behavior or belief ... as a result of real or imagined group pressure."

Solomon Asch (1952) conducted a classic series of conformity studies during the early 1950s. View the two cards with vertical lines drawn on them, shown in Figure 4.10. Which line on card B is the same length as that on card A? If you had been in Asch's study, you and the other seven subjects would announce your decisions in order as you are seated in the room. You are the seventh to answer out of eight. For the first two rounds there is unanimous agreement. However, on the third trial, everyone in the group agrees that line 1 is equal in length to line X. You think it is line 2 instead. What do you do? This goes on through 18 experimental trials. In 12 of the trials you are the only one disagreeing with the others. Actually, the others in the group were Asch's paid stooges, or confederates. The experiment was designed to create pressure on you to conform or yield to the others.

Asch (1955) found that, out of 123 naive subjects, 37 percent conformed to the majority opinion, while control subjects judging independent of group pressure made virtually no errors.

Another technique for constructing a conformity-inducing situation was developed by Crutchfield (Kretch, Crutchfield, and Ballachey, 1962, pp. 504–511). With this method five naive subjects at a time were seated at booths that were partitioned from

FIGURE 4.10

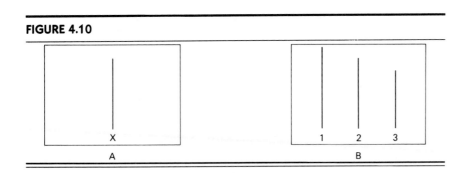

each other. The front of each booth had panels of signal lights and switches. The lights supposedly indicated the responses the others made to the stimuli presented to them (these also indicated that the subject's judgment would be different from the four others). Actually, none of the panels was connected to any other panel. Rather, the investigator rigged the signal lights so that the subject would always be a minority of one. In several studies a total of more than six hundred people participated as naive subjects. Some of the results are summarized below.

1. Group pressure does indeed produce conformity.

2. Yielding can be induced even on attitudes having personal relevance to them.

3. Yielding is greater on difficult decisions than on easy ones.

4. There are large differences in amounts of yielding for different individuals.

5. When subjects are tested again without the group pressure, a major part of the original yielding disappears.

Some situational factors that were found to be pertinent to the conformity process include group size, perceived competence of group members, group unanimity, extremity of group opinion, and group cohesiveness. The size of the group affects conformity in that group pressure increases to a maximum with 4 people comprising the opposing majority. Numbers larger than 4, even up to 15, produce only slightly more yielding. Higher perceived group competence produced more conformity pressure. For example, Crutchfield (1959) found that some high-level mathematicians conformed to group pressure (from other mathematics experts) on the answers to simple arithmetic problems, giving answers that were wrong and that would very likely not have been given under normal circumstances. Group unanimity appears to have a highly significant effect on conformity. Asch (1956) found that when at least one other member of the group reinforced the one-member minority, the resistance to group pressure was significantly increased. With regard to extremity of majority opinion, Tuddenham (1961) found that when the majority opinion lies well outside the range of acceptable judgments, yielding occurs among fewer individuals and to a lesser degree. Group cohesiveness caused an increase in conformity, and the second highest status group member conformed the most of anyone in the group (Harvey and Consalvi, 1960).

Individual personal factors have also been studied in relation to conformity (see also Chapter 2). Some of the results of the conformity research include the following (Tuddenham 1961):

1. Conformists are less intelligent.

2. Conformists are lower in ego-strength and in their ability to work in stress situations.

3. Conformists tend toward feelings of personal inferiority and inadequacy.

4. Conformists show an intense preoccupation with other people, as opposed to more self-contained, autonomous attitudes of the independent person.

5. Conformists express attitudes and values of a more conventional (conservative) nature than nonyielders.

The pressure to conform is eloquently described by Walker and Heynes (1967, p. 98) in the following way:

> If one wishes to produce Conformity for good or evil, the formula is clear. Manage to arouse a need or needs that are important to the individual or the group. Offer a goal which is appropriate to the need or needs. Make sure that Conformity is instrumental to the achievement of the goal and that the goal is as large and as certain as possible. Apply the goal or reward at every opportunity. Try to prevent the object of your efforts from obtaining an uncontrolled education. Choose a setting that is ambiguous. Do everything possible to see that the individual has little or no confidence in his own position. Do everything possible to make the norm which you set appear highly valued and attractive. Set it at a level not too far initially from the starting point of the individual or group and move it gradually toward the behavior you wish to produce. Be absolutely certain you know what you want and that you are willing to pay an enormous price in human quality, for whether the individual or the group is aware of it or not, the result will be *Conformity*.

Have you ever noticed what happens to the person who does try to deviate from the group? By definition this person is a *nonconformist*. He or she gets many times more comments directed toward him or her as these variables increase (that is, group cohesion and relevance of topic, as well as the acting in a noticeably different way). Think of Suicidal Tendencies and Violent Femmes and others of the "punk rock" genre as examples.

In a quantitative study of the group's reaction to a deviant, Schachter (1951) predicted that the deviant would be talked to the most (frequency of communication) and that the reaction to the deviant would depend upon (1) relevance of the discussion topic, (2) degree of group cohesiveness, and (3) degree to which the person deviated. These predictions are summarized in the chart in Figure 4.11, which is included since the actual data supported virtually all the predictions.

In other words, we are more likely to get hot under the collar when a person deviates from a neighborhood group discussing cross-district busing of our children (high cohesion, high relevance), than if a person deviates from a group of strangers deciding on what color to paint the walls in the school gymnasium (low cohesion, low relevance). Notice that the deviant gets many times more comments directed toward him as these variables increase (that is, group cohesion and relevance of topic, as well as the degree of deviation on the topic). Notice also that in the most extreme case (the solid curved line at the top), the frequency of communication tends to diminish after about two-thirds of the 45-minute discussion (30 minutes). This leads us to believe that a certain amount of rejection or ostracism results if the deviant doesn't come around.

While this study represents a quantitative analysis of a group discussion, Leavitt (1964) offers a qualitative analysis of the four stages of conformity pressure. The first stage might be called *reason*. We do not like hearing our ideas disconfirmed, but we are interested in logically convincing the deviant that he or she is wrong. Even at this stage, it is clear we expect the deviant to change to conform to the group and not vice

FIGURE 4.11   THEORETICAL CURVES OF COMMUNICATIONS FROM STRONG REJECTORS, MILD REJECTORS, AND FOUR NONREJECTORS TO THE DEVIANT IN THE FOUR EXPERIMENTAL CONDITIONS.

From Schacter 1951, Deviation, rejection, and communication. *Journal of Abnormal and Social Psychology* 46: 202. American Psychological Association, © 1951.

versa. The second stage is *seduction*. During this stage we attempt to appeal to the deviant's social needs. The comments begin to take on the tone of, "Aw, come on, be a sport, we know you don't want to put the whole group on the spot just for the sake of this little issue." It isn't long before the group enters stage three, which is *coercion*. During this stage the group members lose their smiles and good nature. The comments begin to take on the air of threat, something like, "Now look, this has gone far enough. If you won't play ball, then we are going to have to clip your wings but good the next time you want help from us." The fourth and final stage is *isolation*. At this point the group gives up on and ignores the deviant. This tactic may finally bring conformity if the ostracism is prolonged.

Leavitt (1964, pp. 273–274) summarized the four stages when he writes:

> It's as though the members of the group were saying "Let's reason with him; if that doesn't work, let's try to tease him by emotional seduction; and if even that doesn't work, let's beat him over the head until he has to give up. Failing that, then we'll excommunicate him; we'll amputate him from the group; we'll disown him."

One student wrote of her experience with this conformity influence:

> As a high school band member I experienced all four of these stages when we were to march in the Apple Blossom Parade.
>
> The band master told everyone to wear saddle shoes. When I explained to him that I had none, he said, "Get some, since everybody needs to be dressed the same" (step 1). I told

him I had no money. "Then borrow some," another band member suggested. "Come on, we need you" (step 2). I told them I couldn't borrow any because of an unusual foot size. "Then if you don't get them, you can't march in the parade," said someone else (step 3).

I didn't; I hid when the band came down the street. I never returned to the band again. I felt alone, isolated, and ostracized (step 4), and that ended my musical career. Although it was over twenty years ago, it still hurts when I think about it.

A different case in point was that of a Michigan state senator who began to criticize his fellow senators for overspending tax dollars for refurbishing the Senate offices in Lansing. He reported to the news media that he experienced exactly these four stages as his colleagues tried to stop him from revealing their indulgences. He did not conform, however, because of the overwhelming support from his constituents, who believed that he was right.

Janis (1982, p. 9) has conducted a thorough investigation of the problems that conformity pressure brought to some major American historical events. He refers to the results as *groupthink,* which he defines as

> a quick and easy way to refer to a mode of thinking that people engage in when they are deeply involved in a cohesive in-group, when the members' strivings for unanimity override their motivation to realistically appraise alternative courses of action.

Janis cites several major political decisions that were characterized by groupthink, including the escalation of the Vietnam war and the 1961 American invasion of Cuba (the Bay of Pigs). Although he did not include it in his book, Watergate was another example that fits his definition. (The 1987 Iran-Contra arms scandal may also be another example.)

Groupthink tends to occur when several factors are operating at once. These are called the symptoms of groupthink, and they can occur in any group. The eight symptoms are summarized below.

Type I: Overestimations of the group—its power and morality

1. An illusion of invulnerability, shared by most or all of the members, which creates excessive optimism and encourages taking extreme risks.
2. An unquestioned belief in the group's inherent morality, inclining the members to ignore the ethical or moral consequences of their decisions.

Type II: Closed-mindedness

3. Collective efforts to rationalize in order to discount warnings or other information that might lead the members to reconsider their assumptions before they recommit themselves to their past policy decisions.
4. Stereotyped views of enemy leaders as too evil to warrant genuine attempts to negotiate, or as too weak and stupid to counter whatever risky attempts are made to defeat their purposes.

"I'm awfully sorry. Dick. but we've all just had a little meeting. and we've agreed that perhaps it's best that you leave the commune."

Drawing by Weber: © 1973 The New Yorker Magazine, Inc.

Type III: Pressures toward uniformity

5. Self-censorship of deviations from the apparent group consensus, reflecting each member's inclination to minimize to himself the importance of his doubts and counterarguments.

6. A shared illusion of unanimity concerning judgments conforming to the majority view (partly resulting from self-censorship of deviations, augmented by the false assumption that silence means consent).

7. Direct pressure on any member who expresses strong arguments against any of the group's stereotypes, illusions, or commitments, making clear that this type of dissent is contrary to what is expected of all loyal members.

8. The emergence of self-appointed mindguards—members who protect the group from adverse information that might shatter their shared complacency about the effectiveness and morality of their decisions. (Janis, 1982, pp. 174–175)

For corrective measures for avoiding groupthink, see the article by Janis at the end of this chapter.

Certain groups are particularly vulnerable to groupthink. Those with members who are high in need for affiliation (see Chapter 2); those that are very cohesive (see Chapter 7); or those that have an autocratic leadership style (see this chapter) are likely candidates. However, there are procedures that can be employed to minimize the possibilities of groupthink (Janis 1982, pp. 260–276). Some of these precautions are:

- Assign one member to be the "devil's advocate" or critical evaluator to allow disagreements and criticism of the leader.

- Leaders should not reveal their preferences to the group at the beginning of the discussion.

- Several groups with different leaders can work independently on common problems to offer different perspectives.

- Group members should discuss the group's processes with trusted friends and report their reactions to the group.

- Outside experts should be called in periodically as resource persons. They should be encouraged to disagree with the group's assumptions.

- Whenever issues involve relations with rival groups (e.g., labor and management) time should be spent discussing all warning signals from the rivals and hypothesizing alternative "scenarios of the rivals' intentions."

- After preliminary decisions have been reached, the group should adjourn and hold a "second chance" meeting at a later date to let their ideas "incubate."

Although these suggestions may not always be applicable (even if they are, they may not always work), they do offer a constructive alternative to reduce the dangers of groupthink.

GROUP DEVELOPMENT

A number of writers have been interested in the social influence process as it is manifested in different stages or phases of group development. Group development seems to be partly the result of individual psychological needs and partly the result of the social influences manifested in the group. The various theories on group phases are somewhat incompatible, in that some writers identify three phases and others identify four. Also, some writers identify the phases that occur during the course of one group discussion (Tuckman 1965; Fisher 1980), while others identify the phases that occur over the course of the life of a group, including several meetings (Bennis and Shepard 1956; Thelen and Dickerman 1949). Still another viewpoint is that the phases occur in each meeting and continue to occur throughout the group's life history (Schutz 1958; Bales and Strodbeck 1951). This last viewpoint seems the most profound in providing insight into the phenomenon of group development.

With these differing frames of reference in mind, let us look at the four group phases that seem representative of the literature. *Phase one* (orientation) seems to be a period in which group members simply try to break the ice and begin to find out enough about one another to have some common basis for functioning. It is variously referred to as a period of orientation, inclusion, or group formation. In this phase people ask questions about one another, tell where they are from, what they like and dislike, and generally make small talk. An excerpt from a student paper reveals this:

> Even though we had a task to accomplish for the class, we began by talking about ourselves (one guy and girl found they both liked moto-cross racing, and two others found that they had both been to Daytona Beach last spring vacation). After we had a chance to "break the ice" we were more willing to throw out ideas on how to go ahead with the group project without being afraid of having our ideas shot down in flames.

Phase one seems to be characterized by the establishing of some minimal social relationship before group members feel comfortable getting down to work. However, some executives who have experienced many years of decision-making meetings may begin work with little or no social orientation, and only the barest minimum of group orientation. With these exceptions, the vast majority of us feel better having some period to build relationships prior to launching into the group's work.

Phase two (conflict) is frequently characterized by conflict of some kind or another. After the orientation phase passes, the pressure to accomplish something sooner or later intensifies whatever differences may exist. This student's description illustrates the transition from phase one to phase two:

> We talked about personal interests until some common ground was established, then we found we could talk about the assignment more freely. But after talking about nonsubject things, it was hard to keep the line of talk on the problems at hand. Some wanted to get the assignment accomplished while two guys in the group continually swayed the conversation to things that were easier to talk about, but had nothing to do with the subject (Howard has a big thing for John Deere farm machinery). At first we were constantly trying not to hurt anyone's feelings, so we let the conversation drift. We didn't question or reject each other's ideas, and I feel we often settled for less than we should have. The longer we were in the group together, the more we got to know each other and the more times we voiced our real opinions. That's when the tempers started to flare!

Typically, in phase two the group begins to thrash out decisions for procedures as well as for determining the solution to the group task. Conflict over procedures may be one way in which group members fight for influence or control in the group.

After a period of small talk in one middle-aged encounter group, one member suggested that they go around the group and introduce themselves in some detail, telling what their jobs were, what part of the country they were from, and so on. Just as they were about to begin, another member suggested that they *not* tell these things, to avoid the stereotyping that would inevitably result. A heated argument resulted. Eventually they decided to assume their fantasized identities—that is, they adopted nicknames and behaviors and job titles that represented the type of person they wished they could be. Much later in the group they decided that the new procedure had been much better in helping them to try out behaviors they normally would have been too inhibited to attempt. For example, one female psychiatrist assumed the identity of "Bubbles," a cocktail waitress, since she had always wondered what it would be like to be a sex object and get outside her role as a professional person. The conflict regarding procedures turned out to be very productive for the group in the long run.

Phase three (emergence) involves a resolution of the conflict experienced in phase two. Group cohesiveness begins to emerge and the group settles in to working more comfortably as a unit. This phase is described by three different sources in the following ways.

> Perhaps the major pitfall to be avoided at this point is that of glossing over significant differences for the sake of harmony ... behavior is essentially a kind of polite behavior which avoids upsetting the group. (Thelen and Dickerman 1949)

> Resistance is overcome in the third stage in which ingroup feeling and cohesiveness develop, new standards evolve, and new roles are adopted. In the task realm, intimate, personal opinions are expressed. (Tuckman 1965)

> Social conflict and dissent dissipate during the third phase. Members express fewer unfavorable opinions toward decision proposals. The coalition of individuals who had opposed those proposals which eventually achieve consensus also weakens in the third phase. (Fisher 1974)

Phase four (reinforcement) is the phase of maximum productivity and consensus. Dissent has just about disappeared and the rule of the moment is to pat each other on the back for having done such a good job. Group members joke and laugh and generally reinforce each other for having contributed to the group's success. Student reactions to a group project in this phase include the following typical comments: "At first I thought this assignment would be a waste of time, but now I think it was the most worthwhile thing we have done in the course so far." "Everybody I have talked to feels like the group exercise was really good. We are looking forward to doing more of these."

Psychologically, we all need to feel that what we do is somehow justified or worthwhile (this is referred to in Chapter 3 as rationalizing or reducing cognitive dissonance). Thus, even if we have had bad experiences with a group, we tend to repress those and remember the good things we have experienced. The various group development theories are summarized in the chart in Figure 4.12 and in the following quotation from the earliest of the group development theorists (Thelen and Dickerman 1949, p. 316):

> Beginning with individual needs for finding security and activity in a social environment, we proceed first to emotional involvement of the individuals with each other, and second to the development of a group as a rather limited universe of interaction among individuals and as the source of individual security. We then find that security of position in the group loses its significance except that as the group attempts to solve problems it structures its activities in such a way that each individual can play a role which may be described as successful or not in terms of whether the group successfully solved the problem it had set itself.

FIGURE 4.12   SUMMARY OF LITERATURE ON GROUP PHASES.

	Phase 1	Phase 2	Phase 3	Phase 4
Thelen and Dickerman (1949)	Forming	Conflict	Harmony	Productivity
Bennis and Shepard (1956, 1961)	Dependence	Interdependence	Focused work	Productivity
Tuckman (1965)	Forming	Storming	Norming	Performing
Fisher (1980)	Orientation	Conflict	Emergence	Reinforcement
Bales and Strodbeck (1951)	Orientation	Evaluation		Control
Schutz (1958)	Inclusion	Control		Affection

Although Seeger (1983) argues that group phases do not really exist, Osborn and Harris (in Cathcart and Samovar, 1984) conclude:

> The consensus of numerous systematic observations in . . . group dynamics is that phases or cycle regularities exist in the natural development of small groups. . . .
>
>   It must be kept in mind that the phases are general patterns of development and not distinct stages neatly accomplished. In fact, it is frequently difficult to determine the end of one phase and the beginning of another. (p. 111)

THE SYSTEMS PERSPECTIVE

In this chapter we examined the complicated and fascinating questions of who influences whom and why. In the discussion of status and power we saw that the two go hand in hand; that is, high-status individuals tend to have more power. An obvious extension of this is the notion that due to differing group norms, different characteristics bring about status in different groups. On a football team, the best athlete has the most status. Among college professors, the smartest person usually has the most status. In street gangs, the toughest member typically has the highest status. And so it goes from one group to another.

A major portion of this chapter dealt with the issues of leadership and followership. Although these two are not always discussed together, they are interrelated. Here the systems principle of *equifinality* applies. In other words, the leadership style that would be appropriate in one situation with one set of followers may not be the most appropriate in a different situation with a different set of followers. A great deal of study has led to the belief that the democratic leadership style is the most likely to get the best results in a great many cases. However, our systems perspective reminds us that some situations point to the authoritarian style as the most appropriate. In situations involving life-or-death decisions, or in times of crisis requiring rapid decisions, the democratic approach may be too slow or simply impractical. As we saw earlier, two popular theoretical syntheses regarding leadership styles are offered by Fiedler (1967, 1974) and Hersey and Blanchard (1982). They each suggest a contingency theory of leadership. In other words, the best leadership style is one flexible enough to adapt to the situation. If asked which leadership style is best, they would answer, "It depends."

This chapter also dealt with the topics of social influence and conformity. Systems theory concepts are beautifully illustrated in this literature. Conformity pressure differs depending on the type of group (for example, military vs. the commune), the style of leadership (say, authoritarian vs. democratic), the personalities of the group members (dominant vs. acquiescent), and a number of other factors. We know from the research literature that conformity is more likely (1) in a group in which membership is highly valued by its participants; (2) among members with dependent, obedient, and acquiescent personalities; (3) when the leader is more authoritarian; (4) when the group is unanimously against the deviant member; and (5) to produce public compliance than actual private acceptance. Conformity is clearly dependent on an entire constellation of other variables.

One study analyzed conformity in a systems way (although the authors did not identify their analysis as a systems analysis). Rarick, Soldow, and Geizer (1976) looked at conformity as a result of the combination of the person's personality and the situation in which he or she is placed. The personality variable was self-confidence (they call it self-monitoring) and the situational variable was group size (dyad or three- to six-person group). They found that less confident people conform more in three- to six-person groups than highly confident people. This confirms numerous previous findings. However, they also found that in a dyad, confident people did not conform any more or less than those lacking in confidence. This study very nicely illustrates the systems perspective that all these variables (and others) simultaneously influence one another.

The last section of this chapter dealt with group development. We know that groups go through some fairly common phases, depending on the type of group. As we saw earlier, some writers assume that all the phases occur during the course of one group discussion. Other writers believe that these phases evolve slowly over the group's lifetime. However, the systems theory approach would agree with writers such as Schutz (1958) and Bales and Strodbeck (1951) that these phases are simply parts of a recurring *cycle* of events that probably occur during a single meeting and tend to be repeated throughout the group's lifetime as well. This point of view seems to be the most theoretically valid and is supported by other authors who apply the systems approach to the analysis of small group interaction (see, for example, Fisher and Hawes, 1971).

EXERCISES

1. Leadership Case Studies

Break into small groups and discuss one of the following leadership case studies. Attempt to reach agreement on one of the five comments on the case. Have each group report its choice to the class and the reasons for the choice. What issues in leadership from Chapter 4 are illustrated in these cases?

Case A   In the men's sportswear department of the Arcade Department Store, two men and four women are employed regularly as sales personnel. In addition to salary they receive a bonus determined by the amount by which the individual's daily volume of sales exceeds a quota. Mr. Stone, the buyer, is head of the department, but during his frequent absences his assistant buyer, Mr. Jones, is in charge. In addition to the six regulars, the department also employs several extra salespersons during the summer. These are college students on vacation who have been given some training by the store's personnel department. They are eager beavers and often outsell the regulars. They also work for a salary plus a bonus.

During Mr. Stone's absence on a buying trip the regulars complained to Mr. Jones that the extras were making it difficult for them to make their quotas, that they mixed up the stock and generally were a nuisance. Mr. Jones, a close personal friend of one of the regulars, ordered the extras to take care of the stock and to sell only when customers were waiting. On his return, Mr. Stone countermanded this order; he told the extras to get in there and sell or look for other jobs. A competitive spirit, he said, was good for the department. The regulars are now more resentful than ever; customers are beginning to notice the bad feeling, and some of them have taken their trade elsewhere.

Which one of the following comments on this situation seems to you most sound?

1. Mr. Stone should return to the position taken earlier by his assistant: that is, instruct the extras to work on stock and handle customers only when no regular is free to do so.

2. In addition to telling the extras to sell to the top of their capacity, Mr. Stone should call the regulars in, take a firm stand with them, and advise them to increase their sales or look elsewhere for work.

3. Mr. Stone is right; a competitive spirit is good for the department. Beyond making this point clear, he should continue to have a hands-off policy and let the situation work itself out.

4. Mr. Stone should put the extras on a straight hourly basis of compensation.

5. Mr. Stone should investigate the activities of the extras and the sales methods and compensation plan of all employees.

Case B   Mr. Welty, publisher of a newspaper, employs a total staff of about 200. He prides himself on the high morale among his employees and on their loyalty to him and to the paper. "You may call my kind of management paternalism," he once said, "but I know all of my employees personally and don't have to buy their friendship and loyalty." Though unaware that he had any personnel problem, Mr. Welty had a personnel consultant make a survey and evaluation of the organization.

To his astonishment, Mr. Welty learned that in the pressroom morale was very low, that nearly all of the 38 employees there had bitter feelings against the foreman, Harry Fitzpatrick. They considered him arbitrary, vindictive, and indifferent to their welfare. As evidence of his indifference, they pointed to the deplorable condition of the locker room. Six of the apprentices, former servicemen, were especially sour on Fitzpatrick. He was down on all ex-servicemen, they said, and constantly abused and insulted them.

Shocked by these disclosures, Mr. Welty toured the pressroom and locker room with Fitzpatrick, putting questions to some of the workmen. He then ordered the locker room repaired and cleaned up, and in a long talk with Fitzpatrick reprimanded him sharply. After 23 years with the firm and 13 as foreman, he insisted, Fitzpatrick should know better than to treat employees in that way.

A few months later, on again checking the situation in the pressroom, Mr. Welty found no improvement in employee morale and no improvement in Fitzpatrick's relationship with the workmen. Obviously something more drastic than a verbal reprimand was necessary. Reluctant to dismiss Fitzpatrick, Mr. Welty appointed an acting foreman for the pressroom and for a one-year period assigned Fitzpatrick to supervise the installation of new presses in another part of the plant. "This may be a cowardly decision," he admitted to himself, "but a lot can happen in a year and I'll cross that bridge when I come to it a year from now."

How should Mr. Welty have handled this situation?

1. Exactly as he did. In the course of a year something may well happen to solve the problem.

2. He should have transferred Fitzpatrick for one year to the new job of installing presses but with the understanding that he would not again be foreman of the pressroom.

3. He should have transferred him to the new job for a year, trying in the meantime to help him improve as a foreman, but leaving open the question of what to do with him at the end of the year.

4. He should have fired Fitzpatrick immediately on making the second checkup.

5. He should have kept Fitzpatrick as a journeyman printer, if he cared to stay, but should have relieved him of the foremanship.

2. Interaction Analysis Exercise

Observe a group discussion and try to use the Bales Interaction Process Analysis scoring sheet (Figure 4.13) to make your observations more systematic. Start by observing and recording only one person in the group. Simply place a check mark in the appropriate row when a person says something in the group. As

FIGURE 4.13   BALES INTERACTION PROCESS ANALYSIS SCORING SHEET.

Scoring of Interaction (Bales)	Person 1	Person 2	Person 3	Row totals
1. *Seems friendly,* raises other's status, gives help, reward				
2. *Dramatizes,* jokes, laughs, shows satisfaction				
3. *Agrees,* shows passive acceptance, understands, concurs, complies				
4. *Gives suggestions,* direction, implying autonomy for other				
5. *Gives opinion,* evaluation, analysis, expresses feeling, wish				
6. *Gives information,* repeats, clarifies, confirms				
7. *Asks for information,* repetition, confirmation				
8. *Asks for opinion,* evaluation analysis, expresses feeling				
9. *Asks for suggestion,* direction, possible ways of action				
10. *Disagrees,* shows passive rejection, formality, withholds help				
11. *Shows tension,* asks for help, withdraws "out of field"				
12. *Seems unfriendly,* deflates other's status, defends or asserts self				
Column totals				

you gain more experience, record two or three group members. You may also want to try having several people observe the same person to check the reliability of your observations.

3. Group Development Exercise

Observe a real-life problem-solving group. Listen carefully for statements that indicate the four phases of group development. You might take notes to record exact statements that illustrate the four phases. Notice also if the group does *not* seem to go through these four phases. Compare your observations with others who have observed different groups. Do most of the observations correspond to the research findings?

READINGS: OVERVIEW

In the first article, Hersey and Blanchard offer further elaboration on how to identify the maturity of group members, which influences the choice of an appropriate leadership style.

The second article, by Irving Janis, describes a classic social influence phenomenon. The description of the ways to prevent "groupthink" provide a bit more depth for ways in which groups can improve their performance.

Situational Leadership

Paul Hersey
Kenneth H. Blanchard

The need for a significant Situational Model in the leadership area has been recognized in the literature for some time.

A. K. Korman, in his extensive review of studies examining the Ohio State concepts of Initiating Structure and Consideration, concluded that:

> What is needed . . . in future concurrent (and predictive) studies is not just recognition of this factor of "situational determinants" but, rather, a systematic conceptualization of situational variance as it might relate to leadership behavior [Initiating Structure and Consideration].

In discussing this conclusion, Korman suggests the possibility of a curvilinear relationship rather than a simple linear relationship between Initiating Structure (task behavior) and Consideration (relationship behavior) and other variables. Situational Leadership, which is an outgrowth of our Tri-Dimensional Leader Effectiveness Model, has identified such a curvilinear relationship.

Situational Leadership is based on an interplay among (1) the amount of guidance and direction (task behavior) a leader gives; (2) the amount of socio-emotional support (relationship behavior) a leader provides; and (3) the readiness ("maturity") level that followers exhibit in performing a specific task, function or objective. This concept was developed to help people attempting leadership, regardless of their role, to be more effective in their daily interactions with others. It provides leaders with some understanding of the relationship between an effective style of leadership and the level of maturity of their followers.

Thus, while all the situational variables (leader, follower(s), superior(s), associates, organization, job demands, and time) are important, the emphasis in Situational Leadership will be on the behavior of a leader in relation to followers. As Fillmore H. Sanford has indicated, there is some justification for regarding the followers "as the most crucial factor in any leadership event." Followers in any situation are vital, not only because as a group they actually determine whatever personal power the leader may have. . . .

When discussing leader/follower relationships, we are not necessarily talking about a hierarchical relationship, that is, superior/subordinate. The same caution will hold during our discussion of Situational Leadership. *Thus, any reference to leader(s) or follower(s) in this theory should imply potential leader and potential follower.* As a result, although our examples may suggest a hierarchical relationship, the concepts presented in Situational Leadership should have application no matter whether you are attempting to influence the behavior of a subordinate, your boss, an associate, a friend, or a relative.

Maturity of the Followers or Group

Maturity is defined in Situational Leadership as the ability and willingness of people to take responsibility for directing their own behavior. *These variables of maturity should be considered only in relation to a specific task to be performed.* That is to say, an individual or a group is not mature or immature in any *total* sense. All persons tend to be more or less mature in relation to a specific task, function, or objective that a leader is attempting to accomplish through their efforts. Thus, a saleswoman may be very responsible in securing new sales but very casual about completing the paperwork necessary to close on a sale. As a result, it is appropriate for her manager to leave her alone in terms of closing on sales but to supervise her closely in terms of her paperwork until she can start to do well in that area too.

In addition to assessing the level of maturity of individuals within a group, a leader may have to assess the maturity level of the group as a group, particularly if the group interacts frequently together in the same work area, as happens with students in the classroom. Thus, a teacher may find that a class as a group may be at one level of maturity in a particular area, but a student within that group may be at a different level. When the teacher is one-to-one with that student, he or she may have to behave very differently than when working with the class as a group. In reality, the teacher may find a number of students at various maturity levels. For example, the teacher may have one student who is not doing his work regularly; when he turns work in, it is poorly organized and not very academic. With that student, the teacher may have to initiate some structure and supervise closely. Another student, however, may be doing good work but is insecure and shy. With that student, the teacher may not have to engage in much task behavior in terms of schoolwork but may need to be supportive, to engage in two-way communication, and help facilitate the student's interaction with others in the class. Still another student may be psychologically mature as well as competent in her schoolwork, and thus can be left on her own. So leaders have to understand that they may have to behave differently one-on-one with members of their group from the way they do with the group as a whole.

Basic Concept of Situational Leadership

According to Situational Leadership, there is no one best way to influence people. Which leadership style a person should use with individuals or groups depends on the maturity level of the people the leader is attempting to influence, as illustrated in Figure 1.

Style of Leader versus Maturity of Follower(s)

The attempt in Figure 1 is to portray the relationship between task-relevant maturity and the appropriate leadership styles to be used as followers move from immaturity to maturity. As indicated, the reader should keep in mind that the figure represents two different phenomena. The appropriate leadership style (*style of leader*) for given levels of follower maturity is portrayed by the prescrip-

FIGURE 1   SITUATIONAL LEADERSHIP.

tive curve going through the four leadership quadrants. This bell-shaped curve is called a *prescriptive curve* because it shows the appropriate leadership style directly above the corresponding level of maturity.

Each of the four leadership styles—"telling," "selling," "participating," and "delegating"—identified in Figure 1, is a combination of task and relationship behavior. . . . Task behavior is the extent to which a leader provides direction for people: telling them what to do, when to do it, where to do it, and how to do it. It means setting goals for them and defining their roles.

Relationship behavior is the extent to which a leader engages in two-way communication with people: providing support, encouragement, "psychological strokes," and facilitating behaviors. It means actively listening to people and supporting their efforts.

The maturity of followers is a question of degree. As can be seen in Figure 1, some bench marks of maturity are provided for determining appropriate leadership style by dividing the maturity continuum below the leadership model into four levels: low (M1), low to moderate (M2), moderate to high (M3), and high (M4).

The appropriate leadership style for each of the four maturity levels includes the right combination of task behavior (direction) and relationship behavior (support).

"Telling" Is for Low Maturity   People who are both *unable and unwilling* (M1) to take responsibility to do something are not competent or confident. In many cases, their unwillingness is a result of their *insecurity* regarding the necessary task. Thus, a directive "telling" style (S1) that provides clear, specific directions and supervision has the highest probability of being effective with individuals at this maturity level. This style is called "telling" because it is characterized by the leader's defining roles and telling people what, how, when, and where to do various tasks. It emphasizes directive behavior. Too much supportive behavior with people at this maturity level may be seen as permissive, easy and, most importantly, as rewarding of poor performance. This style involves high task behavior and low relationship behavior.

"Selling" Is for Low to Moderate Maturity   People who are *unable but willing* (M2) to take responsibility are confident but lack skills at this time. Thus, a "selling" style (S2) that provides directive behavior, because of their lack of ability, but also supportive behavior to reinforce their willingness and enthusiasm appears to be most appropriate with individuals at this maturity level. This style is called "selling" because most of the direction is still provided by the leader. Yet, through two-way communication and explanation, the leader tries to get the followers psychologically to "buy into" desired behaviors. Followers at this maturity level will usually go along with a decision if they understand the reason for the decision and if their leader also offers some help and direction. This style involves high task behavior and high relationship behavior.

"Participating" Is for Moderate to High Maturity   People at this maturity level are *able but unwilling* (M3) to do what the leader wants. Their unwillingness is often a function of their lack of confidence or *insecurity*. If, however, they are competent but unwilling, their reluctance to perform is more of a motivational problem than a security problem. In either case, the leader needs to open the door (two-way communication and active listening) to support the follower's efforts to use the ability he already has. Thus, a supportive, nondirective, "participating" style (S3) has the highest probability of being effective with individuals at this maturity level. This style is called "participating" because the leader and follower share in decision making, with the main role of the leader being facilitating and communicating. This style involves high relationship behavior and low task behavior.

"Delegating" Is for High Maturity   People at this maturity level are both *able and willing, or confident,* to take responsibility. Thus, a low-profile "delegating" style (S4), which provides little direction or support, has the highest probability of being effective with individuals at this maturity level. Even though the leader may still identify the problem, the responsibility for carrying out plans is given to these mature followers. They are permitted to run the show and decide on the how, when, and where. At the same time, they are psychologically mature and therefore do not need above average amounts of two-way communication or supportive behavior. This style involves low relationship behavior and low task behavior.

It should be clear that the appropriate leadership style for all four of the maturity designations—low maturity (M1), low to moderate maturity (M2), moderate to high maturity (M3), and high maturity (M4)—correspond to the following leadership style designations: *telling* (S1), *selling* (S2), *participating* (S3), and *delegating* (S4). That is, low maturity needs a *telling* style, low to moderate needs a *selling* style, and so on. These combinations are shown in Table 1.

In using the shorthand designations (S1, S2, S3, S4) and labels ("telling," "selling," "participating," and "delegating") for leadership styles that are identified in Figure 1 and Table 1, one must keep in mind that they should only be used when referring to behaviors represented by the effective face of the Tri-Dimensional Leader Effectiveness Model. However, when discussing basic or ineffective styles, we shall refer to them only by quadrant number: Q1, Q2, Q3, or Q4. For example, when a low relationship/low task style is used appropriately with the corresponding maturity level M4, it will be referred to as S4 or "delegating." But when that same style is used inappropriately with any of the other three maturity levels, it will only be called Q4 and might be better described as abdication or withdrawal rather than "delegating."

Situational Leadership not only suggests the high probability leadership style for various maturity levels, but it also indicates the probability of success of the other style configurations if a leader is unable to use the desired style. The probability of success of each style for the four maturity levels, depending on how far the style is from the high probability style along the prescriptive curve in the style of leader portion of the model, is as follows:

M1   S1 high, S2 2nd, Q3 3rd, Q4 low probability
M2   S2 high, S1 2nd, S3 2nd, Q4 low probability
M3   S3 high, S2 2nd, S4 2nd, Q1 low probability
M4   S4 high, S3 2nd, Q2 3rd, Q1 low probability

In indicating the probability of success of each style above, in some cases the "S" designation was used for a style, and in other cases the "Q" designation was used. As discussed, the shorthand designations (S1, S2, S3, S4) and labels ("telling," "selling," "participating," and "delegating") should only be used when referring to behaviors represented by the effective face of the Tri-Dimensional Leader Effectiveness Model. Thus, the high probability style and the 2nd (secondary) styles were indicated by an "S" designation, while the 3rd and low probability styles were indicated by a "Q" designation. In most cases, there are at least two leadership styles in the effective range. At the same time, there are usually one or two leadership styles that are clearly in the less effective range.

TABLE 1   LEADERSHIP STYLES APPROPRIATE FOR VARIOUS MATURITY LEVELS

Maturity Level	Appropriate Style
M1 *Low Maturity* Unable and unwilling or insecure	S1 *Telling* High task and low relationship behavior
M2 *Low to Moderate Maturity* Unable but willing or confident	S2 *Selling* High task and high relationship behavior
M3 *Moderate to High Maturity* Able but unwilling or insecure	S3 *Participating* High relationship and low task behavior
M4 *High Maturity* Able/competent and willing/confident	S4 *Delegating* Low relationship and low task behavior

Preventing Groupthink

Irving L. Janis

1. *The leader of a policy-forming group should assign the role of critical evaluator to each member, encouraging the group to give high priority to airing objections and doubts. This practice needs to be reinforced by the leader's acceptance of criticism of his or her own judgments in order to discourage the members from softpedaling their disagreements.*

2. *The leaders in an organization's hierarchy, when assigning a policy-planning mission to a group, should be impartial instead of stating preferences and expectations at the outset. This practice requires each leader to limit his or her briefings to unbiased statements about the scope of the problem and the limitations of available resources, without advocating specific proposals he or she would like to see adopted. This allows the conferees the opportunity to develop an atmosphere of open inquiry and to explore impartially a wide range of policy alternatives.*

3. *The organization should routinely follow the administrative practice of setting up several independent policy-planning and evaluation groups to work on the same policy question, each carrying out its deliberations under a different leader.*

4. *Throughout the period when the feasibility and effectiveness of policy alternatives are being surveyed, the policy-making group should from time to time divide into two or more subgroups to meet separately, under different chairpersons, and then come together to hammer out their differences.*

5. *Each member of the policy-making group should discuss periodically the group's deliberations with trusted associates in his or her own unit of the organization and report back their reactions.*

6. *One or more outside experts or qualified colleagues within the organization who are not core members of the policy-making group should be invited to each meeting on a staggered basis and should be encouraged to challenge the views of the core members.*

7. *At every meeting devoted to evaluating policy alternatives, at least one member should be assigned the role of devil's advocate.*

8. *Whenever the policy issue involves relations with a rival nation or organization, a sizable block of time (perhaps an entire session) should be spent surveying all warning signals from the rivals and constructing alternative scenarios of the rivals' intentions.*

9. *After reaching a preliminary consensus about what seems to be the best policy alternative, the policy-making group should hold a "second chance" meeting at*

From Irving L. Janis, Groupthink, 2nd ed. (Boston: Houghton Mifflin, 1982), pp. 260–276. Copyright © 1982 by Houghton Mifflin Company. Adapted by permission of the publisher.

which the members are expected to express as vividly as they can all their residual doubts and to rethink the entire issue before making a definitive choice.

Is a Little Knowledge of Groupthink a Dangerous Thing?

Even if we had more than a little knowledge of groupthink, my answer to this question would be a categorical "yes" if we have in mind a naive person in a position of power who might be led to believe that groupthink is the only major source of error in policy-making and therefore that decisions can be made better by just one man (notably himself) than by a group of colleagues. I would also answer "yes" if I thought that a substantial number of policy-makers might be misled into believing that preventing groupthink should be given high priority, so that all sorts of safeguards should be introduced into the decision-making process without regard for hidden costs. Finally, I would wearily say "yes" if I discovered that many executives were being subjected to a lot of nonsense from overly eager faddists on their staff who were taking up precious time trying to introduce some kind of group therapy in the conference room, like an earlier generation of faddists who tried to inflict parlor-room psychoanalysis on their friends.

But my answer is "no" for anyone who takes the trouble to examine the fragmentary evidence on which I have drawn inferences about the conditions that give rise to groupthink. My two main conclusions are that along with other sources of error in decision-making, groupthink is likely to occur within cohesive small groups of decision-makers and that the most corrosive effects of groupthink can be counteracted by eliminating group insulation, overly directive leadership practices, and other conditions that foster premature consensus. Those who take these conclusions seriously will probably find that the little knowledge they have about groupthink increases their understanding of the causes of erroneous group decisions and sometimes even has some practical value in preventing fiascoes. (If I didn't think so, I wouldn't have bothered to write this chapter.)

A little knowledge of groupthink might be valuable for anyone who participates in a group that makes policy decisions, whether it is the executive committee of an international organization, an ad hoc committee set up by a government agency, the steering committee of a local business, professional, or political organization, or a student committee at a college. Such knowledge can be especially useful if it inclines the participants to consider introducing antidote prescriptions, provided, of course, that they are aware of the costs in time and effort and realize that there are other disadvantages they must also watch out for before they decide to adopt any of them as a standard operating procedure.

Sometimes it may even be useful for one of the members of the group to ask, at the right moment, before a decision is definitely made, "Are we allowing ourselves to become victims of groupthink?" I am not proposing that this question should be placed on the agenda or that the members should try to conduct a group therapy session. Rather, I have in mind making salient the realization that the desire for unity within the group can be discussed frankly and that agreement within the group is not always desirable. This open acknowledgment may enable some members to adopt a psychological set that inclines them to raise critical questions whenever there are signs of undue complacency or a premature consensus. One such question has to do with the consensus itself. A leader or a member who is aware of the symptoms of groupthink, for example, might ask to hear from those who have not yet said anything, in order to get all points of view onto the table before the group makes a final decision. In addition to this common-sense application, some ingenious procedures may be worked out or spontaneously improvised so that the symptoms of groupthink are counteracted by participants who know about the groupthink hypothesis, without constantly reminding the group of it.

With these considerations in mind, I suggest that awareness of the shared illusions, rationalizations, and other symptoms fostered by the interaction of members of small groups may curtail the influence of groupthink in policy-making groups, including those that meet in the White House. Here is another place where we can apply George Santayana's well-known adage: "Those who cannot remember the past are condemned to repeat it." Perhaps a better understanding of group dynamics among government leaders will help them avoid being condemned to repeat the fiascoes of the recent past described in this book.

Internal Influences

Communication Processes

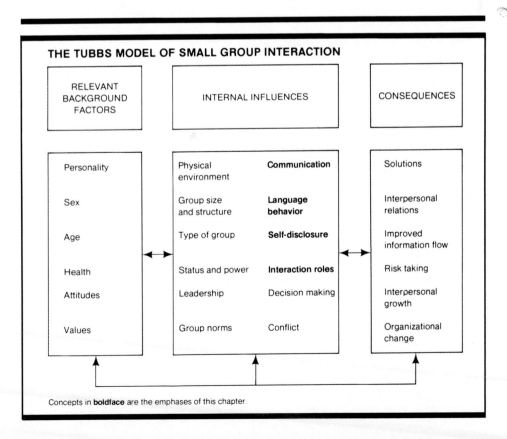

THE TUBBS MODEL OF SMALL GROUP INTERACTION

RELEVANT BACKGROUND FACTORS	INTERNAL INFLUENCES		CONSEQUENCES
Personality	Physical environment	**Communication**	Solutions
Sex	Group size and structure	**Language behavior**	Interpersonal relations
Age	Type of group	**Self-disclosure**	Improved information flow
Health	Status and power	**Interaction roles**	Risk taking
Attitudes	Leadership	Decision making	Interpersonal growth
Values	Group norms	Conflict	Organizational change

Concepts in **boldface** are the emphases of this chapter.

CASE STUDY

A committee of university faculty members were deciding whom to have vote on an important new policy statement. They had worked for several months to develop and refine this policy statement and they wanted to send a copy to all people in the university who would be affected by this policy. The committee had not anticipated any difficulty deciding whom to send the memo to. Then this problem occurred.

Prof. Brown: Now that we have all agreed on the final policy to be communicated, let's decide which method should be used to convey the policy.

Prof. Smith: Let's use an interorganization memo. (The group all agreed.) Let's send a ballot to each person through the faculty mail. (Again, general agreement.)

Prof. Brown: OK, the subject of the memo is adoption of the new faculty senate operating procedures, right? (General agreement.) All right, let's address this to all members of the faculty.

Prof. Jones: Whom are you including in the faculty?

Prof. Brown: That's obvious.

Prof. Jones: No, I don't think so. Are department chairmen included as faculty or are they administrators?

Prof. Brown: Well, they teach, don't they?

Prof. Jones: Yes, but they also serve as administrators.

Prof. Brown: What does it matter what category they go by?

Prof. Jones: OK, let me put it this way. Do the deans and the president qualify as faculty or administrators?

Prof. Thomas: Well, they are listed in the catalog as faculty.

Prof. Jones: OK; however, this policy is the first major step in allowing greater *faculty* governance at this school. How can we get greater faculty governance if we include members of the administration in our definition of faculty?

Prof. James: Yeh. What if it's a close vote and all the administrators vote as a block to defeat our new policy?

Prof. Brown: I still think we are making a mountain out of a molehill.

Prof. Jones: (Getting irritated.) We work for almost a year getting a faculty senate organized and now you think it's a trivial matter whether or not the proposal gets defeated?

Prof. Brown: I didn't say anything of the kind. I only meant that I think it is unlikely that the administration has enough votes to make much difference no matter how we define the term *faculty.*

Prof. Jones: Well, I strongly disagree. I think this is a *crucial* point. Are we, the faculty, going to have a hand in running this place once and for all, or are we going to let this little bit of progress be eroded by allowing administrators to vote on *our faculty senate?*

Prof. Smith: I'm afraid our time is running out for today's meeting. Since many of us have classes to go to I think we should table this discussion until our next meeting. In the meantime let's all try to rethink our positions on this.

Prof. Jones: I don't have to do any rethinking! If we are going to go back to being dictated to by the administration, I don't want any further part of this committee. I volunteered to be on this committee because I thought we had a chance to improve things around here. I can see now I have wasted my time.

Chairperson: Do I have a motion for adjournment?

Prof. Thomas: So moved.

Chairperson: Is there a second?

Prof. Smith: Second.

Chairperson: Meeting adjourned until next week.

1. What is the major problem for this group?

2. How could they have avoided this outcome?

3. If you could role play this discussion, what would you say to help resolve this situation?

This group discussion, which actually occurred, illustrates one type of problem groups may encounter: language-related problems and the relationship between language, thought, and behaviors. The committee members could not agree on how to interpret the word *faculty*. This disagreement led to emotional reactions and eventually to one member's resignation. This problem is just one type of difficulty related to problems of communication. But before we go any further, let us stop and define *our* terms so we don't run into the same problem this committee did.

COMMUNICATION

Communication Defined

Communication within the small group is both similar to and different from communication in other settings. Group communication involves the process of creating meanings in the minds of others. These meanings may or may not correspond to the meanings we intend to create. Group communication involves the sending and receiving of messages between and among the participants. Group communication includes both verbal and nonverbal message stimuli. In all these ways, group communication is similar to communication that occurs in other contexts, such as interpersonal communication (informal communication between two or more people); public communication (between a speaker and an audience); organizational communication (or communication in an organizational setting); or mass communication (in which a source attempts to communicate with large numbers of people, usually through some electronic or written medium). This chapter will focus on communication principles as they relate to the small group context.

Ruch and Goodman (1983) argue persuasively that communication skills are the most important skills of all for managers and leaders. They write:

> Our advice to chief executive officers in any business is to never settle for anything less than the best in communication. Don't put in position second-rate managers as professional communicators. Find the bright stars and give them room to grow and be creative. And then back them up and follow their judgment and instincts within the framework of their professional expertise. (p. 133)

Intentional–Unintentional

Most of the time we communicate for a purpose. It may be to get our point across, to persuade another, to prompt action, or simply to have fun. These types of messages are known as *intentional;* that is, we intend to communicate in order to achieve our purpose. However, we may also transmit messages that are unintentional. The slip of the tongue, or Freudian slip, is one well-known phenomenon. On October 15, 1986, Vice Admiral Poindexter of the U.S. Navy was interviewed by Bryant Gumbel on the *Today* show. Gumbel asked about the recent exposé on the so-called disinformation campaign to discredit Libya. Gumbel said: "Don't you think you have a credibility problem from this?" Admiral Poindexter replied: "I don't think I have any credibility at all." He obviously meant to say that he had no credibility *problem* at all. All of us can sympathize with a situation in which we say something quite different from what we had intended to say.

According to Freud, our id or pleasure center leads us to reveal what we really feel, while our ego, the rational data processing part of our personality, tends to limit or censor what we utter. When the id forces win out over the rational ego forces, the Freudian slip results. Ruch (1972) explains that Freudian slips may occur in the form of malapropisms and spoonerisms. A *malapropism* is an inappropriate use of a word that sounds similar to the correct word, for example, "I illiterate him from memory" for "eliminate"; "a progeny of learning" for "prodigy"; and "the cat sautées across the floor" for "saunters." Comedian Norm Crosby has made an art of using malapropisms as the basis for his humor.

It is also possible for a Freudian slip to occur in the form of a spoonerism. A *spoonerism* is the interchanging of sounds in two or more words. Some examples include "blushing crow" for "crushing blow" and "it is kistomary to cuss the bride," as stated by the groom's former girl friend. Freud (Ruch 1972, p. 102) stated that such unintentional verbal messages more than likely result when we are "distracted, confused, embarrassed, or simply not psychically engaged [or] when the thought is insufficiently worked out or the problem particularly complicated."

Unintentional messages may be transmitted by action as well as by words. The person who crosses his arms in front of him while rearing back in his chair may be unknowingly communicating his disapproval of events occurring in a group discussion. Frequently, group members will direct their remarks (through eye contact) to those members that they prefer, or that they feel have influence in the group. This is often done unconsciously and unintentionally.

The best-selling book *The Making of a Psychiatrist* (Viscott 1972) includes the description of a patient characterized by unintentional, compulsive gestures. Viscott (pp. 50–54) describes him in the following manner:

> "Mr. Parker, I'm going to be taking over from Dr. Meredith and I will try to be as helpful to you as I can. . . . " "Good, good," he said, reaching over and touching me on the knee with his hand, tapping me twice. . . .
>
> In order to control his inner world, Harold Parker had developed an intricate system of rituals which he repeated to ward off bad luck . . . he would touch something solid twice.
>
> "What do you think is going to happen with your company, Mr. Parker?" I asked.
>
> "I think things will turn out well, as they always do. It's a sound company." He tapped my desk twice again and smiled an artificial smile. . . .
>
> "I'm running it," said Harold Parker, tapping his right foot once. Once? Where's the second tap? I was pretty sure there would be another tap coming. There's *supposed* to be another tap coming. The first tap supposedly symbolizes a bad wish and the second supposedly erases it. Where was it? Maybe he didn't tap his foot magically at all. Maybe he just liked to tap his foot. Maybe I was reading a lot into all of this. Maybe this was all bullshit. Paying attention to so many details of a patient's behavior was trying.
>
> "You're running the company from here?"
>
> "I'm on the phone a couple of times a day to Edgar. He's my manager. That's how I'm running it." Mr. Parker tapped my desk twice.

This brief account illustrates one way in which actions can communicate without our even knowing it. This example also illustrates the potential pitfalls in trying to over-interpret or read too much into a person's verbal or nonverbal slips.

Communication is not one-way, especially in groups. Members react to messages. They respond to each other. This response is called *feedback*. Stech and Ratliffe (1985) say feedback is just as complicated as sending the message. Like the intended message, feedback also has content and relationship levels. Actually, when person 2 gives feedback to person 1, that feedback is actually person 2's intended message. In a continuing interaction, the two people continue to shift roles as sender and receiver, alternately providing each other with messages and feedback (p. 22).

Aronson (in Cathcart and Samovar 1984) points out that the value of feedback is not limited to the recipient.

> Frequently in providing feedback, a person discovers something about himself and his own needs. If a person feels, for example, that it's wrong to experience anger, he may block out his awareness of this feeling. When the expression of such feelings is legitimized, he has a chance to bring them out in the open, look at them, and to become aware that his expression of anger has not caused the world to come to an end. Moreover, the direct expression of a feeling keeps the encounter on the up-and-up and thus helps to prevent the escalation of negative feelings. (p. 336)

Groups are one context in which we get feedback on behaviors that helps us eliminate unintentional cues. The gap between what we intend to communicate and what is actually received is called the *arc of distortion* (Bennis 1961). The larger the gap, the less effective we are in our relations with others. We can reduce the gap if we are receptive to feedback from others, and if others are willing to share their impressions with us. In order for the arc to be reduced, the feedback must be of high quality. Miles (1967) suggests that effective feedback must "(1) be clear and undistorted, (2) come from a trusted nonthreatening source, and (3) follow as closely as possible the behavior to which it is a reaction."

Verbal–Nonverbal

As indicated above, we communicate not only with words (verbal messages), but by nonverbal means as well. In Chapter 3 we discussed the importance of environmental influences on small group interaction. Later in this chapter we will discuss verbal cues under the heading "Language Behavior." In addition, visual and vocal nonverbal cues will vary as a part of the process of discussion, and will influence the eventual results of the discussion.

Visual Cues

Visual cues are highly influential in interpersonal communication. *Facial expression* and *eye contact* are probably the two most important types of visual cues. Those who avoid looking at us communicate disapproval or disinterest. Those who look at us may still indicate a negative reaction, based on their facial expression. Probably the most rewarding cue is a smiling face and a head nod in combination with direct eye contact. From these and other cues we infer support, confirmation, and agreement. Knapp (1972, p. 119) emphasizes the importance of the face:

> The face is rich in communicative potential. It is the primary site for communication of emotional states; it reflects interpersonal attitudes; it provides nonverbal feedback on the comments of others; and some say it is the primary source of information next to human speech.

Barnlund (1968, p. 521) echoes this feeling:

> Of all the features that identify a man, none is as differentiating as his face; of all the parts of the body, none is as richly expressive.

Although facial expression is usually a critical factor in nonverbal communication, there are some rare occasions in which other factors may take precedence. Note the following news item:

> Los Angeles (AP) The braless robber has struck for the second time in two days. . . .
> Police said the robber, wearing a sheer blue blouse without a bra, robbed a South Pasa-

dena branch of the Bank of America of about $400 Tuesday. . . . On Monday, a person believed to be the same woman held up a Los Angeles savings and loan office and escaped with $2,600. Police said a red-faced teller was unable to describe the robber's face, noting only that she was braless under a light-colored blouse.

One study confirmed the finding that the general tendency to look into a person's eyes can be preempted by other factors. Wahlers and Barker (1973) conducted an interview study and found that braless women got significantly less eye contact from males than their bra-wearing counterparts.

Eye contact, however, is a powerful type of nonverbal cue. Argyle (1967) estimates that in group communication we spend between 30 and 60 percent of the time exchanging mutual glances with others. Many of these may last less than a second. He summarizes (pp. 115–116) several unstated rules about visual interaction:

a. A looker may invite interaction by staring at another person who is on the other side of a room. The target's studied return of the gaze is generally interpreted as acceptance of the invitation, while averting the eyes is a rejection of the looker's request.

b. There is more mutual eye contact between friends than others, and a looker's frank gaze is widely interpreted as positive regard.

c. Persons who seek eye contact while speaking are regarded not only as exceptionally well-disposed by their target, but also as more believable and earnest.

d. If the usual short, intermittent gazes during conversation are replaced by gazes of longer duration, the target interprets this as meaning that the task is less important than the personal relation between the two persons.

Several other principles have been borne out by experimental studies as well as by systematic observation of ongoing behaviors. For example, females consistently give more eye contact than males (Mehrabian 1969). Also, we are able to assert dominance over others almost exclusively with eye contact in a matter of seconds when we first encounter one another (Strongman and Champness 1968). We tend to direct our comments toward those from whom we expect or would like feedback (Kendon 1967). Conversely, avoiding eye contact is a way of protecting oneself from the contact of others. Argyle and Dean (1965) summarize the functions of eye contact by stating that it signals information seeking, openness to communication, concealment or exhibitionism, recognition of social relationships, and conflicts in motivation.

Hand gestures are another type of visual cue. Barnlund (1968) states, "Next to the face, the hands are probably the most expressive part of the human body." Entire books have been devoted to the study of the hands in oral communication. It was once thought that hand gestures could be taught as a means of developing greater expressiveness. For example, the outstretched hands with the palms up indicated a request for help, while the clenched fist indicated a threat. The study of gestures today is more descriptive, and leans less in the direction of trying to prescribe which gestures should be used in certain situations.

In one company, for example, a union grievance was filed based on a gesture of the employee's boss. The grievance charged:

> Animus toward the grievant can be demonstrated by the Department Head's handling of the application. . . . The application was tossed across the desk by the Department Head in the direction of the grievant. The Department Head's manner was offensive, embarrassing and unprofessional to both the grievant and the [union president]. (1986)

This grievance went through several steps of the grievance procedure and tied up dozens of hours of managerial time for the better part of a year. There were also threats of legal action.

Physical appearance includes facial attractiveness as well as body shape and size and styles of dress. In one study of physically attractive vs. unattractive people, Widgery (1974) found that on the basis of faces alone, more attractive people are consistently assumed to have higher credibility than their homely counterparts. Walster et al. (1966) found that among 752 college students at a freshman dance, physical attractiveness was by far the most important factor in determining the extent to which a date would be liked by his or her partner. Perhaps some homely soul rationalized this by creating the old saying:

> Beauty is only skin deep,
> But ugly's to the bone.
> Beauty soon will fade away,
> But ugly holds it own.

B. F. Skinner has argued that beauty is a form of reinforcer, since it encourages us to look once again. Certainly most fashion models of both sexes are reinforcing to look at!

As we saw in Chapter 4, body shape has been described in three basic categories by Sheldon (1954). The mesomorph is muscular and athletic looking and would be considered the most attractive. The ectomorph is tall, thin, and fragile looking. The endomorph is soft, round, and fat. Three representative examples of the respective body types would be Burt Reynolds, Don Knotts, and Buddy Hackett. Our body shapes are usually some mixture of these three types. Jack Lalanne, the famous physical fitness personality, once said on a television show that if you raid the refrigerator every night, even if you are alone, your body itself communicates to everybody every day that you eat too much. So you're not fooling anybody.

Styles of dress also communicate about us. We are often judged as "straight" or "punkers" based on our clothing choices. Lefkowitz, Blake, and Mouton (1955) conducted an interesting study of the influence of a person's dress on jaywalking behavior. They collected data on jaywalking on three different days for three different one-hour periods. They wanted to determine if pedestrians (these happened to be in Austin, Texas) would violate the "wait" signal more if they saw someone else violate it than if there were no violator. They were also interested in any differential effects that would result from differences in the violator's dress. The experimenters made use of a confederate who jaywalked while dressed one of two ways. First, he dressed in a high-status manner with a freshly pressed suit, shined shoes, white shirt, tie, and straw hat (Mr. Clean). The low-status dress consisted of an unpressed blue denim shirt, soiled and patched pants, well-worn shoes, and no hat (Mr. Dirty). Observations were made on 2103 pedestrians who crossed the intersection during the hours of the experiment.

The study revealed several interesting results. Ninety-nine percent of the pedestrians obeyed the "wait" signal when no confederate was present, or when the confederate also obeyed. When "Mr. Dirty" jaywalked, 4 percent of the other pedestrians also violated the signal. When "Mr. Clean" jaywalked, 14 percent of the other pedestrians also disobeyed. Some students replicated this study in 1973 and found quite similar results. Although these studies are dated, it is still valid today that a person with multicolored hair, or spiked hair and punk appearance would not get very far in a job interview in most companies.

To summarize, our appearance through facial attractiveness, body shape, and choice of clothing will determine to some extent our influence on others.

Body movements are also an influential type of nonverbal cue. Each of us can probably remember having someone say, "You seem kind of down today," as a reaction to our slumped shoulders and slightly bowed head. Probably one of Peter Falk's most memorable roles is his slouchy interpretation of the character Columbo. Although there are a wealth of other cues (gestures, raincoat, cigar), body movements stand out very vividly, as did John Wayne's swagger or Vanna White's walk.

Body orientation is an important factor in small group interaction. Knapp (1972, p. 97) defines body orientation as "the degree to which a communicator's shoulders and legs are turned in the direction of, rather than away from, the addressee." Mehrabian (1969) found that a seated communicator who leaned forward was perceived as having a more positive attitude than one who leaned backward and away from the person judging. Goffman (1961) noted that higher-status persons were more relaxed in staff meetings in a psychiatric hospital than lower-status individuals, who sat straighter in their chairs. Body position may also add to our perceiving a person as being "uptight." Schutz (1971, p. 212) describes this in the context of an encounter group.

> If a person is holding himself tight, I would either move on to someone else and count on the group interaction to loosen him up so that he can work better later, or perhaps choose to try to help him break through that defense. . . . A first step is to ask the person to relax by unlocking his arms and legs if he has them crossed, perhaps to stand up and shake himself loose, jiggle and breathe very deeply for several minutes.

Inclusiveness is another important aspect of body orientation. In a small group discussion, subgroups frequently form that are usually annoying to at least some in the group. Subgroups may be the result of one person directing comments to only one or two others. This term *directing comments* refers to body orientation and the direction of eye contact. Those who feel excluded from the discussion will sooner or later begin to withdraw their participation from the group, and the benefit of their contributions will be lost. Thus body orientation can be a potent factor in determining the discussion's outcome.

Vocal Cues

In addition to the verbal message and the visual cues, vocal cues affect small group interaction. There is usually some confusion between the terms *vocal cues* and *verbal cues.* Perhaps it would be helpful to remember that vocal cues are lost when a verbal (word) message is written down. Vocal cues include regional dialects, methods of pronunciation, and the five major factors of (1) volume, (2) rate and fluency, (3) pitch, (4) quality, and (5) inflection.

Try to imagine the sound of your voice saying, "Now that we are all here, we can get the meeting started." Now think of how it would sound as stated by Bill Cosby, Sammy Davis, Jr., David Brinkley, Humphrey Bogart, W. C. Fields, Elizabeth Taylor, Mae West, Mary Tyler Moore, Valerie Harper, or by some of your own friends. Each person's voice is unique; sometimes voice prints are used like fingerprints for identification. This individuality results from the complex combination of vocal cues mentioned above. Speaking with adequate *volume* or loudness is the first responsibility of any communicator. Conversely, the first responsibility of listeners is to let speakers know they can't be heard. Speakers should be asked to speak more loudly and to repeat the part that was missed (Tubbs and Moss 1986). This requires some tact, however. The intent should be to communicate, "I want to know what you're saying," rather than, "Listen, dummy, I'm important and you're not taking my listening convenience into sufficient account."

Groups tend to have more problems with adequate volume than, say, people involved in personal conversations. As the size of the group increases, the hearing difficulties may also increase, since there are more potential sources of interfering noise and the distance from the speaker to any given member in the group tends to be greater.

A second critical vocal cue is *rate and fluency.* Rate refers to words uttered per minute (WPM), and fluency refers to the lack of interruptions (which may influence the rate). We have all suffered the unpleasantness of listening to a person who injects long pauses in the middle of sentences, or who frequently throws in such distracting verbal fillers as "ah," "um," "er," "why I," "and-uh," "like," among others. An average speaking rate is between 125 and 175 words per minute. If the person is able to articulate well—that is, to speak distinctly—a faster rate seems to be more interesting to listen to. Studies in listener comprehension indicate that we can understand rates two and three times the normal speed with little difficulty. In group discussion, the fluent speaker is usually more pleasant to listen to.

Vocal *pitch* refers to the frequency in cycles per second (CPS) of the vocal tones. Mary Tyler Moore and Frank Perdue have high-pitched (or high-frequency) voices; John Wayne and Mae West had lower-pitched voices. There is probably no such thing as the perfectly pitched voice; however, most successful professional announcers seem to have lower-pitched voices.

Vocal *quality* refers to the resonance of the voice. Different examples would include breathiness (Connie Stevens), harshness (George C. Scott), nasality (Sylvester Stallone), and huskiness (Deborah Winger). Vocal quality may determine the extent to which people may want to listen to us for any length of time. Johnny Carson's laugh was once described as being "like the sound of cracking plastic." The voice of comedian Don Adams was once compared to "the sound of scratching your fingernail across a blackboard." On the other hand, some people who try to make their voices sound more deep and resonant come across as phony and artificial.

Inflection refers to the relative emphasis, pitch changes, and duration in uttering different word parts of words in a sentence. The American southerner's accent is characterized by a drawn-out vowel sound: for example, Atlanta (northern pronunciation) versus Atlaaanta (southern pronunciation). Inflections also include the rise in vocal pitch at the end of an interrogative sentence:

Are you coming?

Probably the most critical thing to remember about vocal inflections is that they may indicate a lot of the emotional tone of a statement. The statement "Oh, great" can be said with true enthusiasm or great disgust. We can use our voices to indicate sarcasm, ridicule, and superiority, and what we convey may be counterproductive to the group's progress.

Leathers (1976) reports that several emotions can be reliably detected in most speakers. He has groups of students rate ten different vocal messages according to the emotions they convey. The rating instructions are as shown in Figure 5.1. While Leathers's technique is for the purpose of research, the practical aspect is that vocal cues do accurately convey emotions. As we become more aware and in control of our nonverbal cues, we may improve our effectiveness in groups. For example, several students complained about a professor who was being quite abusive in his tone of voice to them. They were considering quitting his class because of this. When he was told, he was shocked. He had been unaware of the negative consequences his vocal tone had had on his teaching effectiveness.

Tessa Warschaw (1980) has developed a questionnaire designed to help us become more aware of our own nonverbal cues. She recommends monitoring your own behaviors in each of three settings: at home, at work (or at school if you are not working), and in social settings. Her guidelines are as shown in Figure 5.2.

Clearly, not all the cues in Figure 5.2 are exhibited in the small group setting. However, as we become more aware of our nonverbal behavior overall, we can begin to change some of these cues in situations that appear to need improvement. We can also begin to develop our sensitivities to the nonverbal behaviors of others. For example, if a meeting has been going on for a long time, you can detect tiredness and low level of energy through bored facial expressions, yawns, or unenthusiastic vocal tones. These cues may indicate that the group needs to take a break in order to continue at peak efficiency. But the person not sensitive to these cues may try to keep pushing a tired group, only to accomplish less and less.

In summarizing this section on verbal and nonverbal cues, we need to point out that all these cues are perceived as a whole. We do not dissect them in reality as we

FIGURE 5.1   THE VOCALIC MEANING SENSITIVITY TEST

Source: Reprinted with permission of the author from Dale Leathers, *Nonverbal Communication Systems* (Boston: Allyn and Bacon, 1976).

The communicator you are listening to—either live or on tape recording—is attempting to communicate ten different classes or kinds of meaning to you. Each attempt to communicate a class of meaning will begin with the words "This is vocal message number_____." You are to listen very carefully and place the number of the vocal message in the blank across from a word, such as disgust or happiness, which comes closest to representing the meaning which has just been communicated to you vocally. Follow the same procedure for each of the ten vocal messages.

Class of Vocalic Meaning	Number of Vocal Message
Disgust	_____
Happiness	_____
Interest	_____
Sadness	_____
Bewilderment	_____
Contempt	_____
Surprise	_____
Anger	_____
Determination	_____
Fear	_____

have done in this analysis. For example, it has been found that when we say one thing, but nonverbally indicate something else (for example, "I really appreciate that" spoken sarcastically), the *nonverbal* message is more likely to be believed (Keltner 1970). In this same context, subjects in one study who were told to lie showed several nonverbal changes. There were more errors in their speech, they had less direct eye contact, and talked for shorter durations than they had when they were telling the truth (Mehrabian 1971). Obviously, nonverbal communication plays a significant role in small groups. As one source puts it, whether you talk or not, "You can't *not* communicate" (Watzlawick, Beavin, and Jackson 1967). Let us keep in mind the importance of both verbal and nonverbal messages. This discussion has dealt mainly with nonverbal messages; the importance of verbal messages will be dealt with later in this chapter.

Defensive–Supportive

For several years it has been an established fact that when someone threatens you psychologically, you react by throwing up a barrier against that threat. That barrier is referred to as a *defense mechanism.* Once that defensive barrier has been erected,

FIGURE 5.2 YOUR SYMBOL-AND-SIGN INVENTORY

Source: From Tessa Warschaw, *Winning by Negotiation* (New York: McGraw-Hill, 1980), pp. 88–92. Reprinted by permission of McGraw-Hill Book Company; copyright 1980.

Our bodies give off different clues at different times. The signals we flash vary depending on whether the environment we're in is formal or informal. Whether we're at home or in the office, whether we're on public display or in a one-to-one encounter, whether the people we're with are known to us or strangers. To understand the effect we produce on others, we must first be aware of how we appear and react in different settings.

Following are lists of fifteen different aspects of ourselves through which we broadcast signals. Check the words that best describe your attitudes, manner, or physical response in each of three different settings—home, work, and social gatherings. Think about your answers. Take your time. Be objective.

Body

Home	Work	Social Setting	
____	____	____	tense
____	____	____	relaxed
____	____	____	drooping
____	____	____	mobile
____	____	____	athletic
____	____	____	stiff
____	____	____	graceful

Eyes

Home	Work	Social Setting	
____	____	____	downcast
____	____	____	squinting
____	____	____	roving
____	____	____	darting
____	____	____	expressive
____	____	____	staring
____	____	____	blinking

Overall Appearance

Home	Work	Social Setting	
____	____	____	calm
____	____	____	flamboyant
____	____	____	casual
____	____	____	conservative
____	____	____	femme fatale
____	____	____	macho male
____	____	____	negligent

Eye Contact

Home	Work	Social Setting	
____	____	____	direct
____	____	____	indirect
____	____	____	avoiding
____	____	____	confrontive
____	____	____	seductive
____	____	____	scrutinizing
____	____	____	glancing

FIGURE 5.2   YOUR SYMBOL-AND-SIGN INVENTORY (Continued)

Hand Movement

Home	Work	Social Setting	
___	___	___	constant hand movement
___	___	___	on body or shaping the air
___	___	___	appropriate gestures
___	___	___	rubbing together
___	___	___	covering mouth
___	___	___	pounding table or backs
___	___	___	finger pointing
___	___	___	no movement

Handshake

Home	Work	Social Setting	
___	___	___	cordial
___	___	___	firm and responsive
___	___	___	quick and wet
___	___	___	brotherhood/sisterhood grip
___	___	___	overgrip
___	___	___	barely brushing
___	___	___	limp and cold

Stance

Home	Work	Social Setting	
___	___	___	stooped and burdened
___	___	___	elastic
___	___	___	erect
___	___	___	relaxed and grounded
___	___	___	hands on hip
___	___	___	arms crossed
___	___	___	feet apart

Walk

Home	Work	Social Setting	
___	___	___	fast
___	___	___	slow
___	___	___	youthful
___	___	___	heavy
___	___	___	light
___	___	___	fatigued
___	___	___	shuffling

Voice—Message

Home	Work	Social Setting	
___	___	___	hesitant
___	___	___	understanding
___	___	___	threatening
___	___	___	confusing
___	___	___	confident
___	___	___	unfeeling
___	___	___	encouraging

Voice—Tone and Quality

Home	Work	Social Setting	
___	___	___	tranquilizing
___	___	___	piercing
___	___	___	monotone
___	___	___	whining
___	___	___	loud
___	___	___	modulated
___	___	___	strained

Head

Home	Work	Social Setting	
——	——	——	shaking
——	——	——	nodding
——	——	——	rigid
——	——	——	responsive
——	——	——	swaying
——	——	——	drooped
——	——	——	tilted

Face

Home	Work	Social Setting	
——	——	——	grimacing
——	——	——	frowning
——	——	——	smooth-lined
——	——	——	laugh-lined
——	——	——	stress-lined
——	——	——	twitching
——	——	——	clenched

Smile

Home	Work	Social Setting	
——	——	——	intense
——	——	——	broad
——	——	——	quick
——	——	——	constant
——	——	——	twitch
——	——	——	frozen
——	——	——	tight-lipped

Sit

Home	Work	Social Setting	
——	——	——	slump
——	——	——	rigid and straight
——	——	——	legs crossed
——	——	——	legs apart
——	——	——	chair straddled
——	——	——	informal curl
——	——	——	comfortable

Touching

Home	Work	Social Setting	
——	——	——	avoids physical contact
——	——	——	hesitant
——	——	——	loving
——	——	——	patronizing
——	——	——	conciliatory
——	——	——	pat and peck
——	——	——	invading

effective communication is reduced. Thus it is valuable to learn how we can avoid arousing others' protective psychological shields. Gibb (1961) described six differences between what he called defensive and supportive communication climates. These six differences are:

Supportive Climates	Defensive Climates
Description	Evaluation
Problem orientation	Control
Spontaneity	Strategy
Empathy	Neutrality
Equality	Superiority
Provisionalism	Certainty

When we feel we are being evaluated, especially when someone is criticizing us, we are likely to rise to our own defense. However, when we feel that a person is objectively describing us without adding an evaluation, we are not as likely to become defensive. When someone tries to control or coerce us, we become more uncomfortable than when a person seeks to solve a problem without forcing us to go along with the solution. Then too, a person who has a preset plan usually turns us off, as opposed to one who reacts spontaneously to situations. Strategy often implies a gimmick or some deception. Similarly, when a person is neutral toward us, as opposed to empathic or sympathetic, it usually makes us more defensive. When a person acts in a superior manner instead of treating us as an equal, we say that person is on an ego trip. Such superior behavior is deflating to our self-esteem and arouses our defenses. Finally, when someone acts as a "know-it-all," this attitude of certainty or dogmatism is less pleasant than when the person is willing to have an open mind and act with a degree of provisionalism. Gibb found that groups with defensive climates got more bogged down in worthless ego-protecting discussion and accomplished less than those with more supportive climates.

See also Cushman and Cahn (1985) and Cahn and Tubbs (1983). See the article by Gibb at the end of this chapter for a more complete description, and the one by William Peace for a good explanation of the use of the supportive style of communicating.

Content and Process

One rather difficult distinction to make about group discussion is the difference between the content of the discussion and the process. Suppose a group is discussing this topic: "How can political corruption in the United States be reduced?" When the discussion is over, the professor asks others in the class to comment on the discussion. Comments concerning the *content* of the discussion might include the following:

- I think political corruption will always be with us.

- I think politics are not more dirty now than in the past.

- The political system has shown its strength by catching its own offenders.

These comments are typical of an untrained observer. They all deal with the topic of the discussion, and the observer frequently gets into the heat of the discussion topic himself.

Comments regarding the *process* of the same discussion are quite different, as illustrated by the following:

- Joe dominated the group, while the others couldn't get a word in edgewise.

- Most of your comments were based on opinions. Few actual facts were brought out.

- I think you got bogged down in defining the problem and never really got to any conclusion as to how to solve the problem.

These comments deal with the process or manner in which the discussion was conducted. This type of observation usually requires more insight into group interaction. Also, this type of comment allows both participants and observers to learn from one sample discussion some principles of group interaction that can be generalized to other discussions. Thus it is important to be able to distinguish discussion content from the discussion process.

Notice the difference in the following two students' descriptions of a group discussion. They were asked to describe the group processes in their small group. (The topic was the ethics of cloning humans—exercise 3 in Chapter 1.)

Student 1
I feel a certain resentment towards the idea of *producing* life, which I consider cloning to be. I especially feel a resentment toward producing beings to act as slaves or to be used by us in any way. My group discussed the idea of controlling the traits of cloned human beings for specialized purposes. I do not feel that God appreciates his children tampering with the miracle of life.

Student 2
The group started with the usual "I guess we're supposed to's" and after only a minimal amount of paper shuffling, got down to the subject at hand.

Of the five-person group, only four participated. It was interesting to note who assumed the leadership role, for how long, for what reasons, how effectively, etc. I feel that the member who occupied this role initially usually does not do so in other groups—that members who seemed to know something about this subject successfully opened the discussion and maintained it by asking others questions. What I looked for but did *not* see was direct eye contact, an authoritative tone of voice (I didn't say authoritarian), and backbone enough to justify occupying the leader's role. I think she was assuming this behavior to get a good grade.

Notice how student 1 discusses only the *topic* of the discussion content. Student 2, however, really discusses the group's *process* or behavior, and therefore does a much better job of fulfilling the assignment.

Therapeutic–Pathological

We are more and more coming to realize that some communication patterns are psychologically more healthy or unhealthy than others. One popular way of determining the difference is called *transactional analysis*. This method is described in the bestselling book *I'm OK—You're OK*, by Thomas Harris (1967). A *transaction* is defined as when "I do something to you and you do something back" (pp. 11–12). Transactions can be analyzed in terms of three types of brain functions (called ego states)—namely, the Parent, Adult, and Child (P-A-C). For example, the child-child transaction is shown in Figure 5.3.

According to the theory, transactions that occur between the two participants' adult ego states are more likely to produce an I'm OK—You're OK, or a psychologically healthy outcome. The adult ego state represents the rational data-processing state of the brain. It is comparable to the *descriptive, provisional, problem-oriented,* and *equal* type of comment described by Gibb. The parent ego state is more like Gibb's *evaluative* comment and often implies *control, certainty,* and *superiority*. An example of a parent comment in a small group would be a participant's saying while waving a pointed finger at the group, "You two are always goofing around; I want you to shape up!" This type of comment is likely to produce a response from the child ego state of those on the receiving end, which might be something like, "Oh yeah, well who's gonna make me?" "What do I need with you and this dumb group anyway?"

The child ego state is defined as the location of feelings such as anger, happiness, fear, or love. Harris describes the four possible life conditions as: (1) I'm OK—You're OK, which is the desirable situation, basically a psychology of live and let live; (2) I'm Not OK—You're OK, the situation in which a person lacks self-esteem and considers others to be superior; (3) I'm OK—You're Not OK, wherein the person has feelings of superiority; and (4) I'm Not OK—You're Not OK, in which the person takes a pathological kill-or-be-killed position of defensiveness based on insecurity.

The objective of transactional analysis is to teach us the difference among these

**FIGURE 5.3   CHILD–CHILD
                 TRANSACTION.**

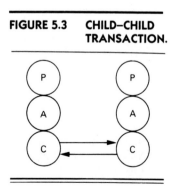

different types of transactions so that we can improve our communication effectiveness by keeping more of our transactions in the adult ego state. This, however, is often easier said than done. In one discussion a group member asked, "What's important here?" This question is usually generated from the adult ego state and is supposed to help group members focus their attention on the main issues before the group. However, in this case it was stated with an exasperated tone of voice and an angry facial expression. The comment did not help the group, but made other group members feel "Not OK," actually diverting attention from the significant issue under discussion. Incidentally, transactional analysts would probably argue that the comment was an ulterior transaction (Figure 5.4) that on the surface was on the adult-adult level, but that was really motivated by the critical parent to punish the child in the group who was holding up the group's progress. (See also Tubbs and Carter 1977.)

Literally thousands of discussions begin with an adult level of problem analysis and degenerate to something less productive. Let us look at a series of statements in two actual discussions. The first exemplifies a deterioration of exchanges between the participants' parent ego states to the point where they are playing the game "Ain't it awful?" (Berne, 1964). The second series represents comments on the same topic that are reality-based and were generated from the participants' adult ego states. In both cases, the discussion topic was "What can be done to create better job equality among the races?"

Discussion I (Parent Level: "Ain't It Awful?")

A: All I know is, racism is racism. A white male today is discriminated against in finding a job.

B: I know what you mean. I've heard of cases where entrance exam results are fudged so that minorities can get in.

C: It's always the way. You work your guts out trying to get ahead and what good does it do you?

D: You're right. There's no justice!

FIGURE 5.4   AN ULTERIOR TRANSACTION.

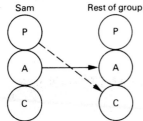

Sam: "What's important here?"

Discussion 2 (Adult Level: Rational Thinking)

A: Earlier in our discussion we defined job equality as an equal opportunity to obtain a job assuming equal qualifications.

B: What about affirmative action programs designed to increase minority employment to a certain percentage of a work force within a certain time period, say, a year?

C: Does anybody have a thought on that?

D: Well, on one hand it does not meet our definition of equality in the short run, because some less qualified person may be given an unfair advantage. But in the long run, it eradicates the effects of several years of discrimination in the other direction.

A: In other words, we need short-term inequality to bring about long-term equality?

C: I guess it's a little like procrastination in studying. If you ignore your homework for several weeks, you have to study extra hard to catch up and then maintain some moderate study effort from then on.

D: In other words, once the percentage of the work force in any given job reaches the percentage of that group in the general population, then "true equality" can be realized.

A: I think that makes sense.

B: It will be uncomfortable in the meantime, but it seems to be a desirable goal.

As you can see, the second discussion focuses on the issues and avoids generalizations or such platitudes as, "It's always the way. You work your guts out trying to get ahead and what good does it do you?" The second type of discussion leads to an action plan, while the first type often ends with nothing much accomplished and with final comments such as, "Well, it's a crazy world, but what can you do about it?"

As we conclude this section on communication, let us keep in mind that as hard as we try to avoid breakdowns, they are an inherent part of the process. Eisenberg (1984) reminds us:

> People within organizations confront multiple situational demands and, therefore, develop multiple and conflicting goals and the resulting communicative strategies do not always minimize ambiguity, but are, however, effective. Strategic ambiguity is essential to organizing in that it: (1) promotes unified diversity, (2) facilitates organizational change, and (3) amplifies existing source attributions and preserves privileged positions. (p. 227)

LANGUAGE BEHAVIOR

The study of the interaction between verbal symbols and the thought patterns associated with them is referred to as *general semantics.* If you have ever become bogged down in a group discussion due to a difficulty in defining terms or dealing with any problems with language, as in the case study at the beginning of this chapter, you will immediately see the relevance of this topic to the study of small group interaction. In fact, some discussions may even have as their task the problem of choosing the appropriate verbal symbol to represent a concept. New products frequently have several proposed names that may be market-tested for consumer response. The intermediate-sized Ford Granada, for example, had several other potential names that apparently were not popular. According to Smith (1974):

> Ford tested Eagle, Fairmont, Stallion, Lucerne, Gibraltar, Scándia, and many other monikers before selecting [the name] Granada for its new compact luxury car. Chrysler Corporation's design studios have flirted with special models carrying such names as Boca Raton, Gatsby, Gandy Dancer, Easy Rider and Magnum.

Committees spend hours brainstorming possible names and then determining procedures for testing market reaction to the main contenders.

Although few of us will ever make decisions concerning product names, each of us will undoubtedly be involved with language problems of one sort or another in group discussions. Our discussion will focus on four specific problems that frequently plague groups: (1) bypassing, (2) inference making, (3) polarizing, and (4) signal reactions.

Bypassing

A husband and wife invited to a party were told the dress was to be "casual." They both wore comfortable slacks and sweaters. When they arrived, they could see through the window that the men at the party were dressed in sport coats and dress slacks, while the women all had floor-length skirts or long dresses. The couple felt so underdressed that they went home and changed before going in to the party.

Two students met on a college campus. One was from a foreign country. As they finished their conversation, the American student departed, saying, "I'll see you later." The foreign student came back to that spot later in the day and waited for some time for the other person—who, of course, never appeared.

A group of housewives got together for their monthly gourmet cooking club meeting. One woman gave instructions for baking peanut butter cookies with chocolate kisses on top. She said, "Just put the chocolate candy right into the peanut butter when you make them." Several in the group misinterpreted her instructions and put the candy on top before rather than after baking. The results were very disappointing.

Each of these cases illustrates a situation in which a misunderstanding occurred due to a language problem. This sort of misunderstanding is referred to as *bypassing.*

It is defined as "the miscommunication pattern which occurs when the *sender* (speaker, writer, and so on) and the *receiver* (listener, reader, and so forth) *miss each other with their meaning*" (Haney 1986). In group discussions, the entire focus of the discussion may be diverted by a difference in interpretation of a given word. Note the incredible problems arising in the group as seen by one participant:

> At the start of our meeting I introduced a definition of communication (communication is an expression of ideas). While the basics were appreciated, Ed and Al requested a revision as the statement was too simple. They decided to drop the words *an expression of ideas.* I didn't believe this was a very good revision and said so. A slight altercation developed lasting about five minutes. It was resolved that other ideas would be considered.
>
> After sufficient waiting (about 30 seconds) I realized no great ideas were forthcoming, so I subtly suggested that my idea be reconsidered and this time Pete and John were on my side. Still my full idea could not survive Al and Ed so it was given new form. . . . In the process of getting a communication definition they had to satisfy me that their changes were justified, while I was attempting to show my original as the best. "Well, you haven't done any better," was surprisingly effective. While I had been using sword points, the best they could muster was a safety pin.
>
> After the mutilation of my last idea, I decided I would not volunteer any more material and thus "watch them squirm."

It seems hard to believe that such intense reactions could result from a difference of opinion over the definition of the term *communication*. However, this reaction is more typical than atypical.

Ogden and Richards (1946) inspired the diagram in Figure 5.5, which helps us understand the relation between an object (or referent) and a symbol used to represent that object. As Figure 5.6 shows, the symbol may vary, but the object remains the same. The object has a word chosen to represent it, but that word and the object have

FIGURE 5.5   THE RELATIONSHIP BETWEEN AN OBJECT AND THE SYMBOL FOR THE OBJECT.

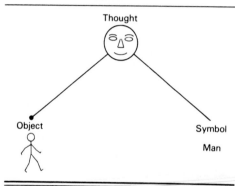

FIGURE 5.6   THE SAME OBJECT MAY BE REPRESENTED BY MORE THAN ONE SYMBOL.

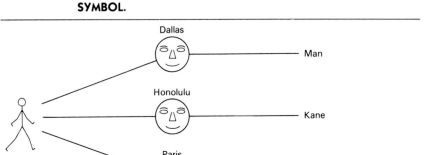

no necessary inherent relationship. It is a little like selecting a name for a newborn baby. At first the choice seems arbitrary, but after a few years it seems impossible to think of that person having a different name. The relationship is indirect between symbol and referent; it exists only in the mind. Since each of us has a different brain and nervous system, the relationship between any given referent and any given word will vary to some extent from person to person.

Part of the bypassing problem is that we frequently assume words contain meaning. A different view is that words are symbols arbitrarily designated to represent concepts or referents. Over time, we begin to associate the word with its referent so strongly that they become inseparable. It is easy enough to say that the word is not the thing and that we should be able to separate the symbol from the referent, but it is difficult in practice not to respond emotionally when another person refers to us as a fascist pig, a nigger, a stupid hillbilly, or a honky.

Two problems related to bypassing occur when we use the same word to mean different things (dress "casually"), and the opposite, when different words are used to express essentially the same idea. For example, we may argue that company employees are not performing properly due to a "communication problem" as opposed to a "lack of motivation." It may be that we are really talking about related problems (that is, employees would be better motivated to perform [motivation problem] if they could suggest some new job procedures to their supervisors [communication problem]), but the issue may be clouded by arguments over the labels used to describe the problem.

Haney (1986) suggests two outcomes that can result from bypassing. On one hand, we may have apparent agreement when in fact we are calling different things by the same name (dressing casually). On the other hand, we may have actual agreement but apparent disagreement, as in the employee problem described above. Given these possible outcomes, here are some guidelines (slightly modified) that Haney (1986) suggests to remedy the potential difficulties.

- Be person-minded, not word-minded.

- Question and paraphrase.

- Be receptive to feedback.

- Be sensitive to contexts.

McCormack (1984), in his best-selling book *What They Don't Teach You At Harvard Business School*, confirms Haney's advice when he writes:

> Insight demands opening up your senses, talking less and listening more. I believe you can learn almost everything you need to know—and more than other people would like you to know—simply by watching and listening, keeping your eyes peeled, your ears open. And your mouth closed. . . . Watch your listen/talk ratio. (pp. 8–9)

These points also corroborate the ancient rhetorician who observed: "We have two ears and only one tongue, so that we might listen more than we speak."

In a nutshell, these guidelines focus on the idea that not all of us use words precisely the same way, and that all words have the potential for multiple usage and interpretation. When you suspect that there may be a difference in word usage, ask questions, and be willing to try to restate or paraphrase the person's message. Remember to use different words in your restatement to see if the basic intent is understood. Also, be receptive to feedback. If we are too impervious or insensitive to allow for the possibility that we may not have stated something perfectly clearly, then we are unlikely to get much feedback to that effect. However, if we are willing to admit to fallibility, we invite feedback and can benefit from that information. Finally, we can often guess the intended meaning of a given statement based upon its use in a given context. For example, one supervisor frequently bade goodbye to his employees with the common phrase, "Well, take it easy now." It was quite obvious from the context that he meant this only as a casual expression. He did *not* intend employees to work less hard. By employing the four techniques mentioned above, we can reduce the frequency of bypassing.

Inference Making

Each of us makes numerous inferences every day. For example, we infer (1) that the sun will rise tomorrow; (2) that a chair won't collapse when we sit down; (3) that the sun is shining on the other side of town, since it is shining at our location; (4) that a car coming at us from a side street will stop at the stop sign and not run into the side of our car; (5) that a person who consistently fails to show up for a group discussion is not committed to our group task. In each of these five cases, there is some probability that our inference will be borne out by the actual events. However, these five examples illustrate quite a range from most probable (number 1) to least probable (number 5).

Statements of inference go beyond what we know through observations. They represent only some degree of probability of coming true. This idea is illustrated in the diagram in Figure 5.7.

FIGURE 5.7

Observational statements	Inferential statements
◄────────────────────────	──────────────────────►
Approaching certainty	Approaching uncertainty

One of the major problems in groups is being able to recognize our own inference making. You can test your own ability on the following sample story. True (T) means that the inference drawn is definitely true, based upon the information in the story. False (F) means that the inference is definitely wrong based upon the information in the story. A question mark (?) means that you cannot be certain of the inference, based upon the story.

Sample Story
A customer handed the pharmacist a prescription for birth control pills. "Please fill this quickly. I have someone waiting in the car."

The pharmacist hurried to fill the order.

Statements about the Story
1. A woman was having a prescription filled
for birth control pills.   T   F   ?
2. She did not want to become pregnant.   T   F   ?
3. She was in a hurry to have the order filled.   T   F   ?
4. The pharmacist did his best to speed up the order.   T   F   ?

If you answered T to any of the statements, you probably assumed or inferred that the customer and the pharmacist were female and male, respectively. Yet there is no statement in the story to support that assumption. Actually, a man is ordering birth control pills for his wife. The pharmacist, a female, cannot do "his" best to fill the order.

Another way of describing inference making is to say that it involves certain assumptions or conclusion drawing (sometimes jumping to the wrong conclusion). This becomes a problem in groups when we react to each other on the assumption that a person is behaving a certain way for the reason that seems obvious or apparent. However, the person may be acting that way for reasons other than the obvious. For example, a person may aggress against another by saying, "I'm sick and tired of your holding us back in our work." On the surface, this appears to be a comment intended to help the group get more accomplished. Beneath the surface, however, it may be part of an effort to undermine the other person's status in the group, and may be a part of the struggle between the two for leadership in the group. These levels can be diagrammed as shown in Figures 5.8 and 5.9. While it is helpful to recognize that all behaviors are motivated, and that they may be motivated by multiple causes, it is also dangerous to attempt to infer too much. Even if we make such an inference, we must recognize the possibility of error.

On the other hand, it is often difficult to analyze the group process without making

FIGURE 5.8   SURFACE AND HIDDEN AGENDAS COMPARED.

Surface agenda

Hidden agenda

some inferences. For example, one encounter group was having its last meeting and the discussion somehow got around to the subject of death. After a somewhat extended discussion on this subject, the group leader intervened by saying: "I wonder if this discussion of death is motivated by the reluctance we are all feeling tonight about saying good-bye for the last time." Although this comment was initially rejected by the group, it turned out a lot of people were reluctant to end the friendships that had grown out of this group, and the topic of the discussion shifted to directly expressing and resolving those feelings.

Some inference making may be useful to the group, while at other times it may be harmful. A person who tries to read too much into behaviors may become a "psycho-pest" (Luft 1969). For example, a person crossing arms across the chest may do this for no reason but increased comfort. An overinterpretation might be that the person is becoming defensive and is trying to put up a barrier between self and others. In attempting to analyze behaviors, it is wise to recognize that analyses often involve inferences that go beyond what we have observed and involve some probability for error.

Polarizing

Perhaps one of the most common problems in groups is polarization. It is difficult to exchange differences in viewpoint without tending to overstate or exaggerate to make

FIGURE 5.9

Levels of Discussion Analysis

Surface agenda

                         * Perceptive observation

                         * Shallow observation

Hidden agenda

                         * Superficial interpretation of motives

                         * Perceptive interpretation of motives

our point. When this happens, it encourages the others to exaggerate a bit more in the opposite direction to make their point. Before long the sides are so far apart that constructive discussion of the issues is often discontinued for the time being. Consider the following example:

Kyle: I can't see why women should get a job just to avoid the boredom of housework, when a man who needs to support his family goes without a job.

Sue: Just because your masculinity is threatened is no reason to keep women out of work!

Kyle: My masculinity? You women's libbers are always hung up on trying to be the dominant sex!

Sue: You men are all alike. You can't stand being bettered by anyone, especially a woman. You want us to tell you how brilliant you are because you know what day of the week it is.

This exchange actually occurred in a student discussion. The topic was, "How can greater job equality be achieved in this country?" The discussion had been progressing well until this polarization occurred. Polarization has three distinct characteristics. First, the statements get more emotionally intense. Second, they go from being specific to being more general ("You men are all alike!"). Third, they tend to move away from the topic at hand (job equality) to other issues ("You can't stand being bettered by anyone").

A simple method usually nips polarization in the bud. It is described by Rogers and Roethlisberger (1952) in the following way:

> The next time you get into an argument with . . . a small group of friends, just stop the discussion for a moment and, for an experiment, institute this rule. "Each person can speak up for himself only *after* he has repeated the ideas and feelings of the speaker accurately and to that speaker's satisfaction." You see what this would mean. It would simply mean that before presenting your own point of view, it would be necessary for you to achieve the other speaker's frame of reference—to understand his thoughts and feelings so well that you could summarize them for him. Sounds simple doesn't it? But if you try it, you will discover that it is one of the most difficult things you have ever tried to do.

After you have tried this restating exercise, notice the effects. First, the tendency for statements to gain emotional intensity is significantly reduced. The calmness is quite dramatic when compared with the interchange between Kyle and Sue above. Second, the discussion tends to stay with manageable specifics, rather than moving to gross generalities that are quite frequently based on stereotypes (men are not all alike any more than women are all alike). Third, the discussion is more likely to remain focused on the group's discussion topic than to go off on a tangent that may be much less relevant to the group's task. This simple technique can actually be quite potent in reducing the problem of polarization.

Signal Reactions

Signal reactions are learned responses to certain stimuli. Perhaps the best-known example of a signal reaction is the salivation of Pavlov's dogs. Ivan Pavlov was a Nobel-prize-winning Russian physiologist. He accidentally stumbled on a very important concept of learning known as classical conditioning. He noticed that the carefully calibrated measurements of his test animals' salivation started to break down because his experienced dogs began to salivate in anticipation of the food when he opened the door to the room before he fed them. His coming in the door was the *conditioned stimulus* or signal that triggered the salivation response. Eventually, he brought the salivation response under stimulus control by associating a bell with food so that the dogs learned to salivate at the sound of the bell even when the food was *not* present.

It is interesting that the founder of general semantics, Alfred Korzybski, wrote that the signal response was an animal-like response. He wrote (1948, p. 249):

> In Pavlov's experiments a dog is shown food and a bell rung simultaneously. At the sight of food, saliva and gastric juice flow. Associations soon *relate* the ringing of a bell and the food, and, later, simply the ringing of the bell will produce the flow. In another animal some other signal, a whistle, for instance, would produce similar effects. In different people, through experience, associations, relations, meanings, and s.r. [stimulus response] patterns are built around some symbol. Obviously in grown-up humans the identification of the symbol with the thing must be pathological.

Actually, Korzybski was a little extreme in saying that we are pathological to allow such strong connections between signal and response. One study showed that the repetitive sound of a gong produced marked emotional responses in former sailors (as measured by their perspiration levels), but very little emotional reaction among former soldiers. Edwards and Acker (1962) write:

> This signal was used as a call to battle stations aboard U.S. Navy ships during the war, and it continued to elicit a strong autonomic response from the Navy veterans. Even though more than fifteen years had elapsed since this stimulus had signaled danger. . . .

Although this study did not involve reactions to verbal symbols, it does demonstrate the natural, not pathological, tendency toward strong signal reactions.

A study that directly tested emotional reactions to verbal symbols also proved that strong physiological reactions to symbols are typical rather than pathological. Subjects were exposed to various words on a screen and their perspiration was measured as an index of their reactions. There were no significant differences between reactions to positive words such as *beauty, love,* and *kiss,* and negative words such as *cancer, hate,* and *death.* However, some words did cause significant responses. These were referred to as "personal" words and included the person's first and last names, father's and mother's first names, major in school, year in school, and school name. Subjects were significantly aroused by these "personal" words (Crane, Diecker, and Brown 1970).

Certainly nobody would argue that these college students were pathological or that they "confused" their own name with themselves as physical beings. Yet these studies collectively indicate that all of us learn to react to certain verbal and nonverbal stimuli in some strong and predictable ways. When the response becomes habitual, it is like a reflex action. At this point, the so-called signal, or automatic response, may create problems.

In group discussions, certain phrases may produce signal reactions that are counterproductive. Such phrases have been referred to as "idea killers" (Bittel 1956) or communication stoppers. They include, among others:

- "That's ridiculous."

- "We tried that before."

- "That will never work."

- "That's crazy."

- "It's too radical a change."

- "We're too small for it."

- "It's not practical."

- "Let's get back to reality."

- "You can't teach an old dog new tricks."

- "We'll be the laughingstock."

- "You're absolutely wrong."

- "You don't know what you're talking about."

- "It's impossible."

- "There's no way it can be done."

On the other hand, "igniter phrases" that seem to promote group productivity would include some of the following:

- "I agree."

- "That's good!"

- "I made a mistake. I'm sorry."

- "That's a great idea."

- "I'm glad you brought that up."

- "You're on the right track."

- "I know it will work."

- "We're going to try something different today."

- "I never thought of that."

- "We can do a lot with that idea."

- "Real good, anyone else?"

- "I like that!"

- "That would be worth a try."

- "Why don't we assume it would work and go from there."

Other specific terms that are likely to produce signal reactions are such words as *weirdo, queer, honky, racist, male chauvinist pig,* and many swear words. In fact, even swear words have different levels of offensiveness that vary from culture to culture. Profane words have been classified as (1) religious, (2) excretory, and (3) sexual (Bostrom and Rossiter 1969). In our culture the sexual words are usually the most offensive, but in Italy, where the Roman Catholic Church is very strong, religious words are considered much more offensive, and in Germany excretory swear words are considered to be the worst. Several studies indicate that those who swear may reduce their credibility in the eyes of others (Bauduin 1971). It also seems advisable to avoid communication stoppers and idea killers whenever possible.

Since we know that words do have a great deal of potential for influencing thought and subsequent action, note the set of terms in Figure 5.10. Just pick any three-digit number at random and pick the corresponding three words from the lists. These terms all have some relevance to small group interaction. If all else fails, they can be used for fun. For example, 2, 6, 9 would be *Machiavellian managerial transactions.* Numbers 8, 4, 3 would be *stagnated interpersonal relations.* So if you want to impress your friends with how much you have learned by reading this book, try the *SNOW* index.

SELF-DISCLOSURE

Perhaps one of the greatest dilemmas facing a group member is the choice between openly expressing his or her thoughts and feelings versus concealing or distorting inner feelings, thoughts, and perceptions. In a discussion on racial equality, we may not openly reveal our true feelings for fear of sounding like a racist or bigot. Nobody wants to be labeled an Archie Bunker if it can be avoided! On the other hand, if every person in the group conceals his or her thoughts, there will be little said and therefore little accomplished. The question is not whether to reveal or conceal, but *how much* to reveal or conceal. *Self-disclosure* has been defined by Tubbs and Baird (1980) as

> a process, whereby an individual voluntarily shares information in a personal way, about his or her "self" that cannot be discovered through other sources.

You may wonder why a person should bother to let himself or herself be known to others. Jourard (1964) studied mentally disturbed individuals and concluded that a great deal of human energy is consumed in attempts to keep from being known by others. That energy could be used for other purposes, but neurotic individuals are so "wrapped up in themselves" that they are seldom able to devote sufficient energy to other problems (such as a group problem-solving discussion). All of us are periodi-

FIGURE 5.10 SYSTEMATIC NEW ORDER (OF) WORDS.

(*SNOW* INDEX)

0 external	0 bureaucratic	0 acceptance
1 authoritarian	1 group	1 solutions
2 Machiavellian	2 functional	2 consensus
3 energetic	3 logistical	3 relations
4 situational	4 interpersonal	4 commitment
5 socialized	5 instrumental	5 responsibility
6 systematic	6 managerial	6 development
7 dynamic	7 organizational	7 coordination
8 stagnated	8 executive	8 power
9 transparent	9 homogeneous	9 transactions

cally faced with such situations. When we get bad news from home or from a friend, it is much harder to concentrate on such mundane problems as how to budget our study time for tomorrow's exam. However, the mentally unhealthy person is habitually in this state of mind.

Part of returning to mental health involves sharing oneself with others. Jourard (1964, p. 24) states:

> Self-disclosure, or should I say "real" self-disclosure, is both a symptom of personality health . . . and at the same time a means of ultimately achieving healthy personality. . . . I have known people who would rather die than become known. . . . When I say that self-disclosure is a symptom of personality health, what I mean really is that a person who displays many of the other characteristics that betoken healthy personality . . . *will also display the ability to make himself fully known to at least one other significant human being.*

Perhaps a less self-centered motive for self-disclosure is the desire to improve the quality of communication within a group. Keltner (1970, p. 54) states:

> We probably do not reveal enough of ourselves in speech-communication to enable our co-communicators to understand us better. The complexities of the world we live in demand better communication than we have known. *To communicate better, we must understand each other better. To understand each other better, we must reveal more of ourselves through speech and speech-communication events.*

Countless students in group discussion feel that they don't know what to contribute to a discussion. They often feel that they have no good or new ideas to add to what has already been said. Yet, as we will see in the last section of this chapter, numerous roles may be adopted by group members, several of which involve some degree of self-disclosure. For example, if an idea is initiated by another, you may make a substantial contribution by offering your *reaction* to the idea (opinion giving)—by encouraging or showing agreement or disagreement. Counterproductive role behaviors may also involve self-disclosure (for example, aggressing, reporting a personal achievement, confessing a personal ideology that is irrelevant to the discussion topic, or seeking sympathy from the group).

Self-disclosure is not always desirable. An optimum amount of self-disclosure seems a desirable goal to achieve. Some of us are too closed (concealers); others of us "wear our hearts on our sleeves" (revealers). Culbert (1968, p. 19) describes the problem of overdisclosing rather vividly:

> The revealer is likely to react by immediately disclosing any self-information to which he has access. The revealer, too, is attempting to master the problem, but for him mastery seems to be attained by explicitly acknowledging and labeling all the relevant elements comprising the situation. While a concealer runs the risk of having insufficient external feedback, a revealer runs the risk of overlabeling the limited number of objective elements present or of labeling them so early that their usefulness in the relationship is nullified.

Encounter groups usually proceed under the assumption that people have learned to be too closed too often. Thus participants are encouraged to share their feelings and perceptions as openly and honestly as they can. Much of the self-disclosure involves giving feedback to others concerning the ways in which they "come across." This feedback is often useful in reducing the size of the arc of distortion, discussed earlier in this chapter.

The Johari Window

Perhaps the most useful model for illustrating self-disclosure in groups is the Johari window (named after its originators, Joe Luft and Harry Ingham) (Luft 1970). See Figure 5.11 for this model.

FIGURE 5.11   THE JOHARI WINDOW.
From *Group Processes: An Introduction to Group Dynamics,* by Joseph Luft, by permission of Mayfield Publishing Company. Copyright © 1963, 1970 by Joseph Luft.

This window classifies an individual's relating to others according to four quadrants (or windowpanes). The size of each quadrant represents the person's level of self-awareness. Quadrant one, the open quadrant, represents our willingness to share with others our views on such things as current national or world events, current movies, sports, and what is generally referred to as "cocktail party" conversation.

The second quadrant is referred to as the blind quadrant or the "bad breath" area. This area represents the things that others may know about us, but that we do unintentionally and unknowingly. We may continually dominate meetings, or bore people with long-winded accounts of how good our high school was. Conversely, we may annoy people by our silence, since they may feel that they have opened themselves up to the group, while we have "played our cards pretty close to the chest" by revealing little. Group members seem to resent both those who talk too much and those who talk too little.

The third quadrant is the hidden area that is most likely to be changed (reduced) by self-disclosure. It represents the feelings about ourselves that we know but are unwilling to reveal to others. It may represent our greatest fears, some past experiences we would like to forget, or our secret sexual fantasies, among other things.

The fourth quadrant is called the area of the unknown. It represents all the areas of potential growth or self-actualization. This includes almost anything outside our experience, such as the sport we've never played, the places we have never seen, the hobby we haven't taken the time to try, the organization we have never joined, the style of behaving we have never been willing to risk, and others.

Luft advocates changing the shape of the window so that quadrant one enlarges while all the others become smaller. I once participated in an encounter group in which we tried to grow interpersonally along the lines suggested by this model. One participant introduced herself as "Mickey" and told us what city she was from, and so on. She was dressed in slacks and a sweater. Only after 15 weeks did we find out that she was a nun. She had been trying to develop herself as a person without having the rest of us react to her role rather than to her. Thus her unknown quadrant was diminished by her efforts to try new, less inhibited behaviors. She also reduced her blind quadrant by asking for interpersonal feedback. We might have been more inhibited in our feedback had we known she was a nun. She also destroyed the stereotypes most of us had toward nuns.

Luft (1970) illustrates the Johari window as it applies to groups in Figure 5.12. Each window represents a person.

Appropriateness

Within this framework, the question still arises as to when and how much self-disclosure there should be. Luft (1969, pp. 132–133) answers this question when he proposes the following guidelines designating situations in which self-disclosure is appropriate:

1. *When it is a function of the ongoing relationship.* What one shares with another belongs in the particular relationship; it is not a random or isolated act.

FIGURE 5.12   ONE WAY OF LOOKING AT A GROUP.

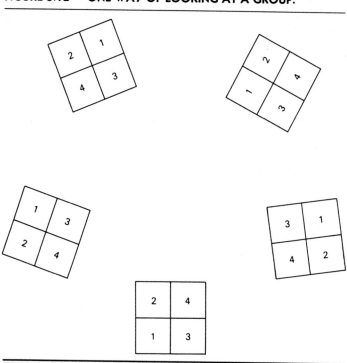

---

2. *When it occurs reciprocally.* This implies that there is some degree of interdependence and mutuality involved.

3. *When it is timed to fit what is happening.* The self-disclosure grows out of the experience that is going on between or among the persons involved. The timing and sequence are important.

4. *When it concerns what is going on within and between persons in the present.* Some account is taken of the behavior and feelings of the participants individually and of the persons collectively. There is a recognition of the relationship as an emergent phenomenon in addition to the individual selves.

5. *When it moves by relatively small increments.* What is revealed does not drastically change or restructure the relationship. The implication is that a relationship is built gradually except in rare and special cases.

6. *When it is confirmable by the other person.* Some system is worked out between the persons to validate reception of that which has been disclosed.

7. *When account is taken of the effect disclosure has on the other person(s).* The disclosure has not only been received; there is evidence of its effect on the receiver.

8. *When it creates a reasonable risk.* If the feeling or behavior were really unknown to the other, it may have been withheld for a reason bearing on differences which have yet to be faced by the participants.

9. *When it is speeded up in a crisis.* A serious conflict jeopardizing the structure of the relationship may require that more quadrant 3 material be quickly revealed to heal the breach or help in the reshaping of the relationship.

10. *When the context is mutually shared.* The assumptions underlying the social context suggest that there is enough in common to sustain the disclosure.

Probably the most difficult problem for members of encounter groups to resolve when they go "back home" is knowing how to apply what they have learned without overdoing it. One encounter group graduate said, "How do I use this openness with my boss when he hasn't read the book?" His concern was warranted. It may be quite difficult to put into practice any new behaviors when the others "back home" haven't changed and are still as closed and perhaps as devious as ever.

The most logical advice would be to try to use what you can, when you can. Not all of our learnings will be usable all the time. But certainly some new behaviors (such as increased openness and sensitivity) will be appropriate some, if not most, of the time. Experiences in groups frequently teach us lessons we can't possibly unlearn. Once we have experienced a greater level of personal intimacy with others, day-to-day superficiality may compare rather badly. Schutz (1971, p. 284) puts it this way:

> Relating to people more honestly is certainly possible. Find someone you have withheld something from and tell it to him. See what happens. Next time you feel like touching someone, do it. Next time you are hurt or frightened, express it. When you catch yourself trying to project an image, stop, and see if you can be real instead. If you're embarrassed to pay someone a compliment, do it anyway. If you want to know how people respond to you, ask them.

Another way to put it is that the competent communicator has a higher level of rhetorical sensitivity. That is, he or she learns when and with whom to disclose, and when and with whom to refrain from disclosure (Hart and Burks 1972; Hart, Eadie, and Carlson 1975). Total disclosure at all times with all people is obviously not desirable.

INTERACTION ROLES

Each of us is required to enact multiple roles in our everyday living. Usually we are able to function effectively in these different roles, which require or expect certain behaviors. We are at different times student, son or daughter, friend, counselor, leader, follower, and some are spouses, parents, and employees as well. It is important to realize that roles are simply sets of identifiable behaviors. When we say that a person is assuming a role, this does not imply that he or she is faking it or acting in a way that is not within that person's true character. In fact, some writings (Hart and

Burks 1972) indicate that the more interpersonally sensitive person is one who is able to develop a considerable degree of role flexibility. It is desirable to learn to widen our repertoire of roles and to discover those roles we most enjoy.

A student relatively new to the small group field indicated an awareness of a few interaction roles:

> This group discussion was a real experience for me. I have never been mixed in with a complete group of strangers and have things work out so smoothly. In most groups you get a few quiet shy ones, who don't say anything, and opposed to them, there's usually one big mouth, normally found in a group, who says everything and has all of the ideas without giving anyone else a chance to give their opinion. It was good to work in a group that was well balanced and one in which everyone participated.

As we mentioned in the discussion of leadership, different functions can be performed by any group member. This is another way of saying that individuals assume different roles in helping the group move toward its goal. We discussed the task roles and socioemotional functions or roles in Chapter 3. Benne and Sheats (1948) proposed a classification of roles into three broad categories: (1) task roles, (2) group building and maintenance roles, and (3) individual roles. Although other sets of categories have been developed for research purposes (McCroskey and Wright 1971; Leathers 1969), this time-tested approach is still one of the most useful for learning to identify roles and to develop role flexibility.

Group Task Roles

These behaviors are directed toward accomplishing the group's objective through the facilitation of problem solving.

- *Initiating-contributing:* Proposing new ideas or a changed way of regarding the group goal. This may include a new goal or a new definition of the problem. It may involve suggesting a solution or some way of handling a difficulty the group has encountered. It may also include a new procedure for the group to better organize its efforts.

- *Information seeking:* Asking for clarification, for authoritative information and facts relevant to the problem under discussion.

- *Opinion seeking:* Seeking information related not so much to factual data as to the values underlying the suggestions being considered.

- *Information giving:* Offering facts or generalizations based on experience or authoritative sources.

- *Opinion giving:* Stating beliefs or opinions relevant to a suggestion made. The emphasis is on the proposal of what ought to become the group's values rather than on factors or information.

- *Elaborating:* Expanding on suggestions with examples or restatements, offering a rationale for previously made suggestions, and trying to determine the results if a suggestion were adopted by the group.

- *Coordinating:* Indicating the relationships among various ideas and suggestions, attempting to combine ideas and suggestions or trying to coordinate the activities of group members.

- *Orienting:* Indicating the position of the group by summarizing progress made, deviations from agreed-upon directions or goals, or by raising questions about the direction the group is taking.

- *Evaluating:* Comparing the group's accomplishments to some criterion or standard of group functioning. This may include questioning the practicality, the logic, or the procedure of a suggestion.

- *Energizing:* Stimulating the group to action or decision, attempting to increase the level or quality of activity.

- *Assisting on procedure:* Helping or facilitating group movement by doing things for the group, such as performing routine tasks like distributing materials, rearranging the seating, or running a tape recorder.

- *Recording:* Writing down suggestions, recording group decisions, or recording the outcomes of the discussion. This provides tangible results of the group's effort.

Group Building and Maintenance Roles

The roles in this category help the interpersonal functioning of the group. They help alter the way of working, to strengthen, regulate, and perpetuate the group. This is analogous to preventive maintenance done to keep a mechanical device such as a car in better working order.

- *Encouraging:* Praising, showing interest in, agreeing with, and accepting the contributions of others; showing warmth toward other group members, listening attentively and seriously to the ideas of others, showing tolerance for ideas dif-

FRANK AND ERNEST   by Bob Thaves

CITY PLANNING COMMISSION

SO FAR, THEN, WE HAVE TWO SUGGESTIONS FOR RAISING CITY REVENUE: A WORLD'S FAIR OR A SPEED TRAP.

Reprinted by permission. © 1976 NEA, Inc.

ferent from one's own, conveying the feeling that one feels the contributions of others are important.

- *Harmonizing:* Mediating the differences between the other members, attempting to reconcile disagreements, relieving tension in moments of conflict through the use of humor.

- *Compromising:* Operating from within a conflict situation, one may offer a compromise by yielding status, by admitting a mistake, by disciplining oneself for the sake of group harmony, or by coming halfway toward another position.

- *Gatekeeping and expediting:* Attempting to keep communication channels open by encouraging the participation of some or by curbing the participation of others.

- *Setting standards or ideals:* Expressing standards for the group and/or evaluating the quality of group processes (as opposed to evaluating the content of discussion).

- *Observing:* Keeping a record of various aspects of group process and feeding this information, along with interpretations, into the group's evaluation of its procedures. This contribution is best received when the person has been requested by the group to perform this function. The observer should avoid expressing judgments of approval or disapproval in reporting observations.

- *Following:* Going along with the group, passively accepting the ideas of others, serving as an audience in group discussion.

Individual Roles

These behaviors are designed more to satisfy an individual's needs than to contribute to the needs of the group. These are sometimes referred to as self-centered roles (Brilhart 1974).

- *Aggressing:* Deflating the status of others, disapproving of the ideas or values of others, attacking the group or the problem it is attempting to solve, joking maliciously, resenting the contributions of others and/or trying to take credit for them.

- *Blocking:* Resisting, disagreeing, and opposing beyond reason, bringing up dead issues after they have been rejected or bypassed by the group.

- *Recognition seeking:* Calling attention to oneself through boasting, reporting on personal achievements, acting in inappropriate ways, fighting to keep from being placed in an inferior position.

- *Self-confessing:* Using the group as an opportunity to express personal, non-group-related feelings, insights, ideologies.

- *Acting the playboy:* Showing a lack of involvement in the group's task. Displaying nonchalance, cynicism, horseplay, and other kinds of "goofing-off" behaviors.

- *Dominating:* Trying to assert authority or superiority by manipulating others in the group. This may take the form of flattery, of asserting a superior status or right to attention, giving directions authoritatively, and/or interrupting others.

- *Help seeking:* Attempting to get sympathy from other group members through expressions of insecurity, personal inadequacy, or self-criticism beyond reason.

- *Special interest pleading:* Speaking on behalf of some group such as "the oppressed," "labor," "business," usually cloaking one's own prejudices or biases in the stereotype that best fits one's momentary need. (Adapted from Benne and Sheats 1948.)

It is generally desirable to learn to perform the task roles as well as the group building and maintenance roles, while avoiding the individual roles. However, even the first and second sets of roles may be misused and abused. For example, there is a fine line between initiating and dominating, between encouraging and flattering, and between opinion giving and recognition seeking. The way in which the role is enacted can make a crucial difference in whether the behavior is viewed as constructive or self-serving. One student attempted to be a gatekeeper by asking silent members if they had any ideas they would like to contribute. After his attempts were rebuked, he wrote the following analysis of his behavior.

> On one occasion, I tried to involve another group member in the discussion against his will. The conflict was resolved in a later discussion, but my bad feelings during the intervening period made me realize that this was an area for attention. . . .
>
> This "expansiveness" and disregard for another person's feelings is an amazing trait to find in myself, because it is something I dislike in other people. It has caused me to resolve that (1) I will not be "overbearing" with quiet people, (2) I will listen more, (3) I will attempt to be more aware of the feelings of others.

Even behaviors motivated by the best intentions may go astray in producing a desired contribution to the group effort.

THE SYSTEMS PERSPECTIVE

In this chapter we examined some issues close to the hearts of many modern communication scholars. The chapter began with an analysis of five critical issues in the study of communication. We looked at the differences between intentional-unintentional, verbal-nonverbal, defensive-supportive, content-process, and therapeutic-pathological communication. While these issues apply to all communication contexts, our examples and specific applications were focused on the small group context. These issues have considerable overlap with topics discussed in other chapters in this book. For example, how does one express leadership behavior, or establish a group

norm, or manifest one's personality, or express one's values? All of these are manifested through behaviors that communicate to others in the group.

The systems perspective fits very well with the new emphasis in communication
theory on the transactional model of communication. Recent writings of Sereno and
Bodaken (1975), Wilmot (1975), and Tubbs (1976) stress that the participants in any
communication event are highly dependent upon one another. They are simultaneously influencing one another and are both senders and receivers at all times. Wilmot
(1975) goes so far as to state that "the process of your creating a message may affect
you *more* than it does the person receiving it." The transactional point of view can
be summarized by stating that a person's communication can be defined only *in relation* to some other or others.

In this chapter we discussed the verbal-nonverbal distinction in communication.
The systems nature of this relationship is stressed by Barnlund (1968, p. 535):

> In particular, Birdwhistell has emphasized that no physical motion is meaningless, but
> that its significance derives from the *interactional context* in which it is evoked. Persons
> are engaged in physical conversation even when verbally silent, modifying their positions
> continually in response to perceptible movements in others [emphasis added].

Knapp (1972, pp. 8–9) adds further support for this viewpoint:

> We are constantly being warned against presenting material out of context. . . . There is
> a danger that the reader may forget that nonverbal communication cannot be studied in
> isolation from the total communication process. Verbal and nonverbal communication
> should be treated as a total and inseparable unit.

We might add that each of the communication factors discussed in this chapter is
similarly related to all the others.

In the second section of this chapter we looked at four issues related to language
behavior—bypassing, inference making, polarizing, and signal reactions. Each of
these factors is related to both the background factors of the individuals and the eventual consequences of group discussion. We saw that background factors were related
to signal reactions in the study showing that former sailors experienced a physiological reaction to an alarm bell they had not heard for 15 years. We also saw that similar
reactions can be elicited by such verbal stimuli as our own names, or our parents'
names. The influence of language on group consequences was shown by the use of
"idea killers" such as "It's impossible," "That's crazy," or "That will never work."
The net effect of these types of statements is to reduce potential group productivity
in terms of both idea production and interpersonal relations, as we saw in the case
study at the beginning of this chapter.

The third section of this chapter dealt with the question "How much should I
reveal and how much should I conceal in a group?" The Johari window was offered
as a helpful model for understanding one's relationship to others. Guidelines for
appropriate self-disclosure were included. Obviously, appropriate self-disclosure will
vary considerably from group to group. Probably high self-disclosure is appropriate

in an encounter group with a highly supportive atmosphere and a norm of openness and trust. However, social groups, educational groups, work groups, and especially problem-solving groups are hardly the place for a high degree of very personal self-disclosure. Personality also interacts with self-disclosure. If we open up to those who are highly Machiavellian, they will turn around and use those revelations to benefit themselves and possibly to harm us. Appropriate self-disclosure, then, is very much contingent on a number of relevant variables. For this reason, Tubbs and Baird (1980) have developed a contingency model of self-disclosure that suggests how much to disclose and under what circumstances.

The final section discussed the issue of which roles members may adopt in groups. Task and maintenance roles were indicated as useful roles to learn and to use. Individual or self-centered roles were identified to help indicate communication behaviors that are typically *not* useful to the group. These roles undoubtedly interact with people's personality traits. For example, the person who is dominant and achievement-oriented will probably adopt the task roles quite comfortably. The affiliators will naturally gravitate toward the group maintenance roles. Finally, the hostile or acquiescent personality types will be tempted to adopt the self-centered roles of aggressing and blocking or help seeking and special interest pleading, respectively. One of the reasons for studying different types of roles is to increase our ability to adopt different roles in accordance with the demands of the situation. Barnlund (1968, p. 170) summarizes a great deal of literature on role taking:

> A number of studies show that role insight is associated with social maturity and a high level of general adjustment. Commenting on the close connection between role sensitivity and interpersonal effectiveness, Cameron has written, "To the extent that an individual, in the course of personality development, learns to take social roles skillfully and realistically, acquires an adequate repertory of them, and becomes adroit in shifting from one role to another when he is in difficulty, he should grow into a flexible, adaptive social adult with minimum susceptibility to behavior disorders."

The readings for this chapter deal with improving communication skills and with defensive communication.

EXERCISES

1. Nonverbal Communication

(a) Eyelogue   Group members form two lines facing each other. Without talking, express your feelings for a few seconds to the person facing you. Then move one line so that each person is facing someone different. Repeat until you have expressed a feeling toward every person in the group.

(b) Group Grope   Have group members mill around the room encountering each other nonverbally while blindfolded. Afterward discuss and have group members share their impressions.

(c) Nonverbal Sociogram   Have group members move around and stand near others to whom they feel psychologically close. One person may want to diagram the standing positions on the board for discussion.

(d) Hand-Holding Go-around   Stand in a circle with all group members holding hands with eyes closed. Have the instructor (or a volunteer) go around the outside of the circle putting his or her hands on each pair of clasped hands, one pair at a time. After the person has gone all the way around, discuss the impressions experienced.

2. Transactional Analysis Exercise

Observe any discussion in the class and attempt to identify the ego states that seem to motivate various comments. Write down several representative comments for each of the three ego states (Figure 5.13).

3. Self-Disclosure Exercise

Pair off with someone you feel close to. Begin to talk about the topics listed below. Feel free to stop if you feel the topics are too close for comfort. Discuss the following by taking turns before moving to the next topic.

FIGURE 5.13

Ego states   *Sample comments*

Parent

Adult

Child

(a) Your hobbies and interests

(b) Your attitude toward your body—likes and dislikes

(c) Your family's financial status

(d) Attitudes toward your parents and others in your family

(e) Attitudes toward religion

(f) Your love life, past and present

(g) Personal problems that really concern you

(h) How you react to your partner on the basis of this exercise*

4. Member Roles Exercise

Have a group discussion using the fishbowl format (a group of observers sur-rounding a group of discussants). Try to identify the roles each member plays by placing a check mark in the appropriate box in the chart shown in Figure 5.14. These observations should be fed back to the group members and dis-cussed in a supportive way. For a variation, some group members can be briefed in advance to act out certain roles to test the observers' abilities to recognize the behavior.

READINGS: OVERVIEW

Much has been written about the importance of developing a supportive style of personal communication in and outside small groups. In the first article, Wil-liam Peace describes his attempts to use supportive communication in an orga-nizational context.

Jack Gibb offers valuable insights in the second article, "Defensive Com-munication." Many discussions have gone astray because of this problem. Both articles go further into topics discussed in the body of the chapter.

---

*The topics are similar to those developed by Sidney Jourard (1971) and published in *Self-Disclosure: An Experimental Analysis of the Transparent Self* (New York: Wiley), pp. 177–178.

FIGURE 5.14   MEMBER ROLES EXERCISE CHART.

Roles Members	A	B	C	D	E	F	G	H
Group Task Roles								
1. Initiator-contributor								
2. Information seeker								
3. Information giver								
4. Coordinator								
5. Orientor								
6. Evaluator								
7. Energizer								
8. Opinion giver								
Group Building Roles								
9. Encourager								
10. Harmonizer								
11. Compromiser								
12. Gatekeeper and exploiter								
13. Standard setter								
14. Follower								
Self-centered Roles								
15. Aggressor								
16. Blocker								
17. Recognition-seeker								
18. Playboy (playgirl)								
19. Dominator								
20. Help-seeker								

I Thought I Knew What Good Management Was

William H. Peace

In August 1980, I was named general manager of the newly created Westinghouse Synthetic Fuels Division (SFD). The division's nucleus was a department engaged in coal gasification research and development and supported, in part, by the U.S. Department of Energy. The technology was highly regarded, and the outlook for synthetic fuels was promising. Oil prices were continuing to rise; worldwide oil shortages were forecast, as were crude oil prices of $100 per barrel; and the Carter administration had just created the Synthetic Fuels Corporation to stimulate the production of synfuels from domestic resources and reduce U.S. dependence on imported oil.

Before my assignment at SFD, I had been general manager of a division that marketed turbine generators and related services worldwide. My 16 years with Westinghouse had been spent selling complex, high-technology systems to sophisticated customers. My charge from the president of Westinghouse's Power Systems Company (then my boss's boss) was straightforward: "We think we have a very promising coal gasification technology—maybe one of the best in the world. See what you can do to make it into a good business. You may conclude that we can't, and that's an okay answer. See what you can do. I'm always available to consult and help. Keep me informed."

When I first arrived at SFD, I had mixed feelings. The Waltz Mill site, located 35 miles southeast of Pittsburgh and set in rolling hills dotted with small farms and houses, was (and is) beautiful. At the tine, about 100 people worked on the site, which included the coal gasification pilot plant, its support buildings, and offices. An additional office building and a test facility were under construction. Looking around the site, I felt both the challenge of a great opportunity and the threat of a situation that in many respects, notably technology and market, was foreign to me. (In fact, it took me nearly four years before I could feel comfortable discussing the technology with a knowledgeable customer.)

My first impressions of the people at SFD were also mixed. Some employees made me feel welcome; with others, I sensed skepticism, perhaps even resentment of my intrusion. And in a way, I felt like a hired gun, an outsider brought in to win a position for a group I barely knew. Further, while the technical people were highly competent, I thought the marketing, financial, and personnel functions were underdeveloped. So early in the assignment, I brought in a new controller and new marketing and human resource managers. They, in turn, bolstered their staffs to develop the organization's commercial capability.

Other than staff, what concerned me most was the need for a strategic plan to transform our promising, fledgling technology into a competitive, profitable business. Accordingly, I spent much of my first year learning the business and beginning to formulate a transition plan with my staff. (A chronology of key events at SFD appears in the *Exhibit.*) We concluded that a full-scale demonstration project that would prove the technical and economic feasibility of the fluid bed gasifier was an essential stepping-stone. By late 1981, we had identified a partner who had the technical and financial muscle to supplement Westinghouse strengths and to make the demonstration a success.

After much soul-searching as to what customers wanted, what Westinghouse could accept, and what had a reasonable chance of yielding good financial returns, we chose a system supply concept to approach the market. We would sell coal gasification systems in much the same way that Westinghouse sells nuclear steam supply systems: we would design them to satisfy the customer's coal resources and application; Westinghouse would build the proprietary components; and we would buy the balance of the hardware outside. We would provide some construction, start-up, and training services, but others would be responsible for many of the field man-hours and bulk materials.

Thus my assignment, as I saw it in 1980, was to tackle a set of business issues: to develop a strategic plan that would position the business technically and commercially and to become profitable in a new and unfamiliar environment. That there might be people problems that were even more challenging didn't occur to me. After all, if there were such problems, somebody would have told me about them.

Trouble Brewing

An employee attitude survey taken several months before my arrival at Waltz Mill seemed to confirm this reasoning. Compared with other attitude surveys I had seen, it didn't look particularly unfavorable. Most of the issues, like the need for better communication and for a site cafeteria, seemed resolvable, and my staff and I drew up plans to address them. We then prepared a presentation for all the employees to air the survey findings and our plans. At several of these sessions, which were held in small groups to foster discussion, I was struck by the employees' attitudes—they seemed distrustful of management, perhaps even hostile.

I found this hostility difficult to understand. It seemed inappropriate, ungrateful. "Can't the employees see," I thought, "that Westinghouse is trying to do something with this business, to make it good for everyone, including them? Can't they see the forest for the trees? Why all the petty complaining?"

Still, the problem didn't seem pressing, and I had too many other things on my mind to look for trouble.

By the fall of 1982, however, I was beginning to wonder. We had signed a contract in August to build a commercial scale demonstration project, and successful performance of that project could be our doorway to future commercial markets. But to move through this doorway, we needed to think more competitively, to get closer to our customers, to develop new business skills, and to take new risks. In other words, the employees had to change the way they thought about themselves and their jobs. From my perspective, that was looking more and more difficult.

For one thing, not all the employees supported the change from an R&D venture to a commercial enterprise. Probably the commercial enterprise seemed riskier since the organization now had to be competitive, and each task had to be done right the first time. For another, rifts were appearing in the organization: between the "old-guard" technology developers and the "new-guard" financial, marketing, and human resource staff; and between the "upper-site" office professionals and the "lower-site" technicians at the coal gasification pilot plant.

These rifts were apparently based on each group's assumption that its opponents had a secret agenda. For example, the old guard suspected that the new guard would give the technology away to get the division on a commercial footing, while the new guard was concerned that the old guard would cling to the same old R&D and resist the changes needed to carry the organization into the future.

There were some grains of truth in these fears, of course. But they were exacerbated by poor communication and an uncertain and rapidly changing environment: synthetic fuels were becoming less and less attractive economically, and doubts were proliferating about Westinghouse's willingness to give us the management commitment and financial resources we needed. At the time, however, I assumed that we had resolved the rifts in my staff meetings. Only in retrospect did I realize how often we had been shadowboxing. And with hidden agendas left unchallenged, there was ample opportunity for suspicion and distrust to develop, particularly at the lower levels of the hierarchy.

To ease the transition from lab to business, I had instituted biweekly meetings with small groups of employees. At first, these were homogeneous groups of technicians, engineers, or managers; later, they were representative cross-sections of employees selected by Human Resources. We had no agenda; rather, we discussed whatever issues the attendees wanted to raise. I called these get-togethers "employee meetings"; the employees called them "Peace talks." Whatever the name, the meetings were eye-opening. As problems that I thought had been resolved kept recurring, I began to see that my managers weren't using the same agenda I was. Employees often complained, for example, that their innovative ideas were vetoed by their management as being too risky, too expensive, or too impractical.

This lack of management follow-through annoyed me. I knew that the goals and objectives of the business plan had been well articulated, and I felt that the

EXHIBIT	CHRONOLOGY OF EVENTS AT SYNTHETIC FUELS DIVISION
August 1980	Peace appointed general manager
December 1980	New staff appointments complete
February 1981	Demonstration project (SASOL) first discussed
March 1981	SFD strategic plan prepared
May 1981	"Peace talks" begin
June 1981	Initial agreement on SASOL project
April 1982	SASOL project restructured
May 1982	Keystone project proposed to Synthetic Fuels Corporation (SFC)
July 1982	SFC drops Keystone as technically immature
August 1982	SASOL contract signed
October 1982	Consultants brought in
November 1982	Vandalism incident; employee surveys
January 1983	Revised Keystone project proposed to SFC; consultants present findings
February 1983	Change in Westinghouse top management
April 1983	Westinghouse decides to divest SFD
June 1983	SASOL project abandoned
October 1983	SFC declares Keystone technically mature
December 1983	SFC drops Keystone because equity commitment lacking
April 1984	Kellogg Rust acquires SFD
June 1984	Keystone project again proposed to SFC
September 1984	$34 million contract signed with Department of Energy
July 1985	Keystone meets SFC equity commitment requirements
September 1985	Contract drafts prepared for SFC assistance to Keystone

managers were simply fighting the system. I held quarterly meetings with all of them to review progress on key plans, discuss issues of management style, and answer questions. Evidently, I wasn't getting through to them.

Looking back, I can see that the Peace talks themselves created problems since only a few employees got the word from any one meeting, and some managers felt bypassed (even though one of their peers usually attended). So today, we give every employee a copy of each session's questions and answers. This practice doesn't alleviate managers' anxiety about loss of control, but it does ensure that everyone gets the same version of what has been said.

Trouble Erupts

The undeclared war within the division might have gone on indefinitely had an act of vandalism not brought matters to a head. In November 1982, several unidentified people (reportedly lower-site employees) slashed the tires of two managers' cars while they were parked off-site. The only explanation we were given was that some employees resented the managers' tight-ship discipline and iron-fisted style. Clearly, things were getting out of hand.

During the next week, I met with a great many people, including all the lower-site managers and employees. The picture that emerged from these meetings shocked me even more than the vandalism incident.

The Lower Site

Morale at the lower site was abysmal. Cliques of technicians had formed, some of which, Mafia-like, made the real decisions about what would be done. Pranks and hazing were common and, to some extent, managers felt captive: if they enforced discipline, the "Mafia" would retaliate or, worse yet, upper management might not support their disciplinary measures. First-level supervisors usually knew who was responsible for problems but found it difficult to catch the culprits in the act. (In one rare case, when two employees were caught stealing, the manager told them to return the goods and failed to take disciplinary action.)

I was furious. I didn't understand how things could have gotten so far out of kilter. Yet much as I disliked what I was hearing, I knew it was true. I saw that I was no more in control than lower-site management was. But I was going to put a stop to that!

Every manager agreed that the hazing and pranks had to stop. I met with all the employees and told them in plain terms that damaging personal or corporate property would be grounds for immediate dismissal. My position was clear, and it got results. The pranks stopped immediately, although hostilities lingered for a time.

The second image was harder to deal with: it had to do with me—and my management style.

The Boss

As far as the lower-site technicians were concerned, I just didn't care about them or SFD. They thought I had lost interest in everything but the demonstration project, and they accused me of forgetting that they were the people who had made the technology what it was. They also saw me as using my position as a stepping-stone to corporate headquarters at Gateway. "After all," went the reasoning, "he's the executive vice president's fair-haired boy, and he lives in that fancy neighborhood."

These impressions stung, but I could see where they came from. Take my alleged lack of interest in the lower site: today, I spend at least one hour on the lower site almost every week, walking around, listening, observing, asking questions. But I didn't do that then. I had forgotten a lesson I'd learned years before when, as chief engineer of a U.S. Navy destroyer, I could often be found in the fire room or engine room, dressed in coveralls, talking to the enlisted men and watching their work. In every category, that destroyer had the highest engineering readiness scores of any ship in the squadron; we won everything.

Commitment, which was central to the stepping-stone issue, is hard to measure from a distance, but I surely wasn't as committed to SFD in 1980 as I was in 1982 or 1984. My commitment grew the more I believed in our business plan, the more attached I felt to the people, the more successes we achieved in the face of adversity, and the more I saw the business as my child. In any case, the employees were astonished when I told them in November 1982 that I had turned down a vice president's job to be their general manager. I wanted them to understand that SFD wasn't just a stepping-stone for me and that I really appreciated the opportunity to turn a technology into a business. But I had never said that before in an unambiguous way.

Organizational Problems

As I struggled with these images, a consultant from the University of Pittsburgh added another piece to the puzzle. I had sought his help soon after the Peace talks began because I saw that my efforts to improve morale weren't working and because I thought that my staff was part of the problem. He and his assistant had interviewed about 40 employees (a representative cross-section of the division), and in early December, just after the vandalism incident, he presented the findings to me and my staff.

He reported that our people wanted to work and to contribute and that they were dedicated to the technology and believed it was the best available. But they also felt frustrated by "the system" and by what they saw as management's lack of commitment.

The severity and extent of the problems he described surprised all of us. The charge that top management didn't follow through bothered me for days, and I kept thinking about the examples the employees had given and how they looked from my side:

Inconsistent Goals   Well, we had to reorder our priorities as projects were on or off, or as customers' (or Westinghouse's) priorities changed.

No Results from the Peace Talks   I saw these meetings more as a chance to exchange views than as a vehicle for correcting problems. The employees simply saw them as ineffective.

Quality Circle Recommendations Ignored   It's true we didn't have a reliable mechanism for reacting to quality circle recommendations. At times, in fact, my staff and I responded in ways that reinforced the employees' distrust of us. For example, we had waffled months before when the engineers' quality circle made design recommendations for an office building that was nearly complete. Rather than tell the group, which included a contingent of bright, vocal, and aggressive professionals, that it was too late to accept any changes (or else prepare ourselves for some expensive last-minute redesign), we let them put forth their ideas and then shot them down. The office was completed on time and budget, but the quality circle broke up and the employees had continuing reason to dislike their new offices and distrust management.

Looking back now, I understand a lot more about how these impressions arose. Even so, I suspect that one of the most important factors behind the employees' attitude toward me was something they didn't mention in the interviews—their belief that SFD was a stepping-stone for me. But in any case, it was clear that we needed to improve the ways we communicated, individually and as an organization.

When the consultants presented their findings to all the employees in January 1983, most superiors thought the problems overstated, while subordinates found the presentation right on target. My own view was that the presentation accurately reflected the employees' perceptions; I was still trying to understand how management's perceptions and the employees' perceptions had gotten so far apart.

Changing Our Ways

During the early months of 1983, we made a large-scale effort to change the way things were done at SFD. For example, we asked almost everyone in the division to describe the way the people they worked with behaved and the way they would like them to behave. Then they met together in their work groups to discuss the discrepancies and prepare action plans to correct them.

The consultant also worked with all the managers together to review some basic principles of psychology, communications, decision making, and problem management. This group learning process reflected our commitment to apply these principles, which many of our managers had long since forgotten or else had never learned, and it paid off. For example, one manager told me that completing an exercise with the Myers-Briggs Type Indicator had taught him how fundamentally different people are. (This instrument identifies 16 distinct personality styles according to categories like one's preference for thinking or feeling and the use of intuition.) "Before examining my own style," he explained, "I could never understand why our program manager was so hard to deal with. I knew he was bright, but he just couldn't see things the way I did. Now I realize that he wants data and that the intuition that works for me is pretty much irrelevant for him."

Lastly, the consultant gave me and my staff feedback from the employees. He also spoke with managers who were clearly having style problems and with those who were simply curious.

In some cases, this one-on-one session with the consultant was the first step of a painful experience, since it's hard to be objective when it's your behavior that's being interpreted. One manager met repeatedly with his people, for example, to try to reconcile *his* belief that he let them participate in key decisions with *their* belief that he was autocratic. Not surprisingly, he admitted at the time that he didn't sleep well for several weeks.

At first, many employees viewed these efforts with suspicion: "Do we need this?" "Where's the hidden agenda?" "Shouldn't management change first?" "Is Peace really committed to this?" "What if I don't want to change?" But as the problems became clearer, so did the benefits of change. As one manager put it, "The process exposed a lot of tunnel vision."

People recognized that dramatic actions were needed to break down old walls of distrust. This recognition created a lot of anxiety, but it also led to lighter moments: one manager came to work without his toupee as a way of saying, "I'm going to be different."

For me, these months were a breath of fresh air. I could see and feel the changes from day to day. "Finally, we're getting our act together," I thought. "This is what I wanted all along." I had mixed feelings, though, about the pain I saw in the organization. I wished it could be avoided; but I also saw it as confirmation that people were learning and changing. For my part, I kept trying to reconcile how I saw myself with the way my people saw me. I also tried to understand what I could have done differently to keep the mistrust and hostility from building.

During this period of introspection, I found that the comments of one of my managers gave me a lot to think about. While discussing the vandalism incident, she had pointed out that I wasn't very good at giving recognition. "I hope you don't mind my saying this," she said, "but you really ought to make a special effort to celebrate people's accomplishments. There's not enough hoopla anymore."

I agreed. I admitted I wasn't at ease in situations that called for hoopla, and I told her I had asked my staff to help me out. "The problem," she said, "is that all of you were brought up to take meeting objectives for granted; only outstanding accomplishments are supposed to be noted."

She was right, but there was more to it than that. In our culture, men, particularly ambitious, successful men, become adept at staying out of touch with their feelings. We believe that we can withstand enormous pressure and ambiguity, that we can make decisions using logic alone, and that we are immune to emotion. The problem, of course, is that human beings are emotional creatures (whether we executives like it or not). Maintaining tight control of our emotions (or being out of touch with them) isn't a skill, it's a weakness.

Today, we at SFD are better about celebrating accomplishments, not because we have a formal recognition program, but rather because everyone is a lot more people oriented. Our employees tend to acknowledge one another's special efforts spontaneously, while I find I enjoy celebrations now that I'm more relaxed about expressing my emotions.

In addition, I have come to see that during my first two years at SFD I focused too much on myself and my goals. As a result, my pride demanded that I defend my image of myself as competent, intelligent, successful. As I listened more intently to others, however, and cared about their goals, I found I had less need to be defensive. In effect, I have become a leader who serves others by making *them* successful.

Divestiture

In April 1983, Westinghouse decided to sell the Synthetic Fuels Division. To me, the decision seemed capricious. I thought I had made considerable progress in fulfilling my charge to make a business out of the technology. Unfortunately, the president of the Power Systems Company, who had given me that charge, had just elected to take early retirement. Headquarters seemed to have little concern for our people problems or our problems in finding a buyer. That's a perception, of course, *our* perception; perceptions at headquarters were doubtless different. But little effort was made to resolve these differences: trust was supplanted by anger.

The divestiture process was little short of traumatic for me, and many of my staff felt the same frustration, anger, and bitterness I did. Moreover, my anger at being abandoned after having done what was asked of me only reinforced my by-then strong commitment to SFD. It was a living part of me, and I was part of it. Convinced that SFD should be sold and not shut down (a likely possibility as potential buyers failed to appear), I put everything I had into finding and courting prospective buyers while trying to keep nervous (and valuable) human resources from deserting what appeared to be a sinking ship.

Rumors that I had been (or would be) fired for trying too hard to save SFD circulated repeatedly. The rumors were false, buy they convey the employees' sense of the situation. Even on the lower site people felt that "management may not be able to sell this place, and I may end up on the street if they don't, but I know they're giving it all they've got." By then, it was okay (pretty much) to talk to management again.

By early 1984, I was exhausted physically and emotionally. Preparations were under way to close the Synthetic Fuels Division when Westinghouse accepted an offer from Kellogg Rust Inc., one of the Signal Companies, to purchase 80% of SFD (now known as KRW Energy Systems Inc.).

At the meeting to announce the sale, I received two plaques from the employees as thanks for "saving our jobs." One is a collage of photographs of everyone at SFD; the other, from the lower-site technicians, is a religious message engraved on brass. Those plaques mean a great deal to me because they reflect the changes throughout our company. Not everyone has changed his or her beliefs, of course, but the consensus on how we should behave has shifted dramatically. At every level, our employees are far more supportive of one another, more communicative, more patient, and more trusting. As one manager later said, "If it hadn't been for these efforts, SFD would never have survived: there would have been nothing left to sell."

Looking Back

I can now see several reasons for our problems at SFD. First, people tend to develop ways to resist change and uncertainty. Yet uncertainty was about our only given, and we had to undergo a large-scale strategic redirection.

Second, some of our managers were not well trained. They adopted short cuts like cursory performance evaluations, which made the job of managing easier in the short run but was counterproductive in the long run. Assuming that knowledge is power, they communicated little to their employees. (Today, by contrast, we have a no-secrets approach to information, which we try to share widely among those who can use it.) And they tended to treat employees like children, conveying a "we know what's good for you" attitude that employees resented and distrusted. That they often weren't sure whether the managers were acting in the company's best interest or their own only heightened this distrust.

Finally, as people began to defend themselves against their bosses, change, or "the system," trust broke down. Employees and managers alike assumed the worst about one another and acted accordingly. And as suspicion built on itself, the organization's goals took a backseat to turf and survival. Quality, productivity, and customer satisfaction meant very little.

Personal lessons

For me, the central issue was commitment: my commitment and how it was perceived. One key manager later told me, "You didn't really change—our perception of you did." But that's not true; certainly perceptions changed, but if I too hadn't changed, we would have failed.

In the summer of 1980, I was a kind of hired gun committed to the challenge I'd been given by my boss to make a business out of the technology. In the fall of 1982, I was a general manager under siege. We were on the brink of building our first commercial project, but I had lost the people. My commitment then was to the technology and to making it a commercial success.

By the spring of 1983, I was in a life-or-death struggle. I had been stung by the charge that I wasn't committed, and I was angry with the change in Westinghouse's commitment. By that time, I was committed to the people, to the technology, and to their mutual success.

More than my commitment changed, however. Two years of unremitting stress changed me as a person. It may seem paradoxical, but I'm more at ease with myself than ever before. Seeing my own needs and motivations more clearly gives me a broader perspective, and in a fundamental sense, I'm more in control of my life. In 1980, I thought I was in control and that I made only logical choices. Now I can see the emotional forces that drive all of us toward the choices we later justify logically. I find that I laugh more easily and enjoy people (their virtues and even their faults) as never before. I'm sure I'm helped, too, by feeling that if I could survive *that* I can survive anything.

Other lessons I learned from these experiences have to do with perceptions, communications, and trust. Perceptions form around tiny bits of data and become stronger as supporting evidence accumulates; they are never completely accurate, nor are they completely wrong. Staying in touch with others' perceptions is difficult, however, partly because these may not be wholly conscious and partly because only the tip of what may be a large, threatening iceberg will be known to any one employee. So managers must piece together the overall picture for themselves by listening hard for the tone, or context, or shading that doesn't quite match their own perceptions. Moreover, managers (particularly those at high levels) must consider carefully their decisions will be perceived. If a decision is right in some business sense but wrong (for whatever reason) from the employees' perspective, its implementation will be erratic at best.

The chain of command is an inefficient communication system. Although my staff and I had our goals, tasks, and priorities well defined, large parts of the organization didn't know what was going on. Frequent, thorough, open communication to every employee is essential to get the word out and keep walls from building within the company. And while face-to-face communication is more effective than impersonal messages, it's a good idea to vary the medium and the format so that no one (including top management) relies too much on "traditional" channels of communication.

Trust in organizations is like love in a marriage; it holds people together and makes them effective. From my experience, we have two ways to build trust in us as individuals. First, we can make ourselves vulnerable by setting aside the masks we usually wear and disclosing our true selves. (The fact is, our employees know we're human—regardless of the executive cloaks we wear—and they forget only briefly that we're "the boss.") And second, we can take real risks on behalf of our employees.

As an example, let me tell you one last story. About two years ago, top management ordered that all merit increases scheduled for the fourth quarter be rescinded as an economy measure. I felt that the edict was unfair to employees unfortunate enough to have their raises fall in that quarter. Moreover, we had already told them what merit increases to expect during the year as part of their performance appraisals. We didn't implement the edict, nor did we publicize our insubordination. But employees found out about both. That risk, while it might have cost me my job, went a long way toward building the trust we needed.

Defensive Communication

Jack R. Gibb

One way to understand communication is to view it as a people process rather than as a language process. If one is to make fundamental improvement in communication, he must make changes in interpersonal relationships. One possible type of alteration—and the one with which this paper is concerned—is that of reducing the degree of defensiveness.

Definition and Significance

Defensive behavior is defined as that behavior which occurs when an individual perceives threat or anticipates threat in the group. The person who behaves defensively, even though he also gives some attention to the common task, devotes an appreciable portion of his energy to defending himself. Besides talking about the topic, he thinks about how he appears to others, how he may be seen more favorably, how he may win, dominate, impress, or escape punishment and/or how he may avoid or mitigate a perceived or an anticipated attack.

Such inner feelings and outward acts tend to create similarly defensive postures in others; and, if unchecked, the ensuing circular response becomes increasingly destructive. Defensive behavior, in short, engenders defensive listening, and this in turn produces postural, facial, and verbal cues which raise the defense level of the original communicator.

Defense arousal prevents the listener from concentrating upon the message. Not only do defensive communicators send off multiple value, motive, and affect cues, but also defensive recipients distort what they receive. As a person becomes more and more defensive, he becomes less and less able to perceive accurately the motives, the values, and the emotions of the sender. The writer's analyses of tape-recorded discussions revealed that increases in defensive behavior were correlated positively with losses in efficiency in communication.[1] Specifically, distortions became greater when defensive states existed in the groups.

The converse, moreover, also is true. The more "supportive" or defense reductive the climate, the less the receiver reads into the communication distorted loadings which arise from projections of his own anxieties, motives, and

Reproduced from The Journal of Communication, *Vol. 11, No. 3, Copyright, September, 1961,* 141–148. Reprinted by permission of the International Communication Association.

concerns. As defenses are reduced, the receivers become better able to concentrate upon the structure, the content, and the cognitive meanings of the message.

Categories of Defensive and Supportive Communication

In working over an eight-year period with recordings of discussions occurring in varied settings, the writer developed the six pairs of defensive and supportive categories presented in Table 1. Behavior which a listener perceives as possessing any of the characteristics listed in the left-hand column arouses defensiveness, whereas that which he interprets as having any of the qualities designated as supportive reduces defensive feelings. The degree to which these reactions occur depends upon the personal level of defensiveness and on the general climate in the group at the time.[2]

Evaluation and Description

Speech or other behavior which appears evaluative increases defensiveness. If by expression, manner of speech, tone of voice, or verbal content the sender seems to be evaluating or judging the listener, then the receiver goes on guard. Of course, other factors may inhibit the reaction. If the listener thought that the speaker regarded him as an equal and was being open and spontaneous, for example, the evaluativeness in a message would be neutralized and perhaps not even perceived. This same principle applies equally to the other five categories of potentially defense-producing climates. The six sets are interactive.

Because our attitudes toward other persons are frequently, and often necessarily, evaluative expression which the defensive person will regard as nonjudg-

TABLE 1   CATEGORIES OF BEHAVIOR CHARACTERISTICS OF SUPPORTIVE AND DEFENSIVE CLIMATES IN SMALL GROUPS

Defensive Climates	Supportive Climates
1. Evaluation	1. Description
2. Control	2. Problem orientation
3. Strategy	3. Spontaneity
4. Neutrality	4. Empathy
5. Superiority	5. Equality
6. Certainty	6. Provisionalism

mental are hard to frame. Even the simplest question usually conveys the answer that the sender wishes or implies the response that would fit into his value system. A mother, for example, immediately following an earth tremor that shook the house, sought for her small son with the question: "Bobby, where are you?" The timid and plaintive "Mommy, I didn't do it" indicated how Bobby's chronic mild defensiveness predisposed him to react with a projection of his own guilt and in the context of his chronic assumption that questions are full of accusation.

Anyone who has attempted to train professionals to use information-seeking speech with neutral affect appreciates how difficult it is to teach a person to say even the simple "who did that?" without being seen as accusing. Speech is so frequently judgmental that there is a reality base for the defensive interpretations which are so common.

When insecure, group members are particularly likely to place blame, to see others as fitting into categories of good or bad, to make moral judgments of their colleagues, and to question the value, motive, and affect loadings of the speech which they hear. Since value loadings imply a judgment of others, a belief that the standards of the speaker differ from his own causes the listener to become defensive.

Descriptive speech, in contrast to that which is evaluative, tends to arouse a minimum of uneasiness. Speech acts which the listener perceives as genuine requests for information or as material with neutral loadings is descriptive. Specifically, presentations of feelings, events, perceptions, or processes which do not ask or imply that the receiver change behavior or attitude are minimally defense producing. The difficulty in avoiding overtone is illustrated by the problems of news reporters in writing stories about unions, communists, Negroes, and religious activities without tipping off the "party" line of the newspaper. One can often tell from the opening words in a news article which side the newspaper's editorial policy favors.

Control and Problem Orientation

Speech which is used to control the listener evokes resistance. In most of our social intercourse someone is trying to do something to someone else—to change an attitude, to influence behavior, or to restrict the field of activity. The degree to which attempts to control produce defensiveness depends upon the openness of the effort, for a suspicion that hidden motives exist heightens resistance. For this reason, attempts of nondirective therapists and progressive educators to refrain from imposing a set of values, a point of view, or a problem solution upon the receivers meet with many barriers. Since the norm is control, noncontrollers must earn the perceptions that their efforts have no hidden motives. A bombardment of persuasive "messages" in the fields of politics, education, special causes, advertising, religion, medicine, industrial relations, and guidance has bred cynical and paranoidal responses in listeners.

Implicit in all attempts to alter another person is the assumption by the change agent that the person to be altered is inadequate. That the speaker secretly views the listener as ignorant, unable to make his own decisions, uninformed, immature, unwise, or possessed of wrong or inadequate attitudes is a subconscious perception which gives the latter a valid base for defensive reactions.

Methods of control are many and varied. Legalistic insistence on detail, restrictive regulations and policies, conformity norms, and all laws are among the methods. Gestures, facial expression, other forms of nonverbal communication, and even such simple acts as holding a door open in a particular manner are means of imposing one's will upon another and hence are potential sources of resistance.

Problem orientation, on the other hand, is the antithesis of persuasion. When the sender communicates a desire to collaborate in defining a mutual problem and in seeking its solution, he tends to create the same problem orientation in the listener; and, of greater importance, he implies that he has no predetermined solution, attitude, or method to impose. Such behavior is permissive in that it allows the receiver to set his own goals, make his own decisions, and evaluate his own progress or to share with the sender in doing so. The exact methods of attaining permissiveness are not known, but they must involve a constellation of cues and they certainly go beyond mere verbal assurances that the communicator has no hidden desires to exercise control.

Strategy and Spontaneity

When the sender is perceived as engaging in a stratagem involving ambiguous and multiple motivators, the receiver becomes defensive. No one wishes to be a guinea pig, a role player, or an impressed actor, and no one likes to be the victim of some hidden motivation. That which is concealed, also, may appear larger than it really is with the degree of defensiveness of the listener determining the perceived size of the suppressed element. The intense reaction of the reading audience to the material in *The Hidden Persuaders* indicates the prevalence of defensive reactions to multiple motivations behind strategy. Group members who are seen as "taking a role," as feigning emotion, as toying with their colleagues, as withholding information, or as having special sources of data are especially resented. One participant once complained that another was "using a listening technique" on him!

A large part of the adverse reaction to much of the so-called human relations training is a feeling against what are perceived as gimmicks and tricks to fool or to "involve" people, to make a person think he is making his own decision, or to make the listener feel that the sender is genuinely interested in him as a person. Particularly violent reactions occur when it appears that someone is trying to make a stratagem appear spontaneous. One person has reported a boss who incurred resentment by habitually using the gimmick of "spontaneously" looking at his watch and saying, "My gosh, look at the time—I must run to an appointment." The belief was that the boss would create less irritation by honestly asking to be excused.

Similarly, the deliberate assumption of guilelessness and natural simplicity is especially resented. Monitoring the tapes of feedback and evaluation sessions in training groups indicates the surprising extent to which members perceive the strategies of their colleagues. This perceptual clarity may be quite shocking to the strategist, who usually feels that he has cleverly hidden the motivational aura around the "gimmick."

This aversion to deceit may account for one's resistance to politicians who are suspected of behind-the-scenes planning to get his vote, to psychologists whose listening apparently is motivated by more than the manifest or content-level interest in his behavior, or to the sophisticated, smooth, or clever person whose "oneupmanship" is marked with guile. In training groups the role-flexible person frequently is resented because his changes in behavior are perceived as strategic maneuvers.

In contrast, behavior which appears to be spontaneous and free of deception is defense reductive. If the communicator is seen as having a clean id, as having uncomplicated motivations, as being straightforward and honest, and as behaving spontaneously in response to the situation, he is likely to arouse minimal defense.

Neutrality and Empathy

When neutrality in speech appears to the listener to indicate a lack of concern for his welfare, he becomes defensive. Group members usually desire to be perceived as valued persons, as individuals of speech worth, and as objects of concern and affection. The clinical, detached, person-is-an-object-of-study attitude on the part of many psychologist-trainers is resented by group members. Speech with low affect that communicates little warmth or caring is in such contrast with the affect laden speech in social situations that it sometimes communicates rejection.

Communication that conveys empathy for the feelings and respect for the worth of the listener, however, is particularly supportive and defense reductive. Reassurance results when a message indicates that the speaker identifies himself with the listener's problems, shares his feelings, and accepts his emotional reactions at face value. Abortive efforts to deny the legitimacy of the receiver's emotions by assuring the receiver that he need not feel bad, that he should not feel rejected or that he is overly anxious, though often intended as support giving, may impress the listener as lack of acceptance. The combination of understanding and empathizing with other person's emotions with no accompanying effort to change him apparently is supportive at a high level.

The importance of gestural behavior cues in communicating empathy should be mentioned. Apparently spontaneous facial and bodily evidences of concern are often interpreted as especially valid evidence of deep-level acceptance.

Superiority and Equality

When a person communicates to another that he feels superior in position, power, wealth, intellectual ability, physical characteristics, or other ways, he arouses defensiveness. Here, as with the other sources of disturbance, whatever arouses feelings of inadequacy causes the listener to center upon the affect loading of the statement rather than upon the cognitive elements. The receiver then reacts by not hearing the message, by forgetting it, by competing with the sender, or by becoming jealous of him.

The person who is perceived as feeling superior communicates that he is not willing to enter into a shared problem-solving relationship, that he probably does not desire feedback, that he does not require help, and/or that he will be likely to try to reduce the power, the status, or the worth of the receiver.

Many ways exist for creating the atmosphere that the sender feels himself equal to the listener. Defenses are reduced when one perceives the sender as being willing to enter into participative planning with mutual trust and respect. Differences in talent, ability, worth, appearance, status, and power often exist, but the low defense communicator seems to attach little importance to these distinctions.

Certainty and Provisionalism

The effects of dogmatism in producing defensiveness are well known. Those who seem to know the answers, to require no additional data, and to regard themselves as teachers rather than as co-workers tend to put others on guard. Moreover, in the writer's experiment, listeners often perceived manifest expressions of certainty as connoting inward feelings of inferiority. They saw the dogmatic individual as needing to be right, as wanting to win an argument rather than solve a problem, and as seeing his ideas as truths to be defended. This kind of behavior often was associated with acts which others regarded as attempts to exercise control. People who were right seemed to have low tolerance for members who were "wrong"—i.e., who did not agree with the sender.

One reduces the defensiveness of the listener when he communicates that he is willing to experiment with his own behavior, attitudes, and ideas. The person who appears to be taking provisional attitudes, to be investigating issues rather than taking sides on them, to be problem solving rather than debating, and to be willing to experiment and explore tends to communicate that the listener may have some control over the shared quest or the investigation of the ideas. If a person is genuinely searching for information and data, he does not resent help or company along the way.

Conclusion

The implications of the above material for the parent, the teacher, the manager, the administrator, or the therapist are fairly obvious. Arousing defensiveness interferes with communication and thus makes it difficult—and sometimes impossible—for anyone to convey ideas clearly and to move effectively toward the solution of therapeutic, educational, or managerial problems.

Notes

1. J. R. Gibb, "Defense Level and Influence Potential in Small Groups," in L. Petrullo and B. M. Bass (eds.), *Leadership and Interpersonal Behavior* (New York: Holt, Rinehart and Winston, Inc., 1961), pp. 66–81.

2. J. R. Gibb, "Sociopsychological Process of Group Instruction," in N. B. Henry (ed.), *The Dynamics of Instructional Groups* (Fifty-ninth Yearbook of the National Society for the Study of Education, Part II, 1960), pp. 115–135.

Internal Influences

Conflict Resolution and Decision-Making Processes

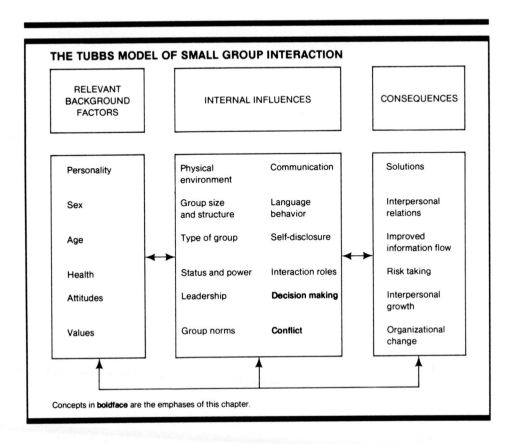

THE TUBBS MODEL OF SMALL GROUP INTERACTION

RELEVANT BACKGROUND FACTORS	INTERNAL INFLUENCES		CONSEQUENCES
Personality	Physical environment	Communication	Solutions
Sex	Group size and structure	Language behavior	Interpersonal relations
Age	Type of group	Self-disclosure	Improved information flow
Health	Status and power	Interaction roles	Risk taking
Attitudes	Leadership	**Decision making**	Interpersonal growth
Values	Group norms	**Conflict**	Organizational change

Concepts in **boldface** are the emphases of this chapter.

CASE STUDY

The situation reported in this case occurred in a classroom of a large state university. Herb Hamilton was a 48-year-old high school biology teacher taking an evening graduate-level psychology course in stress management. Dr. Martin, the professor, was 37 years old, had been teaching for 15 years, and was an adjunct professor of psychology at the university (where he taught one night a week) and a full professor at a nearby engineering college. The class had 19 people in it ranging in age from 25 to 48. (Herb was the oldest member of the class.) This is Dr. Martin's account.

Our first class met on January 12. After covering the basic description of the course, assignments, etc., I began a lecture offering a brief overview of the major sources of stress. I mentioned job, family, and community. As I proceeded to discuss divorce statistics, Herb became very upset and said the following, as best I can recall, "It's easy for you to be smug. You have a job, you are married, and you don't know the first thing about what stress feels like. You can only talk about it in an intellectual vacuum!"

After finishing the class, I talked with Herb for about fifteen minutes. He revealed to me that he was under psychiatric care; had been through a very messy divorce during which his wife broke a milk bottle across his face; was currently on a disability leave from his teaching job after having suffered an emotional breakdown; and was the father of four children who "never bothered to call him unless they wanted some money." I tried to calm him down since he was shaking noticeably. I told him that the course was designed to help each of us cope more effectively with the stresses in our lives.

He continued to be disruptive, abusive, and insulting through the next several weeks of class. Several students complained privately that they couldn't believe how antisocial his behavior was, and that he was violating their right to learn by his behavior.

Then, on the evening of March 2, Herb came to class smelling of alcohol. I was seated directly behind him. Two students were presenting a report on alcoholism. They began with a 35-item test of knowledge about alcoholism. Herb began criticizing the test by stating that he couldn't answer these items because they were statements, not questions. They explained that it was a true-false test and the items were intended to be statements of fact, which could be indicated as true or false.

As one person began to read off the correct answers, Herb debated and criticized virtually every item's answer. After the first item, I asked Herb to let the students go on with the report and then we could discuss the entire report as a class. Herb continued to argue every point. Four or five times, other class members asked Herb to be quiet and quit interrupting the presentation. By the time we got to item 21 on the test, the entire class was getting upset.

The 21st item on the test stated that alcohol is a stimulant. The speaker said that this statement was false, that it was a depressant. This particularly upset Herb, who argued that it was a stimulant in small quantities and a depressant only in large quantities. I corroborated the speaker, explaining that alcohol depressed the inhibitory mechanisms in the central nervous system, which made it *appear* that the drinker was acting like he or she had been stimulated. Herb turned around to the rest of the class and said, "People, can we tolerate this? This is absolutely wrong. We aren't even getting the accurate facts in this class. We are getting garbage," or words very similar to those.

1. What should Dr. Martin do?

2. How could this conflict have been dealt with? In what ways could it have been avoided?

P erhaps one of the most frequent criticisms of committees is that they are a waste of time. By this people usually mean that groups often require a lot of effort without achieving any tangible results. Therefore it is important to note that several techniques have been developed that can help us get better results from the time we spend in problem-solving groups or committees.

DECISION-MAKING PROCESSES

To increase our understanding of organizational behavior in general, it is particularly important to concentrate on organizational decision making. The decision making of the organization is in essence its nucleus, it's what holds the organization together and makes it progress. The goals, tasks, and choices determining the organization's activities are highlighted, broadly illuminating the dynamics of organizational life.

A majority of the really crucial events of the world are a consequence of the organizational decision-making process rather than isolated, individual decision making. An industrial example cited by Bass (1983) is the "delayed decisions by Detroit auto manufacturers to switch to production of small cars." He goes on to say that it can "only be understood in terms of consumer attitudes toward the small car (fostered by a generation of advertising), the gasoline crisis, political support for continued low gasoline prices, differential profitability of small and large autos, short public memory, and long lead times for investment turnarounds." (p. 2). The unanswered question is whether an understanding of better organizational decision-making processes could have produced a better decision under the conditions.

As you no doubt know, decision making is hard work. Often the decision-making models in textbooks are extremely simplified compared to the actual cases that confront us in real life. Some fascinating material has recently been published that reveals that even within our own brains we use two different models or methods for decision making. The left hemisphere of the brain is more prone to logical, factual, sequential, and systematic thinking and decision making. The right hemisphere tends to function more in a holistic, intuitive, emotional manner. For example, one recent advertisement for a new sports car stated that the left side of our brains would like its craftsmanship, good economy, and high resale value, and the right side of our brains would like the fact that it goes like a "bat out of hell."

The right side of the brain would enjoy the pictures and the cartoons in this book, while the left side would like the charts that organize the concepts. The chart in Figure 6.1 compares the right and left brain functioning methods.

FIGURE 6.1   LEFT AND RIGHT BRAIN FUNCTIONS.

	Left	Right	
1	Logical, more like a computer analyzing component bits of information in a systematic manner and sequence, then drawing a conclusion from the premises.	Intuitive, more like an artist looking for an *overall* image, concept, or Gestalt. The conclusions are often reached in a flash of insight, rather than in a systematic method.	1
2	Either/or thinking, one correct answer (such as in mathematics).	Many alternatives, numerous shades of gray, subtle gradations or nuances of meaning.	2
3	Precise, literal meaning, such as in legal documents.	Nonliteral comparisons, such as in metaphors and analogies. (For example, comparing a group's leader to a ship's rudder.)	3
4	Verbally oriented.	Nonverbally oriented, uses graphic or pictorial descriptions.	4
5	Explicit, carefully defined, and fully explained.	Implicit, impressionistic, like a sketch rather than a photograph.	5
6	Controlled, disciplined.	Emotional, sensual, like reacting to music or to fragrances or colors.	6
7	Pragmatic, very practical real-world orientation.	Imaginative, nontraditional, innovative, uses fantasy.	7
8	Dominant.	Passive.	8
9	Intellectual, cerebral.	Sensually oriented, prefers experiencing to intellectualizing.	9
10	Careful with time and the use of time.	Casual with time and the use of time.	10
11	Scientific.	Artistic.	11
12	Preprogrammed, organized.	Ambiguous, nebulous.	12
13	Objective, verifiable.	Subjective, personal, unique.	13
14	Skeptical, preferring evidence and factual proof.	Accepting, preferring intuition and gut-level impressions.	14
15	Comparison against standards of performance.	Comparison against internal private standards.	15

Gibson and Hodgetts (1986) identify four different kinds of creativity which may be applied to group problem solving:

Innovation is original thinking. This is probably the most difficult since by definition it is something never created before. Reportedly, the flip top can was invented by a can opener company which was going broke and needed to think up a new product line.

Synthesis is the combining of information from other sources into a new pattern. A kaliedoscope is somewhat like this. The colored pieces of glass are combined and recombined to make new patterns.

Extension is the expansion of ideas beyond their current boundaries. McDonalds decided a few years back to add breakfast to their existing product lines. This increased their profits by 40 percent!

Duplication is to copy good ideas. Japanese companies have become famous for taking original ideas from American companies and copying them and improving on them. The motorcycle, electronics, watch, and auto industries are but a few examples. (pp. 155–156)

As you look at several decision-making models in this chapter, you will notice that implied in each approach is a bias toward the left brain or the right. It is probably good to remember that both sides of the brain should be used in concert, since their functions complement each other.

Finally, some of the following models are prescriptive—that is, they prescribe a desired way to solve problems. Other models are more descriptive and describe how we tend to solve problems rather than tell us how we should do it. Each model has some research evidence suggesting that it is helpful in improving the decisions that people make. However, our ability to solve problems will probably be helped most if we become familiar with several of these approaches and gain what we can from each, instead of picking only one.

The Reflective Thinking Process

Undoubtedly, the best-known pattern for small group problem solving is the reflective thinking sequence first proposed by John Dewey (1910). It emphasizes the left brain functions. Although the method has several variations, the basic components are: (1) What is the problem? (2) What are its causes and limits? (3) What are the criteria for an acceptable solution? (4) What are the available solutions? (5) What is the best solution? (6) How can it be implemented? A more detailed outline includes the following:

I. Problem Phase

    a. *Identification of problem area, including such questions as:*

        1. What is the situation in which the problem is occurring?

        2. What, in general, is the difficulty?

        3. How did this difficulty arise?

    4. What is the importance of the difficulty?

    5. What limitations, if any, are there on the area of our concern?

    6. What is the meaning of any terms that need clarifying?

  b. *Analysis of the difficulty*

    1. What, specifically, are the facts of the situation?

    2. What, specifically, are the difficulties?

  c. *Analysis of causes*

    1. What is causing the difficulties?

    2. What is causing the causes?

II. Criteria Phase

  a. What are the principal requirements of the solution?

  b. What limitations must be placed on the solution?

  c. What is the relative importance of the criteria?

III. Solution Phase

  a. *What are the possible solutions?*

    1. What is the exact nature of each solution?

    2. How would it remedy the difficulty? by eliminating the cause? by off-setting the effect? by a combination of both?

  b. *How good is each solution?*

    1. How well would it remedy the difficulty?

    2. How well would it satisfy the criteria? Are there any that it would not satisfy?

    3. Would there be any unfavorable consequences? any extra benefits?

  c. *What solution appears to be best?*

    1. How would you rank the solution?

    2. Would some combination of solutions be best?

IV. Implementation Phase

What steps would be taken to put the solution into effect?

While this sequence is well known and widely taught, other approaches that are of value have also been proposed.

The Kepner–Tregoe Approach

A variation of the reflective thinking sequence has been proposed by two business consultants (Kepner and Tregoe 1965). The overall format is similar to the reflective thinking sequence; however, the most important contribution seems to be the way in which a group works through the *criteria phase*.

Let's say that the group is trying to figure out how to cut its departmental spending by 10 percent. In selecting the best solution, several criteria must be considered. There are certain required elements and other desired elements to any solution. Kepner and Tregoe refer to these as the *musts* and *wants*, respectively. For example:

Musts	**Wants**
The budget must be reduced by 10 percent.	We would like to avoid laying people off.
We must have it accomplished within a year.	Sooner would be better.
Any changes must be in line with existing company policies.	We would like to involve people in the decision.
Any changes must not violate our union contract.	We would like people to willingly cooperate.

Using the method described above, the criteria for an acceptable decision could be assigned a numerical value and ranked in order of importance. Then a grid can be constructed on which you can evaluate different solutions against the relevant criteria.

One school district committee, faced with declining enrollments, used this method to determine how to solve the problem. The administrators set up the following grid in the process of conducting their analysis:

Criteria (partial list):

Alternative Solutions (partial list):	1. Cut costs	2. Maintain quality of curricular offerings	3. Utilize existing facilities
1. Close three middle schools	yes	yes	yes
2. Close one high school	yes	no	yes
3. Leave all schools open	no	yes	yes

On the basis of this analysis, they decided to choose solution 1, since it was the only one that met all their important *must* criteria.

One college management department was trying to select a new chairperson. In a series of meetings, the three most important criteria or areas of skill were identified as follows:

> The critical criteria for the chairperson of the department have been structured into three areas of competence: administrative, professional, and personal.

I. Administrative Skills

   a. Leads (motivates and inspires faculty).

   b. Employs participative style of management (whenever possible, consults with faculty prior to making decisions that affect them).

   c. Demonstrates commitment to development of faculty (allows faculty considerable personal freedom, encourages them to share leadership responsibilities and to take on projects).

   d. Recognizes faculty performance and makes recommendations to administration for promotions and merit increases.

   e. Leads department in keeping curriculum abreast of educational needs.

   f. Is well known in the professional field, particularly to administrators in other educational institutions who can assist in recruitment and development of faculty.

   g. Is committed to equal development of disciplines represented in the department.

II. Professional Skills

   a. Demonstrates commitment to excellence in teaching and research.

   b. Is well known and respected through publications and other professional contributions. Is a recognized scholar in his or her field.

   c. Possesses a doctorate.

III. Personal Skills

   a. Possesses a high degree of integrity and maturity.

   b. Is willing to listen and respond to the ideas and opinions of others.

   c. Is willing to express personal and departmental convictions to faculty and administration.

   d. Evokes the acceptance and trust of associates.

Over a period of some time, several potential candidates for the position were selected. Let us call them Tom, Dick, and Harry. Once the criteria had been established, and the potential candidates selected, a chart or grid shows the way in which the candidates were compared to the criteria (see Figure 6.2). On the basis of the data in the chart, which candidate would you have chosen?

The Single Question Form

Larson (1969, p. 453) has found that another, rather brief method is about as good as the methods already described. Larson studied the differences between high- and low-success individual problem solvers and derived a technique that could be used by groups. This method involves using the following format:

> What is the single question, the answer to which is all the group needs to know to accomplish its purpose?
> What subquestions must be answered before we can answer the single question we have formulated?
> Do we have sufficient information to answer confidently the subquestions?
> What are the most reasonable answers to the subquestions?
> Assuming that our answers to the subquestions are correct, what is the best solution to the problem?

This technique evolved out of an analysis of the basic differences in communication behaviors between successful and unsuccessful problem solvers studied by Bloom and Broder (1961). It seems that the successful problem solvers were more willing and interested in getting at solutions and avoided getting bogged down with the trivial detail of the discussion. Their attitudes seemed to be characterized as, "Let's assume for the moment a few things," rather than, "How can we be expected to solve this when those guys who gave us the problem can't solve their own problems?" In other words, there is an eagerness to make progress rather than to alibi out of making progress. Dance and Larson (1972, p. 128) summarize these two different sets of behaviors in Figure 6.3. Notice that this is a descriptive summary that has prescriptive implications.

Each of the problem-solving methods described thus far (that is, reflective thinking, the Kepner-Tregoe approach, or the single-question form) will probably offer you and your group a way to get better results than if you used no systematic method

FIGURE 6.2

Candidates	Criteria (Ranked in Order of Importance)		
	Administrative Skills (1)	Professional Skills (2)	Personal Skills (3)
Tom	Good	Excellent	Excellent
Dick	Excellent	Excellent	Good
Harry	Good	Good	Good

FIGURE 6.3   SOME DIFFERENCES BETWEEN HIGH- AND LOW-SUCCESS PROBLEM SOLVERS.

Used with permission of F.E.X. Dance, *Speech Communication: Concepts and Behavior* (New York: Holt, Rinehart and Winston, 1972), p. 128.

High Success	Low Success
1. Starting the attack on the problem	
Able to select some phrase or concept as a point of departure. Able to state a specific objective toward which to work.	Tried to change the problem to one which they could solve more easily. Tendency to disagree with the problem, for example, "This is a stupid problem."
2. Approach to basic ideas within the problem	
Used analogies and examples to help themselves understand the concepts within the problems. Considered more implications of the ideas which they came up with, such as, "What would result from . . ." "What causes . . ."	Did not attempt to arrive at an understanding of the problem, for example, "We haven't studied that yet." Used more unconnected series of thoughts.
3. General approach to problems	
Set up hypotheses about what the correct answer would do. If unfamiliar terms were used in the problem, made an assumption about the meaning and proceeded.	Selected answers on the basis of feeling and impressions (especially in social problems). Devoted little time to considering the nature of the problem.
4. Attitudes toward solving problems	
"You can figure it out if you try."	"You either know it or you don't." Easily discouraged. Avoided complex problems. Little confidence in their own reasoning abilities.

at all. Try using each of these methods in solving some of the problem exercises in this book. Don't give up—most problems can be solved if we work at them long enough.

Brainstorming

Another popular technique that can be applied to problem-solving is brainstorming (Osborn 1953). This technique is primarily used to generate ideas and can be applied as *part* of the problem-solving process. It emphasizes right brain activity. For example, groups frequently dwell on one or two proposed solutions to a problem, when many more solutions may be available. Brainstorming would be one way to help generate more alternative solutions for the group to consider.

Brainstorming can be applied to any of the phases of the reflective thinking sequence discussed earlier. The problem identification phase includes the need to determine the factors causing the problem; the criteria phase requires identification of the requirements for an appropriate solution; the solution phase requires some alternatives from which to choose; and the implementation phase requires creative

FRANK AND ERNEST by Bob Thaves

THEY OFFERED ME A JOB AS A TOP LEVEL DECISION-MAKER, BUT I CAN'T MAKE UP MY MIND WHETHER OR NOT TO TAKE IT.

application of the chosen solution. The guidelines (adapted from Osborn 1953) for using the brainstorming technique are listed below.

Rules for Brainstorming

1. *Put judgment and evaluation temporarily aside.*

   a. Acquire a "try anything" attitude.

   b. No faultfinding is allowed. It stifles ideas, halts association.

   c. Today's criticism may kill future ideas.

   d. All ideas are at least thought starters.

2. *Turn imagination loose and start offering the results.*

   a. The wilder the ideas, the better.

   b. Ideas are easier to tame down than to think up.

   c. Free wheeling is encouraged; ideas can be brought down to earth later.

   d. A wild idea may be the only way to bring out another really good one.

3. *Think of as many ideas as you can.*

   a. Quantity breeds quality.

   b. The more ideas to choose from, the more chance of a good one.

   c. There is always more than one good solution to any problem.

   d. Try many different approaches.

4. *Seek combination and improvement.*

   a. Your ideas don't all have to be original.

   b. Improve on the ideas of others.

   c. Combine previously mentioned ideas.

   d. Brainstorming is a group activity. Take advantage of group association.

5. *Record all ideas in full view.*

6. *Evaluate at a later session.*

   a. Approach each idea with a positive attitude.

   b. Give each idea a fair trial.

   c. Apply judgment gradually.

Osborn offers a few additional tips to further stimulate the creation of ideas (ideation). After ideas are generated, think of adding, subtracting, multiplying, and dividing as ways of modifying the ideas you already have. Effective toothpaste was improved by adding fluorides. Portable radios were made portable by subtracting size through the use of printed circuits. The common razor-blade market was revamped by the creation of a double-edged razor (multiplying). General Motors decided to divide up the production of the Oldsmobile Cutlass to several assembly plants, since the single plant at Lansing, Michigan, could not expand fast enough to keep up with demand.

One aspect of brainstorming that may be less obvious is the incubation of ideas, allowing ideas to develop during a period of relative relaxation. Sometimes allowing ideas to incubate or "set" creates a new insight into a problem. Many company executives as well as important politicians prefer to be alone before making important decisions. This period of solitude may help you to let all the facts sink in before committing yourself to a decision.

The brainstorming process has a success record that is hard to ignore. Several reactions to brainstorming training have been noted (Osborn 1957, p. ix):

> General Electric—Graduates from our new Creative Engineering Program continue to develop new processes and patentable ideas at an average rate of almost three times that of nongraduates.

> National Cash Register—As a result of 12 seminars our students showed an average improvement of 79% in fluency of ideas.

An important note about brainstorming is that a critical thinking session is often a useful follow-up to brainstorming. During this time, evaluation and sorting of the ideas is conducted. Without this critical thinking session the quantity of ideas may be great, but the overall quality may suffer.

Incrementalism

Braybrooke and Lindblom (1963) have pointed out that many economists, social scientists, political analysts, and other decision makers generally resort to a style of decision making that is far from the rational models described earlier in this chapter.

They argue that numerous decisions concerning governmental policies such as welfare and social security are arrived at partially as a result of adapting to political pressure and expediency, rather than as a result of sheer rational analysis of the available alternatives. Since environmental obstacles frequently prevent groups from choosing a "best" alternative, other alternatives may result by default. A department chairperson vacancy at a university may be filled by a "compromise candidate," one who is clearly not the most outstanding contender, but who is the only one upon whom the group can agree. This is an example of a nonrational decision.

The term *incrementalism* refers to the process of making decisions that result in change. Some decisions result in vast amounts of change, while other decisions progress toward change by small bits or *increments*. A second variable is the amount and quality of knowledge or understanding underlying a decision. When these two factors are taken in combination, the model in Figure 6.4 results.

Braybrooke and Lindblom's analysis is primarily centered on political decisions resulting in societal change. With respect to quadrant 1 in the diagram in Figure 6.4, the researchers contend that few decisions resulting in major social changes can be made with a high level of intellectual understanding of a problem. Numerous "think tanks" are devoted to analyzing what we should be doing to prepare ourselves for the year 2000 and beyond. Yet even the best estimates are "guesstimates" that must be continually revised based on new data. The decision to enact forced busing of schoolchildren to achieve a racial balance in public schools was an attempt to bring about a major social change. Yet the magnitude of resistance to this move was severely underestimated. In another context, the decision to have year-round daylight saving time was implemented in an attempt to save fuel. However, because of the threat of children being run down by cars in the dark early-morning hours, more parents drove their children to school, thus using more energy than daylight saving time was saving. These decisions illustrate the point that attempts to make major changes are not always accompanied by a full realization of the consequences. Thus the majority of decisions resulting in large changes would be depicted in Figure 6.4 as falling in quadrant 4.

FIGURE 6.4   MODEL OF DECISION MAKING.
Reprinted with permission of The Free Press, a Division of Macmillan, Inc. from *A Strategy of Decision* by David Braybrooke and Charles C. Lindblom. Copyright © 1963 by the Free Press of Glencoe.

Quadrant 2 refers to the daily decisions of most groups that result in relatively small changes. Decisions to change the prime lending rate of a bank, to increase social security benefits, to add a few employees to a payroll, are all examples of such decisions. Obviously, defining "small" changes is a matter of judgment. These types of decisions frequently result from the careful study of experts in costing, economics, and management. Thus the chances are increased that the decision will be made with a high level of understanding of the problem. However, this may not always be the case. If the decisions result in unwanted or unanticipated problems such as inflation or unionization, the decision is defined as falling into quadrant 3. Braybrooke and Lindblom (1963, p. 73) offer the following explanation for the tendency toward incremental change:

> For a democracy like the United States, the commitment to incremental change is not surprising. Nonincremental alternatives usually do not lie within the range of choice possible in the society or body politic. Societies, it goes without saying, are complex structures that can avoid dissolution or intolerable dislocation only by meeting certain preconditions, among them that certain kinds of change are admissible only if they occur slowly. Political democracy is often greatly endangered by nonincremental change, which it can accommodate only in certain limited circumstances.

Their point of view is that we make group decisions on the basis of relatively limited information and understanding of the consequences of those decisions. By implication, it would seem that this calls for problem-solving strategies that are flexible and subject to change based on feedback indicating that change is desirable. For example, the United States auto makers at one time committed large amounts of money to the development of a rotary engine as a possible alternative to the piston engine. However, when the demand for more energy-efficient engines became greater, the work on the rotary engine was permanently halted. This type of bit-by-bit planning is representative of the exploratory decision making sometimes required in a continually changing environment.

Mixed Scanning

Etzioni (1968) offers a decision-making strategy that he asserts is "neither rationalism nor incrementalism." Actually it is a combination of the two approaches. Rather than examining a problem comprehensively (rational approach), or part by part (incremental approach), we can combine elements of both of these approaches into a so-called mixed-scanning strategy. Etzioni offers the following example (1968, p. 284) in support of this contention:

> Infantrymen taking positions in a new field in hostile territory scan it for hidden enemy troops. They are trained to scan a field. A rationalistic strategy is likely to be avoided because it would entail examining the whole field bit-by-bit, exhaustively, which would be dangerous and fatiguing and is likely not to be completed. Incrementalists would examine places in which enemy troops have been known to hide and some others near them or similar to them. Unlike the whole field, these places can be prodded by fire. Soldiers who are tired of marching and combat will sometimes follow this procedure.

But armies known for their effectiveness train their soldiers in a different procedure. A major consideration in this regard is that accuracy of aim declines with distance. The infantrymen are taught first to scan the whole field in a rough, nondiscriminating way for some obvious sign of danger (a movement, an unnatural shadow, and so on).—If none is visible, they proceed with a bit-by-bit examination from the left to the right, beginning with subfields closest to them and moving outward to more distant ones. The assumption is that scanning is going to become more superficial the longer it is carried out, which is made to coincide with the scanning of the more remote, less dangerous subfields.

The basic idea is to combine an analysis of the "big picture" with an appropriate amount of attention to detail. In an employment decision, several candidates may be assessed according to specific ratings on several criteria relevant to the job. This would be an example of paying attention to detail. It may be that one person meets all the criteria very well, and he or she would be a strong replacement for the employee who is to be replaced. However, at the same time, perhaps a completely different level of scanning is needed to anticipate the type of employee that might be best several years from now. In one such case, a decision to replace a college debate coach resulted in hiring a professor in interpersonal and small group communication, since the debate program was getting smaller while the interpersonal and small group curriculum was increasing in size and scope.

A similar example of such a mixed-scanning model applies to the technique of efficient reading. The so-called SQ3R method of reading involves these five steps (Robinson 1961):

1. *Survey.* Glance at (or scan) the chapter outline and leaf through the pages to get a general idea of how much material is allotted to each topic in the outline.

2. *Question.* Begin to look more closely at the chapter and ask yourself questions about what the topics might be about.

3. *Read.* Read the chapter straight through once.

4. *Recite.* See how much of the material you can recite or explain to someone (or write down on a blank paper).

5. *Review.* Review the points you were able to recite and check the ones you were not.

This widely recommended study method contains elements of Etzioni's mixed-scanning model. It involves a general overview as well as an appropriate amount of attention to the necessary details. Etzioni urges that this alternating between levels of analysis enables us to "see the forest for the trees." Many groups seem to have trouble either getting down from the clouds of ambiguities and abstractions or getting up out of the quagmire of trivia long enough to see the overview. This ability to maintain a balance between attention to the general versus the specific appears to be a major factor in successful problem solving.

Tacit Bargaining

Still a third strategy for decision making that is considered an alternative to the rational-thinking approach is advanced by Schelling (1960). This strategy is referred to (p. 53) as "tacit bargaining," or "bargaining in which communication is incomplete or impossible." Examples of such situations (Schelling 1960, pp. 56–57) include the following:

1. Name heads or tails. If you and your partner name the same, you both win a prize.

2. Circle one of the numbers listed in the line below. You win if you all succeed in circling the same number.
   7   100   13   261   99   555

3. You are to divide $100 into two piles, labeled A and B. Your partner is to divide another $100 into two piles labeled A and B. If you allot the same amounts to A and B, respectively, that your partner does, each of you gets $100; if your amounts differ from his, neither of you gets anything.

In his research Schelling found that in the first problem 36 participants chose heads and only 6 chose tails. In problem 2, the first 3 numbers got 37 out of 41 votes (7 got the most, then 100, then 13). In problem 3, 36 out of 41 split the money into two equal piles of $50 each. The data suggest that people can cooperate fairly successfully in some problem-solving situations if it is to their advantage to do so. However, numerous situations exist in which the participants have divergent interests. For example, several fraternity representatives meet together on an interfraternity council; each member is interested in promoting the entire Greek system, but his primary loyalty is to his own fraternity. This divided loyalty creates an arena of "politicking" such that most members will choose *not* to communicate in a completely open and honest way.

This is often referred to as a "mixed-motive" situation, in which there is simultaneous pressure to cooperate and to compete. Thus many proposed solutions are likely not to be prompted by the most honorable intentions, but to be motivated by the interests of a single person. Similar situations exist in congressional committees, which often split according to partisan (Republican and Democrat) affiliations. In these situations, decisions are frequently based on compromises and a philosophy of, "I'll support you on this issue, but you owe me support on the next issue." Rational and objective choices are less likely to prevail under these circumstances.

These bargaining situations imply communication procedures that are distinctly different from those in other kinds of problem-solving situations.

Negotiations between union and management are often characterized by each side's making highly publicized statements of extreme positions in order to strengthen its respective bargaining position. Thus the union president will call for a minimum wage increase of 10 percent and the company's representative will state flatly that 3 percent is all it can afford to give. In reality, both parties exaggerate their public position and privately acknowledge that a 6 or 7 percent agreement is what they are really trying to achieve. Keltner (1970) has graphically depicted this form of information exchange in Figure 6.5.

Assuming that in these bargaining situations it would be naive to advise participants to simply "give in," still some reasonable suggestions can be made to increase the effectiveness of communication as well as the quality of decisions made. A good negotiator should learn to master the following abilities (adapted from Keltner, pp. 241–242):

- He should be willing to face the issues directly and precisely.

- He should be convinced of the position he represents.

- He must have considerable self-confidence.

- He must be reasonably skeptical.

- He must inspire trust in his counterparts at the bargaining table.

- He desires respect rather than popularity.

FIGURE 6.5   DIFFERENCE BETWEEN THE DESIRED AND ACTUAL AMOUNT OF INFORMATION COMMUNICATED DURING A CONFLICT SITUATION. THE DIFFERENCE WIDENS AS THE HOSTILITY INCREASES AND INFORMATION DECREASES OUT OF FEAR OF REPRISAL.

From *Interpersonal Speech-Communication, Elements and Structures* by John W. Keltner. © 1970 by Wadsworth Publishing Company, Inc. Reprinted by permission of Wadsworth Publishing Company, Belmont, California 94002.

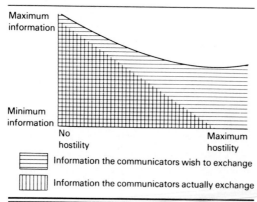

Information the communicators wish to exchange

Information the communicators actually exchange

In concluding this section on problem solving, we should point out that, to some extent, the situation will affect the strategy of decision making chosen. In some situations one of the rational-thinking approaches will be most appropriate; in other more tentative situations, the incremental approach may be preferable. The mixed-scanning strategy seems to have application in most situations, and the tacit-bargaining strategy will be most likely in situations allowing little or no free communication among participants. In using any strategy you should know which one you are using, and understand the underlying assumptions and requirements of each. You should also expect some problems with each and realize the communication requirements inherent in each. Also, as you attempt to make decisions, you will undoubtedly encounter many types of conflict, which is the subject of the next section.

CONFLICT AND CONFLICT RESOLUTION

It has been said that conflict is an inevitable part of people's relating to one another. As Johnson (1973, p. 145) puts it, "A conflict-free relationship is probably a sign that you really have no relationship at all, not that you have a good relationship." It has also been said that where there is movement there is friction, and where there is friction, heat is produced. Certainly many small groups involve movement, especially if their task is to solve and act on problems. It appears obvious that in such cases the heat referred to is the emotional heat that results from conflicts.

> Group processes themselves do not insure that top managers will adequately explore available information. Groups frequently avoid uncertainty and prematurely smooth over conflict. (Brodwin and Bourgeoss 1984, p. 167)

In our society, conflict is usually considered to be bad, that thing that results in wars, divorces, worker strikes, and bloody noses. However, several authors agree that conflict within and among groups has some *desirable* effects. Both the desirable and undesirable aspects of conflict will be discussed in this section. However, we look first at the sources from which conflicts arise.

Sources of Conflict

According to Deutsch (1969), conflict exists whenever incompatible activities occur. An incompatible action prevents, obstructs, interferes with, injures, or in some way reduces the effectiveness of the other action. Incompatible actions may occur within a single person (intrapersonal), a single group (intragroup), between two or more people (interpersonal), or between two or more groups (intergroup). Conflicts may originate from a number of different sources, including: (1) differences in information, beliefs, values, interests, or desires, (2) a scarcity of some resource such as money, power, time, space, or position, and (3) rivalries in which one person or group competes with one another (Deutsch 1969). To these sources could be added the difficulty of the task, the pressure to avoid failure, the relative importance of a group's or individual's decision, and differences in skill levels that may cause more skilled individuals to become irritated at the less skilled; this often leads to a reciprocal irritation. In an earlier chapter we discussed personality differences. These differences lead to incompatibilities among certain members of a group. Members may be incompatible because of their differences—or they may be incompatible because of their similarities, such as in the need to achieve or dominate others. All these factors tend to instigate conflict.

See also the article by Folger and Poole at the end of this chapter for more on the constructive use of conflict.

Desirability of Conflict

As mentioned above, many writers believe that conflict in a group is desirable. For example, in Chapter 4 we discussed the very real problem of groupthink, which can occur in any group. Conflict helps eliminate or reduce the likelihood of groupthink. Furthermore, Deutsch (1971, pp. 42–55) cites Simmel (1955) in his argument that conflict has other desirable functions, such as preventing stagnation; stimulating interest and curiosity; providing a medium through which problems can be aired and solutions arrived at; causing personal and social change; being part of the process of testing and assessing oneself and, as such, being highly enjoyable as one experiences the pleasure of full and active use of one's capacities; demarcating groups from one another and thus helping to establish group and personal identities; fostering internal cohesion in groups involved in external conflicts; resolving tension among individuals and thus stabilizing and integrating relationships; eliminating sources of dissatisfaction in social systems by permitting immediate and direct resolution of rival claims; revitalizing existing group norms or helping the emergence of new norms in order to adjust adequately to new conditions; and ascertaining the relative strengths of antagonistic interests within a social system, thereby constituting a mechanism for the maintenance or continual readjustment of the balance of power.

Alfred Sloan was one of the early executives who helped make General Motors successful. He recognized the importance of idea conflict in decision making. Once, Sloan was chairing a meeting of the GM board of directors in which someone presented an idea for buying a small company. After the presentation Sloan asked each member around the table for an opinion. Not one gave an objection to the proposal; they all agreed the company should buy at the earliest possible moment. Finally, Sloan looked at the other board members and said: "Gentlemen, I don't see any reason not to adopt the idea either. Therefore, I suggest we postpone this decision for thirty days while we do some more thinking." Thirty days later the board decided against the plan—after finding out many negatives they had not known earlier. (See Goldhaber et al., 1979, p. 28).

Conflict clearly plays an important role in small group interaction. However, it is a double-edged sword, as we shall see.

Types of Conflict

Many people fail to differentiate between two very different types of conflict—namely, conflict of ideas versus conflict of feelings (often called personality conflict). As we saw in the example above, Alfred Sloan recognized the importance of idea conflict in making a decision. If there is too little conflict of ideas, groupthink can occur, as we saw in Chapter 4. Idea conflict, however, can very easily turn into conflict of feelings. We can call this personal conflict. Notice the difference between the conflicts in these two conversations in a group discussion.

Conversation 1

Judy: Why don't we have our next meeting at my sorority house?

Dave: I think the campus center meeting room might have fewer interruptions. I know how hard it is to have meetings at my fraternity house.

Conversation 2

Judy: Why don't we have our next meeting at my sorority house?

Dave: And have people interrupting us all the time? No, thanks, I'd rather meet in the campus center.

In the first situation there was a conflict of ideas. In the second, the conflict could have escalated to the personal level, depending on Judy's reaction. The personal animosity that may have been created by Dave is the kind that tends to get in the way of group success. As shown in Figure 6.6, our goal in using conflict successfully is to avoid turning idea opponents into personal opponents.

Undesirability of Conflict

Our society frequently considers conflict to be undesirable. Millions of dollars are lost each year due to work stoppages and strikes. Thousands of divorces result from unchecked marital conflicts. And every once in a while a disaster like that at Kent State occurs as a result of conflict that has gotten out of control. Even in meetings, discussions, and conferences, conflict may cause reactions similar to that of one student who said, "I don't even want to go to publication council meetings anymore. Every week it is just one hassle after another. Nothing ever gets accomplished because every time we end up arguing."

Conflicts are often hard to keep under control once they have begun. There is a definite trend toward escalation and polarization. Once conflict escalates to a point at which it is no longer under control, it almost always yields negative results. In this same vein, one conflict tends to lay the groundwork for further conflicts at a later time. Part of this is because of defensive reactions. Defensiveness leads us to distort our perceptions so that ambiguous acts are more frequently misconstrued as threatening when they may in fact not be intended that way. Watzlawik, Beavin, and Jackson (1967, pp. 103–104) cite the following example of developing trust in a risky situation:

> We have established a very interesting communication pattern for the establishment of trust between humans and bottle-nosed porpoises. While this may be a ritual developed "privately" by only two of the animals, it still provides an excellent example for the analogic communication of "not." The animals had obviously concluded that the hand is one of the most important and vulnerable parts of the human body. Each would seek to establish contact with a stranger by taking the human's hand into his mouth and gently squeezing it between his jaws, which have sharp teeth and are powerful enough to bite the hand off cleanly. If the human would submit to this, the dolphin seemed to accept it as a message of complete trust. His next move was to reciprocate by placing the forward ventral portion of his body (*his* most vulnerable part, roughly equivalent to the human

---

FIGURE 6.6   OPPOSITION AND SUPPORT.

	Idea Supporter	Idea Opponent
Personal Supporter	1 + +	2 + −
Personal Opponent	3 − +	4 − −

AVOID TURNING IDEA OPPONENTS
INTO PERSONAL OPPONENTS

throat) upon the human's hand, leg, or foot, thereby signaling his trust in the friendly intention of the human. This procedure is, however, obviously fraught with possible misinterpretation at every step.

Nye (1973) identifies three conditions that both cause and result from conflicts. First is *competition.* In many instances there is a win-lose arrangement so that both competitors cannot possibly win. Any athletic contest illustrates that fact. Similarly, several people may seek a promotion, while only one can actually be promoted. In politics one candidate must lose, and this often produces bitter feelings, as illustrated by Nixon's famous remark after the 1962 California gubernatorial election, "You won't have Dick Nixon to kick around anymore."

Second, *domination* is related to conflict. Zimbardo (1972) conducted an experiment in which about two dozen normal, well-adjusted college students acted as either guards or prisoners (half in each group) in a simulated prison. After only four days, three of the "prisoners" had to be released because they suffered such extreme depression and anxiety. At the end of six days, extreme hostility had developed between the prisoners and guards. Zimbardo (1972, p. 8) described the situation in the following way:

> We were horrified because we saw some boys ("guards") treat others as if they were despicable animals, taking pleasure in cruelty, while other boys ("prisoners") became servile, dehumanized robots who thought only of escape, of their own individual survival, and of their mounting hatred of the guards.

The third factor is *provocation,* which Nye (1973, p. 8) defines as "intentional or unintentional harm to other persons or groups." This specific factor is most likely to promote further future conflicts. Harmful acts produce grudges that may last for years before conflict has a chance to resume. In any case, the three factors described above illustrate the negative side of conflict. The logical question that arises is, "How do we reduce conflict and keep it at a manageable level?"

Toward Conflict Resolution

A number of systems have been proposed for improving our abilities to resolve conflict. Two famous psychologists (Blake and Mouton 1970) have proposed a scheme whereby we can try to avoid win-lose situations and, when it is possible, apply a win-win approach. This can best be illustrated with their model, called the Conflict Grid® (Figure 6.7).

See the article by Roy Lewicki and Joseph Litterer at the end of this chapter for a further elaboration on conflict resolution.

The Conflict Grid clearly illustrates the possibility of having *both* concern for results and concern for people at the same time. Intuitively, it would seem difficult to "have your cake and eat it too" when it comes to conflict resolution. Alternative

FIGURE 6.7 BLAKE AND MOUTON'S CONFLICT GRID.®

Reproduced by permission from "The Fifth Achievement," Robert R. Blake and Jane Srygley Mouton. *Journal of Applied Behavioral Science,* 6(4), 1970.

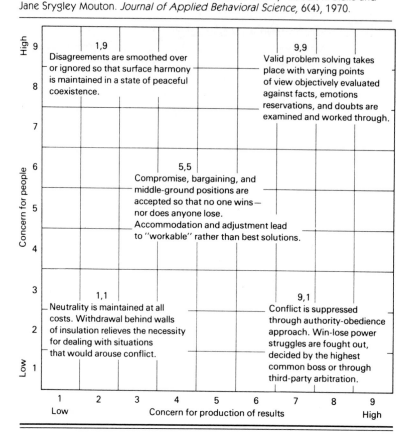

strategies of dealing with conflict are also depicted on the grid. Try to identify where your style would fit.

The 1,1 style is the "hands-off" approach. Neutrality is maintained with an attitude of, "the less said about it the better." The 1,9 position is excessively person oriented. Its goal is to maintain the *appearance* of harmony at all cost. In reality deep conflicts exist but are never dealt with. An uneasy state of tension exists, which is frequently characterized by lots of smiling and nervous laughter (but members avoid looking at each other). The 5,5 position represents the willingness to compromise. While compromise may be a viable alternative in some cases, it should not be a chronic way of avoiding deeper levels of conflict resolution. The bull-headed approach is depicted by the 9,1 position. This style is even worse than the compromise. Since absolute stalemates often occur, a group full of these types may get nowhere fast.

The optimum style for reducing conflict is the 9,9 approach. Here the individuals attempt to be both person and results-oriented. Conflicts are not ignored, but individuals don't go around with a chip on their shoulder either. Differences are discussed with such comments as, "I don't agree with the position that . . . " At the same time, personally insulting statements such as "Anybody who believes that is nuts," are avoided. Tubbs and Moss (1987, p. 223) offer four guidelines for implementing the 9,9 style:

- Make sure you agree on the use of your terms or definitions.
- Build on areas of mutual agreement.
- Determine the specific changes necessary for a satisfactory resolution of the issues.
- Avoid personal attacks and stick to the issues.

Charles Osgood (1969) has proposed a theory based on gradual behavior modification, which he calls the GRIT theory. GRIT not only describes a quality necessary to carry out the program, but also stands for Graduated Reciprocation in Tension-Reduction. If both sides in a dispute want to reduce conflict, they can do so by setting up a series of gradual steps toward de-escalation. Two groups of diplomats representing the United States and Russia might decide to take the following actions over a period of months: (1) the release of medical data from space programs, (2) the removal of certain trade and travel restrictions, and (3) the deactivation of an overseas military base. The technique may be applied to any conflict situation and seems practical in that parties would be likely to de-escalate on small issues first to build trust before moving on to more risky issues. This technique seems to have been a part of Henry Kissinger's famous "shuttle diplomacy" in the early 1970s.

Stech and Ratliffe (1985) recommend the following three steps in managing conflict:

1. Recognize and confront.
2. Bring the issues out in the open and deal with them directly.
3. Work out a way to allow everyone to feel respected and needed in the work situation. (pp. 156–157)

These steps represent an assertive way to manage conflict. However, many people run away from conflict. That can make the situation worse because differences do not simply disappear with time; sometimes they get worse. It is important to confront conflict.

Tannenbaum and Schmidt (1972) propose that one frequent source of conflict is the leadership struggle between superior and subordinate in decision making. They argue that the leader has to be flexible enough to modify his or her decision-making style to fit the "followership" of the group. Their discussion focuses primarily on the business setting, but the implications are valid for any small group setting in which conflict arises from a leadership struggle. They propose a continuum of decision-making styles that can serve as a model for the leader (in conjunction with the group) so that the group can choose the style most appropriate for their situation and that would reduce unnecessary conflict. This model (Figure 6.8) has also been described

FIGURE 6.8   CONTINUUM OF LEADERSHIP BEHAVIOR.
Reprinted by permission of the *Harvard Business Review*. An exhibit from "How to Choose a Leadership Pattern" by Robert Tannenbaum and Warren H. Schmidt (March/April 1958). Copyright © 1958 by the President and Fellows of Harvard College; all rights reserved.

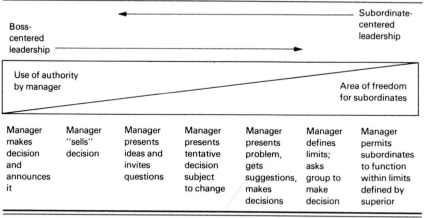

as including four styles of decision making: (1) tells, (2) sells, (3) consults, and (4) joins.

A related system of conflict prevention through better decision making includes four other styles: (1) railroading, (2) teaming up, (3) majority vote, and (4) consensus. *Railroading* occurs when one or more group members force their will on the group. This technique is very likely to produce resentment and result in unnecessary conflict. *Teaming up* refers to a situation in which various minority members within a group form a coalition to help each other achieve mutually advantageous goals. This pattern is frequently used in Congress when politicians make trades through which they agree to support each other's bills. This may have short-term success, but may also result in further conflict once the scheme is discovered. *Majority vote* represents the wishes of at least 51 percent of a group's members. However, the remaining minority may be bitterly opposed to the outcome of the decision. This bitterness often results in conflict at a later time. *Consensus* denotes agreement among all members of a group concerning a given decision. Consensus is generally considered to yield the best resolution of conflict in a group decision. Few groups are as concerned as they should be about trying to reach consensus on decisions. Juries represent one of the few types of groups that are required to reach consensus. Those that don't—hung juries—are dismissed. Pfeiffer and Jones offer four relatively simple rules to help group members achieve consensus:

- Avoid *arguing* for your own individual judgments. Approach the task on the basis of logic.

- Avoid changing your mind *only* in order to reach agreement and avoid conflict. Support only solutions with which you are able to agree somewhat, at least.

- Avoid "conflict-reducing" techniques such as majority vote, averaging, or trading, in reaching your decision.

- View differences of opinion as helpful rather than as a hindrance in decision making.

Gouran (1969) found that groups that were able to reach consensus better had a greater proportion of "orientation statements" explicitly directing the group toward the achievement of its goal or helping to resolve conflicts. A follow-up study by Kline (1970) reported that orientation statements contained fewer self-referent words and phrases—"I," "me," "my," "I think," and so on—and that highly opinionated statements, which were characteristic of groups that had difficulty reaching consensus, contained more self-referent words.

Consensus does not come quickly or easily. Agreement generally results from careful and thoughtful interpersonal communication between group members. To achieve complete group consensus, some individual preferences of group members must be surrendered. The group as a whole must decide if consensus can be achieved. If several members are adamant in their positions and refuse to change their minds in agreement with the others, the group may decide that reaching complete consensus is not worth the effort. In this case it may be better to postpone the group decision, particularly if the group making the decision will also be implementing the decision. If several group members are not in favor of the solution, they will be less anxious to put it into practice.

Conflict resolution seems to improve as we engage in certain types of behaviors. These can be summarized as follows:

1. Focus on the problem, not on personalities.

2. Build on areas of agreement. Most groups have at least some positions or goals that are not mutually exclusive.

3. Attempt to achieve consensus. Try consensus testing by taking a nonbinding straw vote. Then discuss why the minority might be objecting to the decision.

4. Avoid provoking further conflict. Avoid "hitting below the beltline," as one book puts it (Bach and Wyden 1968, p. 80).

5. Don't overreact to the comments of others. Extreme statements on either side tend to destroy consensus and produce a "boomerang effect" (Sherif, Sherif, and Nebergall 1965).

6. Consider compromise. This is often the best way to go from a win-lose to a win-win situation.

While these are not hard-and-fast rules, and they may not work in all cases, they should improve a group's chances of keeping conflict at a manageable level so that the group can move forward toward its goal.

Finally, Schweiger, Sandberg and Ragan (1986) cite results of a laboratory study which compared the effectiveness of the dialectical inquiry, devil's advocacy, and consensus approaches to strategic decision making by groups:

> The following is a brief description of: dialectical inquiry and devil's advocacy: (consensus has already been defined).
>
> *Dialectical inquiry*—Relies on the use of constructive group conflict through debates between contrary sets of recommendations and assumptions. Formalized argumentation and debate among group members allow assumptions and recommendations to be systematically evaluated. The strengths and weaknesses of each is made explicit.
>
> *Devil's Advocacy*—Relies on the use of constructive group conflict through critiques on a single set of recommendations and assumptions.
>
> Results showed that both dialectical inquiry and devil's advocacy led to higher quality recommendations and assumptions than consensus. Dialectical inquiry was also more effective than devil's advocacy with respect to the quality of assumptions brought to the surface. However, subjects in the consensus groups expressed more satisfaction and desire to continue to work with their groups and greater acceptance of their groups' decisions than did subjects in either of the two other types of groups studied.

THE SYSTEMS PERSPECTIVE

In this chapter we have examined the very difficult task of improving our ability to make decisions. Most untrained groups do not follow a disciplined path toward a decision. Instead, we frequently find ourselves either off the track or bogged down in conflicts that keep us from accomplishing a task. The focus in this chapter has been biased toward problem-solving groups. However, other types of groups also have to make decisions and deal with conflicts. Certainly these issues arise for families, learning groups (as we saw in the case at the beginning of this chapter), social groups planning events, and work groups solving organizational problems. Conflict, too, is present in each of these types of groups.

It is probably apparent by now that the decision-making process in most groups can be improved. In this chapter we examined seven alternative problem-solving strategies: (1) the reflective thinking process; (2) the Kepner-Tregoe approach; (3) the single question form; (4) brainstorming; (5) incrementalism; (6) mixed scanning; and (7) tacit bargaining. You might want to become familiar enough with all of these methods so that you would be able to use whichever one seems most appropriate for a given problem and a given group. Again, this illustrates the systems principle of *equifinality* in that several alternative methods may be used to reach the same desired end result, namely, the solution to the group's problem.

By now you may have wondered how one *does* decide which of the seven problem-solving strategies to use. Should you use a rational strategy like the reflective thinking process or brainstorming, or should you use incrementalism or tacit bargaining? The systems perspective suggests that the appropriateness of any method will depend on the demands of the specific situation. Therefore we need to be familiar with all the alternatives in order to increase our tool kit of behavioral science "tools."

The rational problem-solving methods work well in most cases, but seem particularly suited to an autonomous group trying to satisfy its own needs while being allowed to do so by a democratic leader. By comparison, governmental groups are not autonomous and must answer to the taxpayers. Thus incrementalism may be appropriate, since major changes may be demanded without the luxury of enough time to gather exhaustive amounts of data on the problem. It's a little like the old story that when you are up to your hips in a swamp full of alligators, you don't want a systematic estimate of the probability of danger, you want somebody to throw you a rope!

Tacit bargaining seems to be primarily appropriate in the mixed-motive situations we described earlier. Notice the assumptions and viewpoints expressed in the following quotations. Karrass (1970, p. 4), in his book on negotiating, writes, "In a successful negotiation both parties gain, but more often than not one party wins more than the other." In a similar vein, Korda (1975, p. 4) writes, "No matter who you are, the basic truth is that your interests are nobody else's concern, your gain is inevitably someone else's loss, your failure someone else's victory." The viewpoint expressed in these two quotations indicates some of the attitudes and values relevant to the mixed-motive situation. These statements also describe the outcomes or consequences of bargaining types of problem-solving situations. Obviously, these types of competitive situations suggest very different communication behaviors and skills than would the encounter group, which stresses trust, mutual self-disclosure and risk taking. Thus the demands of the situation will play a great part in suggesting which problem-solving strategy we will want to employ.

The second part of this chapter dealt with conflict and conflict resolution. It should be emphasized that conflict may have some desirable consequences for the group. However, conflict that gets out of control may be destructive. Also, conflict between ideas is usually more productive than conflict between personalities.

In terms of personality and its relation to conflict, we would expect more conflict-producing behaviors from those high in aggression, dominance, and need for autonomy. Conversely, we would expect less conflict and more conflict-resolving attempts from those high in need for affiliation and nurturance. Other background factors that would probably relate to conflict include the degree of differences or heterogeneity in group members' ages, sex, values, attitudes, and beliefs. Consistency theories would lead us to believe that the greater and more numerous these differences, the greater the group conflict and the lower the satisfaction level resulting from the discussions.

Perhaps one of the most important factors related to conflict is the style of leadership and the resulting group norms regarding conflict. In this chapter we examined Blake and Mouton's (1970) Conflict Grid and Tannenbaum and Schmidt's (1972) tells, sells, consults, and joins model. Both models seem to suggest practical methods for developing some leadership expertise in resolving conflicts.

EXERCISES

1. Problem-Solving Discussion Assignment

Each group should decide on a topic and should formulate a discussion question that cannot be answered yes or no. A sample question would be: "What can be done about the problem of current marijuana laws?" This form of discussion question is preferable, since it poses a problem to be answered by the group. A less desirable discussion question would be: "Should marijuana be decriminalized?" Notice that this question can be answered yes or no and is less open-ended and therefore less helpful in prompting discussion.

Each group may want to gather some preliminary information on the topic. (This is optional.) Select a moderator and work up an agenda for your discussion, including the following:

(a) Define the nature and limits of the problem. *Analyze* causes and important aspects of the problem.

(b) Determine the criteria by which to judge an acceptable solution to the problem.

(c) Identify several alternative solutions to the problem.

(d) Decide which is the best solution (based on the criteria you have identified).

(e) How might this solution be implemented?

The discussion will be approximately 30 minutes long. Moderators will be responsible for introducing and concluding the discussion as well as for moving the group along their agenda.

As a guide, you may want to review the following questions, which show in greater detail the various issues to be encountered at each phase of the agenda. Application of this pattern depends upon such factors as:

(a) Whether the discussion is one of fact, value, or policy

(b) The general scope of the problem

(c) The amount of time available

(d) The knowledge of the participants

   I. Problem Phase

      A. *Identification of problem area, including questions:*

         1. What is the situation in which the problem is occurring?

         2. What in general is the difficulty?

         3. How did this difficulty arise?

         4. What is the importance of the difficulty?

         5. What limitations, if any, are there on the area of our concern?

         6. What is the meaning of any terms that need clarifying?

B. *Analysis of the difficulty:*

  1. What, specifically, are the facts of the situation?

  2. What, specifically, are the difficulties?

C. *Analysis of causes:*

  1. What is causing the difficulties?

  2. What is causing the causes?

II. Criteria Phase

  A. What are the principal requirements of the solution?

  B. What limitations must be placed on the solution?

  C. What is the relative importance of the criteria?

III. Solution Phase

  A. *What are the possible solutions?*

   1. What is the exact nature of each solution?

   2. How would it remedy the difficulty? by eliminating the cause? by offsetting the effect? by a combination of both?

  B. *How good is each solution?*

   1. How well would it remedy the difficulty?

   2. How well would it satisfy the criteria? Are there any that it would not satisfy?

   3. Would there be any unfavorable consequences? any extra benefits?

  C. *Which solution appears to be best?*

   1. How would you rank the solution?

   2. Would some combination of solutions be best?

IV. Implementation Phase
  What steps would be taken to put the solution into effect?

2. Adjunct of Exercise 1

In conjunction with Exercise 1, some members of the class may want to fill out the evaluation forms (Figures 6.9 and 6.10) on the discussion group. These forms can serve as the basis of a postdiscussion feedback session by which the group can analyze its own strengths and weaknesses in conducting their assignment.

FIGURE 6.9   JUDGE'S EVALUATION REPORT ON THE LEADER.

Judge's Evaluation Report on the Leader

Name of leader _____

Evaluator _____

Assign for each criterion one of the following ratings:

5—Superior
4—Excellent
3—Average
2—Below average
1—Poor

Criteria	Rating
1. *Attitude.* Impartiality, fairness; ability to help group maintain discussion attitude.	_____
2. *Knowledge.* Understanding of the problem. Knowledge of discussion method.	_____
3. *Thinking.* Ability to think quickly, to see relationships.	_____
4. *Introducing.* Skill in getting the discussion off to a good start.	_____
5. *Speaking.* Ability to express ideas clearly, rephrase unclear contributions.	_____
6. *Guiding.* Ability to keep discussion "on the track"; maintain progress; make internal summaries.	_____
7. *Regulating.* Ensuring evenness of contribution, maintaining equanimity.	_____
8. *Ending.* Summarizing group effect.	_____
General comments	

---

3. Brainstorming Exercise

Utilizing the rules for brainstorming given in Chapter 6, try to answer the following question: How can we limit growth in population, industrial productivity, pollution, and use of natural resources in such a way as to ensure the preservation of the human race?

For further practice, try brainstorming other topics for further brainstorming practice discussions.

4. Conflict Resolution Exercise: "Win as Much as You Can"

Directions For ten successive rounds you and your partner will choose either an X or a Y. The "payoff" for each round is dependent upon the pattern of choices made in your cluster.

FIGURE 6.10   JUDGE'S EVALUATION REPORT ON PARTICIPANTS.

Judge's Evaluation Report on the Participants

Name of participant _____

Evaluator _____

Assign the particpant for each criterion one of the following ratings:

5—Superior
4—Excellent
3—Average
2—Below average
1—Poor

Criteria	Rating
1. *Attitude.* Objectivity, open-mindedness; willingness to modify views in light of new evidence.	_____
2. *Knowledge.* Information on the problem.	_____
3. *Thinking.* Analysis, ability to reason about the problem.	_____
4. *Listening.* Ability to understand and interpret view of others.	_____
5. *Speaking.* Ability to communicate ideas clearly and effectively; adaptation to the speaking situation.	_____
6. *Consideration for others.* Tact, courtesy, cooperation, evenness of contribution.	_____

General comments

Strategy You are to confer with your partner on each round and make a joint decision. Before rounds 5, 8, and 10 you confer with the other dyads in your cluster.

Instructions for participants

1. This is a learning exercise. In it, there are ten rounds and there are other teams with which you are playing.

2. The purpose of the exercise is to win as much as you can.

3. When the timekeeper says, "Begin round 1," your team will decide on its vote for the first round. Your vote may be either X or Y, and should be reported secretly on a small piece of paper. The payoff for each round will be determined by how your team's vote is related to the votes of all the other teams. The payoff possibilities are shown at the top of the tally sheet (Figure 6.11).

4. When all votes are collected, the timekeeper will announce the total vote but *will not* disclose how each individual team voted.

FIGURE 6.11   "WIN AS MUCH AS YOU CAN" TALLY SHEET.

Round	Strategy Time allowed	Strategy Confer with	Choice	$ Won	$ Lost	$ Balance	
1	2 min.	partner					
2	1 min.	partner					
3	1 min.	partner					
4	1 min.	partner					
5	3 min. + 1 min.	cluster partner					Bonus round: pay is multiplied by 3
6	1 min.	partner					
7	1 min.	partner					
8	3 min. + 1 min.	cluster partner					Bonus round: pay is multiplied by 5
9	1 min.	partner					
10	3 min. + 1 min.	cluster partner					Bonus round: pay is multiplied by 10

5. As shown on the tally sheet, you will have two minutes to cast your vote for the first round. For all the other rounds, you will have one minute to cast your vote except for Rounds 5, 8, and 10, which are bonus rounds.

6. During each bonus round your team will select as many representatives as it wishes to send to a meeting of the teams. The representatives from all teams will then meet separately for three minutes to discuss their strategy.

7. After the representatives have met, your team will then have one minute to make its final decision about your vote. At the end of each round, when all the votes are in, you will be told the total outcome of the vote (2 X's, 2 Y's, or 4 Y's, and so on).

8. There are three key rules to keep in mind.

   (a) You are not to talk to the other teams or signal them in any way. You may communicate with them but only during Rounds 5, 7, and 10 through your representatives.

   (b) All members of your team should agree on your team's vote or at least be willing to go along with it.

   (c) Your team's vote must be reported on a small slip of paper when it is called for at the end of each round.

4 X's:	Lose	$1.00 each
3 X's:	Win	$1.00 each
1 Y:	Lose	$3.00
2 X's:	Win	$2.00 each
2 Y's:	Lose	$2.00 each
1 X:	Win	$3.00
3 Y's:	Lose	$1.00 each
4 Y's:	Win	$1.00 each

5. Conflict Resolution Exercise: "The Babysitter Case"

Mr. and Mrs. Todd have been using Paula Moore (age 17) as their regular baby-sitter ever since their son Brad was born two years ago. Paula has always been competent and responsible while in the Todd's home. The Todds have a policy that Paula is not to have any visitors while she is babysitting. This is consistent with the policies of other families in the neighborhood where Paula lives and babysits.

Paula babysat for the Todds on Saturday night and everything seemed routine. However, the next morning Mr. Todd's neighbor from across the street told him that two young men and Paula's 16-year-old sister had arrived in a customized van the night before, and the three young people had gone into the Todd's house. The neighbor couldn't say how long the three had been in the house, since he had left shortly after they arrived.

Mr. Todd checked with another neighbor and had the story confirmed. The second neighbor said that the three people had been in the Todd's house. He also added, "We don't use the Moore girls anymore for our kids. They are too boy crazy."

The Todds became quite upset, since this appeared to be a clear violation of their no-visitor policy for their babysitters.

The situation is further complicated by the fact that Paula lives only a few houses down the street from the Todds and Mr. Moore (Paula's father) works in the same office with Mr. Todd. Thus the Todd and Moore families are in the same neighborhood group and Mr. Todd and Mr. Moore are in the same work group. What should the Todds do?

READINGS: OVERVIEW

Probably one of the most troublesome issues in small group interaction is how to resolve conflicts. In the first article Folger and Poole elaborate on the same point discussed in Chapter 6—that conflict isn't all bad. However, trying to change conflict from a destructive to a constructive force in group activities takes some doing.

The second article by Lewicki and Litterer offers several methods for improving conflict-reduction skills. In this article, they show how conflict can be managed more effectively. Both articles provide a useful extension of the ideas presented in the chapter.

Action and Intervention

Joseph P. Folger and Marshall Scott Poole

Until now we have been concerned primarily with understanding the forces behind conflicts. Understanding, however, is of little value unless it can be put into *practice*. This chapter suggests measures members can take to improve their group's chances of dealing with conflict productively.... These guidelines will not be pat answers, because there are simply too many variables in conflicts. To present formulas would be both wrong and misleading. In each case we will explore the rationale behind the principle in question and consider problems and needs governing its use in groups and organizations.

Self-Regulation of Group Conflicts

Self-regulation refers to group behavior which checks destructive conflict interaction and turns it in a constructive direction. The previous discussions of the forces shaping conflict—trained incapacities, climate, power, and face-saving—suggest action principles to counteract whatever negative influence these forces may exert and to turn them into positive influences. In order to work with the four forces members must be able to (a) diagnose emerging problems, and (b) act on their diagnoses to successfully alter group interaction patterns. Accordingly, this section will present suggestions for both diagnosis and action for each force. Before proceeding, however, here are two reminders:

First, it is often difficult to determine when group interaction has made a turn in a destructive direction. As we have seen, conflict interaction can develop by gradual and often subtle steps. A group can suddenly find itself caught in an escalating spiral without suspecting it. The cues for recognizing destructive conflict which were outlined at the end of chapter 2 can help members avoid such situations. *Members must be constantly on the alert for signs of destructive patterns and act quickly to alter them.*

Second, changing conflict interaction patterns require *structural* change in the group. Often, discussing a problem in the group will prompt members to apologize and promise to change their attitudes and feelings about others: "Really, it's just a matter of taking a different perspective and respecting each

From Joseph P. Folger and Marshall Scott Poole, Working Through Conflict *(Glenview, Ill.: Scott-Foresman, 1984), pp. 168–184. Copyright © 1984 by Scott, Foresman and Company. Reprinted by permission.*

other's opinions." This change in attitude is admirable and represents an important first step, but more often than not it is ineffective. In order to alter a group's methods of dealing with conflict, *it is necessary to structurally change the group's interaction patterns by altering its working habits, its climate, its power relations, or its members' need to save face.* Changes in attitude are important, but they are usually insufficient to sustain more productive patterns of conflict interaction. Too easily, existing structures re-exert their influence on member interaction and undermine resolutions made in more reflective moments. This occurred in the Riverdale Halfway House conflict discussed in chapter 3. After talking with the consultant, both George and Carole attempted to put a new face on things and take more constructive attitudes toward each other. Over the long run, however, their attempts proved fruitless, because the suspicious climate at Riverdale prevented serious work on their problems. After a while both George and Carole fell back into their old patterns of sniping and misunderstanding, which persisted until George left. Only when the *forces* moving group interaction in destructive directions are eliminated or neutralized is lasting change possible. For this reason, the principles we discuss are oriented toward *unfreezing and changing* the structures which shape group interaction.

Working with Trained Incapacities

Trained incapacities are work habits inflexibly applied in response to conflict. The key to diagnosing the effect of trained incapacities is therefore to examine the group's "standard operating procedures"—its habitual methods of conducting its affairs—for traps. The discussion in chapter 2 of task requirements, the five incapacities, and the problems they imply supplies a systematic set of starting points for this search: groups can monitor discussions for problems due to goal-centeredness (such as insufficient analysis of problems underlying the conflict), evaluative tendencies, dependence on objective standards, destructive redefinition, or reliance on procedural rules. This monitoring process must go on continually, because groups can slip into harmful patterns without recognizing it. Because trained incapacities are "second nature," they are subtle and hard to detect: members know something is wrong, but they cannot put their finger on the source. The chair of an administrative committee in one midwestern social service agency keeps a checklist of possible problems to help her overcome this difficulty. It includes questions such as the following: "Is there too little dissent to have a balanced discussion?" "Are votes being used to suppress minority views?" and "Are differences discussed in win-lose terms?" The chair goes over this list (or parts of it) during and after every meeting, carefully monitoring the group's process. Although her answers are negative for most meetings, the list has turned up several unexpected problems that could have been damaging if unchecked.

One dangerous symptom of trained incapacities is a high level of tension in the group. Recall from chapter 2 that differentiation of positions in the early stages of a conflict creates tension which can lead to inflexible behavior and reinforce trained incapacities. Although there is not a perfect cause-effect relationship between tension level and the problems of trained incapacities, tension increases their likelihood immensely. Situations which create tension—a serious threat from outside the group, a rapidly-approaching time limit, or a severe and important disagreement—are ripe for the dangers discussed in chapter 2.

The most straightforward method of counteracting trained incapacities is for the group to adopt *procedures that correct* for the biases they introduce. The widely-used *Reflective Thinking Process* for group decision-making is one such procedure (Scheidel & Crowell, 1979, pp. 25–51; Gouran, 1982, pp. 29–30). Basically, the Reflective Thinking Process is designed to avoid three errors that may be produced by trained incapacities: (1) over-focusing on solutions before the problem is thoroughly understood (which stems from goal-centeredness), (2) premature evaluation of ideas (which stems from the tendency to evaluate), and (3) destructive redefinition of disagreements. The process avoids these problems by positing a five-step problem-solving procedure and requiring the group to go through the steps in order, keeping deliberations on each step separate:

1. Definition of the Problem or Task—the group assesses the nature of the problem before it and determines if the problem is significant enough to act on.

2. Analysis of the Problem—once the problem is defined, the group analyzes its causes. Only after these are understood, does the group move on to step C.

3. Suggestion of Possible Solutions—the group researches and develops a wide array of possible solutions. No serious evaluation or elimination of solutions occurs at this stage.

4. Solution Selection—the group evaluates and selects the best solution.

5. Implementation—the group plans how to put the solution into effect.

This procedure closely parallels logical thought processes and is the basis for most group decision-making methods (see also, Etzioni, 1968) and conflict management sequences (see also, Filley, 1975). By requiring the group to analyze the problem prior to developing solutions and to develop a long list of solutions prior to evaluating them, it counteracts over-focusing on solutions and premature evaluation. By focusing the group's attention on a well-defined pattern of thought about a common problem, it also helps avoid destructive redefinition.

Hall and Watson (1970) present another procedural format that works against the ill effects of trained incapacities. Rather than focusing on *what* the group talks about at particular stages of decision-making, they attempt to develop a set of ground rules for *how* members should work on a problem. Their *consensus-*

seeking rules (p. 304) are designed to help groups work through differences and disagreements in a constructive fashion:

1. Avoid *arguing* for your own position. Present your position as clearly and logically as possible, but consider seriously the reactions of the group in any subsequent presentations of the same point.

2. Avoid *"win-lose"* stalemates in the discussion of positions. Discard the notion that someone must win and someone must lose in the discussion; when impasses occur, look for the next most acceptable alternative for both parties.

3. Avoid changing your mind *only* to avoid the conflict and to reach agreement. Withstand pressures to yield which have no objective or logically sound foundation. Strive for enlightened flexibility; avoid outright capitulation.

4. Avoid suppressing conflicts by resorting to voting, averaging, coin-flipping, and the like. Treat differences of opinion as indicative of an incomplete sharing of information and viewpoints and press for additional exploration and investigation.

5. View differences of opinion as both natural and helpful rather than as a hindrance in decision-making. Generally, the more ideas expressed the greater the likelihood of conflict will be, but the richer the array of resources will be as well.

6. View initial agreement as suspect. Explore the reasons underlying apparent agreements; make sure that people have arrived at similar solutions for either the same basic reasons or for complementary reasons before incorporating such solutions in the group decision.

These rules encourage members to air and work out differences rather than to come to agreement quickly. They counteract several problems of trained incapacities, including over-evaluation, premature convergence on a single solution (from goal-centeredness), and reliance on objective standards where none exist. Hall and Watson tested these procedures and found that groups trained in the rules produced better answers on a problem-solving task than did untrained groups. They attributed this to a "synergy bonus" from the procedure which allowed trained groups to make use of all their members' skills and knowledge. Untrained groups fell prey to difficulties which precluded effective involvement of all members.

Although these and other formats are invaluable in helping groups to avoid trained incapacities, it is important to remember that they can themselves become procedural incapacities. Neither format is appropriate under all conditions. For example, Reflective Thinking does not work well when members have fundamental disagreements over values, because it presumes agreement on criteria used to evaluate solutions. The consensus-seeking rules would not be appropriate for members with long-standing dislike of each other. In such cases sticking to either procedure would only compound the conflict; although protecting against some possible problems, they can unintentionally introduce others.

The effectiveness of procedural formulas is limited by the fact that they can only counteract those trained incapacities which are *explicitly* permitted in their rules. Reflective Thinking, for example, does nothing to control overemphasis on objective criteria because its rules do not take this incapacity into account. A much more effective method is to give the group *critical tools for recognizing and surmounting trained incapacities, whatever their particular form might be.* Trained incapacities feed on the group's lack of self-awareness; critical methods that make members *conscious* of their own possibly narrow thinking offer a powerful means of controlling destructive habits.

In response to this need Volkema (1981; 1983) developed the *Problem-Purpose Expansion Technique,* a critical method to help members recognize and transcend their own narrow thinking. Volkema argues that the effectiveness of any conflict management strategy depends on how people *formulate* the problems they face. Problem formulation has at least two effects on conflicts. First, it channels members' thinking and can severely limit the range of solutions considered by the group. In the research and development case discussed in chapter 4 (Case 4.2) the problem was expressed as "selection of the best possible procedure for making decisions in the research meetings." This problem formulation constrained members to search for a *single* procedure to be used by *all* project teams, a problem that provoked the conflict. The formulation implicitly ruled out several solutions that would have allowed members to work on common grounds, such as adopting two procedures and testing each in half of the project teams or adopting several procedures and allowing the project directors to choose whichever they liked best. As we have seen, groups tend to converge on solutions prematurely, and an overly-narrow problem formulation encourages this. Second, problem formulations also influence conflicts by setting up the relationship between people when a conflict emerges. The research committee's problem formulation set up a win-lose situation once members became divided over the two candidate programs. Since only one program could be adopted given this approach, a win-lose fight became inevitable with the manager forcing an end to the conflict.

Volkema shows that problem formulations vary along a continuum from a very narrow scope to a very broad scope. For the research and development committee, the formulation "Selection of Tom's procedure for the project teams" would be the narrowest scope possible, because it focuses on a *single* solution and specifies *what* must be done in that solution, that is—selection. Problem formulations of a broader scope ask the question "What are we trying to accomplish by the narrower formulation?" So the formulation given in the previous paragraph "Selection of the best possible procedure for making decisions in the research meetings" is a bit broader than the first, because it encompasses what selection of Tom's procedure would accomplish. Notice also that the second formulation admits a greater number of possible solutions than the first, because it does not specify *which* procedure should be chosen and opens up a range of possibilities. The second formulation also focuses the group's attention on a different set of actions than does the first. If we take the first formulation, the group is likely to focus on how it can get project teams to like Tom's procedure; if we take the second, the group concentrates on searching for alternative procedures and choosing one. A still broader problem formulation than the second would be "selection of the best possible procedures which can be used by the teams." Broader still is "To make the best possible decisions in the project teams." Both of these formulations open up a wider range of possibilities and imply different actions than do the first two (indeed, the fourth opens up the possibility of chucking the procedures altogether).

Volkema argues that in every conflict some levels of formulation promote better and more acceptable solutions than others. Exactly which formulations are best varies depending on the group, the nature of the conflict, the group's environment, and other factors; at present we do not know enough to identify the best formulations. However, our discussion of trained incapacities suggests a way to identify which formulations are *not desirable,* namely, those that promote trained incapacities.

The trained incapacities at work in a group are usually evident in its problem formulations. When groups are goal-centered, they begin discussions of the problem by suggesting specific solutions. Goal-centeredness could lead a discussion of problems with an office record-keeping system to an early consideration of specific changes before all of the real difficulties with the system are identified. If discussion begins with the suggestion of specific solutions, problem formulation is likely to be excessively narrow and focused on only one aspect of the problem. If group members fall prey to the objectivity incapacity, they assume that there are objective or "correct" standards that the solution must meet, when, in fact, the problem requires a judgment call based on the values or preferences of the group. If the group operates under this misconception, the formulation of a problem can easily reflect the objective standards the group hopes will resolve the problem. For example, a group in conflict over whether to hire a male or a female for a position might phrase its problem as "to hire a person who can raise productivity by 10 percent in three years," in an attempt to get around the issue. When destructive redefinition is likely, the formulation will often be so narrow as to preclude a cooperative solution (as in the research and development committee) or phrased in either-or terms (such as "To decide whether a man or woman can best fill our needs"). Such formulations can undermine even the best procedures, because they can easily slip in undetected during a problem definition step.

Identification of problem formulations is a complex process. For one thing, problems are not always explicitly stated by a group. Sometimes, in fact, groups consciously *avoid* clear problem statements in an attempt to avoid bringing the conflict out. In these cases members must try to infer the group's definition of the problem from its discussions. Figuring out the definition is fairly easy once one is familiar with some examples of problem formulations: hypothetical examples can be compared to the group. An additional complication is introduced by the fact that problem formulations may change as the group works on an issue. In the research and development committee the problem was initially "selection of the best possible decision-making procedure for the project teams" but over time shifted to "should we adopt the manager's preference?" which implied confrontation. Clearly these shifts reflect significant occurrences in the conflict and changes in the relationship of members to one another. Indeed, several researchers have proposed that group work is nothing more than a series of redefinitions and reconceptualizations of problems leading gradually toward a narrow solution statement (Lyles & Mitroff, 1980; Poole, 1982). Members must be sensitive to these shifts and their implications for the direction the conflict takes.

Volkema has developed a method called *Problem-Purpose Expansion* to help groups generate a range of formulations. The method makes members aware of their assumptions and makes it possible to recognize trained incapacities by comparing different levels of problem formulations. The *Problem-Purpose Expansion Method* (PPE) has two basic parts. The first is a format for stating the problem. The format is as follows: an infinitive + an object + a qualifier. For example, if the problem is presently thought to be how to convince the residents of a neighborhood that a sidewalk should be installed along their block, the problem might be stated as:

to convince	neighbors	that a sidewalk is needed
Infinitive	Object	Qualifier

This statement then becomes the focus of an initial brainstorm of solutions (see Figure 8).

The second part of PPE expands this problem by reformulating it so that a brainstorming of solutions can be repeated at another level. This is done by asking the following:

What are we trying to accomplish by this?
We want (Most recent formulation)
In order to (Reformulation)

The group might decide it wants to *convince neighbors that a sidewalk is needed* in order *to get neighbors to pay for sidewalk installation*. This reformulation becomes a second level and can be brainstormed. This process is then repeated to generate a whole set of formulations and solutions (see Figure 8). Comparison of the levels can enable the group to recognize where its thinking was narrow and what incapacities may be operating. By making the group aware of different formulations, PPE can disclose the values and assumptions hidden in the group's current way of looking at its problem and suggest innovative viewpoints that cut through existing tangles.

PPE can also be used when the problem in question is "about" the group itself rather than about something the group might do. For example, in the Riverdale Halfway House case (chapter 2) the problem was formulated as how

FIGURE 8   A HIERARCHY OF EXPANDED PROBLEM STATEMENTS.
From Volkema (1982).

	Problem Statements	Possible Solutions
Increasing Problem Scope	TO CONVINCE NEIGHBORS THAT A SIDEWALK IS NEEDED	Gather data; hold public hearings; go door-to-door
	TO GET NEIGHBORS TO PAY FOR SIDEWALK INSTALLATION	Go to the Transportation Department; sue neighbors; introduce a resolution at City Hall
	TO GET A SIDEWALK INSTALLED	Pay for sidewalk yourself; install sidewalk yourself
	TO MAKE THE AREA WHERE A SIDEWALK WOULD GO PASSABLE	Level off area; build boardwalk
	TO MAKE PEDESTRIAN TRAFFIC SAFE	Reroute auto traffic; partition off part of street; stop auto traffic for pedestrians; put up caution signs for autos

"to resolve the animosities between George and Carole." PPE might lead to other formulations more conducive to constructive dialogue, such as how "to clarify lines of authority at Riverdale" or how "to create a more supportive climate at Riverdale." In both cases the broader reformulations change the focus of the problem from Carole and George to the group as a whole and provide a common problem the entire group can work on.

PPE moves the group out of its well-worn, unreflective channels and encourages it to consider new ideas. As we noted in chapter 2, a surprising or startling move can also do this. A former chair of the board of General Motors is reputed to have said during a particularly docile meeting, "Well, it appears as if we're all in agreement. Why don't we all try to work up some conflicts over the weekend so when we come back on Monday we'll be able to think this proposal through thoroughly?" The chair's statement was designed to surprise the other members and jolt them out of their premature convergence. Because it is surprising it is also likely to arouse members to shock, laughter, or incredulity; as a result of this increased energy, when members return to their task they most likely will do so with greater concentration and renewed vigor.

Finally, trained incapacities may be neutralized by reducing the tensions which sustain them. There are, in principle, three ways to reduce tension in conflicts. One method involves *removing the parties from the conflict situation,* in the hope that distance from the conflict will allow them to calm down and recompose themselves. The well-known tactics of a "cooling off period" and of "taking time out" are designed to facilitate this process. The second tack is the opposite of the first: *members are encouraged to vent their tensions* as a means of working through them. This approach is used in some training groups employed by consultants to build cohesive management teams. Obviously, it can easily run out of control, and must be handled very skillfully. The third approach involves reducing tension by *reassuring members that their tension is natural* and does not represent permanent problems or rifts in the group. In one group engaged in planning an educational conference, numerous conflicts arose over the format and scheduling of events. One member was instrumental in enabling the group to confront and work out its differences. She played a "parental" role, reminding other members that each was valuable in his or her own right and that she cared about everyone. This reassurance noticeably reduced tensions and enabled the group to confront and resolve issues it was reluctant to deal with.

Working with Climate

Diagnosis of climates was considered at great length, . . . so this section will advance three measures for *changing* climate to influence conflict interaction. Our earlier analysis of climate clearly implies the first principle: *small, cumulative changes in interaction can eventually result in major changes in climate.* For example, many members report that their first feeling of belonging to their group occurred when members began using "we" when talking about group activities. This subtle difference signals a change in identification from "individual" to "member"; it promotes a more relaxed climate in the group by indicating to members that others are well-disposed toward them and that there is a common ground for working together. In the psychological evaluation unit analyzed in chapter 3, Jerry maintained his dominant position and the group's authoritarian climate through a series of moves which enabled him to control the issues the group worked on. In the same way members could have changed the group's climate by being more assertive and making "bids" to have a say in controlling the group. Jerry might not have noticed these changes, but they will gradually alter the group's climate to encourage more equal participation by members.

A second tactic for working on climates is *to discuss openly themes which trouble members.* Much of the climate's influence on group interaction depends on members' inability to recognize it. If they can bring its effects out in the open and consciously move to counteract them, climate can be used to channel conflict interaction in constructive directions. Often this "consciousness raising" is done by one insightful member.

CASE 6.1

In a small, twelve-person consulting agency, two important members, the program coordinator (Joe) and the publications manager (Jim) were having serious problems getting along together because an outside business they had been running for three years was failing. Joe and Jim decided not to bring up their problems in front of the group, because they believed it could only disrupt the operations of the ordinarily harmonious group. Their suppression of the problems certainly kept their antagonism from becoming an open issue in the group, but it did not prevent their tensions from influencing the group's climate. The agency's weekly meetings were marked by uncomfortable pauses and evasions of pressing issues. Relationships in the group became cautious and artificial; authority relations were also ambiguous because two central members, Joe and Jim, were reluctant to talk to each other and fought over small issues. Finally, at one tension-filled meeting another member, Karen, openly stated that she felt uncomfortable and that she wanted to talk about Joe and Jim's problems and its effect on the group. In the ensuing discussion many issues and feelings emerged. Members were relieved to talk openly, and both Jim and Joe were able to unburden themselves and get support from the group. The tension between Joe and Jim did not subside as a result of Karen's intervention (in fact, it continued until Joe left the agency), but the group's climate improved markedly and members were better able to cope with their co-workers' relationship problems.

There are also formal procedures for member evaluation of the group's climate and functioning (Auvine, Densmore, Extrom, Poole, & Shanklin, 1979). Self-evaluation questionnaires on which members rate their own and others' performance and weaknesses are often used (see Johnson & Johnson, 1975, for several good forms). The questionnaire provides a structured and legitimate way to raise criticisms of the group and open them up for discussion. This "survey-feedback" process can be used to set goals for changing the group's interaction and, ultimately, its climate.

A third tactic for altering a group's climate was mentioned [before]—a member can create a *critical incident* that shifts the entire direction of the group's climate. Recall the example in chapter 1 of the faculty brown bag discussion where the student suddenly challenged the speaker: the climate shifted from congenial to tense. In the same vein, members can attempt to create critical incidents to alter unfavorable climates. Several considerations must be taken into account in order to do this effectively. For one thing, *timing* is critical. Members must be able to recognize propitious moments for acting on the group's climate. Bormann (1972) gives a good example of the importance of timing. In the groups he studied he found a certain point in discussion at which one member would venture a favorable comment or joke about the group. In cases where the other members responded with other favorable comments or followed up on the joke, the group generally developed an open, inclusive climate. When members let the favorable comment drop, the group usually took a much *longer* time to develop cohesion, if it did so at all. Timing is vital in these cases; if the critical moment passes it is gone and members may not get another chance.

Along with timing, *salience* is also important. The move must hold the group's attention if it is to be a watershed. The student's attack on the brown-bag lunch speaker captured the attention of other members; thereafter, they were reacting to the student's move, and their reactions reinforced the tension his statement originally interjected. There are many ways of enhancing the salience of a move—including raising the volume of one's voice, using colorful or symbolic language, being dramatic, or saying something surprising. Used properly, these tactics increase the probability that the move will prove effective. Finally, a member who aspires to create a critical incident should have *credibility and respect* in the eyes of other group members. The actions of a respected member are likely to receive attention from other members and therefore have a good chance to influence the group's interaction. In addition, making an effort to change the group's climate can be interpreted as manipulation; moves of a respected and trusted member are unlikely to be rejected as self-serving.

Of the three approaches, creating a critical incident is the most *uncertain.* It is hard to do, and it has the potential to backfire: other members may reject the person who attempts to maneuver the group. When effective, however, it brings results quickly and it can be initiated by a single member without having to rely on others. Small, cumulative changes and open discussion are more certain, but also have problems. Small changes operate piecemeal through day-to-day group interaction; therefore, it is easy to lapse back into old patterns. To use this technique successfully requires a clear sense of purpose and patience. It does not work quickly and is of limited utility in situations where climate is causing an immediate crisis in a group. Open discussion works much more quickly than cumulative change, but it may add fuel to a conflict by introducing a new issue: members satisfied with the present climate may side against those who are dissatisfied. The emotions associated with discussions of power relations or the group's supportiveness may generalize to the conflict and intensify disagreements on other issues. In using any of the approaches it is important to be aware of possible problems and take measures to circumvent them.

Working with Power

There are a number of barriers to accurate diagnosis of the role of power in conflicts. For one thing, members are often unwilling to talk about power or to provide honest and accurate assessments of their own or others' power, for several reasons. Given our culture's emphasis on democracy and equality, the open use of power is not socially sanctioned. Members may be unwilling to admit that they use "force" or that their group is controlled by only a few members because they believe it makes them look bad. Further, since power depends on endorsement, powerful members often try to keep their power unobtrusive, in order not to alienate those they influence. If weaker members cannot see the member's power, or if they do not understand how it "works," they can do nothing to upset the present balance. In addition, as we noted in chapter 4, many moves (such as issue control) use power indirectly and it is hard to determine how power figures in or who is influencing the situation. Finally, power and endorsement processes depend on relationships *between* members rather than being properties of individuals, so it is often hard to grasp where the source of power is. If power stems from relationships it is often misleading to try to identify a particular person who holds power. The more important question may be who assents to the use of power or who withholds endorsement.

These barriers make the assessment of power a complex process for which there can be no set formula. It is best to look for several different types of indicators to determine which one works best in a given situation. One approach for assessing power is to *determine the possible power resources in the situation and identify who holds them.* This involves identifying both obvious resources like status, knowledge, personal attractiveness, or formal authority *and* more subtle sources of power, such as confidence or ability to predict the other's behavior (Frost & Wilmot, 1978). A second, complementary approach is to *identify power through its effects.* Those members whose *preferences consistently win out* and who are accommodated by other members are generally those who control influential resources and use them effectively. As Frost and Wilmot (p. 60) note, the *ability to label the conflict* is also a sign of power. If a conflict could be interpreted either as a minor difference of opinion or as a major matter of principle, and it ends up being interpreted as a minor difference, the members who favored this view are likely to hold the high ground. A third indicator of power is *conservatism.* If power is relational, then changes in existing relationships generally alter the balance of power, while stability preserves it. Members who are against change are likely to believe they will lose by it, and these are generally the members with power under the status quo.

None of these three indicators is foolproof and each can support mistaken assessments. However, as a set they provide a good starting point for thinking about power. Judgments about power ultimately rest on knowledge of the group or organization, its particular history, and the nuances that signal dominance and subordination. Diagnoses cannot be programmed and must be continually revised in light of ever changing relationships in the group.

[Earlier,] we illustrated how conflict interaction can head toward destructive escalation when members draw upon *unique* resources as a basis for influence. We also discussed several ways that a group can encourage its members to use resources that the group as a whole *shares* when any attempt at influence is made. More specifically, we suggested that the group can try to develop consensus on what the major goals or objectives of the group are, work toward making power resources accessible to all members, and increase awareness that the members, as a community, are the source of power in the group. In one sense, these suggestions are preconditions; they are what must be in place in a group if the members can hope to develop shared power resources and use them as a basis for moves in any conflict interaction. In another sense, these suggestions offer long-term intervention strategies; they are areas that the group can work on in the long run and can establish as part of the general expectations for how the group operates. They can govern what members consider doing when they try to sway each other's thinking about any issue that is in front of the group.

What happens, however, when these preconditions have not been established in a group or they fall through when some particular conflict issue arises that is so important to some member that he or she draws upon resources as a basis for influence that the group as a whole does not share? Although no intervention is guaranteed of success in this situation, there are several approaches members can take to help prevent the possible escalation that can result from this type of move.

Members of the group may need to *anticipate and state* what the group's likely reaction to the member's use of unique resources may be. It may be wise for members to acknowledge explicitly, for example, that they are likely to have trouble seeing the member as someone who has the best interest of the group in mind if such an attempt is made. Or they can warn of possible escalation because they feel that the power move may lead other members to believe that they have no alternative but to use their own unique power resources to regain control. Although this approach is an attempt to encourage members to reflect on how moves are being made in the conflict rather than introducing structural changes in the way people are actually behaving, it can at least force the group to recognize that its interaction may be about to shift dramatically. It also points to the possible dangers or pitfalls that might result when the shift occurs.

A second approach is aimed at developing structural changes in interaction when power moves are based on uniquely held resources. Chapter 4 shows that one of the most effective tools for changing the influence of power in conflicts is to increase members' *awareness* of their own role in creating and sustaining power relations. If members become aware of how their endorsement is shaped by social categorization, the mystique of power, and their own interaction, they are well on their way to "seeing through" the existing power structure. Their understanding enables them to withdraw their support from unwarranted power and work to change the group's power structure. The value of "consciousness-raising" is illustrated by the support groups that spring up in professions which are undergoing rapid change and its accompanying struggles. These groups, which range from groups of female executives in male-dominated corporations to groups of nurses and medical orderlies attempting to gain more input into hospital decisions, give their members a chance to share problems and fears and give each other advice. Members help each other understand how the dominant groups maintain their positions, work out ways of being more effective, and build resolve and courage to face difficult situations. They encourage members to question what was previously unquestionable, the taken-for-granted relations of authority and obedience, strength and weakness in the group. Nor are formal support groups the only thing that can serve this function: a conversation over drinks after work can have the same effect and lead to important insights. Just realizing they are not alone and comparing experiences is an important step for members who wish to change their group.

As Janeway (1980) observes, in addition to awareness, mutual support is another way for weaker members to counterbalance stronger ones. People generally associate coalitions with open shows of strength and solidarity against others, as in a union vote, but open shows may be ineffective in group and organizational contexts. By raising a flag of defiance, members may threaten the stronger members and cause them to overreact, sending the conflict into an escalating spiral. Those who have greater resources stand to lose if the current balance tips in a new direction, and they will fight against moves they perceive as harmful. A coalition is more likely to be successful in moving a conflict in a productive direction if it is unobtrusive. The pact between members should not be openly displayed, and, if possible, any coordination or support should not be obvious. In addition, a coalition is more likely to turn conflict in a productive direction if it aims for a balance of power with shared endorsement, than if it tries to win. If the powerful members' interests are not threatened, and if they do not face serious losses, they are more likely to cooperate with efforts to achieve a balance of power.

Working with Face-Saving Issues

The key to diagnosing face-saving issues successfully lies in members' ability to recognize two major symptoms in group interaction. First, when face-saving is a concern, *the interaction in the group becomes centered on a secondary issue, and this issue prevents members from addressing substantive decisions and agenda items.* The substantive problems the group must resolve are buried by statements and reactions that indicate members are resentful of each other, or are clouded by arguments that defend individuals' positions but do little to advance the group's understanding of the problem or decision it faces. Since the secondary, face-saving issues are related to the more substantive problems the group is addressing, they can consume a group's energy and predominate the interaction before the group realizes that a face-saving issue has diverted its attention. For example, members can defend alternative solutions to a problem in what appears to be a heated debate. But the members may do so only because they feel that if they back away from their positions, they will carry less weight in future discussions or decisions. In this case, the most pressing issue, the one that has greatest influence over the interaction is, "how will the group treat members who change their minds?" However, the content of the discussion remains focused on an agenda item in front of the group. If members fail to see that a secondary issue is driving the interaction, the face-saving concern can produce destructive escalation and threaten the working relationships in the group.

Second, . . . *face-saving issues turn members away from group-centered interaction and toward individually centered interaction.* This is an important symptom in diagnosing face-saving issues. When face-saving is an issue, the relationship between an individual member (or several members) to the group as a whole becomes salient and the interaction becomes focused on this relationship. The relationship issue (that is, how the group will view the member) is being raised even though the group may not make any explicit comments about the fact that it is being raised or about how it should be resolved. There may be, in other words, no explicit attempt to talk about what the relationship of the individual member to the group is or why it is in dispute even though the members are negotiating how someone will be seen.

A concern for the image of an individual in the group is not always problematic; it becomes problematic when it prevents members from pursuing a discussion of more critical issues or ignites those discussions into heated but pointless arguments. If there is a prolonged focus on the relationship of the individual to the group, issues can become easily personalized, members can become overly cautious about making any comments, or the group may make little progress on important issues despite heated discussion. Any of these symptoms suggest that some action must be taken to redirect interaction that has been triggered by face-saving concerns.

Establishing *climates that prevent face-saving concerns from emerging* is, perhaps, the most effective means for eliminating the potentially destructive influence of these issues. The climate established in the group plays a critical role in determining whether face-saving concerns will emerge and become problematic for the group. Members have shared expectations about whether it is safe to move away from a stated position, whether conflict issues can be raised without threatening the group, and whether a member's feelings of unjust treatment can be discussed openly. These expectations arise from events that have occurred in the group—from previous reactions that the group has had to members' comments and concerns, or assumptions people make about how the group would react, to concern about a member's image in the group. While establishing a "healthy" climate is something the group can work towards on an act-by-act basis, the difficult interventions are those that are needed when *a preventative climate has not been established or when some event in the group calls the climate into question* (when, for example, a member is unsure about whether he or she can step back from a position and still be seen as an important, contributing member).

Interventions that attempt to stop the destructive effects of face-saving issues must be built on a recognition that face-saving centers around the *negotiation* of a member's image in the eyes of the group. All three forms of face-saving we have discussed carry a "statement" about an image that the speaker does not want to have the group assign to him or her. Consider the following characterizations of these statements:

Resisting Unjust Intimidation: "Don't see me as someone who accepts unfair treatment or intimidation."

Stepping Back from a Position: "Don't see me as someone who is indecisive" (easily beat, weak, and so on).

Raising Unacknowledged Conflict Issues: "Don't see me as someone who is willing to *cause* problems by raising conflict issues."

Each of these statements makes an assumption or guess about the likely reactions of the group and each indicates that the member feels threatened by the image he or she assumes will be assigned by other group members. However, because each of these statements is founded on an assumption about how the group will react, these assumptions can either be confirmed or rejected by other group members. The interaction that occurs when face-saving is an issue is always a negotiation; it is an attempt to settle what image the speaker can assume the group will hold of him or her.

Interventions that treat *the face-saving issue as a negotiation process* may have the greatest chance for success. We see three steps that can be taken to help facilitate this process. First, the negotiations can occur with less chance of continued escalation *if defensiveness is reduced.* A person who is trying to save face is always under some perceived threat—the threat of having an undesirable image assigned to him or her by the group. Defensiveness is a likely reaction to perceived threat (Gibb, 1961). People feel they must be on guard because a mistaken move on their part can bring about some undesirable consequence. Research by Rapoport (1960) suggests that defensiveness can be reduced by having an opponent indicate an understanding of another's stand on an issue and recognizing some area of validity in the other's position. In the face-saving context, group members can show that they understand why someone feels unfairly treated or worried about appearing weak or indecisive. They can also recognize ways in which the belief may actually be legitimate. If the group has handled similar incidents poorly in the past, acknowledging that these incidents occurred can show a sympathetic understanding for the members' concern. Acknowledging another's position as legitimate and indicating an understanding of it does not ensure that the issue can be settled easily, but it does allow for the possibility of an open discussion as the negotiation unfolds.

Second, the negotiation of a face-saving concern can be facilitated *if the group opens the door for an exchange of concessions on the issue.* Pruitt (1971) has demonstrated the importance of letting both parties in a negotiation tell each other (either implicitly or explicitly) that an exchange of concessions is possible and safe. The parties need to know that there will be some reciprocity of moves if both sides begin making offers toward a settlement. Although face-saving issues are not the same as formal bargaining situations where offers can be made in increments, it is useful to think of the negotiation of a face-saving issue in the same general terms. Take as an example, the face-saving situation where someone is hesitant to step back from a position. The person who is concerned about losing face needs some assurance that moving away from a position is a safe move. A member who is afraid of losing face in the eyes of the group if they back away from a stand needs some assurance that shifting positions will not reduce their role or importance in the group. Comments or reactions that give a member a "way out" of these fears are likely to reduce the concern for face that may be keeping someone from moving from a position they, themselves, no longer want to defend. To encourage an exchange of concessions, there are several tacks members in the group can take: they can acknowledge the importance of the concerned member by requesting information from him or her about important issues that the group is addressing, they can stress the importance of the member in the group's current or future work, or they can actually increase the member's role in future projects. A supervisor in a large record-keeping office at a corporation recently dealt with a difficult face-saving issue by trying to reassure a concerned employee that it was safe to back away from a position.

CASE 6.2

An office worker was assigned the task of putting together an extensive report that described the productivity and performance of people in various divisions of a corporation. When the report was printed, a copy was sent to each division head for their inspection before the book was distributed generally in the corporation. One division head called the research office after reading the report and was irate about an error that he found in the description of his department. He saw the mistake as a significant problem that could cause considerable damage to his division's reputation and future development.

The complaint was discussed by several supervisors in the research office before it reached the person who had actually compiled the book. When this person was told about the error, she became very defensive and argued that the information that appeared in the book was accurate. It was clear to her supervisors that the information was in error and that the employee was trying to save face. The worker was defending her position, not because she firmly believed that it was correct, but because acknowledging that she had made a mistake could mean that she would be seen as incompetent.

The approach her immediate supervisor took in handling this situation was to point out to the employee that compiling the report was an immense and difficult task because the information had to be drawn from so many different sources and often had to be inferred from sketchy notes or letters that various people in the departments submitted to the records office. She congratulated the employee for putting together a catalogue that had ten thousand pieces of *correct* information. These comments allowed the woman to admit the error because it reduced the threat of being seen as incompetent and, more importantly, it allowed the two of them to begin discussing possible ways that the error could be handled so that the irate division head would be satisfied and accurate information would be disseminated about the unit.

Signalling that an exchange of "concessions" is possible is important in the other two face-saving situations we have discussed, although the way this signalling occurs would, of course, be different. The person who is trying to save face because he or she feels that they have been treated unfairly by the group is often preoccupied with making this point known. Letting others know that they feel they have been mistreated can take precedence over any desire to discuss whether or how the treatment occurred. As a result, other members in the group must provide some assurance that if the concerned person stops "saying" that he or she has been treated unfairly, the issue will not be lost or forgotten. There has to be assurance that the group is willing to discuss the matter in order for the person to concede that they have made their point known. This is often more difficult than it may appear at first glance. If a member feels they have been treated unfairly in the past, it may be difficult for that member to believe that the group actually wants to address the issue. But until this assurance is given, the face-saving issue may continue to escalate as the member criticizes the group without allowing for a productive discussion of the issue.

When someone raises a conflict issue in a group that typically avoids potentially divisive issues or believes that none occur, a concern for face can continue as the conflict is being addressed. The member can believe that they are being seen as someone who is the cause of the group's problems rather than someone who raises an issue that was already present and affecting the group's interaction. If this concern for face is not alleviated, the member who raises the issue may feel less a part of the group or could be hesitant to address the conflict openly during differentiation. At least *one* other member in the group must step forward and say that they believe it is important that the issue be addressed. If such a signal is not sent, the person who is concerned about his or her image in the group has no assurance that the group does not still hold him or her responsible for the conflict. The group has to offer some signal that it is beginning to *own* the conflict.

If defensiveness cannot be reduced, or if the group cannot facilitate negotiation through an exchange of concessions, there is a third step that can be taken to help stop the possible destructive effects of face-saving interaction. One or more members can *stress the consequences of not settling the issue that is in front of the group.* This strategy is frequently offered as a way to increase tension or sharpen a conflict so that members will become more motivated to deal with the issue (Walton, 1969). When face-saving is an issue, increasing tension by pointing to the consequences of an unresolved conflict can encourage the member who is concerned about face to care more about the substantive issue that is in front of the group than the potential threat to his or her image. It can, in other words, help direct the interaction away from an individual focus and toward a group focus.

Relations among the Forces

It should be clear that the forces are often interrelated and that work on one can be counteracted by the effect of others. Climate pervades everything that happens in the group, so an unfavorable climate can undermine work in other forces. A competitive group with great differences in members' influence and little supportiveness will have great difficulty avoiding destructive redefinition and problems related to face-saving. At the same time, forces that shape immediate interaction can prohibit changes in climate, because climates depend on interaction. The use of unique sources of power may reinforce an authoritarian and suspicious climate, despite the best efforts of members to relax the climate. Premature evaluation may anger members and introduce a competitive atmosphere as well as face-saving concerns. In the same way all four forces may intersect and reinforce one another under certain circumstances. It is important to take this possibility into account when attempting to turn conflict in productive directions. . . .

REFERENCES

Auvine, B., Densmore, B., Extrom, M., Poole, S., & Shanklin, M. *A manual for group facilitators.* Madison, Wis.: The Center for Conflict Resolution, 1977.

Avery, M., Auvine, B., Streidel, B., & Weiss, L. *Building united judgment.* Madison, Wis: The Center for Conflict Resolution, 1981.

Bartunek, J., Benton, A., & Keys, C. B. Third party intervention and the bargaining behavior of group representatives. *Journal of Conflict Resolution,* 1975, *19,* 532–557.

Bormann, E. G. Fantasy and rhetorical vision: The rhetorical criticism of social reality. *Quarterly Journal of Speech,* 1972, *58,* 396–407.

Delbecq, A., Van de Ven, A., & Gustafsen, D. *Group techniques for program planning.* Glenview, Ill.: Scott, Foresman, 1975.

Etzioni, A. *The active society.* New York: Macmillan, 1968.

Filley, A. *Interpersonal conflict resolution.* Glenview, Ill.: Scott, Foresman, 1975.

Fisher, R. J. Third party consultation: A method for the study and resolution of conflict. *Journal of Conflict Resolution,* 1972, *16,* 67–94.

Frost, J. H., & Wilmot, W. W. *Interpersonal conflict.* Dubuque, Iowa: William C. Brown, 1978.

Gibb, J. Defensive communication. *Journal of Communication,* 1961, *2,* 141–148.

Goldmann, R. B. *Round table justice: Case studies in conflict resolution.* Boulder, Colo.: Westview Press, 1980.

Gouran, D. S. *Making decisions in groups.* Glenview, Ill.: Scott, Foresman, 1982.

Guetzkow, H., & Gyr, J. An analysis of conflict in decision-making groups. *Human Relations,* 1954, *7,* 367–381.

Hall, J., & Watson, W. H. The effects of a normative intervention on group decision-making performance. *Human Relations,* 1970, *23,* 299–317.

Hollander, E. P., & Julian, J. W. Contemporary trends in the analysis of leadership processes. *Psychological Bulletin,* 1969, *71,* 387–397.

Janeway, E. *Powers of the weak.* New York: Morrow-Quill, 1980.

Johnson, D. W. & Johnson, F. P. *Joining together.* Englewood Cliffs, New Jersey: Prentice-Hall, 1975.

Kerr, S., Schriesheim, C. A., Murphy, C. J., & Stogdill, R. M. Toward a contingency theory of leadership based upon the consideration and initiating structure literature. *Organizational Behavior and Human Performance,* 1974, *12,* 62–82.

Lindskold, S. Trust development, the GRIT proposal, and the effects of conciliatory acts on conflict and cooperation. *Psychological Bulletin,* 1978, *85,* 772–793.

Lyles, M. A., & Mitroff, I. I. Organizational problem formulation: An empirical study. *Administrative Science Quarterly,* 1980, *25,* 102–119.

Morley, I. E., & Stephenson, G. M. *The social psychology of bargaining.* London: George Allen and Unwin, 1977.

Osgood, C. E. Suggestions for winning the real war with communism. *Journal of Conflict Resolution,* 1959, *3,* 295–325.

Osgood, C. E. *An alternative to war or surrender.* Urbana: University of Illinois Press, 1962.

Osgood, C. E. *Perspective in foreign policy.* Palo Alto, California: Pacific Books, 1966.

Poole, M. S. *A multiple sequence theory of decision development.* Paper presented at Conference on Small Group Communication Research, Pennsylvania State University, April 1982.

Pruitt, D. Indirect communication and the search for agreement in negotiation. *Journal of Applied Social Psychology,* 1971, *1,* 205–239.

Pruitt, D., & Johnson, D. F. Mediation as an aid to face saving in negotiation. *Journal of Personality and Social Psychology,* 1970, *14,* 239–246.

Rapoport, A. *Fights, games and debates.* Ann Arbor: University of Michigan Press, 1960.

Scheidel, T., and Crowell, L. *Discussing and deciding.* New York: Macmillan, 1979.

Stogdill, R. *Handbook of leadership.* New York: Free Press, 1974.

Tannenbaum, R., & Schmidt, W. H. How to choose a leadership pattern. *Harvard Business Review,* 1958, *36,* 95–101.

Volkema, R. J. *An empirical investigation of problem formulation and problem-purpose expansion.* Unpublished Ph.D. Thesis, University of Wisconsin, Madison, 1981.

Volkema, R. J. *Problem-purpose expansion: A technique for reformulating problems.* Unpublished manuscript, University of Wisconsin, Eau Claire, 1983.

Walton, R. *Interpersonal peacemaking: Confrontations and third party consultation.* Reading, Mass.: Addison-Wesley, 1969.

Wehr, P. *Conflict regulation.* Boulder, Colo.: Westview Press, 1979.

Converting Win/Lose to Win/Win: The Tactics of Conflict Resolution

Roy J. Lewicki and Joseph A. Litterer

. . . [I]ntegrative bargaining, leading to a win/win outcome, is a very attractive process. For each party, it holds out the prospect of a larger, more satisfactory gain than might be realized through distributive bargaining. Further, by establishing a cooperative rather than a competitive relationship, integrative bargaining supports many societal expectations and values. In Chapter 5, we discussed the strategies and tactics of integrative bargaining that may be used once commitment to the process is established. In this chapter, we address ways to convert a win/lose relationship into a win/win relationship; that is, getting out of distributive bargaining and into integrative bargaining.

Let us begin by reviewing the structure of distributive and integrative bargaining (Table 1). The difference between the two processes is substantial. The primary concern is how to convert distributive bargaining into integrative given this difference. Distributive bargaining begins with a fundamental conflict over the allocation of limited resources; the accompanying tension, hostility, defensiveness and distrust perpetuates and magnifies the conflict even further. For productive negotiating to occur, this conflict must be handled in a way that arrests the escalation, reduces conflict, opens lines of communication, and increases trust and cooperativeness.

Put simply, in order to successfully convert a win/lose to a win/win situation, we must effectively deal with the dynamics of escalating, polarizing conflict. In this chapter, we will explore a variety of approaches and techniques that can be used to put derailed negotiations back on the track. Many of these techniques are applicable to a broader range of conflict settings than negotiation. Some of the approaches are predominantly directed at reducing the level of emotional tension and hostility; others are designed to enhance accurate communication between the parties, and still others help to create new alternatives for agreement on the substantive issues. Initially, we will discuss all of these techniques as actions that the parties themselves can take to move from unproductive polarization to productive deliberation. However, as we shall also point out, it is often difficult for negotiators to initiate these actions "in the heat of battle." Under conditions of high mistrust and suspicion, overtures of cooperation and conflict reduction are frequently seen as strategic ploys, tricks to lure the other party

---

From Roy J. Lewicki and Joseph A. Litterer. Negotiation *(Homewood, Ill.: Irwin, 1985), pp. 279–280, 290–299.*

TABLE 1

	Distributive Bargaining	Integrative Bargaining
Pay-off structure	Fixed amount of resources to be divided.	Variable amount of resources to be divided.
Primary motivation	Gains of one will be the sacrifices of the other.	Parties concerned about maximizing joint outcomes.
Interests	Diametrically opposed.	Convergent or congruent.
Relationships	Short term relationship; people do not need to work together in the future.	Long term relationship; parties expect to work together in the future.

into a false sense of trust and vulnerability. As a result, intervention by neutral third parties is often necessary. At the end of the chapter, we will examine the approaches that third parties traditionally take in breaking negotiation deadlocks. . . .

Controlling Issues

. . . [A] third major difficulty that inhibits parties from resolving conflict is that as conflict intensifies, the size and number of the issues expand. As conflict escalates, it snowballs; bits and pieces of other issues are accumulated in a large, unmanageable mass. While smaller conflicts can be managed one at a time, each in a way satisfactory to the details of the incident, larger conflicts become unwieldy and less amenable to any easy resolution. The problem for negotiators in escalated disputes, therefore, is to develop strategies to contain issue proliferation, and reduce the dispute to manageable proportions.

Roger Fisher has been a major advocate of strategies of issue control in negotiation, particularly in international affairs. In a well-known article on *fractionating conflict,* Fisher suggests six major approaches for reducing a large conflict into smaller parts:

1. Reduce the Number of Parties on Each Side.   When conflict escalates, each side seeks to build alliances for strength, or to bring their constituencies into the dispute; either they increase the number of parties at the negotiation or they bring more clout to the table. Additional parties, such as lawyers, expert witnesses, etc. are often brought into negotiations for the information they can provide. Rather than having them present their testimony and leave, however, experts often remain on the scene to provide additional input. Since the sheer number of parties at the table can make negotiations considerably more complex (more parties = more perspectives on the issues, more time needed to hear each side, more opportunities for disagreement, etc.), groundrules are needed for ways to limit the number of parties. One way to control conflict size is to return the dispute to the original negotiating parties. The fewer the actors present, or the more the conflict can be limited to two individuals, the more likely the parties will be to reach a favorable settlement.

2. Control the Number of Physical Issues Involved.   A second way to control the size of a conflict is to keep the number of issues small enough to manage. When conflict escalates, the size and number of issues proliferate. Some conflicts escalate to the point where there are too many issues to constructively manage. At the same time, keeping negotiations limited to a very few issues also raises problems. Single issue conflicts are frequently harder to manage because they quickly lead to win-lose polarization over the issue. Achieving a win-win solution requires a negotiating situation where all parties can win. In such circumstances, it is often desirable to expand the number of issues, in order to permit each side to view itself as having gained. This can be done by (a) defining the issue more broadly so that resolution can benefit both sides, or (b) coupling the issue with another issue so that two issues are involved, and each party can receive a preferred settlement on one of the issues. Small packages of two or three issues are frequently easier to resolve because multiple issues facilitate packaging and trading off on concessions.

3. State Issues in Concrete Terms Rather Than as Principles.   A third way that conflict issues become difficult to control is when events or issues are treated as matters of "principle." Small conflicts can rapidly become intractable disputes when their resolution is *not* treated as an isolated event, but instead must be consistent with a broader "policy" or "principle." Since any deviation from policy is viewed as a threat to that policy, and since broad policy is far more difficult to change than a concession on a single issue, negotiations are immediately problematic. For example, a union may request binding arbitration of grievances in a labor dispute; management not only does not want to grant the request, but states that the request is inconsistent with management's rights to handle discipline cases. "It's a matter of principle," they assert. Resorting to arguments of "principles" and "policies" is often a strategic defense by high power parties against any change from the status quo; the more arguments are conducted at that level alone, the less likely those disputes can be successfully resolved.

There are, of course, times when a single event is properly seen as an indicator of new principles or policy. That being the case, the negotiations should be arranged to specifically address the policy or principle. Many times, people are reluctant to do this, because they know negotiations over principles are difficult and lengthy. However, to attempt to negotiate a concrete issue when the negotiation is really on the "hidden agenda" of a major principle only results in frustration. If this is occurring, it is wise to face the issue and raise it directly. There are at least two strategies:

- Question whether the issue needs to be addressed at the principle or policy level. Ask with which established policy or principle the issue is closely connected. If none exists, and one party wants to look at the matter from a policy or principle level, suggest that the immediate concrete issue be handled and discussed separate from the underlying principle or policy. If need be, the parties can agree that the concrete issue can be settled in this instance, with no expectation as to how the policy will later be established.

- Point out that exceptions can be made to all policies, and that principles and policies can be maintained even if minor deviations are permitted to exist. For example, while "honesty is the best policy," there are often times when we know that deviations from the truth may be necessary. The parties may be willing to agree that this might be one of those times.

4. Restrict the Precedents Involved—Both Procedural and Substantive.   The final type of issue magnification is that the parties treat concessions on a single issue as violations of some substantive or procedural precedent. When a substantive precedent is at stake, one party will imply that to concede on this issue at this time will render him vulnerable to conceding on the same issue, or a similar issue, in the future. "If we give one inch on a cost-of-living clause this year," management argues, "you will be back wanting a foot next year." In contrast, procedural precedents are at stake when parties agree to follow a process they haven't followed before. For example, a procedural precedent may be set when the parties agree to negotiate in a relationship that previously has not been characterized by negotiation, and/or one has more power than the other. Parents are confronted by their children, who no longer wish to "obey orders;" teachers find their authority challenged by students. Belief in the domino theory is strong. The high power party, who supports the precedent, believes that if he/she negotiates now, rather than "quelling the rebellion," there will be no end to the number and types of demands in the future.

Issues of precedent are usually as thorny to control as issues of principle. Once again, a negotiator trying to move a conflict toward de-escalation and resolution should try to keep single issues from becoming translated into major questions of precedent. Focus the dialogue on the key issue, and persist in arguments that concessions on *this* issue at *this* time do not necessarily dictate any precedents—substantive or procedural—for the future.

5. Search for Ways to "Fractionate" the Big Issues.   Fisher calls these "salami tactics"—ways to slice a large issue into smaller pieces. Issues that can be expressed in quantitative terms are easy to slice—wage demands, for example, can be cut down to pennies per hour increment, or lease rates can be sliced down to pennies per square foot. When trying to fractionate issues of principle or precedent, use time horizons (when the principle goes into effect or how long it lasts) and the number of different applications of the principle as ways to slice the issues. Thus, a cost-of-living escalator may seem like an all-or-nothing issue. However, a cost-of-living escalator can be "sliced" according to *when* it is introduced, or to the *number of different worker classifications* to which it applies.

6. Issues Are Resolved Quickly When They Are "Depersonalized,"—Separated from the Parties Who Are Advocating Them.   The most common approach to negotiation—positional bargaining—tends to create conflict over both the issues and the relationship between negotiators. People become identified with positions on issues, and vice versa. Effective negotiation requires separating the issues from the parties, not only by working to establish a productive relationship between the parties (leaving only the issue conflict at stake), but by trying to resolve the issues without regard to the people.

Establish Commonalities

As we noted earlier, escalated conflict tends to magnify (in the parties' eyes) their perceived differences and to minimize their perceived similarities. The parties tend to see themselves as farther apart and having less in common than may be true. Therefore, a fourth major action that parties can take to de-escalate conflict is to establish commonalities or focus on common objectives. Several approaches are possible.

Superordinate Goals

Superordinate goals are common goals; they are desired by both parties and require the cooperation of both parties to achieve. In a corporation, for example, people do different jobs (e.g., marketing, manufacturing) which have different objectives, yet they must work together in some basic ways (for example, to get the product to the customer) or the corporation will not survive. A local city council and community members may disagree as to the ways to spend limited funds for community development; however, they may be able to agree if it is possible for them to write a joint grant proposal that will provide enough money to meet all objectives. Two negotiators may be in a heated conflict over how to resolve an issue, but if they share the common objective of completing negotiations by a certain deadline, then the deadline will increase the likelihood of concession making.

In order to have significant impact on negotiations, superordinate goals must be jointly desired by both sides, and must not be seen as benefiting one side more than the other. In a research study, Johnson and Lewicki showed that superordinate goals which were closely related to the issues of the conflict, and which were introduced by one party in the dispute, often became caught up in the conflict dynamics and lost their effectiveness. Random events (under neither party's control) or events created by neutral third parties, are frequently better superordinate goals than those which are searched for and planned by the parties. For example, natural disasters such as floods, storms, blackouts, fires, etc. bring divisive people and communities together in a common purpose of survival; the same impact can be seen in negotiations.

Common Enemies

A common enemy is a negative form of superordinate goal. The parties find new motivation to resolve their differences in order to avoid intervention by a third party, or to pool resources to defeat a common enemy. Political leaders of all persuasions have often provoked outside enemies to attack in order to bring their own constituencies together. Managers who are in conflict are sometimes told by their superiors that if they do not reach agreement, someone else will make the decision for them. Labor and management may behave more collaboratively when threatened with binding arbitration or government intervention in their dispute.

Agreement on the Rules and Procedures

A third way parties can establish commonalities is by mutual agreement on the rules by which negotiations will be conducted. Escalated conflict tends to exceed its bounds; as parties become more upset, they may be more likely to resort to any and all tactics to defeat their opponents. Efforts at effective conflict de-escalation and control may require that the parties rededicate themselves to basic ground rules for how they will manage their dispute. These include:

- Determining a site for a meeting. Changing the site or finding "neutral turf" may be helpful to get things moving again.

- Setting a formal agenda as to what may be discussed, what may *not* be discussed, and agreeing to abide by that agenda.

- Determining who may attend the meetings. Changing key negotiators or representatives may be a "signal" of intention to change negotiation approach or tactics.

- Setting time limits for the individual meeting, and for the overall negotiations session. As we have pointed out, progress in negotiation is paced according to the time available; therefore, setting limits is likely to create more progress than if no limits are set.

■ Setting procedural roles—who may speak, how long they may speak, how issues will be approached, what facts may be introduced, how records or "minutes" will be kept, how agreements will be affirmed, what clerical or support services are required, etc.

Finally—and perhaps a very radical step for some negotiators—the parties may agree to set aside a short period of time during negotiations for the expressed purpose of critiquing *how they are doing*. This mechanism effectively designates a selected time for the parties to critically evaluate their own progress in negotiation, and to suggest a time when groundrules may be reevaluated, procedural mechanisms changed, or perhaps even changing negotiator behavior. This "process orientation" may provide the opportunity for the parties to self-correct the procedural mechanisms that will allow them to make greater progress on their substantive disagreements.

Integrative Frameworks

Superordinate goals, common enemies and mutual commitment to rules are factors *outside* the boundaries of the dispute; they transcend the specific issues and bring the parties together in unified action. However, superordinate goals and common enemies do not establish the foundation for long-term cooperation; when the common goal or common enemy is removed, the parties may find that they have no greater basis for resolving their dispute than they did before. Hence, other mechanisms must be pursued to establishing a common ground for deliberation.

There are two primary vehicles for developing commonalities in disputes: first, by focusing on similarities between the parties rather than on differences; and second, by searching for cognitive ways to redefine the dispute such that all parties' interests may be accommodated.

Maximizing similarities is simply a process of refocusing the parties' attention on what they have in common, rather than where they disagree. As noted earlier, conflict processes tend to highlight perceived differences and magnify the importance of these differences. The longer the parties are in dispute, the more they quibble about the differences, and the more they recognize other differences that are then drawn into the dispute. One way to control this escalation is to re-emphasize what the parties have in common—objectives, purposes, overall philosophies and viewpoints, long-range goals, styles of operation, etc. Another is to review what they have accomplished together. Reemphasizing the commonalities tends to put the differences back into their proper perspective, and de-emphasizes their importance. This process either defuses the emotionality tied to the differences, or creates a positive emotional bond based on similarities that will allow differences to be bridged.

Integrative frameworks are ways of redefining the issues to create a common perspective from which initial positions appear more compatible. Eiseman refers to this process as creating an integrative conceptual framework, while

Fisher and Ury state that successful negotiators focus on *interests,* not positions. By defining negotiated issues in terms of positions—my position on this issue is X—parties tend to treat complex phenomena by simplistically defining a single point, and then refusing to move from it. In order to create movement, parties must establish ways of redefining the conflict so that they can explore compatible interests. Fisher and Ury use the simple example of two women quarreling in a library. One wants the window open and the other wants it closed. They bicker back and forth about how much to leave it open: a crack, halfway, three quarters of the way. No solution satisfies them.

Enter the librarian. She asks one why she wants the window open: "To get some fresh air." She asks the other why she wants it closed: "To avoid the draft." After thinking a minute, she opens a window in the next room, bringing in fresh air without a draft.

Eiseman notes that there are several ways to create integrative frameworks out of polarized positions:

1. Dimensionalize the Problem.   Instead of treating the conflict as distinctly different categorical viewpoints, treat it as points along a continuum. In the above example, the parties were in dispute about whether the window would be open or closed. In fact, there are almost an infinite number of degrees that the window can be open, from very slightly to a great deal. Once the parties redefine the issue as the amount it will be open, they can then "negotiate" more easily over the size of the opening.

2. Increase the Number of Dimensions.   The successful intervention of the librarian in the above example is predicated on her imaginative solution, that fresh air and no draft can be accommodated if one does not restrict the solution to opening a window in the same room. Multiple dimensions allow one party to "win" on one dimension and the other to "win" on the second. Increasing dimensions allows for the possibility that an additional dimension can be identified on which the parties can more easily reconcile their differences. It may also provide an entirely new way of looking at the problem, so that both sides can now recognize degrees, shades, and variations that may satisfy all parties.

3. Construct an "Ideal Case."   Sometimes parties are in dispute because each is proposing a solution which meets only his/her own needs but not those of the other side. One way to break this deadlock is to construct an ideal case that would meet the needs of both sides. In the above example, the librarian did this by saying to herself, "Ideally, how can one party get fresh air while the other avoids a draft?" Negotiating parties can construct ideal solutions by creatively devising ways that both parties could ideally have their needs met, and then determining how that ideal scenario might be attained.

4. Search for Semantic Resolutions.   Particularly in cognitive conflicts, where parties are negotiating over contract language, setting policy or establishing memoranda of agreement, conflict frequently intensifies over key words, phrases and expressions. Sometimes this conflict can be reduced to irrelevant hairsplitting, yet to the parties the wording has significance in its meaning and intent. Discovering how parties attach different meanings to some words, or exploring language that can accommodate both sides, is another alternative for achieving an integrative framework.

Make Preferred Options More Desirable to the Opponent

A final alternative method that parties can use to increase the likelihood of agreement is to make their desires and preferences more palatable to their opponent. We have noted that as conflict escalates, the parties become more locked into defining their *own* position on an issue. Moreover, as this position is formulated over time, negotiators try to remain consistent with the original position—that is, to establish clearcut "policy" which applies in all circumstances. Because these policies are designed to apply to a variety of circumstances, of necessity they become broader rather than more specific. If the other does not readily comply with a negotiator's position or policy, the negotiator's tendency is to escalate and rigidify his demands, or increase the magnitude of the threat for noncompliance. These actions heighten conflict.

Roger Fisher suggests that most influence situations can be characterized by a "demand" (what we want), and offers and threats that state or imply the consequences of meeting or not meeting the demand. The basic dynamics of this process are depicted in Table 2.

Fisher suggests that this emphasis is greatly misplaced and self-destructive. Rather than focusing on their own positions, demands, and threats, negotiators should direct their effort to the following question: how can we get them (our opponents) to make a choice which is best for us, given that our interests diverge? This approach is largely a matter of perspective-taking—focusing on the other's interests rather than one's own. Like role-reversal, it requires negotiators to focus less on their own position, and more on a clear understanding of opponent's needs. Moreover, once those needs are understood, parties should invest their efforts *not* in the tactics of getting the opponent to come to us, but in the ways we can move toward them. Several alternatives can be pursued to accomplish this objective:

1. Give Them a Yesable Proposal.   Rather than increasing the emphasis on *our* position, a negotiator's efforts should be directed at creating a position that *opponents* will find acceptable. Rather than stating our position and letting *them* suggest alternatives which we may approve or overrule, a negotiator should give

TABLE 2

	Demand	Offer	Threat
	The decision desired by us	The consequences of making the decision	The consequences of not making the decision
Who?	Who is to make the decision?	Who benefits if the decision is made?	Who gets hurt if the decision is not made?
What?	Exactly what decision is desired?	If the decision is made, what benefits can be expected? —what costs?	If the decision is not made, —what risks? —what potential benefits?
When?	By what time does the decision have to be made?	When, if ever, will the benefits of making the decision occur?	How soon will the consequences of not making the decision be felt?
Why?	What makes this a right, proper, and lawful decision?	What makes these consequences fair and legitimate?	What makes these consequences fair and legitimate?

Every feature of an influence problem can be located somewhere on this schematic map. The nature of a given problem can be discovered through estimating how the presumed adversary would answer the above questions.

attention to understanding *their* needs and devising a proposal which will meet those needs. Fisher terms this a "yesable" proposal—one to which their only answer can be, "yes, it is acceptable." To succeed, however, this approach requires a negotiator to begin to think about what the other party would want or would agree with, rather than exclusively considering his own goals and needs.

2. Ask for a Different Decision. Rather than making demands more general, to fit with our "position" or "policy," negotiators should endeavor to make demands more specific. Negotiators must determine what specific elements of the demands are most palatable or offensive to the opponent, then use this information to *refine the demand.* "Ask for a different decision," asserts Fisher. Reformulate, repackage, reorganize, rephrase. Fractionate, split, divide, make more specific. Making demands more specific is not making them more rigid; they *would* be rigid if it were the *only* demand to be made. Rather, specific demands which can be reformulated are easier to recast to meet the other's needs.

Fisher and Ury describe an analogous procedure in their recommendation that successful negotiators be skilled at inventing options for mutual gain. This principle has already been discussed several times in our review of integrative bargaining. By inventing and refining ways that both parties can succeed, and by providing a variety of these options to the opponent, the likelihood that both parties can select a desirable option is greatly enhanced.

3. Sweeten the Offer Rather Than Intensifying the Threat.   Negotiators can also make options more palatable by enhancing the attractiveness of accepting them. Again, this is a matter of placing the emphasis on the positive rather than the negative; in the traditional "carrot and stick" tactics of managerial motivation, it is making the carrot more attractive rather than enlarging the stick. Promises and offers can be made more attractive in a variety of ways: maximizing their attractive qualities and minimizing their negative ones, showing how they meet the opponent's needs, reducing the disadvantages to them of accepting an offer, making offers more credible (i.e., that it will actually be given if they accept), or setting deadlines on offers so that they expire if not accepted quickly. Many would argue that these are common "sales tricks" akin to rebates, "two for the price of one" offers, "today only" sales, "extra added attraction" elements, etc. They are. The same techniques that salesmen use to move their products can and should be used by negotiators to get their position accepted by an adversary. Many of these techniques were described in the chapter on persuasion.

4. Use Legitimacy or Objective Criteria to Evaluate Solutions.   Finally, negotiators may insist that alternative solutions and settlements be evaluated by "objective" criteria that meet the test of fairness and legitimacy. Each side should be able to demonstrate that its "demands" are based on sound facts, calculations and information, and that preferred solutions are consistent with those facts and information. This procedure will frequently require disclosing and sharing facts, rather than disguising and distorting them. "Here's how we arrived at our proposal. Here are the facts we used, the cost data we estimated, the calculations we made. You can verify these by the following procedures." The more this data is open to public verification, and demonstrated to be within the bounds of fairness and legitimacy, the more convincing will be the position "independent" of the negotiator who advocates it, and the more persuasive it will be in achieving a settlement. . . .

Consequences

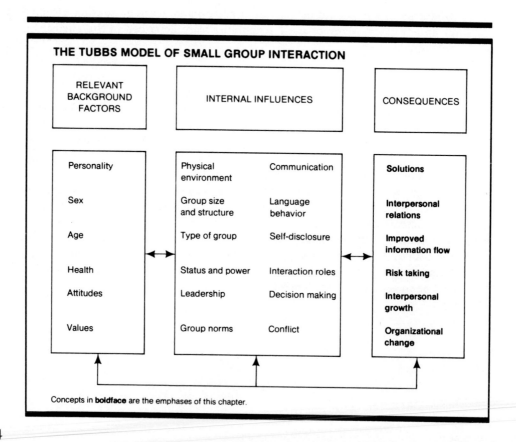

THE TUBBS MODEL OF SMALL GROUP INTERACTION

RELEVANT BACKGROUND FACTORS	INTERNAL INFLUENCES		CONSEQUENCES
Personality	Physical environment	Communication	**Solutions**
Sex	Group size and structure	Language behavior	**Interpersonal relations**
Age	Type of group	Self-disclosure	**Improved information flow**
Health	Status and power	Interaction roles	**Risk taking**
Attitudes	Leadership	Decision making	**Interpersonal growth**
Values	Group norms	Conflict	**Organizational change**

Concepts in **boldface** are the emphases of this chapter.

CASE STUDY

Dave King is president of XYZ fraternity, which has 60 members living in the house. The house has room to sleep 75, but membership has declined somewhat in recent years and several rooms in the house are unfilled.

The fraternity house is located near a river that periodically floods its banks. When this happens, one room of the house gets water-soaked. This room has four members residing in it at the present time. These four have put a sign on the door of their room calling themselves the "swamp rats," and labeling the room "the Riverfront Apartment."

Dave and the other fraternity officers (vice-president, treasurer, and house manager) decided in an executive council meeting to use some of the unoccupied rooms in the house by letting the "swamp rats" move to drier quarters. They announced this plan at a chapter meeting on a Tuesday evening. That night, several members went to the "swamp rats'" room to help them move out. The "swamp rats" had barricaded themselves in their room by placing their mattresses against the inside of the locked door. When Dave and the others tried to reason with the "swamp rats" to move out of the water-soaked room, the "swamp rats" opened the door and a fight broke out. The "swamp rats" insisted that they did not want to be evicted from their "riverfront apartment." Now there is a high degree of hard feelings among the fraternity members and two factions have emerged. One group backs the officers, who feel that they were only trying to help. The other group backs the "swamp rats," who feel that the officers are overstepping their authority in trying to move them out of their room.

1. What should Dave have done differently?

2. How would you go about correcting the situation as it now exists?

This case study points to the fact that not all problem-solving attempts have positive outcomes or consequences. Dave King found out the hard way that even well-intentioned leaders sometimes live to see their best efforts backfire. This chapter deals with the potential outcomes or consequences of group interaction. These are sometimes referred to as the *end results*. However, our systems theory perspective reminds us that groups are ongoing and that today's end results are simply the new *inputs* for tomorrow's activities. The consequences of this particular decision eventually led to the deterioration of Dave's effectiveness as fraternity president. The interactions among the fraternity members led to increased polarization between the two factions. This problem eventually resolved itself when the senior class graduated and a river flood control program eliminated the flooding problem altogether. Now the fraternity is troubled with a whole set of new problems, and so it goes with the ongoing cycle of small group events.

After wading through six chapters on small group interaction, you should be able to answer such questions as, "Why use groups anyway? Wouldn't it be easier to just do the job yourself?" Certainly by now you are more aware of the many difficulties and complexities involved with group behavior. Before you throw up your hands and give up, read this chapter. At this time we will begin to elaborate upon the advantages of group interaction by determining the end results or potential consequences of group discussion. In this chapter we will examine six of these end results: (1) solutions to problems, (2) changes in interpersonal relations, (3) improved information flow, (4) increased risk taking, (5) interpersonal growth, and (6) organizational change.

SOLUTIONS TO PROBLEMS

Quality of Solutions

A clear result of small group research is that groups have the potential to make better-quality decisions than the same individuals would make if working alone. Group performance does not always surpass individual performance, but in those instances, the group process has been counterproductive. This notion has been stated in the following formula (Steiner 1972, p. 9):

$$\text{Actual productivity} = \text{potential productivity} - \text{losses due to faulty process}$$

When the group process is functioning well, group productivity tends to be as good or better than the individual's productivity.

In an early test, Shaw (1932, p. 492) studied the relative effectiveness of individuals and groups in solving this problem (see if you can solve it):

> On one side of a river are three wives and three husbands. Get them all across the river by means of a boat carrying only three at a time. No man will allow his wife to be in the presence of another man unless he is also there.

Shaw found that 60 percent of her groups were able to determine the correct solution, while only 14 percent of the individuals were able to.

In a related study, Maier and Solem (1952, p. 280) asked individuals and groups to solve this task:

> A man bought a horse for $60 and sold it for $70. Then he bought it back for $80 and again sold it for $90. How much money did he make?

About 45 percent of individuals solved the problem, while 72 percent solved it in a leaderless group discussion, and 83 percent solved it in a discussion group with a leader who encouraged discussion and raised questions that promoted the group effort. Thus the study indicated that the groups surpassed the efforts of individuals, and that a leader helped improve the group effectiveness.

In addition to the type of tasks described above, some studies have examined tasks that could be subdivided (for example, assembly line production), tasks that involved guessing the number of objects in a jar, and tasks in which individuals compared the length of lines. Other studies have examined the effect of the presence of onlookers on a person's performance. It was found that some people are encouraged by the presence of others, while others are stimulated negatively, and some are unaffected. It has also been found that groups are better at solving complicated tasks requiring reasoning and elimination of poor solutions. In addition, it would seem that simply having several individuals solving a problem would increase the probability that a good solution would emerge. In other words, "two (or more) heads are better than one." Luft (1970, p. 30) summarizes the issue of group versus individual productivity:

> Problems calling for a wide variety of skills and information or the cross-checking of facts and ideas seem to call for a group approach. Feedback and free exchange of thinking may stimulate ideas that would not have emerged by solo effort.

A good example of this type of decision is in the work of credit committees in lending institutions such as banks and credit unions. These committees are made up of individuals who have a high degree of technical knowledge—yet the committee must meet to consider all applications for loans larger than a certain dollar amount. Another good example would be surgical teams in hospitals. Here again, each person is highly educated, yet the collective wisdom of the group is superior to any one of the members acting alone. Finally, most large corporations are run by executive committees comprised of top-level executives. Here again, the reason is that committees make more effective decisions than individuals.

One ancient author stated the point eloquently when he wrote:

> Nowadays I make it a practice to call my workers into consultation on any new work ...I observe that they are willing to set about on a piece of work on which their opinions have been asked and their advice followed. (Columella, 100 A.D.)

Finally, Collins and Guetzkow (1964, p. 55), summarizing the research on this issue, state:

> Group members may collectively achieve more *than the most superior members are capable of achieving alone.* (Emphasis added.)

As we saw in Chapter 6, there are four methods for reaching decisions: (1) railroading, (2) teaming up, (3) majority vote, and (4) consensus. Consensus typically is the best method, since it optimizes good-quality decisions as well as a high degree of acceptance.

Acceptance of Solutions

The plant manager of a large manufacturing plant decided that his supervisors were using far too many pens, and that this was an unnecessary cost. He wrote a memo to all supervisory personnel indicating that each one would have to turn in a completely empty pen to an assistant plant manager in order to get a new pen. The intent was to save money. Actually, the pens cost about 50 cents apiece and the supervisor's salary figured out to about $10 per hour, so if a foreman had to spend more than 3 minutes searching for the assistant plant manager, the cost was actually *greater* than if the foreman had just gotten a new pen from the immediate area. The foremen determined that it usually took them about 30 minutes to find the assistant plant manager. Thus, under the new policy, the cost of replacing the pen had increased by ten times.

An even greater cost was the foremen's loss of positive attitude toward the plant. They felt that they were being treated like children, and several foremen went out of their way to do a poor job in retaliation. After less than one month, the plant manager rescinded his new policy in favor of the old practice of replacing pens. A university department that moved into new offices encountered the same sort of problem. Professors were allocated offices by a combination of rank and seniority. The full professors got first pick in order of seniority. Then the associate professors, by seniority, then the assistant professors, and so on. One associate professor ended up with one of the few offices without a window. He went into the department chairman's office to complain and commented that although he had over twenty years seniority, some of the full professors, who were considerably younger, had window offices. As he continued to plead his case for a window office, he began to cry. He said he felt he had given the best years of his life to the school. He had even won an outstanding teaching award once. But since he had not published much, he had not received the promotion to full professor. As badly as the chairman felt, and as much as he sympathized with the professor, it was too late to rectify the situation without evicting someone else from a new office and making the other person feel cheated. Since acceptance or satisfaction with the decision was the key criterion for effectiveness in this decision, how could this situation have been avoided?

These cases illustrate one of the most common problems suffered by organizations: namely, employees rejecting solutions to problems. For solutions to be effective, they must be of high quality and they must be accepted by those who must carry them out. If a solution is weak on either of these two dimensions, its overall effectiveness is reduced. Maier (1963, p. 5) offers the following formula and explanation for determining a decision's effectiveness:

$$ED = Q \times A$$

where ED represents effective decision, Q represents quality, and A represents acceptance.

Three types of problem situations can be identified from this frame of reference. The first includes problems requiring a high quality but low acceptance. These problems are best solved by persons with a high level of technical knowledge and expertise. They might include important financial decisions involving setting prices, determining expenditures, and so on.

Second, some solutions require high acceptance but low quality. These might include fair ways of distributing new equipment, vacation schedules, undesirable work assignments, new offices or office equipment, or a new vehicle such as a truck. Decisions such as these may include all individuals who may be affected by the results of the decision.

Third, some decisions require both high quality and high acceptance. It would appear that the majority of problems fall into this category. Since this is the case, Maier recommends that problem-solving groups rather than isolated individuals be used, since the acceptance of the solution is likely to be higher when people are involved in formulating a solution, and because we have already seen that groups tend to produce better-quality solutions than individuals.

Participative decision making (PDM) not only can result in high-quality decisions and increased acceptance of the solutions, but may also result in increased levels of satisfaction, commitment, and loyalty to the solution and to the group. Let us return to the pen replacement problem. The chances are that if the foremen were made aware of the problem and were asked to help find a way to reduce it, several things would occur. First, they might suggest a good solution. Second, they would be more likely to accept the new solution. Third, they probably would use peer pressure on one another to see that the new solution was followed. In each case, the result might have been better than what actually happened.

See the article at the end of this chapter in which Norman Maier more fully explains the use of the ED = Q × A formula. This article also shows the relevance of small group interaction to organizations and their effectiveness.

Mossholder, Bedian, and Armenakis (1982) summarize results from the following studies:

> Bowers and Seashore (1966) demonstrated that team oriented intermember behaviors positively affected group members' satisfaction and performance.
>
> In an exhaustive review of group productivity literature, Stogdill (1972) found positive intragroup relationships to be associated with increased organizational productivity when group esprit and drive were high.
>
> The study conducted by the authors Mossholder, Bedian, Armenakis in 1982 indicated that the "performance of low self-esteem (compared to that of high self-esteem) persons is more likely to be enhanced by high peer group interaction and diminished by low PGI."
>
> These results have important implications from a managerial perspective: Those involved in managing groups should recognize explicitly the importance of individual differences in attempting to affect work related outcomes. It appears that peer group interaction not only provides socio-psychological support of lower self-esteem individuals, but also mitigates the effects of job strain.
>
> The present study also suggests that managers may facilitate performance by differential selection of the job assignments of low versus high self-esteem individuals. The placement of low self-esteem individuals in roles requiring interpersonal interaction and teamwork would seem advised. In contrast, high self-esteem individuals, less dependent on their peers for task and socio-psychological support, may be more compatibly assigned tasks requiring independence of judgement or action. (p. 583)

During World War II a group of social scientists was assigned to persuade house-wives to serve more kidneys, beef hearts, and sweetbreads to their families, thus better utilizing the scarce supply of meat. Six groups of housewives were studied. Three groups heard a persuasive lecture showing how the use of these foods at home would help the war effort and would still be nutritious and tasty for their families. The other three groups were drawn into discussions of the difficulties of using these meats, and ways of overcoming these difficulties. In both sets of groups, the housewives were asked to indicate (by a show of hands) how many thought that they would actually serve these meats in the upcoming week. A follow-up study revealed that 3 percent of the women in the lecture groups actually served the unfamiliar meats, while 32 percent of the discussion-group members actually served the meats (Lewin 1953). Although this study had some methodological defects, it has become a classic in that it demonstrated the dramatic increase in commitment to an action plan that resulted from participating in a group discussion compared to listening to a persuasive speech. Many other studies have confirmed this powerful phenomenon (Tubbs and Carter 1977).

A related study in industry was conducted with an assembly-line operation. Workers were to paint parts of wooden toys and hang them on an overhead conveyor belt of hooks that carried the toys to a drying area. The speed of the conveyor line had been carefully calculated by plant engineers. The employees were paid on the basis of how many toys they painted (piecework). Problems developed in that the job produced high turnover of employees, high absenteeism, and low job satisfaction.

A consultant was called in to arrange a series of meetings between supervisors and employee representatives. As a result, the operators were given permission to vary the conveyor belt speed from "slow" to "medium" to "fast." The results were that employee satisfaction increased, product quality remained high, and overall productivity was higher than before (Whyte 1955).

These studies indicate two things. First, people generally are resistant to changes that affect their lives, especially if these changes are initiated by others. Second, group decision making and "people involvement" can be a powerful asset in increasing satisfaction and overcoming resistance to change. Let us look at each of these in more detail.

Resistance to change is a phenomenon that some would argue begins with the so-called birth trauma in which the fetus resists being plucked from the warm, dark security of the womb only to be exposed to the shock of the cold, bright, noisy world

FRANK AND ERNEST   by Bob Thaves

"..AND THAT'S MR. FITZIMMONS ...OUR VICE-PRESIDENT IN CHARGE OF RESISTANCE TO CHANGE."

outside. Over time and experience, most of us develop a "separation anxiety" when we are forced to leave (or be separated from) any place or set of circumstances in which we feel comfortable. Each time we move or change schools or jobs, a certain amount of this is experienced. Try to remember how threatening your first day of high school (or college) was, compared to the comfortable security of your immediate past.

Resistance to change is normal, and tends to increase when we do not understand the need for change, or if we are not instrumental in bringing about the change. A good example of such resistance, writes Zander (1961), "was furnished by a farmer in the TVA [Tennessee Valley Authority] area. He assured us that he knew all about contour plowing, the rotation of crops, and the use of what he called 'phosaphate' for improving the soil. He allowed as how these were good ideas. 'But,' he said, 'I don't do it that way.'"

More recently, many major American companies have increased their use of quality circles to increase both their product quality and worker involvement and commitment. A quality circle is simply a small group of employees (usually 10 to 15) who get together on company time to talk about how they can do their jobs better. Main (1981, p. 76) quotes one top executive in Westinghouse as saying:

> The point is, we are making much better decisions than before ... we are getting a contribution and commitment from larger numbers of people. The management team becomes excited and it works. When participative management catches on, ... decisions are carried out by enthusiasts who have helped shape them, who feel they "own" the decisions, rather than by unwilling subordinates who have simply been told what to do without really knowing why.

In a study conducted by Brockner and Hess (1986) it was found that "the mean self-esteem level of the individuals in each quality circle was highly predictive of the group's task performance. Successful and unsuccessful circles did not differ in their size, longevity or organizational function. Moreover, self-esteem was uncorrelated with group size, longevity, or function, thereby discounting the possibility that the relationship between self-esteem and performance was a spurious function of any of these variables" (p. 620).

The results of the study do not indicate any cause of the relationship between self-esteem and the quality circles. The first possibility is that self-esteem caused the performance; second: performance within the quality circle caused the high self-esteem; or third: self-esteem and performance are related because of their common covariation with other factors.

Beebe (1986) cites three of the hundreds of companies which are successfully using quality circles to overcome resistance to change:*

> Problem: A mountain of paperwork was building on desks at CH2M Hills Boise office last year. Employees were slow to file reports and other documents in loose-leaf binders favored by the consulting engineering firm. The forms were not pre-punched.
> Solution: A volunteer group of workers suggested to the company that it switch to pre-

---

*By Paul Beebe; reprinted with permission of *The Idaho Statesman*.

punched forms. Doing so would relieve employees of an annoying chore and speed filing, they said.

Savings: Pre-punched forms save the Boise office 60 man-days a year, Edward Sloan, CH2M Hill's district coordinator of construction management services said. Company-wide it probably saves 2,400 man-days, he said.

Problem: It took 15 to 20 minutes to unload each potato truck that entered the Ore-Ida Foods Inc. processing plant at Ontario, Ore. Employees estimated hundreds of hours were being wasted as potatoes moved down truck-mounted conveyors into the building.

Solution: A group of Ore-Ida workers in Ontario last year recommended to managers that belly-dump trucks should be used to haul potatoes to the plant. Potatoes could be unloaded into bays in only a few minutes.

Savings: Within one year, Ore-Ida realized $130,000 in labor savings and lost time, said John Walhof, the company's productivity manager.

Problem: Could the error rate of machines that place electrical components on printed circuit boards at Hewlett-Packard Co.'s disc memory division in Boise be improved?

Solution: The employees who operate the machines thought so. One group suggested a series of modifications that improved the manufacturer's error rating of its machines from 3,000 improperly mounted components per million to 500 parts per million, a six-fold improvement.

Benefit: Far fewer components are being mounted incorrectly. Board rejection rates are down and employee morale is up, said Jim Stinehelfer, manufacturing manager in H-P's disc memory division.

Ore-Ida and CH2M Hill teams consist of six to ten people who meet once a week. Hewlett-Packard quality circles contain up to thirty people. Most of the groups are comprised of workers from the same area of the company. "We wanted to create an environment where employees are free to offer suggestions about their working environment, ideas on ways our products are produced, new products," said Ore-Ida's productivity manager of the company's People–Excellence–Products program. Ore-Ida has organized 138 PEP teams in all of its U.S. operations, including 35 at its Ontario plant and 35 at its Burley plant. Teams tackle everything from safety issues to product quality. Hewlett-Packard spokesmen have said their company has seen big increases in morale and productivity that can be related to quality circles. Line inspectors have been eliminated in many areas because employees now monitor the quality of their work. The manufacturing manager of Hewlett-Packard stated the fundamental reason for the quality circles was to "make the people on the lines feel responsible for the quality of the product. The best way to have them feel that responsibility is to give it to them."

There are several important factors to remember in *overcoming resistance to change.* First, people will accept changes that they have a part in planning. Obviously it is much easier to live through the trauma of going to college if we choose to go and if we like the college or university than if we are forced by our parents to go, or to go someplace we don't like. Second, changes will be accepted if they do not threaten our security. Many office work groups resist innovations such as computer systems for fear that the computer will eventually take away some of their jobs. Third, changes will be more readily accepted when people are involved in gathering facts that indicate the need for change. Farmers who notice decreasing crop yields will be more receptive to farming innovations than those who are prospering. Finally, greater acceptance and commitment will result when the changes are kept open to further revision based on the success or failure of the new procedures. None of us is very enthusiastic about adopting changes for a lifetime. However, if we feel the changes are on a trial basis, subject to modification, we are usually more willing to give them a try. Obviously, to the extent that these conditions are *not* met, resistance to change will be increased.

Many firms are beginning to take a step beyond quality circles with the self-managing work team concept. Sims and Dean (1985, p. 26) consider self-managing work teams the logical extension of quality circles: "Operating under several labels—self managing work groups, autonomous work groups, and sometimes simply "teams"— this organizational innovation has as its fundamental theme the attempt to place a remarkably high degree of decision making responsibility and behavior control in the hands of the work group itself."

A self-managing team usually elects its own leader and often management appoints an external leader who acts as a coordinator/facilitator rather than a supervisor. Teams frequently take on responsibilities which have not traditionally been the topic for work groups in the past. Some of these include: (1) preparation of the annual budget, (2) timekeeping functions, (3) recording of quality control statistics, (4) solving technically related problems, (5) adjusting production schedules, (6) modifying or redesigning production processes, and (7) setting team goals and assessing internal performance.

For long-term success, teams must function in a responsible manner and management must possess a high degree of trust and confidence in the system. To help ensure successful teams, organizations typically design them with "well defined physical and task boundaries, sometimes using socio-technical design concepts to ensure an appropriate match between technical systems and the conventions, rules, and norms governing interaction. Task interdependence within teams is usually higher than between teams." Sophisticated computerized information systems are frequently used in measuring inputs and outputs across team boundaries. This provides extensive and rapid feedback about the quantity and quality of team performance while reducing secrecy between teams. Teams are provided with as much information as possible.

Management typically initiates the self-managing work concept while striving for additional productivity, improving quality, reducing overhead, and reducing conflict. For the employee, the concept provides the opportunity to exercise more control over aspects of daily work life. Are these teams successful? There is no single conclusive answer to this question, but according to Sims and Dean (1985, pp. 26–27):

> The consensus of many managers is that self-managing teams provide a 20% to 40% productivity edge over the traditional system. Savings come about not because employees are working harder, but because they require less surveillance (therefore, there is less overhead), and scrap, lost time, and poor-quality products are significantly reduced. The old cliché "working smarter, not harder" seems to hold true.

Many other benefits of the team approach seem to manifest themselves: Teams become very flexible and adapt well to changing conditions and new startups. Also, plants with the team concept generally have very high responses to job satisfaction and attitude surveys.

Sims and Dean report that an informal estimate of plants in the United States using the self-managing team concept was over 200. The question to be asked is, Why hasn't the use of this innovation been more widespread? Sims and Dean report several reasons: "Managers, particularly middle managers, feel highly threatened by the concept because they believe it will reduce their power and influence. Perhaps an even more important reason is that startup costs for the team concept can be significant, and patience—a typical wait is 18 months to two years—is required before the rewards of successful implementation can be reaped." Furthermore, union support has not been uniform; some unions have seen the concept as a potential threat to their power. Finally, there has been little media attention given to the teams. Some companies consider this team concept an advantage over competitors and are therefore extremely secretive about their experiences.

Franecki, Catalanello, and Behrens (1984, p. 69) state that participative management (PM) techniques are becoming increasingly popular:

> PM techniques . . . range from the more basic ones, such as joint setting of job-performance goals by supervisor and subordinate, to more elaborate ones, such as establishing work teams whose employee-members assign job tasks, acquire new members, and set quality standards.

A field survey of 200 private-sector employers was conducted to analyze the use and benefits of the PM techniques. In general it was found that "respondents to the survey use a variety of employee committees, and they perceive positive effects for their firms: cost savings, improved operating statistics, and better employee relations were all reported. It also appears that employees approve of committees . . . This conclusion is significant because participation has sometimes resulted in overly high expectations by those it serves."

CHANGES IN INTERPERSONAL RELATIONS

Probably the most notable difference between a television interview with a professional golfer who has just won a major tournament and a baseball team that has won the World Series (or a football team that has won the Super Bowl) is the tremendous amount of energy, enthusiasm, and esprit de corps of the group versus the low-keyed response of the lone golfer. The backslapping, hugging, and champagne splashing of the group are some of the most obvious signs that interpersonal relations are an important by-product of group activity. Sensitivity training groups frequently provide powerful emotional experiences for group members. One group participant wrote of his experience (Tubbs and Moss 1974, p. 243):

> I thought we had a good meeting. Afterward several people came up and we walked across campus together, which made me feel that they weren't resentful about my getting emotional. . . . I am feeling happier about myself in the group.

In Chapter 6 we examined the positive and negative aspects of conflict. Group discussion may improve interpersonal relations through the successful resolution of conflict. Conflict may be intragroup or intergroup. In either case, resolving conflict tends to affect interpersonal relations favorably.

A common technique for improving intergroup relations is to have members of each group get together and write down their perceptions of (1) themselves, (2) the others, and (3) how they think the others view them. Production and service groups in manufacturing plants frequently need to have such meetings to coordinate their activities more effectively. The production groups frequently feel that a service department (such as maintenance) does not act quickly enough to get defective machinery working. On the other hand, maintenance people feel as if they are always put under unreasonable pressures, since every time a piece of machinery breaks down, each production supervisor wants immediate attention to his or her problems even though several machines require repair simultaneously.

Meetings designed to share perceptions of one another and to inform each other of particular problems can potentially clear up and reduce areas of misperception and misunderstanding. After one such meeting, one man said to another from a different department, "After drinking coffee with you and hearing your side of the story, it's going to be hard for me to cuss you out tomorrow the way I usually do." This comment is typical of the increased quality of interpersonal relations that can come out of group problem solving conducted in an atmosphere of support and mutual gain. However, if the meetings are conducted in an atmosphere of blame placing and fault-finding, the relations are likely to be even worse than if the meetings had not been held. In other words, the intermediate influences discussed in Chapters 5 and 6 have a significant influence on the end results.

A subset of interpersonal relations is group cohesion. *Cohesiveness,* according to Schachter et al. (1968, p. 192):

> has been defined variously as referring to morale, "sticking together," productivity, power, task involvement, feelings of belongingness, shared understanding of roles, and good teamwork.

This definition covers a lot of territory and can be further clarified by the definition offered by Cartwright (1968, p. 91):

> Most agree that group cohesiveness refers to the degree to which the members of a group desire to remain in the group.

Group cohesion can also be a by-product or end result of group activity. Generally, a prestigious or successful group is more attractive to belong to and results in higher levels of cohesion. The Boston Celtics basketball team and the Los Angeles Raiders football team are two examples of successful groups that could be expected to have high levels of cohesion.

Cohesion is a result of group interaction, but it in turn influences other things. As we saw in Chapter 4, cohesive groups tend to have stricter norms and tolerate smaller amounts of deviance from the group values. Cohesive groups may have high or low productivity, depending on the group norm regarding productivity. Cohesiveness increases the loyalty of each member to that particular group, but frequently breeds deeper cleavages *between* groups. This may become a problem if the groups happen to be part of a single organization in which integration of several groups is necessary.

As with so many topics in this book, cohesiveness has been identified as one type of variable (consequence). However, it also has an influence on other variables. Cartwright (1968, pp. 106–107) describes the complexity of classifying cohesiveness:

> In our attempt to discover some theoretical order among the many findings related to group cohesiveness, we have identified certain factors as determinants and others as consequences of cohesiveness . . . . Factors that increase cohesiveness lead to consequences that, in turn, lead to greater cohesiveness. Several examples . . . come readily to mind. Similarity of beliefs and values tend to generate interpersonal attractions among members, and the resulting cohesiveness gives the group power to influence members toward greater similarity. As a group becomes more cohesive its ability to satisfy the needs of members increases, thereby raising the incentive value of the group. And cohesiveness tends to generate frequent interaction among members, which, under certain conditions at least, heightens interpersonal attraction and thus cohesiveness.

Cartwright goes on to say that the opposite spiral may also occur—that is, negative experience may lead to negative attitudes, which in turn may cause more negative experiences.

In summary, it is important to note that small group interaction has the potential of increasing interpersonal relations and cohesiveness. The great emphasis on "team building" in management training illustrates the usefulness of this concept. In terms of learning theory, the behaviors of talking and cooperating rather than avoiding and competing with one another have been reinforced, and the cooperating behaviors are therefore more likely to occur again. Thibaut and Kelley (1986, p. 12) put it this way:

> The selectivity observed in interaction reflects the tendency for more satisfactory interactions to recur and for less satisfactory ones to disappear. The consequences of interaction can be described in many different terms, but we have found it useful to distinguish only between the rewards that a person receives and the costs he incurs.

The critical element in improving interpersonal relations through group interaction is to make the experience as rewarding as possible.

IMPROVED INFORMATION FLOW

Communication in small groups can also result in an increased knowledge level and increased coordination among group members based on the sharing of information. Information may be distorted severely if passed along serially from one person to the next through ten people. However, the distortion will be significantly decreased if the same ten people hear the information simultaneously in a meeting. In addition, active discussion by participants will help them remember the information better than if they heard an announcement or read it in a memo.

Another factor is the tendency for subgroups to form so that information that passes *between* groups is restricted. This is especially true in complex organizations. Lawrence and Lorsch (1969) have referred to problems of this nature as differentiation-integration problems. On one hand, organizations require specialization (differentiation) in order to operate effectively. Thus different groups become specialists in such departments as production, finance, legal, research and development, data-processing inspection, master mechanics, engineering, accounting, sales, or personnel. At the same time, these groups must cooperate and coordinate their efforts to keep from working at cross purposes and generally harming organizational success. Lawrence and Lorsch (1969, pp. 54–55) summarize the results of one such set of four interdepartmental meetings:

> The managers and scientists were generally enthusiastic about what the program had accomplished. They reported that as a result of the program they had developed a more concerted effort to coordinate all of their research activity. . . . They were also using a new set of decision criteria to evaluate research and development projects. This was a direct result of their effort and according to them had facilitated the resolution of conflict . . . . Finally, the members of the integrating group indicated that they were devoting more time to working with other functional groups, enabling research to get a unified new product effort. According to organizational members, all of this added up to improved organizational integration without sacrificing differentiation.

Coordination problems certainly occur among members of a single group as well as among multiple groups in an organization. Almost invariably, groups of students assigned to work on class projects have at least some difficulty in finding (1) each other, (2) a free hour in common in which to meet, (3) the materials necessary to conduct the research for their assignments, and sometimes (4) a suitable place in which to conduct their discussion. In addition, group members may forget that they were supposed to meet, or they may get too busy to prepare for the meeting. A host of other tangential problems may add to the coordination difficulties. Not all of these problems will be solved by group discussions, but they will probably at least be reduced. In some circles it is known as "letting the right hand know what the left hand is doing."

Likert (1967) also points out that group decision making tends to lead to a different type of solution than person-to-person decision making. In the one-on-one setting, the focus of the solution is on the person perceiving an individual problem. In an organization, this approach frequently solves one person's problem while *creating* new problems for others. Suppose that five supervisors all want to take their vacations in June and July. Assuming that all of them cannot be absent at once, any decision regarding one person's vacation will potentially influence the vacation plans of the others. It may be that one person's plan is flexible and could be modified in light of the situations of the others in the group. The group method then focuses on coordinating the best solution for all, considering the limitations of the job demands.

In addition to offering better decisions for more people, the group decision-making method reduces the jealousy and hostility that frequently accompany the person-to-person method. When individuals are awarded decisions in their favor without others knowing the circumstances surrounding the decision, the others frequently feel that "special deals" have been made and the superior is accused of playing favorites. However, this reaction is drastically reduced when all interested parties are witness to the decision and the surrounding circumstances. Although the group method may be time-consuming, the end results of increased knowledge level and increased coordination are frequently worth the time spent. In fact, the total time expenditure may be less, since the related problems of jealousy and resentment do not occur as much and do not have to be solved as offshoots of the original problem.

INCREASED RISK TAKING

Imagine the following situation (Wallach, Kagan, and Bem 1962):

> An engaged couple must decide, in the face of recent arguments suggesting some sharp differences of opinion, whether or not to get married. Discussions with a marriage counselor indicate that a happy marriage, while possible, would not be assured.

In deciding questions such as this, as well as those dealing with career choices, decisions in football games, decisions regarding one's health, and other decisions, it

GRIN AND BEAR IT   by Lichty & Wagner

Courtesy of Field Newspaper Syndicate.

© Field Enterprises, Inc. 1981

"I like to be where the action is...on the Budget Committee!"

has been found that groups tend to take bigger risks than individuals. This concept was first proposed by Stoner (1961) and has become a heavily researched topic known as the *risky shift phenomenon.*

Several theories have been proposed to account for such an occurrence. The "leadership hypothesis" holds that the influence of the group's leader causes the shift. The "diffusion of responsibility" hypothesis argues that since nobody in the group feels as much personal responsibility or accountability for the decision, more risk is taken. The "rationality hypothesis" argues that greater risk is simply a better choice with a greater likelihood of payoff. The "conformity hypothesis" posits that people take more risk as a result of buckling to pressure from others in the group. Finally, the "risk value" hypothesis holds that risk is generally admired or valued in our culture, and this value is reinforced in the group setting.

There is a great deal of contradictory evidence on each of these hypotheses, but some consistent trends can be identified. First, the risky shift itself is a fairly predictable phenomenon. Teger and Pruitt (1970, p. 72) state:

> The difference between the mean level of risk taken initially by the individuals and the mean of their later group decisions is termed a "shift." If there is a change toward greater risk, it is termed a "risky shift." A risky shift is almost always found.

Second, the "leadership hypothesis" seems to have at least some limitations, since not all leaders encourage risk, and since some studies show that risky choices are made even before the leader says anything.

The "diffusion of responsibility" hypothesis has the most intuitive appeal for many. It seems that people would feel more security in numbers and less fear of personal harm if they made decisions as part of a group. However, a summary of the literature on this view indicates that the hypothesis has serious shortcomings (Clark 1971).

The "rationality hypothesis" has also been seriously questioned, since several studies have shown what we might intuitively expect, that not all risky decisions are the better rational choices, and in some cases the groups actually choose the riskier choices that lead to worse consequences (Malmuth and Feshbach 1972).

The "conformity hypothesis" has also been criticized due to the fact that not all groups exert pressure toward risk. The "risk value" hypothesis seems to be one of the most popular views. Brown (1965) argues that our culture values risk and that this value causes group members to want to avoid being seen as "chicken," which results in their making riskier choices. However, Clark (1971) has argued that even this is not always the case. Several other conditions affect the occurrence of the risky shift. In his summary of the literature (1971, p. 264) he identifies four such conditions. The group must (1) actually discuss risk-relevant topics; (2) not have severe consequences for failure; (3) have members who vary in initial riskiness; and (4) have individuals who perceive themselves as being at least as willing to take risks as others in the group.

In your own group experiences you should be aware that groups do tend to cause individuals to take greater risks than they might take as individuals. In some cases this may be good, but in other situations excessive risks might result.

INTERPERSONAL GROWTH

Although we can probably learn to improve our interpersonal skills by observing our behavior and the behavior of others in any group, the encounter group or the sensitivity training group has this as one of its major objectives. Instead of focusing on problem solving (for example, how can we solve the problem of evaluating student performance in a communication course), encounter groups focus on improving interpersonal skills. The Johari window discussed in Chapter 5 is one model used for bringing about greater interpersonal growth.

In order to change a person's interpersonal behavior, a three-phase process must be undertaken. These phases are (1) unfreezing, (2) change, and (3) refreezing (Bennis et al. 1968). In order to better visualize this process, let us look at two actual individuals and their experiences in an encounter group.

The Case of Jim

Jim was a 28-year-old man who worked as a statistician in a manufacturing plant. He explained on the first evening of class that he wanted to be a supervisor and that he wanted a $200,000 home by the time he was 30. He and his wife had no children and lived in an apartment.

In the first class period, the leader stated that the experience would be unconventional and unstructured, with a lot of group discussion and few lectures. Within minutes, Jim began to criticize the leader by asking such questions as, "What are you getting paid for if you aren't going to teach us anything?" and, "Why should we do your job for you?"

The leader responded by saying, "I think it is interesting that you feel that learning can occur only if I lecture to the group. Do you think that it is possible for us to learn together rather than me trying to tell you the 'answers'?" A lively discussion followed in which the assumptions of traditional methods of education and leadership were discussed.

Over several weeks Jim criticized each of his bosses and former bosses and indicated that he had a record of quitting jobs due to conflicts with his supervisors. In each case, the problem (according to Jim) was that the supervisor did not adequately recognize his worth. Each week Jim would criticize the leader in class. Criticisms included the following:

I think you wear striped shirts because you like to get attention.
When are you going to tell us what we are supposed to be getting out of this class?
I suggest if Frank won't tell us what to do, we start for ourselves. Let's go around the room and have everybody tell us one observation he has had about this group so far.

Over time, others in the group commented that Jim's criticism of the leader irritated them, and that they thought that the class procedures were worthwhile. Then one night the leader asked, "Jim, do you see any connection between your dissatisfaction with my leadership and your dissatisfaction with each of your bosses on your jobs?" Jim's face lighted up and he said, "I never thought of that!" Over several weeks Jim began to see that he was struggling for control with leaders and vacillated between exerting control (initiating an exercise in group observation skills) and requesting control ("When are you going to tell us what we should be learning?").

Over time, Jim was encouraged to try leadership behaviors in the group and was encouraged not to always expect the leader to have to lead. At the end of the term, Jim told the group that he felt that he had learned a lot about his problems of relating to authority figures and that he even felt more comfortable with his boss at work.

The Case of Wendy

Wendy was a 19-year-old college sophomore majoring in philosophy. On the first day of class she said that she had been valedictorian of her class and was currently into Nietzsche and Nihilism. According to a sociogram taken in class, she was the least popular person in the class. She asked for feedback as to why and she was told that "she seemed too condescending, cold, and generally snotty." She participated in an exercise called the "trust fall" in which she allowed herself to fall into the arms of a circle of her classmates.

Afterwards the exercise was discussed and she said that she felt that she did not have to try to impress everybody with her superior intellect just to be accepted. Over the course of the term, she was gently reminded when she slipped back into her "superiority complex." For several years after the course, I would see her on campus and she seemed to have retained her new warmth and approachability.

Jim and Wendy had different problems, but the same procedures were used to help them learn to improve their interpersonal skills. In both cases, an *unfreezing* occurred in which the assumptions about how to behave were questioned. Jim assumed that a leader had to be perfect and had to be strong and decisive to be of any value. Wendy assumed that she had to impress people with her intellect to be accepted. Both learned through feedback that their assumptions were not always correct.

The *change* phase came when both people were encouraged to adopt new behaviors that they typically would not have been willing to try. Jim tried leading the group himself and Wendy tried to drop her façade and let people accept her for more reasons than just her brains.

The *refreezing* came when the group tried over time to reinforce or encourage Jim and Wendy's new behaviors. This trial and error learning over time, followed by feedback, tends to increase the likelihood that the new behaviors will be retained after the encounter group experience is over.

As we have said, acquisition of these new interpersonal skills follows the sequence of unfreezing, change, and refreezing. Johnson (1972, p. 6) breaks it down a bit more specifically into five steps.

Unfreezing	1. Becoming aware of the need for and uses of a new skill.
Change	2. Identifying the behaviors involved in the new skill.
	3. Practicing the behaviors.
Refreezing	4. Receiving feedback concerning how well you are performing the behaviors.
	5. Integrating the behaviors into your behavioral repertoire.

It is quite general and vague to say that encounter groups provide an experience for interpersonal growth. Some more specific ways of identifying such growth have been presented by Egan (1973). He states (p. 23): "I grow interpersonally if

- I am freer to be myself in my interactions with others,

- I manage interpersonal anxiety more effectively,

- I learn how to show greater concern for others,

- I can take initiative in contacting others more easily,

- I can share myself more openly and deeply with the significant others in my life,

- I can be less fearful in expressing feelings and emotions in interpersonal situations,

- I can step from behind my façade more often,

- I can learn to accept myself and deal with my deficits in the community of my friends more often,

- Intimacy frightens me less,

- I can endure concerned and responsible confrontation more,

- I can learn to confront those who mean something to me with care and compassion,

- I can come to expect myself and others to work on the phoniness in their lives,

- I can commit myself more deeply to others without fear of losing my own identity,

- I can come to know who I am a bit more in terms of my personal goals and the direction of my life.

Although these goals may not be achieved by all encounter group participants, they are potential outcomes for some.

Numerous studies have been conducted to test empirically the extent to which the goals mentioned above are actually accomplished in encounter groups. An excellent review of these has been published by Cooper and Mongham (1971). Statistically significant positive changes have been documented in a number of studies, including Miles (1965), Bunker (1965), Valiquet (1968), Underwood (1965), Lieberman, Yalom, and Miles (1973), and Burke and Bennis (1961). On the other hand, some writers have shown either no significant changes or some negative changes as a result of encounter groups.

Campbell and Dunnette's (1968) well-known article indicates some areas of weakness in encounter group research. They acknowledge the point that studies have shown that encounter groups do seem to bring about generally desirable results in line with their goals. However, they also point out that more specific behavioral measures should be used to determine success. They call for more research to indicate which *specific* encounter group practices (such as methods of giving feedback) are constructive and which are potentially destructive. They also indicate that encounter groups used for management training do not show any necessary improvement in specific indices of job performance.

Undoubtedly smarting from the sting of such critics as Campbell and Dunnette,

Lieberman, Yalom, and Miles (1973) published an extensive volume of encounter group research. Eighteen different student groups at Stanford were studied in several different varieties of encounter group experiences, each lasting 30 hours. As a result of the experiences, of the total of 206 students who initially participated, 28 changed greatly, 40 changed moderately, 78 were unchanged, 17 changed negatively, 16 were casualties, and 27 dropped out (Lieberman, Yalom, and Miles 1973, p. 118). The results seem to represent moderate support in favor of encounter groups. The 16 casualties were concentrated for the most part in the groups whose leaders were more aggressive and confrontive. Also, the casualties had lower self-esteem and a more negative self-concept prior to the experience.

ORGANIZATIONAL CHANGE

Based on a rapidly increasing rate of change, modern organizations have been put under greater and greater pressure to adapt or go under. Certainly the policies and practices of colleges and universities have to be different today than they were five years ago. Numerous attempts have been made to help "ease the squeeze" felt by organizations. These attempts usually fall under the general label *organization development* (OD), which is another name for planned organizational change.

Over thirty years ago, Kurt Lewin (1951) wrote about the problem of trying to get people to change. He called his analysis *force field analysis,* and it states basically that any situation occurs as a result of the combination of various competing forces. If you have ever tried to live up to your New Year's resolutions, you have experienced this. Figure 7.1 illustrates the concept further. Your motivation to live up to your New Year's resolutions represents one of the arrows labeled "driving forces." If you are thinking about exercising more or losing some weight, several arguments can add to your motivations (better-fitting clothes, more dates, better health). The restraining forces would be all the reasons why you don't live up to your resolutions (it's fun to eat, it's too cold to exercise, you hate to exercise alone).

FIGURE 7.1

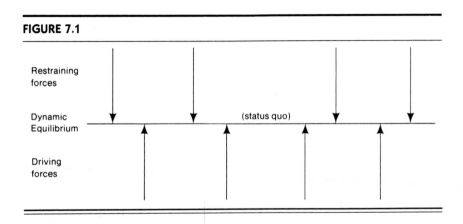

Just as this force field analysis can be applied to individuals, it can be applied to groups and to organizations. In groups, some members may want to get the job accomplished (task-oriented behavior), while others may be much more interested in socializing with an attractive group member of the opposite sex. In fact, they may have joined the group just to meet that person. How much work actually gets accomplished is the status quo where these competing sets of forces meet. If the socializing couple leaves, the restraining forces will go up. Change can occur through either a reduction in the restraining forces or an increase in the driving forces, or both. Various methods of organizational development are designed to move the status quo in the more positive direction.

While OD methods vary, most writers in the field would agree that various group methods play an important part in the process. Argyris (1962) contends that holding encounter groups with top administrators is the most effective tactic for promoting organizational change. Beckhard (1969) uses small groups as the basis of a "confrontation meeting" in which differing factions within an organization are brought together to resolve their mutual differences. Lorsch and Lawrence (1972) focus their OD attempts on diagnosing the problems within and between groups in their differentiation-integration approach discussed earlier. Likert (1967) has shown that group decision making is one of the basic methods of effective management, and that organization development can occur through the use of small groups discussing survey feedback with their supervisors.

In a study of eleven successful and six unsuccessful change efforts, Greiner (1970) found that the successful efforts involved what he called *shared power approaches* (including group problem solving and group decision making). These were found to be more effective than either the *unilateral approaches* (including change by decree, by personnel replacement, or by structure) or the *delegated authority approaches* (including case discussion and encounter group sessions). Greiner (p. 217) describes the shared power approaches as follows:

> More toward the middle of the power distribution continuum, as noted earlier, are the shared approaches, where authority is still present and used, yet there is also interaction and sharing of power. This approach to change is utilized in two forms.

> *By Group Decision Making* Here the problems still tend to be defined unilaterally from above, but lower level groups are usually left free to develop alternative solutions and to choose among them. The main assumption tends to be that individuals develop more commitment to action when they have a voice in the decisions that affect them. The net result is that power is shared between bosses and subordinates, though there is a division of labor between those who define the problems and those who develop the solutions.

> *By Group Problem Solving* This form emphasizes both the definition and the solution of problems within the context of group discussion. Here power is shared throughout the decision process, but, unlike group decision making, there is an added opportunity for lower level subordinates to define the problem. The assumption underlying this approach is not only that people gain greater commitment from being exposed to a wider decision-making role, but also that they have significant knowledge to contribute to the definition of the problem.

Schein and Bennis (1965), in an early work entitled *Personal and Organizational Change through Group Methods,* describe in detail the reasons why groups are so potent in changing organizations. Changes occur in three ways. First, individuals gain an increased *awareness* of problems of which they are a part. This represents an intellectual or cognitive change in their amount of information. Second, there tends to be a change in *attitude* toward the problems. Individuals may be more willing to become a part of the solution rather than expending all their effort trying to place the blame for the problem. This part of the change process is more emotional or gut level. Third, group experiences tend to produce a change in *behavior* that goes beyond the change in knowledge level or attitude.

Schein and Bennis (1965, p. 37) refer specifically to these behavioral changes as "increased *interpersonal competence;* i.e., skill in handling interpersonal and group relationships toward more productive and satisfying relationships." It is perhaps this threefold form of individual change that accounts for the tremendous potential groups have for bringing about organizational change. (See also the Maier and Likert articles that follow this chapter.) Main (1981, p. 93) quotes William Coates, executive vice-president of Westinghouse, as stating that organizational change is best achieved through the group participation method. Although it eats up many hours, Coates says that lost time is recovered later. "We spend a lot of time trying to get a consensus, but once you get it, the implementation is instantaneous." The company has already saved millions of dollars of expenses that would otherwise have to be added to their product costs.

Team building that emphasizes team problem solving is an Organizational Development tool used in today's business world. Organizational Development as defined by Huse and Cummings (1985) is "the deliberate, reasoned, introduction, establishment, reinforcement and spread of change for the purpose of improving an organization's effectiveness and health. Effectiveness refers to setting and attaining appropriate goals in a changing environment; health refers to the motivation, utilization, and integration of human resources within the organization."

See the article by Kotter, Schlesinger, and Sathe at the end of this chapter for a comprehensive discussion of the methods for accomplishing organizational change.

THE SYSTEMS PERSPECTIVE

This chapter dealt with the consequences of group interaction. In Chapter 1 our model indicated that all the other variables tend to culminate in these consequences. However, in ongoing groups, the outcomes or consequences of earlier group interactions tend to have a continuing influence on subsequent activities. Take the fraternity case study at the beginning of this chapter. As a result of the conflict over the "swamp rats," the fraternity developed two subgroups. This cleavage led to a deterioration over time of the entire fraternity's ability to work and play as a team. This example illustrates the systems concepts of *input* and *throughput* resulting in *output* that is fed back into the group as new *inputs,* since many groups represent ongoing *cycles* of events.

In this chapter we looked at six potential consequences of group interaction: (1) solutions to problems; (2) changes in interpersonal relations; (3) improved information flow; (4) increased risk taking; (5) interpersonal growth; and (6) organizational change. Each of these potential consequences may vary considerably depending on the particular combination of the other variables depicted in the model. For example, the quality and acceptance of solutions will vary depending on the degree of group member participation.

A great deal of material has been written about member acceptance of group-derived solutions. The term *consensus* is typically used in this context. Consensus means unanimous agreement with the solution. Conceptually, consensus and acceptance of the solution appear to be roughly equivalent. Gouran (1969) found that consensus is related to fewer opinionated statements (that is, fewer statements that express feeling, belief, or judgment, when the factual basis for the statement is not apparent). Knutson (1972) found that groups containing individuals engaging in "high orientation behavior" will be more likely to reach consensus. Orientation behavior was defined (Knutson 1972, p. 160) as:

> Behavior which reflected an attempt on the part of the individual to resolve conflict, facilitate achievement of a group's goal, make helpful suggestions, or lessen tension.

Hill (1976) conducted a follow-up study on the question of the relationship of opinionatedness and leadership to group consensus. He found two interesting interrelationships: first (p. 257), that

> leadership behavior characterized by moderately opinionated or unopinionated communication will be associated with groups which come closer to total consensus than groups with manifestly opinionated leaders.

The second finding was that

> group leaders who behave in an opinionated manner will be perceived by their fellow group members as significantly less competent than will be unopinionated leaders, and they will also be perceived as significantly less objective than either moderately opinionated or unopinionated leaders.

All the studies cited above confirm our thesis that small group interaction must be viewed as a system of interrelated variables in which a change in any one variable creates changes in the other variables in the system.

The second section of this chapter dealt with interpersonal relations. We saw that group member relations may be improved as a result of group interaction. However, groups comprised of members with highly incompatible personalities or value systems may in fact become even more polarized as a result of small group interaction. This outcome would depend on the style of leadership and quality of conflict resolution in the group. Information flow may also be improved as a result of interaction, but with a highly structured communication network and authoritarian leadership, communication flow might actually diminish. Similar points can also be made regarding risk taking, interpersonal growth, and organizational change. Each of these potential consequences depends to a considerable degree on the quality of the mix of other relevant variables in the model.

What we have attempted to do in this chapter and throughout the book is to indicate ways to better understand and improve your functioning in small groups. There are no guarantees that these improved consequences will occur. However, considerable research cited earlier leads us to believe there is a distinct probability that you can and will become a more effective group participant if you are able to implement the ideas we have discussed.

The readings for this chapter help show how you can improve several small group consequences. Directly or indirectly, these articles touch on how to improve all six consequences discussed in this chapter. The article by Norman Maier even suggests a contingency model consistent with systems theory that suggests which types of problems are more likely to be solved using group decisions and which types of problems can be solved by the leader acting alone.

EXERCISES

1. Getting the Car Home

Divide the class in half. Let one half attempt to solve this problem individually, with no conversation allowed between and among participants. Record the number who solve the problem correctly as well as the average amount of time taken to solve it (sum the times of each person and divide by the number of persons). Have the other half of the class form into groups of four or five people. Record how many groups correctly solve the problem and the average length of time taken per group.

Problem: You are stranded with a flat tire. In attempting to change the tire, you step on the hubcap containing the lug nuts (which hold the wheel on) and all five nuts are lost down a storm sewer. How do you get the car home?

2. Personal Feedback Exercise

On the basis of in-class experiences this term, answer the questions in Figure 7.2 for each person in the class (while every other person in the class does the same thing). Ultimately you will receive feedback from every other class member. These can be anonymous, or your may sign your name if you wish.

FIGURE 7.2   Personal feedback exercise form.

Comments for _____

Following are some general impressions I have formed of your performance over the course of the semester.

1. In the task or problem-solving areas, you seem to have the following
   strengths:

   weaknesses:

2. In terms of your ability to *communicate clearly and effectively* on an interpersonal level, you seem to have the following
   strengths:

   weaknesses:

3. In terms of your ability to *work with others on a social-emotional level,* you seem to have the following
   strengths:

   weaknesses:

4. In the following areas you seem to have improved during the semester:

5. Additional comments:

Most of us who work in small groups are interested to one extent or another in getting results. In the first article, Norman Maier offers a very practical discussion of the formula $ED = Q \times A$ briefly described in this chapter. This article also bridges the gap between communicating in small groups and applying those concepts and skills to meeting the needs of an organization.

In the final article, Kotter et al. offer a comprehensive spectrum of seven methods for bringing about organizational change.

Improving Decisions in an Organization

Norman R. F. Maier

The Pragmatic Test of Decisions

Most management situations are sufficiently complex so that solutions to problems or decisions that are to be made cannot be classified into correct and incorrect categories. Rather the alternative possibilities have relative merits, and the standards by which they are to be judged are not agreed upon. Frequently the criteria for judging them are unclear, or there is a lack of agreement on the correct standards to use. People may favor certain decisions because they fit the facts, because they like them, because they get support from those who must execute them, because they are the only ones that came to mind, because making a change in preference may cause them to lose face, because they like the person who suggested a particular decision, because the alternative favored is their brain child, because they participated in reaching it, and for a variety of other reasons. Some of these reasons may be of assistance in the reaching of effective decisions while others may be a hindrance.

Regardless of why people favor certain solutions or decisions over others, the test of a decision's value is quite a different matter. If the pragmatic test is to be used, an effective decision would be the one that produced the desired objectives most completely, achieved the desired objective most efficiently (costwise, energywise, and with the least undesirable side effects), and carried with it the most valuable by-products. These three measures of success might sometimes be in conflict, but in any event they would all be dependent on the outcome of the decision.

In other words, decisions can best be evaluated in terms of subsequent events, and unfortunately it is then too late to change the decision. For example, General Eisenhower's decision to invade the French coast at a time when the weather report was doubtful is regarded as a good one because it turned out that the weather did not interfere with the plans. Had the weather turned out to be sufficiently unfavorable and created great losses, his decision would have been open to criticism. In this instance the weather information indicated that invasion was risky on the date set for the invasion. However, the alternative was to set another date and go through the costly preparation process again.

From Norman R. G. Maier, Problem-Solving Discussions and Conferences (*New York: McGraw-Hill, 1963*), pp. 1–19. Reprinted by permission of the estate of Norman R. F. Maier.

Decisions of this sort may be regarded as lucky, or we might suppose that the decision maker has some kind of intuition, some special wisdom, or some special information that guides him. Regardless of how we view such decisions, the factor of chance plays a part. Some people are wealthy because their ancestors happened to settle along a river bank that later became a thriving city. Even if we view the ancestors as having the intuition to settle at the right place, the payoff on these decisions did not occur in their lifetimes. It seems unlikely that potential real estate values were factors influencing these decisions, and hence it would be more appropriate to attribute the successes of the decisions to luck than to wisdom.

Granting that chance plays a part in successful decisions, we also must concede that some people seem to be lucky more often than others and that the difference exceeds what one would expect from the laws of probability. Some executives seem to have an uncanny way of making decisions that turn out to be highly successful; others may go through several bankruptcies. Although the borderline between luck and decision-making aptitude may sometimes be narrow, it is important to do what we can to reduce the chance factors to their bare minimum if we are to examine the factors that make for decision-making ability.

Since the final evaluation of the decision is only possible some time after the decision has been made, and since the evaluation of alternatives is often not available, we must confine our speculation to the ingredients of decision that have high probabilities for success. In examining alternate decisions we may appraise them from the point of view of their probable effectiveness.

For example, if a first-place baseball team is to play the seventh-place team, an even-money bet placed on the first-place team would be wiser, even if it turned out that the seventh-place team won. One cannot take unknowns into account in appraising decisions before the actual test. However, failure to consider all the factors and influences that are available before the decision is made will reduce its possibility for success. Thus the illness of two star players on the first-place team should not be overlooked.

The Dimensions of Effective Decisions

Two different dimensions seem to be relevant in appraising a decision's potential effectiveness. One of these is the objective or impersonal *quality* of the decision; the other has to do with its *acceptance* or the way the persons who must execute the decision *feel* about it. The usual conception of effective decisions has emphasized the quality dimension. This approach leads to a careful consideration of the facts of the case. The advice is to "get the facts; weigh and consider them; then decide." It is this emphasis that causes one to assume that there is a correct answer to a problem, a right decision to make. Although this position is sound in technological matters that do not involve people, one cannot assume that it is universally sound. It is this position that causes us to concentrate on getting more information and to assume that when decisions do not work out there must have been some oversight. Thus nations may debate peace plans for the world, attempting to improve the decision, when the fault may lie elsewhere. It is quite possible that any number of plans would be adequate if they received international acceptance. As soon as the behavior of people is involved, opinions and feelings introduce a second dimension.

It is important to clearly separate these two dimensions since, as we shall see, the ways for dealing with them are very different. Failure to differentiate the dimensions leads to complications in discussion because one person may be using terms such as "good" to describe the quality of the decision, another to describe its acceptability; and a third may be thinking in terms of the outcome, which depends on both.

Decisions may have varying degrees of acceptance by the group which must execute them; and it follows that, quality remaining constant, the effectiveness of decisions will be a function of the degree to which the executors of the decision like and believe in them.

For example, let us suppose that there are four ways to lay out a job and that the quality of these methods, from best to poorest, is in the following order: method A, method B, method C, and method D. Suppose further that the persons who must use these methods have a preference order as follows: method D, method B, method C, and method A. It is conceivable under these circumstances that method B would yield the best results even though it is not the decision of highest objective quality. Naturally one must consider the degrees of difference between each alternative; nevertheless, the fact remains that an inferior method may produce better results than a superior one, if the former has the greater support.

The formula for an effective decision *(ED)* therefore would require consideration of two independent aspects of a decision: (1) its purely objective or impersonal attributes, which we are defining as quality *(Q)*; and (2) its attractiveness or desirability to persons who must work with the decision, which we are defining as acceptance *(A)*. The first depends upon objective data (facts in the situation); the second on subjective data (feelings which are in people). Simply stated, the relationship may be expressed as follows:

$$ED = Q \times A$$

This separation of quality and acceptance somewhat alters the meaning of such expressions as "good" decisions and "correct" decisions. The term "goodness" might be used to describe degrees of quality, acceptance, or effectiveness and hence has little meaning when applied to decisions. The term "correct" similarly has different dimensions and in addition is limited because it is an absolute term and suggests that there are no moderately effective decisions, medium-quality decisions, and partially acceptable decisions.

It must also be recognized that the effect of acceptance on performance will vary from one problem to another. It is clear that when the execution of a decision is independent of people, the need for acceptance is less than when the execution is influenced by the motivations and attitudes of the people who must carry it out. Nevertheless, a respect for acceptance may be a worthwhile consideration in all group problem solving since a concern for a participant's satisfaction may influence his motivations and attitudes, which in turn would influence his contributions. For example, a marketing plan may have high quality and still have poor acceptance by a group of persons involved in designing the visual appearance of a package. Since the execution of the design and its reception by the public are independent of the initial planning group, it can be assumed that the success of the decision will be independent of the degree of acceptance of the decision-making group. However, what effect will such a decision have on a group if it has been railroaded through? If some members of the planning group are dissatisfied with the decision, may not this make them less valuable participants in the future? When we take the long-range point of view, dissatisfaction with a perfectly good decision can depress a group's future performance; whereas, high satisfaction with a decision may serve to upgrade future performance.

If we can assume the position that the acceptance of a decision by the group that must implement it is a desirable ingredient, what are the problem issues? First of all, we must examine how this ingredient is related to the other desired ingredient—quality.

It is one thing to say that in striving for effective decisions two criteria must be satisfied, but can one achieve both of these objectives simultaneously? High-quality decisions, on the one hand, require wisdom, and wisdom is the product of intelligence and knowledge. Decisions of high acceptance, on the other hand, require satisfaction, and satisfaction is the product of participation and involvement in decision making. Thus the method for achieving *quality* differs from the method for achieving *acceptance;* as a matter of fact they are in conflict.

Figure 1*A* describes this basic problem in aiming at two objectives. If we aim for both objectives, we may achieve neither. The traditional leadership approach is to aim for quality first, as in Fig. 1*B*. This means that the man responsible for decisions uses whatever resources he feels are needed in obtaining facts and opinions, and he may make free use of experts or consultants. However, the actual decision-making function resides in the leader who finally weighs the evidence and decides. Once a satisfactory quality has been achieved, the next step in this process is to obtain acceptance of the decision.

Traditional methods for achieving this secondary objective have ranged through (1) imposing the decision on subordinates who must execute it (dictatorial methods, using the motivation of fear); (2) playing the father figure and gaining acceptance through a sense of duty and trust (paternalistic methods, using the motivation of loyalty); (3) using persuasion types of approach which explain the virtues of the decision (selling methods, in which personal gains are stressed); and (4) using participative approaches which encourage discussion of decisions by subordinates but leave the final decisions to the superior (consultative management, in which the motivation is based on a limited degree of participation in which there is opportunity to discuss but no right to make a

FIGURE 1   QUALITY AND ACCEPTANCE AS TARGETS.

(A) Aiming at both objectives achieves neither. This is particularly true when the aim is good. As one moves from right to left and approaches the objectives, the directions in which they lie become farther apart. When one is next to them, they lie in opposite directions.(B) The traditional approach is to aim at quality and so assure achieving it. Once this is accomplished, concern turns to acceptance, which thereby becomes a secondary objective.

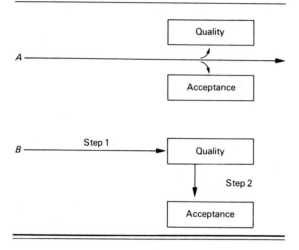

decision). Although this evolution of the decision-making process reveals improvement, the change has been confined to the aspect that is concerned with obtaining acceptance of decisions by subordinates. Throughout the history of the decision-making process, the quality ingredient has remained in the hands of the top man or group leader. Management philosophy is that the person held accountable for the decision should be the one who makes it. The fact that changes in methods for obtaining acceptance have occurred, however, suggests that the adequacy of the acceptance ingredient still leaves something to be desired. Patching up an old method may improve things, but it lacks elegance.

Suppose for the moment we make a fundamental change in our thinking and regard acceptance as the initial objective. This approach is shown in Fig. 2. To ensure success with this objective it is necessary to share the decision making with the subordinates who must execute the decision. Group decision, a method in which problems are solved and group differences are resolved through discussion, now emerges as the appropriate approach. It immediately becomes apparent that in attempting to be sure of obtaining acceptance, one risks the ingredient of quality. At least, that is the first concern of leaders and superiors when the question is raised. This notion of group decision becomes even more

**FIGURE 2   ACCEPTANCE AS PRIMARY
OBJECTIVE.**

When acceptance is the initial target and is
thereby assumed, concern for quality is the major
worry. Will quality suffer if it is made the
secondary objective?

threatening when the leader discovers that he is to be held responsible for decisions made by his immediate subordinates. It is for this reason that he wishes to retain a veto power; yet such a safeguard tends to destroy the value of group problem solving. Yes-men are the products of a superior's tendency to disapprove of decisions made by subordinates.

It appears then that the second objective is endangered whenever the appropriate method for obtaining the first is used. If this conflict is inevitable, it may be well to conclude that there is no one best approach to the problem of effective decision making. Perhaps problems, as well as approaches, should be analyzed. It is possible that the best approach may be a function of the nature of the problem.

Basic Differences in Problems

Problems may be examined with respect to the degree in which quality and acceptance are implicated. For example, in pricing a product it is apparent that a price may be so low that the loss will increase with the volume of business, or it may be so high that the company will be priced out of business. These two fates are possible, regardless of how acceptable the price is to the persons who make or sell the product. Establishing a proper price, therefore, is an illustration of a problem where the quality of the decision is a prime consideration. Although acceptance may influence the manufacture or sale of the product, it is quite clear that satisfaction with company decisions would not depend primarily upon problems of this type.

In contrast, let us select a problem involving the issue of fairness. What is fair is largely a matter of feeling, and it would be difficult for anyone to find an objective criterion that would ensure the achieving of fairness in a group. For example, when a new typewriter is introduced into an office group to replace an old one, who should get it? Should it be the person whose typewriter is replaced, the person with most seniority, the person who is most skilled, the person who is least skilled, the person who does the most work, or should some other criteria be found? Each member of the group might advocate a different scale of values, and invariably the criterion proposed is found to favor the person who advocated it. Thus when people want something, they select the facts and the values that tend to favor their feelings.

If a problem of this kind were solved by group decision, the supervisor would hold a meeting and conduct a group discussion to determine the fair way to introduce the new typewriter into the group. Usually this type of discussion resolves itself into a reshuffling of typewriters so that several persons stand to gain. Furthermore, different groups will solve the same problem in different ways, and each group will be most satisfied with its own solution. Solutions of this kind cannot be generalized, and their merit lies in the fact that they are tailored to fit the groups who make them.

The question of quality is a minor one in such instances. The supervisor need not be concerned with which of several possible solutions is objectively the best; his primary concern is to have a decision that is acceptable. Future performance of the group will depend more upon the way the members accept decisions on such matters than upon their objective qualities. As a matter of fact, it might be difficult to find measures of quality that would be acceptable to everyone.

If we follow this approach to distinguishing between problems, the first step in decision making is to analyze the problem in terms of the important objective—quality or acceptance. Three classifications of problems would seem to emerge.

High-Quality, Low-Acceptance Requirement

These are problems in which the quality of the decision is the important ingredient and the need for acceptance is relatively low. Such problems can be solved effectively by the leader with the aid of experts. The ingredient of acceptance should come up for consideration only after concern with the quality of the decision has been satisfied. Thus the procedure for obtaining acceptance may be regarded as secondary, though necessary.

We shall see later that the quality of decisions often can be improved by the effective use of group participation. This use of the group has additional objectives and raises new problems. For the present we will confine the discussion to the types of problems that can adequately be solved by experts and do not create major acceptance problems. These include:

Decisions regarding expansion, new products, decentralization, plant sites, etc.

Problems concerned with setting prices, determining costs, etc.

Decisions regarding the purchase of materials

Solutions to problems requiring specialized or technical knowledge

Although persons may disagree on the relative importance of the *quality* and *acceptance* requirements, this evaluation must be made by the person who is responsible for the decision. If he feels that a particular decision is required, he is in no condition to permit participation without directly or indirectly imposing his views. In this state of mind he is in a better condition to supply the solution and make acceptance the secondary objective. When the leader strongly favors a particular decision, he is a more effective persuader than conference leader. Thus, regardless of whether quality is the most important factor in a decision or whether the leader thinks it is the most important, the procedure is the same—protecting quality by the effective utilization of the knowledge and intelligence of the decision maker.

Certain decisions that involve acceptance but for which there are no acceptable solutions may also be included in this classification of problems. For example, an airline had the problem of choosing a uniform for stewardesses when the company's new jet plane was introduced. The solution to this problem involves a quality aspect in that the uniform should artistically conform to the design of the plane's interior, and it involves an acceptance decision from the stewardesses, who would have to wear the uniforms. In this instance, the reaction of the stewardesses to the company-imposed decision was quite unfavorable, so that it seemed that the approach used may have been a poor one. On the other hand, could stewardesses have agreed on a solution even if effort had been made to hold group meetings with such a large population?

If we assume that blondes, brunettes, and redheads are favored by different color combinations, it is quite unlikely that all girls would be satisfied with the same uniform, so that any group decision would tend to favor the predominant group. Would such an outcome be a good group decision? Until we know more, it might be best to confine the group decision method to situations that permit a resolution of differences. However, it is important not to assume that all conflicts in a group resist resolution. It is conceivable that if group discussion had been used the girls would have:

1. Evolved a compromise that was artistic

2. Adopted a uniform that permitted variation in some part (such as a scarf) so that complexion differences would have been recognized

3. Been more satisfied because of having had some opportunity to influence the decision

Whether the cost of such meetings would offset the cost of the discontent, which would be temporary, is a decision that the responsible person must make.

High-Acceptance, Low-Quality Requirement

These are problems in which poor acceptance can cause a decision to fail and in which the judgment of quality is influenced by differences in position, experience, attitudes, value systems, and other subjective factors. Problems of this type can best be solved by group decision.

An illustration of a problem falling into this group arose when a supervisor needed two of the three girls in his office for work on a Sunday. He asked them individually, and each claimed that she had made a date that she could not break. The fact that Sunday work paid double did not interest them.

He decided to try the group decision method he had just learned about in the company training program. He asked the girls to meet in his office on Friday morning and told them about the emergency job. Since he needed the help of two of them, he wondered what would be the fairest way to handle it. The girls readily entered into the discussion. It turned out that all had dates, but one had a date with some other girls, and all three agreed that a date with other girls was not a "real" date. Thus this girl agreed that it was only fair that she should work.

One more girl was needed. Further discussion revealed that one girl had a date with the man to whom she was engaged, and the third had a date with a new boyfriend. All girls agreed that a date with a fiancé was a real date, but it was not a "heavy" date. It was decided that the third girl, who had the date with a new conquest, should be excused from Sunday work. Thus she was not required to work, even though she had least seniority, because this was considered fair.

The quality issue does not enter into this problem for two reasons: (1) All girls were qualified to do the work. Had this not been true, the supervisor might have been more reluctant to try out this method. However, it remains to be seen whether the girls would have placed an incompetent girl on the job. (2) The problem was stated in such a way as to limit it to the matter at stake. Had he posed the problem in terms of whether or not anyone should be forced to work on Sunday, the answer might have been "no." We shall see later that a problem should be so stated as to keep it within the bounds of the supervisor's freedom of action. If he has no authority to set such matters as pay rates, he cannot expect the group to solve this type of problem through group decision.

In using group decision the superior serves as the discussion leader and presents the problem to his subordinates. His objective is to have the group resolve their differences through discussion while he remains neutral. He confines his activities to clarifying the problem, encouraging discussion, promoting communication, supplying information that may be at his disposal, and making appropriate summaries. His objective is to achieve unanimous agreement on a decision that is the product of the interaction in a group discussion.

Problems that fall into the high-acceptance category have to do with:

The fair way to distribute something desirable, be it a typewriter, a truck, office space, office furniture

The fair way to get something undesirable accomplished, be it unpleasant work, unattractive hours or shifts

The scheduling of overtime, vacations, coffee breaks, etc.

The fair way to settle disciplinary problems that involve violations of regulations, lack of cooperation, etc.

High-Acceptance, High-Quality Requirement

These are the problems that do not fall into the other two categories. At first this may seem to be the largest category of all, so that little seems to have been achieved by extracting the other two. However, in working with group problem solving, it soon becomes apparent that group decisions are often of surprisingly good quality. It is not uncommon for a supervisor to volunteer the information that the group's solution surpassed not only what he had expected, but what he could have achieved by himself. The fear that group decisions will be of poor quality appears to be greater than the hazard warrants. However, if the supervisor is anxious about the outcome, he is likely to interfere with the problem-solving process, rather than facilitate it. For this reason this category of problems should be handled by group decision only when the leader is experienced. Thus it is a category for which either group decision or leader decision is recommended, depending upon the supervisor's skills.

The fears of people frequently determine the motives they ascribe to others, particularly if they are members of an opposition group. For example, if a manager fears a drop in production, he unjustly assumes that his employees are motivated to produce less. Actually the motivational forces in employees form a complex pattern. They include not only what the employees want, but ways of protecting themselves from what they fear management wants to accomplish. With fear removed by the opportunity to participate, the outcome of a discussion often differs greatly from what is anticipated. Obstacles that seem insurmountable frequently disappear in thin air.

The Dynamics of Group Problem Solving

In order to illustrate the types of forces at work in a problem-solving interaction, it may be best to describe a case in the use of group decision. Specific incidents serve to bring theories and generalizations in closer contact with reality.

This case is selected because it is characteristic of the manner in which men solve problems involving attitudes toward prestige and seniority rights. At the same time it illustrates how the men on the job are aware of company objectives and do not take advantage of the company or of each other when the need for protective behavior is removed.

The problem arose because repair foremen in the telephone industry had a persistent problem in getting their men to clear "wet-weather drops."[1] A wet-weather drop is a defective line that runs from a pole to a building. These lines have to be replaced from time to time because water can seep through a break in the insulation and create a short. After a heavy rain there are reports of trouble, but since the difficulty is present only when the line is wet, the problem is a purely temporary one. During periods of expansion or when replacement material is at a minimum, many lines suffer from this wet-weather difficulty. If a station is out of order for this reason, the loss of service corrects itself and is not as serious as if the station were completely out of order. Hence the company, as well as the men, regards wet-weather drops to be minor and routine jobs in contrast to emergency jobs. Furthermore, repair men do not like to do this unimportant work, and they feel that anyone can do it without thinking. As a consequence, the men make little effort to get these jobs done. If the foreman decides to pressure men into bringing in a few wet-weather drops, he finds himself at a disadvantage. The men may promise to pick up one or two and then fail to do so. When asked why, they claim that they ran into extra difficulty on an emergency job and say, "You wanted me to do a good job on the other first, didn't you, boss?" Although the foreman may know the men are shirking, he never knows on what occasion the excuse is justified. It thus comes about that wet-weather drops are a headache to the foreman. When he gets far enough behind, he puts one man on the job full time and lets him clear wet-weather drops. The man in question feels degraded and wonders why he is picked on. To be as fair as possible, this job is usually given to the man with the least seniority. He may complain violently, but invariably the man with least seniority is in the minority. Among supervisory groups this practice is considered the fairest way to handle the situation, and they believe that the men want seniority to be recognized this way. They are completely unaware of the fact that this practice turns an undesirable job into one that has low status as well.

In a particular crew of twelve men the number of wet-weather drops was gradually increasing, and the time was approaching when something would have to be done about the matter. The foreman decided that this was a good problem on which to try group decision. He told his men that he realized no one liked to clear wet-weather drops and that he wanted to have their reactions on how the problem should be handled.

Of interest is the fact that no one in the group felt that the man with the least seniority should do the whole job. The man with most seniority talked against the idea of picking on the fellow with least seniority, saying that he had hated being stuck with the job when he had the least seniority and that he couldn't see why everybody shouldn't do a share of it. It was soon agreed that the job should be evenly divided among the crew. This crew divided up the job by assigning a work area for each man. In this way each man was to be responsible for the wet-weather drops in his area, and he was to be given a list of those. Each morning the local test desk was to designate for each man the wet-weather drop most in need of replacement. It was understood that he was to clear this one, if at all possible. This condition took care of clearing up the drops that were most essential from the point of view of the office. In addition, all agreed that each man should clear as many additional drops as his load permitted. However, when a man had cleared up all the wet-weather drops in his area, it was specifically understood that he should not be asked to help out another. This last condition clearly reveals an attitude built up over the years. It is evident that the reluctance to clear wet-weather drops hinged on the idea that when a man was conscientious, advantage was taken of him. Soon he got to be the "sucker" in the group or perhaps the foreman's pet. It was evident that all men were willing to do their parts but they did not wish to run the risk of being made a sucker. (Other foremen have testified that this defensive reaction made sense from the manner in which the job is frequently handled. The foreman wants to get the job done, and he begins to rely on those individuals who have cooperated in the past. Soon these men find they are doing all the undesirable jobs. It is just a matter of how long it takes a man to find out that he is losing out with the group.)

The results of this solution were immediately apparent. During the three-month period previous to the discussion, a total of eighty wet-weather drops had been cleared; during the week following the discussion, seventy-eight wet-weather drops were cleared and without any letup on the rest of the work. Within a few months the problem was practically nonexistent. The reaction of the men also bore out the effectiveness of the decision. Men discussed the number of drops they had cleared and showed a friendly competitive spirit. They discussed the time when they expected to be caught up and would only have to take care of wet-weather drops as they arose.

It should be noted that the men's notion of fairness was quite different from what the supervisor had anticipated. Although men strongly urge seniority privileges, they do not wish to give junior men a hard time. Rather, advantage is taken of junior men only when seniority rights are threatened. It is of special interest to note the protective reactions against the possibility that cooperation will lead to abuse. Once the protection was ensured, the men considered customer service. This recognition of the service is apparent from the fact that the crew wanted to clear the drops in the order of their importance. With defensive behavior removed, it is not uncommon for good quality solutions to emerge.

Dependence of the Solution's Quality on the Leader's Skills

The quality of group decisions can further be enhanced by improving the skills and the attitude of the discussion leader. Even with a minimum of skills the group decision approach can be effective with problems such as the following:

Setting standards on tardiness and absenteeism

Setting goals for production, quality, and service

Improving safety, housekeeping, etc.

Introducing new work procedures, changing standards, introducing labor-saving equipment, etc.

It is apparent that both quality and acceptance are needed in solving problems of this type, and for this reason they are the areas of greatest conflict in labor-management relations. However, the requirement of skill is more than methodology because it is something that cannot be decided, adopted, or purchased. It requires additional training in conference leadership, and this means an increase in a company's investment in management talents.

Conclusions

Problems may be divided into the following three types:

Type 1. Q/A problems: those for which the quality of the decision is clearly a more important objective than its acceptance. These may be successfully solved by the leader.

Type 2. A/Q problems: those for which acceptance of the decision is clearly a more important objective than its quality. These may be successfully handled by the group decision method in which the decision is made by the subordinates with the superior serving as a discussion leader.

Type 3. Q-A problems: those for which both quality and acceptance of the decision become major objectives. These problems may be handled in either of two ways, each requiring a different set of skills on the part of the leader. The alternatives are as follows:

Leader decision *plus* persuasive skills to gain acceptance or

Group decision *plus* conference leadership skills to gain quality.

The emphases in this book are on the second alternative because conference skills permit the effective use of a greater range of intellectual resources, thereby achieving high-quality decisions as a by-product.

Note

1. Taken from N. R. F. Maier, *Principles of Human Relations,* Wiley, New York, 1952.

Organizational Change Strategies and Tactics

John P. Kotter, Leonard Schlesinger, and Vijay Sathe

Solving and avoiding organizational problems inevitably involve the introduction of organizational change. When the required changes are small and isolated, they can usually be accomplished without major problems. However, when they are large and involve many people and subunits, they can often bring about significant problems.

The following scenario illustrates a common pattern in the process of organizational change:

1. Some factors in a business situation change over a period of time.

2. A number of aspects of the organization that once fit the situation and worked well no longer are appropriate.

3. Organizational problems begin to surface.

4. Managers become aware of the problems and attempt to take some corrective actions.

5. The management initiative runs into resistance.

6. The managers eventually overcome the resistance, but at a large cost to the organization (and often to themselves).

Though managers may encounter many potential problems while initiating an organizational change, the one that seems to emerge most often is related to human resistance.[1] To understand how managers can successfully manage organizational change, we must begin by examining this central problem area.

From John P. Kotter, Leonard A. Schlesinger, and Vijay Sathe, Organization: Text, Cases, and Readings on the Management of Organizational Design and Change, *2nd ed. (Homewood, Ill.: Irwin, 1986), pp. 349–362.*

[1]See Jay Lorsch, "Managing Change," in *Organizational Behavior and Administration,* ed. Paul Lawrence, Louis B. Barnes, and Jay Lorsch (Homewood, Ill.: Richard D. Irwin, 1976), pp. 669–72.

Human Resistance to Change

Human resistance to change takes many forms, from open rebellion to very subtle, passive resistance. And it emerges for many reasons—some of which are rational and some of which are not. Some reasons are primarily self-centered; others are relatively selfless.

Politics and Power Struggles

One major reason that people resist organizational change is that they see they are going to lose something of personal value as a result of the change. Resistance in these cases is often called "politics" or "political behavior," because people are focusing on their own best interests and not that of the total organization.[2]

After a number of years of rapid growth, for example, the president of one organization decided that its size demanded the creation of a new staff function—new-product planning and development—to be headed by a vice president. Operationally, this change eliminated most of the decision-making power that the vice presidents of marketing, engineering, and production had over new products. Inasmuch as new products were very important in this organization, the change also reduced the status of the marketing, engineering, and production VPs. Yet status was important to those three vice presidents. During the two months after the president announced his idea for a new-product vice president, the existing vice presidents each came up with six or seven reasons why the new arrangement might not work. Their objections grew louder and louder until the president shelved the new job idea.

In another example, a manufacturing company had traditionally employed a large group of personnel people as counselors, "father confessors," and friends to its production employees. This group of counselors exhibited high morale because of the professional satisfaction they received from the "helping" relationships they had with employees. When a new performance appraisal system was installed, the personnel people were required to provide each employee's supervisor with a written evaluation of the employee's emotional maturity, promotion potential, etc., every six months. As some of the personnel people immediately recognized, the change would alter their relationship with most employees—from a peer/friend/helper to more of a boss/evaluator. Predictably, they resisted the new system. While publicly arguing that the new system was not as good for the company as the old one, they privately put as much pressure as

---

[2]For a discussion of power and politics in corporations, see Abraham Zaleznik and Manfred F. R. Kets De Vries, *Power and the Corporate Mind* (Boston: Houghton Mifflin, 1975), chap. 6; and Robert H. Miles, *Macro Organizational Behavior* (Santa Monica, Calif.: Goodyear Publishing, 1978), chap. 4.

possible on the personnel vice president until he significantly altered the new system.

Political behavior emerges in organizations because what is in the best interests of one individual or group is sometimes not in the best interests of the total organization or of other individuals and groups. The consequences of organizational change efforts often are good for some people and bad for others. As a result, politics and power struggles often emerge throughout these change efforts.

While this political behavior sometimes takes the form of two or more armed camps publicly fighting it out, it usually is much more subtle. In many cases, it occurs completely under the surface of public dialogue. In a similar way, although power struggles are sometimes initiated by scheming and ruthless individuals, they more often are fostered by those who view their potential loss as an unfair violation of their implicit, or psychological, contract with the organization.[3]

Misunderstanding and a Lack of Trust

People also resist change when they incorrectly perceive that it might cost them considerably more than they will gain. Such situations often occur when people are unable to understand the full implications of a change or when trust is lacking in the change initiator–employee relationship.[4]

For example, when the president of a small midwestern company announced to his managers that the company would implement a flexible working schedule for all employees, it had never occurred to him that he might run into resistance. He had been introduced to the concept at a management seminar and decided to use it to make working conditions at his company more attractive, particularly to clerical and plant personnel. Shortly after the announcement to his managers, numerous rumors began to circulate among plant employees—none of whom really knew what flexible working hours meant and many of whom were distrustful of the manufacturing vice president. One rumor suggested that flexible hours meant that most people would have to work whenever their supervisors asked them to—including weekends and evenings. The employee association, a local union, held a quick meeting and then presented the management with a nonnegotiable demand that the flexible hours concept be dropped. The president, caught completely by surprise, decided to drop the issue.

Few organizations can be characterized as having a high level of trust between employees and managers; consequently, it is easy for misunderstand-

---

[3]Edgar Schein, *Organizational Psychology* (Englewood Cliffs, N.J.: Prentice-Hall, 1965), p. 44.
[4]See Chris Argyris, *Intervention Theory and Method* (Reading, Mass.: Addison-Wesley Publishing, 1970), p. 70.

ings to develop when change is introduced. Unless misunderstandings are sur-faced and clarified quickly, they can lead to resistance.

Different Assessments of the Situation

Another common reason people resist organizational change is that their own analysis of the situation differs from that of those initiating the change. In such cases, their analysis typically sees more costs than benefits resulting from the change, not only for themselves but for their company as well.

For example, the president of one moderate-sized bank was shocked by his staff's analysis of their real estate investment trust (REIT) loans. Their complex analysis suggested that the bank could easily lose up to $10 million and that possible losses were increasing each month by 20 percent. Within a week, the president drew up a plan to reorganize that part of the bank that managed REITs. However, because of his concern for the bank's stock price, he chose not to release the staff report to anyone except the new REIT section manager. The reorganization immediately ran into massive resistance from the people involved. The group sentiment, as articulated by one person, was "Has he gone mad? Why in God's name is he tearing apart this section of the bank? His actions have already cost us three very good people [who quit] and have crippled a new program we were implementing [which the president was unaware of] to reduce our loan losses."

Those who initiate change sometimes incorrectly assume that they have all the relevant information required to conduct an adequate organizational anal-ysis. Further, they often assume that those who will be affected by the change have the same basic facts, when they do not. In either case, the difference in information that groups work with often leads to differences in analysis, which in turn can lead to resistance. Moreover, insofar as the resistance is based on a more accurate analysis of the situation than that held by those initiating the change, that resistance is obviously good for the organization, a fact which is not obvious to some managers who assume that resistance is always bad.[5]

Fear

People sometimes resist change because they know or fear they will not be able to develop the new skills and behaviors required of them. All human beings are limited in their ability to change their behavior, with some people much more limited in this respect than others.[6] Organizational change can inadvertently

---

[5]See Paul R. Lawrence, "How to Deal with Resistance to Change," *Harvard Business Review*, May–June 1954.

[6]For a discussion of resistance that is personality based, see Goodwin Watson, "Resistance to Change," in *The Planning of Change*, ed. Warren Bennis, Kenneth Benne, and Robert Chin (New York: Holt, Rinehart & Winston, 1969), pp. 489–93.

require people to change too much, too quickly. When such a situation occurs, people typically resist the change—sometimes consciously but often unconsciously.

Peter Drucker has argued that the major obstacle to organization growth is managers' inability to change their attitudes and their behaviors.[7] In many cases, he points out, corporations grow to a certain point and then slow down or stop growing because key managers are unable to change as rapidly as their organizations. Even if they intellectually understand the need for changes in the way they operate, they sometimes are unable to make the transition.

In a sense, all people who are affected by change experience some emotional turmoil, because change involves loss and uncertainty—even changes which appear to be positive, or "rational."[8] For example, a person who receives a significantly more important job as a result of an organizational change will probably be very happy. But it is possible that such a person feels uneasy. A new and very different job will require new and different behavior, new and different relationships, as well as the loss of some current activities and relationships that provide satisfaction. It is common under such circumstances for a person to emotionally resist giving up certain aspects of the current situation.

Still Other Reasons

People also sometimes resist organizational change to save face; to go along with the change would be, they think, an admission that some of their previous decisions or beliefs were wrong. They may resist because of peer group pressure or because of a supervisor's resistant attitude. Indeed, there are many reasons why people resist change.[9]

Because of all the possible reasons for resistance to organizational change, it is hardly surprising that organizations do not automatically and easily adapt to environmental or technological or strategic changes. Indeed, organizations usually adapt only because managers successfully employ strategies and tactics for dealing with potential resistance.

Tactics for Dealing with Resistance

Managers may use a number of tactics to deal with resistance to change. These include education/communication, participation, facilitation and support, negotiation, co-optation, coercion, and manipulation.[10]

---

[7]*The Practice of Management* (New York: Harper & Row, 1954).

[8]See Robert Luke, "A Structural Approach to Organizational Change," *Journal of Applied Behavioral Science,* 1973.

[9]For a general discussion of resistance and reasons for it, see Gerald Zaltman and Robert Duncan, *Strategies for Planned Change* (New York: John Wiley & Sons, 1977), chap. 3.

[10]Conceptually, there are a number of ways that one can label change tactics. This list of

Education/Communication

One of the most commonly used ways of dealing with resistance to change is education and communication. This tactic is aimed at helping people see the need for the logic of a change. It can involve one-on-one discussions, presentations to groups, or memos and reports. For example, as a part of an effort to make changes in a division's structure, measurement system, and reward system, the division manager put together a one-hour audiovisual presentation that explained the changes and the reasons for the changes. Over a four-month period, he made this presentation no less than a dozen times to groups of 20 or 30 corporate and divisional managers.

Education/communication can be ideal when resistance is based on inadequate or inaccurate information and analysis, especially if the initiators need the resister's help in implementing the change. But this tactic requires at least a minimally good relationship between the initiators and the others, or the resisters may not believe what they hear. It also requires time and effort, particularly if a lot of people are involved.

Participation

Participation as a change tactic implies that the initiators involve the resisters or potential resisters in some aspect of the design and implementation of the change. For example, the head of a small financial services company once created a task force to help design and implement changes in the company's reward system. The task force was composed of eight second- and third-level managers from different parts of the company. The president's specific request to them was that they recommend changes in the company's benefits package. They were given six months and were asked to file a brief progress report with the president once a month. After making their recommendations, which the president largely accepted, they were asked to help the firm's personnel director implement them.

Participation is a rational choice of tactics when change initiators believe they do not have all the information they need to design and implement a change or when they need the wholehearted commitment of others in implementing a change. Considerable research has demonstrated that participation generally leads to commitment, not just compliance.[11] But participation does have its drawbacks. Not only can it lead to a poor solution if the process is not carefully managed, but it also can be enormously time consuming.

---

seven tactics is one useful approach. Other writers on this subject have used different variations on that list.

[11]See, for example, Alfred Marrow, David Bowers, and Stanley Seashore, *Management by Participation* (New York: Harper & Row, 1967).

Facilitation and Support

Another way in which managers can deal with potential resistance to change is through facilitation and support. As a tactic, it might include providing training in new skills, giving employees time off after a demanding period, or simply listening and providing emotional support.

For example, one rapidly growing electronics company did the following to help people adjust to frequent organizational changes. First, it staffed its human resource department with four counselors, who spent most of their time talking to people who were feeling "burned out" or who were having difficulty adjusting to new jobs. Second, on a selective basis, it offered people "minisabbaticals," which were four weeks in duration and which involved some reflective or educational activity away from work. And finally, it spent a great deal of money on education and training programs conducted in-house.

Facilitation and support are best suited for resistance due to adjustment problems. The basic drawback of this approach is that it can be time consuming and expensive, and still fail.[12]

Negotiation

Negotiation as a change tactic essentially involves buying out active or potential resisters. This could mean, for example, giving a union a higher wage rate in return for a work rule change, or it could involve increasing an individual's pension benefits in return for an early retirement.

Effective use of negotiation as a change tactic can be seen in the activities of a division manager in a large manufacturing company. The divisions in this company were very interdependent. One division manager wanted to make some major changes in the division's organization. Yet, because of interdependencies, she recognized that she would be forcing some inconvenience and change on other divisions. To prevent top managers in other divisions from undermining her efforts, she negotiated with each division a written agreement that promised certain positive outcomes (for them) within certain time periods as a result of her changes and, in return, specified certain types of cooperation expected from the divisions during the change process. Later, whenever other divisions began to complain about the changes or the change process itself, she pulled out the negotiated agreements.

Negotiation is particularly appropriate when it is clear that someone is going to lose out as a result of a change and yet has significant power to resist. As a result, it can be a relatively easy way to avoid major resistance in some instances. Like the other tactics, negotiation may become expensive—and a manager who

---

[12]Zaltman and Duncan, *Strategies for Planned Change,* chap. 4.

once makes it clear that he or she will negotiate to avoid resistance opens up the possibility of being blackmailed by others.[13]

Co-optation

A fifth tactic managers use to deal with potential or actual resistance to change is co-optation. Co-opting an individual usually involves giving him or her a desirable role in the design or implementation of the change. Co-opting a group involves giving one of its leaders, or someone it respects, a key role in the design or implementation of a change. A change initiator could, for example, try to co-opt the sales force by allowing the sales manager to be privy to the design of the changes and by seeing that the most popular salesperson gets a raise as part of the change.

To reduce the possibility of corporate resistance to an organizational change, one division manager in a large multibusiness corporation successfully used co-optation in the following way. He invited the corporate human relations vice president, a close friend of the president's, to help him and his key staff analyze some problems the division was having. Because of his busy schedule, the corporate VP was not able to do much of the actual information gathering or analysis himself, thus limiting his own influence on the diagnoses. But his presence at key meetings helped commit him to the diagnosis and the solution the group designed. The commitment was subsequently very important because the president, at least initially, did not like some of the proposed changes. Nevertheless, after discussion with his human resource VP, he did not try to block them.

Co-optation can, under certain circumstances, be a relatively inexpensive and easy way to gain an individual's or a group's support (less expensive, for example, than negotiation and quicker than participation). Nevertheless, it has its drawbacks. If people feel they are being tricked into not resisting, they obviously may respond negatively. And if they use their ability to influence the design and implementation of changes in ways that are not in the best interests of the organization, they can obviously create serious problems.

Manipulation

Manipulation, in this context, refers to covert influence attempts. In a sense, therefore, co-optation is a form of manipulation. Other forms do not have specific names but involve, for instance, the selective use of information and the conscious structuring of events so as to have some desired (but covert) impact on the participants.

---

[13]For an excellent discussion of negotiation, see Gerald Nierenberg, *The Art of Negotiating* (New York: Cornerstone, 1974).

Manipulation suffers from the same drawbacks as co-optation, but to an even greater degree. When people feel they are not being treated openly or that they are being lied to, they often react negatively. Nevertheless, manipulation can be used successfully—particularly when all other tactics are not feasible or have failed.[14] With one's back to the wall, with inadequate time to use education, participation, or facilitation, and without the power or other resources to use negotiation, coercion, or co-optation, a manager might resort to manipulating information channels to scare people into thinking there is a crisis coming which they can avoid only by change.

Coercion

The seventh tactic managers use to deal with resistance is coercion. Here they essentially force people to accept a change, explicitly or implicitly threatening them with the loss of jobs or promotion possibilities or raises or whatever else they control. Like manipulation, coercion is a risky tactic because people strongly resent forced change. Yet coercion has the advantage of overcoming resistance very quickly. And in situations where speed is essential, this tactic may be one's only alternative.

For example, when assigned to "turn around" a failing division in a large conglomerate, the chosen manager relied mostly on coercion to achieve the organizational changes she desired. She did so because she felt, "I did not have enough time to use other methods, and I needed to make changes that were pretty unpopular among many of the people."

Using Change Tactics

Effective organizational change efforts are almost always characterized by the skillful use of a number of these change tactics. Conversely, less effective change efforts usually involve the misuse of one or more of these tactics.

Managers sometimes misuse change tactics simply because they are unaware of the strengths and limitations of each tactic (see Figure 7–1). Sometimes they run into difficulties because they rely only on the same limited number of tactics regardless of the situation (e.g., they always use participation and persuasion, or coercion and manipulation).[15] Sometimes they misuse the tactics simply because they are not chosen and implemented as a part of a clearly considered change strategy.

---

[14]See John P. Kotter, "Power, Dependence, and Effective Management," *Harvard Business Review,* July–August 1977, pp. 133–35.

[15]Ibid., pp. 135–36.

FIGURE 7–1   TACTICS FOR DEALING WITH RESISTANCE TO CHANGE

Tactic	Best for:	Advantages	Drawbacks
Education/communication	Resistance based on lack of information or inaccurate information and analysis.	Once persuaded, people will often help with the implementation of the change.	Can be very time consuming if large numbers of people are involved.
Participation	Situations in which initiators do not have all the information needed to design the change and where others have considerable power to resist.	People who participate will be committed to implementing change. And any relevant information they have will be integrated into the change plan.	Can be very time consuming. Participators could design an inappropriate change.
Facilitation and support	Dealing with people who are resisting because of adjustment problems.	No other tactic works as well with adjustment problems.	Can be time consuming, expensive, and still fail.
Negotiation	Situations where someone or some group will clearly lose out in a change and where they have considerable power to resist.	Sometimes is a relatively easy way to avoid major resistance.	Can be too expensive in many cases. Can alert others to negotiate for compliance.
Co-optation	Very specific situations where the other tactics are too expensive or are infeasible.	Can help generate support for implementing a change (but less than participation).	Can create problems if people recognize the co-optation.
Manipulation	Situations where other tactics will not work or are too expensive.	Can be a relatively quick and inexpensive solution to resistance problems.	Costs initiators some of their credibility. Can lead to future problems.
Coercion	When speed is essential and the change initiators possess considerable power.	Speed. Can overcome any kind of resistance.	Risky. Can leave people angry with the initiators.

FIGURE 7–2   STRATEGIC OPTIONS FOR THE MANAGEMENT OF CHANGE.

Rapid changes	Slow changes
Clearly planned	Not clearly planned initially
Little involvement of others	Lots of involvement of others
Attempt to overcome any resistance	Attempt to minimize any resistance

Key Situational Variables

- The amount and type of resistance that is anticipated.
- The position of the initiators vis-à-vis the resisters (in terms of power, trust, etc.)
- The locus of relevant data for designing the change and of needed energy for implementing it.
- The stakes involved (e.g., the presence or absence of a crisis, the consequences of resistance and lack of change)

Change Strategies

In approaching an organizational change situation, managers explicitly or implicitly make strategic choices regarding the speed of the effort, the amount of preplanning, the involvement of others, and the relative emphasis of different change tactics. Successful change efforts seem to be those in which these choices both are internally consistent and fit some key situation variables.

The strategic options available to managers can be usefully thought of as existing on a continuum (see Figure 7–2).[16] At one end of the continuum, the strategy calls for a very rapid implementation of changes, with a clear plan of action and little involvement of others. This type of strategy mows over any resistance and, at the extreme, would involve a fait accompli. At the other end of the continuum, the strategy would call for a much slower change process that is less clearly planned from the start and that involves many people in addition to the change initiators. This type of strategy is designed to reduce resistance to a minimum.[17]

With respect to tactics, the farther to the left one operates on the continuum in Figure 7–2, the more one tends to use coercion and the less one tends to use the other tactics—especially participation. The opposite is true the more one operates to the right on the continuum—the less coercion tends to be used and the more the other tactics tend to be used.

---

[16]See Larry E. Greiner, "Patterns of Organizational Change," *Harvard Business Review,* May–June 1967; and Larry E. Greiner and Louis B. Barnes, "Organizational Change and Development," in *Organization Change and Development,* ed. Gene Dalton and Paul Lawrence (Homewood, Ill.: Richard D. Irwin, 1970), pp. 3–5.

[17]For a good discussion of an approach that attempts to minimize resistance, see Renato Tagiuri, "Notes on the Management of Change," Working Paper, Harvard Business School.

Exactly where a change effort should be strategically positioned on the continuum in Figure 7–2 seems to be a function of four key variables.

1. *The amount and type of resistance that is anticipated.* The greater the anticipated resistance, other factors being equal, the more appropriate it is to move toward the right on the continuum.[18] The greater the anticipated resistance, the more difficult it is to simply overwhelm it and the more one needs to find ways to reduce some of it.

2. *The position of the initiator vis-à-vis the resisters, especially with regard to power.* The greater the initiator's power, the better the initiator's relationships with the others; and the more the others expect that the initiator might move unilaterally, the more one can move to the left on the continuum.[19] On the other hand, the weaker the initiator's position, the more he or she is forced to operate to the right.

3. *The locus of relevant data for designing the change and of needed energy for implementing it.* The more the initiators anticipate they will need information from others to help design the change and commitment from them to help implement it, the more they must move to the right.[20] Gaining useful information and commitment requires time and the involvement of others.

4. *The stakes involved.* The greater the short-run potential for risks to organizational performance and survival, the more one must move to the left.

Organizational change efforts that are based on an inconsistent strategy, or ones that do not fit the situation, tend to run into predictable problems. For example, an effort that is not clearly planned but is quickly implemented will almost always run into unanticipated problems. Efforts that attempt to involve large numbers of people and at the same time try to move quickly will virtually always end up sacrificing either speed or involvement. Efforts in which the change initiators do not have all the information they need to correctly design a change but which nevertheless move quickly and involve few others sometimes encounter enormous problems.

Implications for Managing Organizational Change

Organizational change efforts can be greatly aided by an analysis and planning process composed of the following three phrases:

1. Conducting a thorough organizational analysis—one which identifies the current situation, any problems, and the forces which are possible causes

---

[18]Jay Lorsch, "Managing Change," pp. 676–78.
[19]Ibid.
[20]Ibid.

of those problems. The analysis must clearly specify:

a. The actual significance of the problems.

b. The speed with which the problems must be addressed if additional problems are to be avoided.

c. The types of changes that are generally needed.

2. Conducting a thorough analysis of factors relevant to implementing the necessary changes. This analysis focuses on questions of:

a. Who might resist the changes, why, and to what extent.

b. Who has information that is needed to design the change and whose cooperation is essential in implementing it.

c. The position of the change initiator vis-à-vis other relevant parties in terms of power, trust, normal modes of interaction, etc.

3. Selecting a change strategy based on the analysis in Phases 1 and 2, and a set of change tactics, and then designing an action plan that specifies:

a. What must be done.

b. By whom.

c. In what sequence.

d. And within what time frame.

When initiating and managing an organizational change, it is conceivable that some or all of these steps will need to be repeated if unforeseen events occur or if new and relevant information surfaces. At the extreme, in a highly participative change, the process might be repeated a dozen times over a period of months or years. The key to successful organizational change is not whether these steps are repeated once or many times but whether they are done competently and thoroughly.

References

Adams, W. Clifton, 1972. The interrelationship among need for social approval, persuasibility, and activation. *Central States Speech Journal* **23:** 188–192.

Adler, Alfred, 1956. *The individual psychology of Alfred Adler.* Heinz and Rowena Ansbacher (eds.). New York: Basic Books.

——, 1964. *Superiority and social interest by Alfred Adler.* Heinz and Rowena Ansbacher (eds.). Evanston, Ill.: Northwestern University Press.

Adorno, T. W., Else Frenkel-Brunswik, Daniel Levinson, and R. Nevitt Sanford, 1950. *The authoritarian personality.* New York: Harper & Row.

Albanese, Robert, and David VanFleet, 1985. Rational behavior in groups: The free-riding tendency. *The Academy of Management Review* **11:** 244–255.

Allport, Floyd, 1924. *Social psychology.* Boston: Houghton Mifflin.

Allport, Gordon W., 1967. Attitudes. In Martin Fishbein (ed.), *Readings in attitude theory and measurement.* New York: Wiley, pp. 3–13.

Altman, Irwin, 1975. *The environment and social behavior.* Monterey, Calif.: Brooks/Cole.

Applbaum, Ronald, Edward Bodaken, Kenneth Sereno, and Karl Anatol, 1974. *The process of group communication.* Palo Alto, Calif.: Science Research Associates.

Argyle, Michael, 1967. *The psychology of interpersonal behavior.* Baltimore: Penguin.

——, and J. Dean, 1965. Eye-contact, distance, and affiliation. *Sociometry* **23:** 289–304.

Argyris, Chris, 1962. *Interpersonal competence and organizational effectiveness.* Homewood, Ill.: Irwin.

Aronoff, Joel, and Lawrence A. Messe, 1971. Motivational determinants of small-group structure. *Journal of Personality and Social Psychology* **17:** 319–324.

Aronson, Elliot, 1984. Characteristics of Effective Feedback. In Robert S. Cathcart and Larry Samovar. *Small Group Communication: A Reader* (4th ed.). Dubuque, Iowa: Wm. C. Brown, pp. 336–341.

——, 1973. The rationalizing animal. *Psychology Today* **6:** 46–52.

——, and Judson Mills, 1959. Effect of severity of initiation on liking for a group. *Journal of Abnormal and Social Psychology* **59:** 177–181.

Asch, Solomon, 1952. *Social psychology.* Englewood Cliffs, N.J.: Prentice-Hall.

——, 1955. Opinions and social pressure. *Scientific American* **193:** 31–35.

——, 1956. Studies of independence and conformity: a minority of one against a unanimous majority. *Psychological Monographs* **70:** No. 9 (Whole No. 416).

Atkinson, John W., 1966. Notes concerning the generality of the theory of achievement motivation. In John W. Atkinson and Norman T. Feather (eds.), *A theory of achievement motivation.* New York: Appleton-Century-Crofts, pp. 163–168.

Bach, George, and Peter Wyden, 1968. *The intimate enemy.* New York: Morrow.

Bales, Robert F., 1950. *Interaction process analysis.* Reading, Mass.: Addison-Wesley.

——, 1954. In conference. *Harvard Business Review* **32:** 44–50.

——, 1970. *Personality and interpersonal behavior.* New York: Holt, Rinehart and Winston.

——, and Fred Strodbeck, 1951. Phases in group problem solving. *Journal of Abnormal and Social Psychology* **46:** 485–495.

Barnlund, Dean, 1962. Consistency of emergent leadership in groups with changing tasks and members. *Speech Monographs* **29**: 45–52.

———, 1968. *Interpersonal communication: survey and studies.* Boston: Houghton Mifflin.

———, and Franklyn Haiman, 1959. *The dynamics of discussion.* Boston: Houghton Mifflin.

Bass, B. C. Wurster, P. Doll, and D. Clair, 1953. Situational and personality factors in leadership among sorority women. *Psychological Monographs* **67**: No. 16 (Whole No. 366).

Bass, Bernard M., 1983. *Organizational decision making.* Homewood, Ill.: Richard D. Irwin.

Batchelor, James, and George Goethals, 1972. Spatial arrangements in freely formed groups. *Sociometry* **35**: 270–279.

Bauduin, E. Scott, 1971. Obscene language and source credibility: an experimental study. Paper presented at the annual conference of the International Communication Association. Phoenix, Arizona.

Bay, Christian, 1967. Political and apolitical students: facts in search of a theory. *Journal of Social Issues* **23**: 76–91.

Beckhard, Richard, 1961. The confrontation meeting. In Warren Bennis, Kenneth Benne, and Robert Chin (eds.), *The planning of change.* New York: Holt, Rinehart and Winston, pp. 478–485.

Beebe, Paul, 1986. Going in circles. *The Idaho Statesman,* May 11.

Beebe, Steven A. and John T. Materson, 1986. Communicating in small groups (2nd ed.). Glenview, Ill.: Scott, Foresman.

Benne, Kenneth D., and Paul Sheats, 1948. Functional roles of group members. *Journal of Social Issues* **4**: 41–49.

Bennis, Warren, 1961. Interpersonal communication. In Warren Bennis, Kenneth Benne, and Robert Chin (eds.), *The planning of change.* New York: Holt, Rinehart and Winston.

———, and Herbert Shepard, 1948. A theory of group development. *Human Relations* **1**: 314–320.

———, and Herbert Shepard, 1961. Group observation. In Warren Bennis, Kenneth Benne, and Robert Chin (eds.), *The planning of change.* New York: Holt, Rinehart and Winston, pp. 743–756.

Bennis, Warren, and Burt Nanus. 1985. *Leaders: The strategies for taking charge.* New York: Harper & Row.

———, Edgar Schein, Fred Steele, and David Berlew, 1968. Personal change through interpersonal relationships. In *Interpersonal dynamics: essays and readings on human interaction.* Homewood, Ill.: Dorsey, pp. 333–369.

Berelson, Bernard, and Gary Steiner, 1964. *Human behavior: an inventory of scientific findings.* New York: Harcourt, Brace and World.

Berg, David, 1967. A descriptive analysis of the distribution and duration of themes discussed by task-oriented small groups. *Speech Monographs* **34**: 172–175.

Berg, I. A., and B. Bass (eds.), 1961. *Conformity and deviation.* New York: Harper & Row.

Berne, Eric, 1964. *Games people play.* New York: Grove.

Bilodeau, J., and H. Schlosberg, 1959. Similarity in stimulating conditions as a variable in retroactive inhibition. *Journal of Experimental Psychology* **41**: 199–204.

Bird, G., 1940. *Social psychology.* New York: Appleton-Century-Crofts.

Bird, Lee, 1974. The Nixon years. *Flint Journal,* August 18:D1-D2.

Bittel, Lester R., 1956. Brainstorming. *Factory Management and Maintenance* **114**: 107.

Blake, Robert, and Jane Mouton, 1970. The fifth achievement. *Journal of Applied Behavioral Sciences* **6**: 413–426.

Bloom, Benjamin S., and Lois J. Broder, 1961. Problem-solving processes of college students. In Theodore L. Harris and Wilson E. Schwahn (eds.), *Selected readings in the learning process.* New York: Oxford University Press, pp. 31–79.

Blotnick, Srully, 1986. Survey: Women say affairs of the heart thrive at workplace. *The Idaho Statesman,* March 19, 2.

Bormann, Ernest, 1969. *Discussion and group methods.* New York: Harper & Row.

———, 1970. The paradox and promise of small group research. *Speech Monographs* **37**: 211–216.

Bostrom, Robert, 1970. Patterns of communicative interaction in small groups. *Speech Monographs* **37**: 257–263.

———, and Charles Rossiter, 1969. Profanity, justification, and source credibility. Paper presented at the annual conference of the International Communication Association, Cleveland, Ohio.

Bowers, D. G., and S. E. Seashore, 1966. Predicting organizational effectiveness with a four factor theory of leadership. *Administrative Science Quarterly,* pp. 238–265.

Bradford, David L., and Allan R. Cohen, 1984. *Managing for Excellence: The Guide to Developing High Performance in Contemporary Organizations.* New York: Wiley.

Braybrooke, David, and Charles E. Lindblom, 1963. *A strategy of decision.* New York: Free Press.

Brilhart, John, 1982. *Effective group discussion* (4th ed.). Dubuque, Iowa: Wm. C. Brown.

Brock, A. J. (trans.), 1952. Galen, On the natural faculties. In R. M. Hutchins (ed.), *Great books of the western world.* Chicago: Encyclopaedia Britannica **10**: 163–215.

Brockner, Joel, and Ted Hess, 1986. Self-esteem and task performance in quality circles. *Academy of Management Journal* **29**: 617–623.

Brodwin, D. R., and L. J. Bourgeois, 1984. Five steps to strategic action. In G. Carroll and D. Vogel (eds.), *Strategy and organization: A West Coast perspective.* Boston: Pitman, pp. 167–181.

Brown, Roger, 1965. *Social psychology.* New York: Free Press.

Bruskin, R. H., 1973. Fear. Reported in *Spectra* **9**: 4.

Buchholz, Steve, 1985. *The Positive Manager.* New York: Wiley.

Bunker, Douglas, 1965. Individual applications of laboratory training. *Journal of Applied Behavioral Science* **1**: 131–147.

Burgoon, Michael, 1971. Amount of conflicting information in a group discussion and tolerance for ambiguity as predictors of task attractiveness. *Speech Monographs* **38**: 121–124. (a)

———, 1971. The relationship between willingness to manipulate others and success in two different types of basic speech communication courses. *Speech Teacher* **19**: 178–183. (b)

———, Gerald R. Miller, and Stewart L. Tubbs, 1972. Machiavellianism, justification, and attitude change following counterattitudinal advocacy. *Journal of Personality and Social Psychology* **22**: 366–371.

Burke, Richard, and Warren Bennis, 1961. Changes in perception of self and others during human relations training. *Human Relations* **14**: 165–182.

Bynner, Witter (trans.), 1944. *The way of life according to Lao-tzu.* New York: John Day, Saying 17.

Cahn, Dudley D., and Stewart L. Tubbs, 1983. Management as communication: Performance evaluation and employee self worth. *Communication,* December, pp. 46–54.

Camp, Richard, P. Nick Blanchard, Gregory E. Huszczo, 1986. *Toward a more organizationally effective training strategy & practice.* Englewood Cliffs, N.J.: Prentice-Hall.

Campbell, John, and Marvin Dunnette, 1968. Effectiveness of T-group experiences in managerial training and development. *Psychological Bulletin* **70**: 73–104.

Cartwright, Dorwin, and Alvin Zander, 1953. *Group dynamics: Research and theory.* New York: Harper & Row.

———, 1968. The nature of group cohesiveness. In D. Cartwright and A. Zander (eds.), *Group dynamics* (3rd ed.). New York: Harper & Row, pp. 91–109.

Cathcart, Robert S., and Larry Samovar, 1984. *Small group communication: A reader* (4th ed.). Dubuque, Iowa: Wm. C. Brown.

Champness, Brian, 1969. Communication: What's in a glance? *Time,* October 17, p. 74.

Christie, Richard, and Florence L. Geis, 1970. *Studies in Machiavellianism.* New York: Academic Press.

Clark, Russell, III, 1971. Group induced shift toward risk: A critical appraisal. *Psychological Bulletin* **76:** 251–270.

Collins, Barry, and Harold Guetzkow, 1964. *A social psychology of group processes for decision making.* New York: Wiley.

Cooley, Charles, 1918. *Social process.* New York: Scribner's.

Cooper, Gary, and Iain Mongham, 1971. *T-groups: A survey of research.* New York: Wiley-Interscience.

Couch, A., and K. Keniston, 1960. Yeasayers and naysayers: agreeing response set as a personality variable. *Journal of Abnormal and Social Psychology* **60:** 151–174.

Crane, Loren, Richard Dieker, and Charles Brown, 1970. The physiological response to the communication modes: reading, listening, writing, speaking, and evaluating. *Journal of Communication* **20:** 231–240.

Crockett, Walter H., and Thomas Meidinger, 1956. Authoritarianism and interpersonal perception. *Journal of Abnormal and Social Psychology* **53:** 378–380.

Crowne, D. P., and D. Marlowe, 1964. *The approval motive.* New York: Wiley.

Crutchfield, Richard, 1959. Personal and situational factors in conformity to group pressure. *Acta Psychologica* **15:** 386–388.

Culbert, Samuel A., 1968. *The interpersonal process of self-disclosure: It takes two to see one.* New York: Renaissance Editions.

Cushman, Donald P., and Dudley D. Cahn, 1985. *Communication in interpersonal relationships.* Albany, N.Y. SUNY Press.

Cyert, R. M., and J. G. March, 1963. *A behavioral theory of the firm.* Englewood Cliffs, N.J.: Prentice-Hall.

Dance, Frank E. X., 1972. The centrality of the spoken word. *Central States Speech Journal* **23:** 197–201.

———, and Carl E. Larson, 1972. *Speech communication: Concepts and behavior.* New York: Holt, Rinehart and Winston.

Delbecq, André L., Andrew H. Van de Ven, and David H. Gustafson, 1975. *Group techniques for program planning: A guide to nominal group and Delphi processes.* Glenview, Ill.: Scott, Foresman.

Deutsch, Morton, 1969. Conflicts: Productive and destructive. *Journal of Social Issues* **25:** 7–43.

———, 1971. Toward an understanding of conflict. *International Journal of Group Tensions* **1:** 42–55.

———, and Leonard Solomon, 1959. Reaction to evaluations by others as influenced by self-evaluations. *Sociometry:* 93–111.

Dewey, John, 1910. *How we think.* New York: Heath.

Dill, W. R., 1965. *Decision making: Sixty-third yearbook of the National Society for the Study of Education, Behavioral Science and Educational Administration,* pp. 200–202.

Eakins, Barbara W., and R. Gene Eakins, 1978. *Sex differences in human communication.* Boston: Houghton Mifflin.

Edwards, Allen, 1953. *The Edwards Personal Preference Schedule.* New York: Psychological Corporation.

——, and L. E. Acker, 1962. A demonstration of the long-term retention of a conditioned galvanic skin response. *Psychosomatic Medicine* **24**: 459–463.

Egan, Gerard, 1973. *Face to face: The small group experience and interpersonal growth.* Monterey, Calif.: Brooks/Cole.

Ehninger, Douglas, and Wayne Brocriede, 1963. *Decision by debate.* New York: Dodd, Mead.

Ehrlich, H. J., and Dorothy Lee, 1969. Dogmatism, learning, and resistance to change: A review and a new paradigm. *Psychological Bulletin* **71**: 249–260.

Eisenberg, Eric M., 1984. Ambiguity as strategy in organizational communication. *Communication Monographs* **51**: 227–239.

Etzioni, Amatai, 1964. *Modern organizations.* Englewood Cliffs, N.J.: Prentice-Hall.

——, 1968. *The active society.* New York: Free Press.

Ewbank, Henry, and Jeffrey Auer, 1946. *Discussion and debate.* New York: Crofts.

Exline, Ralph, John Thibaut, Carole Hickey, and Peter Gumpert, 1970. Visual interaction in relation to Machiavellianism and an unethical act. In Richard Christie and Florence L. Geis, *Studies in Machiavellianism.* New York: Academic Press, pp. 53–75.

Faris, Ellsworth, 1932. The primary group: essence and accident. *American Journal of Sociology* **28**: 41–50.

Festinger, Leon, 1954. A theory of social comparison processes. *Human Relations* **7**: 117–140.

——, 1957. *A theory of cognitive dissonance.* Stanford, Calif.: Stanford University Press.

——, and Elliot Aronson, 1968. Arousal and reduction of dissonance in social contexts. In Dorwin Cartwright and Alvin Zander (eds.), *Group dynamics: research and theory* (3rd ed.). New York: Harper & Row, pp. 125–136.

Fiedler, F. E., 1958. *Leader attitudes and group effectiveness.* Urbana: University of Illinois Press.

Fiedler, Fred, 1967. *A theory of leadership effectiveness.* New York: McGraw-Hill.

——, and Martin Chemers, 1974. *Leadership and effective management.* Glenview, Ill.: Scott, Foresman.

Filley, Alan C., 1975. *Interpersonal conflict resolution.* Glenview, Ill.: Scott, Foresman.

Fisher, B. Aubrey, 1970. Decision emergence: Phases in group decision making. *Speech Monographs* **37**: 53–66.

——, 1974. *Small group decision making: communication and the group process.* New York: McGraw-Hill.

——, and Leonard C. Hawes, 1971. An interact system model: generating a grounded theory of small groups. *Quarterly Journal of Speech* **57**: 444–453.

——, 1980. *Small group decision making* (2nd ed.). New York: McGraw-Hill.

Folger, Joseph P., and Marshall Scott Poole, 1984. *Working through conflict: A communication perspective.* Glenview, Ill.: Scott, Foresman.

Following the Leader: Sometimes it's Folly to go Along with the Boss, 1986. *Science,* October 18.

Franecki, Dennis J., Ralph F. Catalanello, and Curtiss K. Behrens, 1984. Employee committees: What effect are they having? *Personnel* July–August: 67–73.

French, John, and Bertram Raven, 1959. The bases of social power. In Dorwin Cartwright (ed.), *Studies in social power.* Ann Arbor: Institute for Social Research, pp. 150–167.

Freud, Sigmund, 1960. The psychopathology of everyday life. In the *Complete Works,* Vol. 6. London: Hogarth Press.

Ganeen, Harold, and Alvin Moscow, 1984. *Managing.* Garden City, N.Y.: Doubleday.

Gardner, Eric, and George Thompson, 1956. *Social relations and morale in small groups.* New York: Appleton-Century-Crofts.

Geier, John, 1967. A trait approach to the study of leadership. *Journal of Communication* **17**: 316–323.

Gibb, Jack, 1961. Defensive communication. *Journal of Communication* **11**: 141–148.

Gibson, Jane Whitney, and Richard M. Hodgetts, 1986. *Organizational communication: A managerial perspective.* New York: Academic Press.

Giffin, Kim, and Kendall Bradley, 1969. Group counseling for speech anxiety: an approach and rationale. *Journal of Communication* **19**: 22–29.

———, and Shirley Masterson Gilham, 1971. Relationship between speech anxiety and motivation. *Speech Monographs* **38**: 70–73.

———, and Bobby Patton, 1974. *Personal communication in human relations.* Columbus, Ohio: Charles Merrill.

Goffman, Erving, 1961. *Encounters.* Indianapolis: Bobbs-Merrill.

Goldberg, Alvin, and Carl Larson, 1975. *Group communication.* Englewood Cliffs, N.J.: Prentice-Hall.

Goldhaber, Gerald, 1971. Communication and student unrest. Unpublished report to the President of the University of New Mexico.

———, 1974. *Organizational communication.* Dubuque, Iowa: Wm. C. Brown.

———, et al., 1979. *Information strategies: New pathways to corporate power.* Englewood Cliffs, N.J.: Prentice-Hall.

Goldhamer, E., and E. Shils, 1939. Types of power and status. *American Journal of Sociology* **45**: 171–182.

Golembiewski, Robert, and Arthur Blumberg, 1970. *Sensitivity training and the laboratory approach.* Itasca, Ill.: Peacock.

Gordon, Thomas, 1955. *Group-centered leadership.* Boston: Houghton Mifflin.

Gouran, Dennis, 1969. Variables related to consensus in group discussions of questions of policy. *Speech Monographs* **36**: 387–391.

———, 1973. Group communication: perspectives and priorities for future research. *Quarterly Journal of Speech* **59**: 22–29.

———, 1974. *Discussion: The process of group decision making.* New York: Harper & Row.

Greiner, Larry, 1970. Patterns of organizational change. In G. Dalton, P. Lawrence, and L. Greiner (eds.), *Organizational change and development.* Homewood, Ill.: Irwin, pp. 213–229.

Gross, Bertram M., 1964. *Organizations and their managing.* New York: Free Press.

Grove, Andrew S., 1983. *High output management.* New York: Random House.

Gulley, Halbert, 1968. *Discussions, conferences, and group processes.* New York: Holt, Rinehart and Winston.

Hailey, Arthur, 1971. *Wheels.* Garden City, N.Y.: Doubleday.

Haiman, Franklin, 1963. Effects of training in group processes on open-mindedness. *Journal of Communication* **13**: 236–245.

———, 1951. *Group leadership and democratic action.* Boston: Houghton Mifflin.

Hain, Tony, 1972. *Patterns of organizational change.* Flint, Mich.: General Motors Institute.

Hall, Edward T., 1959. *The silent language.* Garden City, N.Y.: Doubleday.

Halpin, A. W., and J. Winer, 1957. A factorial study of the leader behavior description questionnaire. In R. Stogdill and A. Coons (eds.), *Leader behavior: Its description and measurement.* Research Monograph No. 88. Columbus, Ohio: Bureau of Business Research, Ohio State University, pp. 6–38.

Haney, William V., 1986. *Communication and organizational behavior* (4th ed.). Homewood, Ill.: Irwin.

Hare, A. Paul, 1962. *Handbook of small group research.* New York: Free Press.

——, and Robert Bales, 1963. Seating position and small group interaction. *Sociometry* **26**: 480–486.

Harnack, Victor, and Thorrel B. Fest, 1964. *Group discussion, theory and technique.* New York: Appleton-Century-Crofts.

Harris, Thomas A., 1967. *I'm OK—you're OK.* New York: Harper & Row.

Hart, Roderick P., and Don M. Burks, 1972. Rhetorical sensitivity and social interaction. *Speech Monographs* **39**: 75–91.

——, William F. Eadie, and Robert E. Carlson, 1975. Rhetorical sensitivity and communicative competence. Paper presented at the annual convention of the Speech Communication Association, December, Houston.

Harvey, Jerry, and C. Russell Boettger, 1971. Improving communication within a work group. *Journal of Applied Behavioral Science* **7**: 1964–79.

Harvey, O. J., and C. Consalvi, 1960. Status and conformity to pressures in informal groups. *Journal of Abnormal and Social Psychology* **60**: 182–187.

Hatvany, Nina, and Vladimir Pucik, 1981. Japanese management practices and productivity. *Organizational Dynamics,* Spring: 5–21.

Hayes, Donald, and Leo Meltzer, 1972. Interpersonal judgments based on talkativeness: fact or artifact? *Sociometry* **35**: 538–561.

"He who runs may read," 1975. *Notes and Quotes,* July–August.

Hearn, G., 1957. Leadership and the spatial factor in small groups. *Journal of Abnormal and Social Psychology* **54**: 269–272.

Heider, Fritz, 1958. *The psychology of interpersonal relations.* New York: Wiley.

Hersey, Paul, and Kenneth H. Blanchard, 1982. *Management of Organizational Behavior* (4th ed.). Englewood Cliffs, N.J.: Prentice-Hall.

Hill, Timothy, 1976. An experimental study of the relationship between opinionated leadership and small group consensus. *Communication Monographs* **43**: 246–257.

Homans, George C., 1961. *Social behavior: Its elementary forms.* New York: Harcourt.

Howell, William, and Donald Smith, 1956. *Discussion.* New York: Macmillan.

Huse, E. F., and T. G. Cummings, 1985. *Organization development and change* (3rd ed.). St. Paul, Minn.: West Publishing.

Huse, Edgar F., and James L. Bowditch, 1973. *Behavior in organizations: A systems approach to managing.* Reading, Mass.: Addison-Wesley.

Jablin, F. M., 1979. Superior-subordinate communication: The state of the art. *Psychological Bulletin* **86**: 1201–1222.

Janis, Irving, 1971. Groupthink. *Psychology Today,* November, pp. 43–46.

——, 1982. *Victims of groupthink,* 2nd ed. Boston: Houghton Mifflin.

Jennings, Helen Hall, 1950. *Leadership and isolation: a study of personality in interpersonal relations* (2nd ed.). New York: Longmans, Green.

Johnson, David W., 1972. *Reaching out: Interpersonal effectiveness and self-actualization.* Englewood Cliffs, N.J.: Prentice-Hall.

——, 1973. *Contemporary social psychology.* New York: Lippincott.

Jones, Richard P., 1981. Nude sunbathing. *Flint Journal,* September 6, p. c6.

Jourard, Sidney M., 1964. *The transparent self: Self-disclosure and well-being.* Princeton, N.J.: Van Nostrand.

Kanter, Rosabeth Moss, 1983. *The change masters: Innovation and entrepreneurship in the American corporation.* New York: Simon & Schuster.

Karrass, Chester L., 1970. *The negotiating game.* New York: T. Crowell.

Kast, Fremont E., and James E. Rosenzweig, 1970. *Organization and management: A systems approach.* New York: McGraw-Hill.

Katz, Daniel, and Robert Kahn, 1978. *The social psychology of organizations* (2nd ed.). New York: Wiley.

Kearney, William, and Desmond Martin, 1974. Sensitivity training: An established management development tool? *Academy of Management Journal* **17**: 755–760.

Keltner, John, 1970. *Interpersonal speech communication.* Belmont, Calif.: Wadsworth.

Kendon, A., 1967. Some functions of gaze-direction in social interaction. *Acta Psychologica* **26**: 22–63.

Keniston, Kenneth, 1967. The sources of student dissent. *Journal of Social Issues* **23**: 108–137.

Kepner, Charles H., and Benjamin B. Tregoe, 1965. *The rational manager: A systematic approach to problem solving and decision making.* New York: McGraw-Hill.

Kibler, Robert, and Larry Barker, 1969. *Conceptual frontiers in speech communication.* New York: Speech Association of America.

———, Larry Barker, and Donald Cegala, 1970. Effect of sex on comprehension and retention. *Speech Monographs* **37**: 287–292.

Kiesler, Charles, and Sara Kiesler, 1969. *Conformity.* Reading, Mass.: Addison-Wesley.

Kinch, John W., 1974. A formalized theory of the self-concept. In Jean Civikly (ed.), *Messages: a reader in human communication.* New York: Random House, pp. 118–126.

Kinkade, Kathryn, 1973. Commune: a Walden-two experiment. *Psychology Today.* January 6: 35–38.

Kinzel, Augustus, 1969. Toward an understanding of violence. *Attitude,* Vol. 1.

Kline, John, 1970. Indices of orientation and opinionated statements in problem-solving discussions. *Speech Monographs* **37**: 282–286.

Knapp, Mark L., 1972. *Nonverbal communication in human interaction.* New York: Holt, Rinehart and Winston.

Knutson, Thomas J., 1972. An experimental study of the effects of orientation behavior on small group consensus. *Speech Monographs* **39**: 159–165.

Korda, Michael, 1975. *Power! How to get it, how to use it.* New York: Random House.

Korzybski, Alfred, 1948. *Selections from science and sanity: An introduction to non-Aristotelian systems and general semantics.* Lakeville, Conn.: Institute of General Semantics.

Kotter, John P., 1986. *Power and influence: Beyond formal authority.* New York: Free Press.

Kreps, Gary L., 1986. *Organizational communication.* White Plains, N.Y.: Longman.

Kretch, D., R. Crutchfield, and E. Ballachey, 1962. *Individual in society.* New York: McGraw-Hill.

Kriesberg, M., 1950. Executives evaluate administrative conferences. *Advanced Management* **15**: 15–17.

Lakin, Martin, 1972. *Interpersonal encounter: Theory and practice in sensitivity training.* New York: McGraw-Hill.

Larson, Carl E., 1969. Forms of analysis and small group problem solving. *Speech Monographs* **36**: 452–455.

———, and Robert D. Gratz, 1970. Problem-solving discussion training and T-group training: an experimental comparison. *Speech Teacher* **19**: 54–57.

Lawrence, P., and D. Dyer, 1983. *Renewing American industry.* New York: Free Press.

Lawrence, Paul, and J. Lorsch, 1969. *Developing organizations: Diagnosis and action.* Reading, Mass.: Addison-Wesley.

Leary, Timothy, 1957. *Interpersonal diagnosis of personality.* New York: Ronald Press.

Leathers, Dale, 1969. Process disruption and measurement in small group communication. *Quarterly Journal of Speech* **55**: 287.

———, 1970. The process effects of trust-destroying behaviors in the small group. *Speech Monographs* **37**: 180–187.

———, 1976. *Nonverbal communication systems.* Boston: Allyn and Bacon.

Leavitt, Harold, 1951. Some effects of certain communication patterns on group performance. *Journal of Abnormal and Social Psychology* **46**: 38–50.

——, 1964. *Managerial psychology* (2nd ed.). Chicago: University of Chicago Press.

Lefkowitz, M. R. Blake, and J. Mouton, 1955. Status factors in pedestrian violation of traffic signals. *Journal of Abnormal and Social Psychology* **51**: 704–706.

——, 1938. The conceptual representation and measurement of psychological forces. *Contributions to Psychological Theory* **1**, No. 4: 62.

Lewin, Kurt, 1948. *Resolving social conflicts.* New York: Harper.

——, 1951. *Field theory in social science.* New York: Harper & Row.

——, 1953. Studies in group decision. In Dorwin Cartwright and Alvin Zander (eds.), *Group dynamics.* Evanston, Ill.: Row, Peterson.

——, Ronald Lippitt, and Ralph White, 1939. Patterns of aggressive behavior in experimentally created "social climates." *Journal of Social Psychology* **10**: 271–299.

Liddell, William W., and John W. Slocum, 1976. The effects of individual-role compatibility upon group performance: An extension of Schutz's FIRO theory. *Academy of Management Journal:* **19**: 420.

Lieberman, Morton, Irwin Yalom, and Matthew Miles, 1973. *Encounter groups: First facts.* New York: Basic Books.

——, Irvin Yalom, and Matthew Miles, 1972. The impact of encounter groups on participants: Some preliminary findings. *Journal of Applied Behavioral Science* **8**: 29–50.

Likert, Rensis, 1961. An emerging theory of organization, leadership, and management. In Luigi Petrutto and Bernard Bass (eds.), *Leadership and interpersonal behavior.* New York: Holt, Rinehart and Winston, pp. 290–309.

——, 1961. *New patterns of management.* New York: McGraw-Hill.

——, 1967. *The human organization.* New York: McGraw-Hill.

Lomranz, Jacob, Martin Lakin, and Harold Schiffman, 1972. Variants of sensitivity training and encounter: diversity or fragmentation. *Journal of Applied Behaviorial Science* **8**: 399–420.

Lowell, Jon, 1985. Saturn. *Ward's Auto World,* February, pp. 35–37.

Luchins, A. R., 1942. Mechanization in problem solving. *Psychological Monographs* **54**: No. 6 (Whole No. 248).

Lorsch, Jay, and Paul Lawrence, 1972. *Managing group and intergroup relations.* Homewood, Ill.: Irwin.

——, 1984. *Group processes: An introduction to group dynamics* (3rd ed.). Palo Alto, Calif.: National Press.

McClelland, David C., 1961. *The achieving society.* Princeton, N.J.: Van Nostrand.

—— (ed.), 1955. *Studies in motivation.* New York: Appleton-Century-Crofts.

——, J. W. Atkinson, R. A. Clark, and E. L. Lowell, 1953. *The achievement motive.* New York: Appleton-Century-Crofts.

McCormack, Mark H., 1984. *What they don't teach you at Harvard Business School.* New York: Bantam Books.

McCroskey, James, 1971. Human information processing and diffusion. In Larry Barker and Robert Kibler (eds.), *Speech communication behavior: perspectives and principles.* Englewood Cliffs, N.J.: Prentice-Hall, pp. 167–181.

——, Carl Larson, and Mark Knapp, 1971. *An introduction to interpersonal communication.* Englewood Cliffs, N.J.: Prentice-Hall.

——, and David W. Wright, 1971. The development of an instrument for measuring interaction behavior in small groups. *Speech Monographs* **38**: 335–340.

McGrath, Joseph E., and Irwin Altman, 1966. *Small group research: A synthesis and critique of the field.* New York: Holt, Rinehart and Winston.

McKeachie, W., 1952. Lipstick as a determiner of first impressions of personality: An experiment for the general psychology course. *Journal of Social Psychology* **36**: 241–244.

McLaughlin, David, and Jay Hewitt, 1972. Need for approval and perceived openness. *Journal of Experimental Research in Personality* **6**: 255–258.

Maier, Norman R. F., 1963. *Problem-solving discussions and conferences.* New York: McGraw-Hill.

———, and A. R. Solem, 1952. The contributions of a discussion leader to the quality of group thinking: The effective use of minority opinions. *Human Relations* **5**: 277–288.

Main, Jeremy, 1981. Westinghouse's cultural revolution. *Fortune,* June 15, pp. 74–93.

Malmuth, Neil M., and Seymour Feshbach, 1972. Risky shift in a naturalistic setting. *Journal of Personality* **40**: 38–49.

Markham, Steven E., Fred Dansereau, Jr., and Joseph A. Alutto, 1982. Group size and absenteeism rates: A longitudinal analysis. *Academy of Management Journal* **25**: 921–927.

Maslow, Abraham, 1970. *Motivation and personality* (2nd ed.) New York: Harper & Row.

———, and N. Mintz, 1956. Effects of esthetic surroundings: I. Initial effects of three esthetic conditions upon perceiving "energy" and "well-being" in faces. *Journal of Psychology* **41**: 247–254.

Mayo, Elton, 1933. *The human problems of an industrial civilization.* New York: Macmillan.

Mead, Margaret, 1935. *Sex and temperament in three primitive societies.* New York: Dell.

Meerloo, Joost, 1956. *The rape of the mind.* New York: Grosset and Dunlap.

Mehrabian, Albert, 1956. Significance of posture and position in the communication of attitudes and status relations. *Psychological Bulletin* **71**: 359–372.

———, 1971. Nonverbal betrayal of feeling. *Journal of Experimental Research in Personality* **5**: 64–73.

Michaelson, Larry K., 1985. Introduction to the special issue on using groups in teaching. *Organizational Behavior Teaching Review,* Fall, pp.1–2.

Mikol, Bernard, 1960. The enjoyment of new musical systems. In Milton Rokeach (ed.), *The open and closed mind.* New York: Basic Books, pp. 270–284.

Miles, Matthew B., 1965. Changes during and following laboratory training: a clinical-experimental study. *Journal of Applied Behavioral Science* **1**: 215–242.

———, 1967. *Learning to work in groups.* New York: Teacher's College Press, Columbia University.

Milgram, Stanley, 1974. *Obedience to authority: An experimental view.* New York: Harper & Row.

Miller, Gerald R., and Paula Bacon, 1971. Open and closed-mindedness and recognition of visual humor. *Journal of Communication* **21**: 150–159.

Miller, Katherine I., and Peter R. Monge, 1985. Social information and employee anxiety about organizational change. *Human Communication Research* **11**: 365–386.

Mills, Judson, and Elliot Aronson, 1965. Opinion change as a function of the communicator's attractiveness and desire to influence. *Journal of Personality and Social Psychology* **1**: 73–77.

Mills, Theodore, 1967. *The sociology of small groups.* Englewood Cliffs, N.J.: Prentice-Hall.

Mitroff, I. I., 1982. Dialectic squared: A fundamental difference is perception of the meanings of some key concepts in social science. *Decision Sciences* **13**: 222–224.

Mitroff, I. I., and R. O. Mason, 1981. The metaphysics of policy and planning: A reply to Cosier. *Academy of Management Review* **6**: 649–651.

Mohr, William L., and Harriet Mohr, 1983. *Quality circles: Changing images of people at work.* Reading, Mass.: Addison-Wesley.

Morris, Charles, and J. Richard Hackman, 1969. Behavioral correlates of perceived leadership. *Journal of Personality and Social Psychology* **13**: 350–361.

Mortenson, C. David, 1970. The status of small group research. *Quarterly Journal of Speech* **56:** 304–309.

Moseley, Ray, 1974. Soviet monkey business: Aping American execs. *Flint Journal* January 13, p. A-8.

Mossholder, Kevin W., Arthur G. Bedian, and Achilles A. Armenakis, 1982. Group process–work outcome relationships: A note on the moderating impact of self-esteem. *Academy of Management Journal* **25:** 575–585.

Mosvick, Roger, 1971. Human relations training for scientists, technicians, and engineers: A review of relevant experimental evaluations of human relations training. *Personnel Psychology* **24:** 275–292.

Murray, Henry, 1938. *Explorations in personality.* New York: Oxford University Press.

Myers, Gail E., and Michele Tolela Myers, 1973. *The dynamics of human communication.* New York: McGraw-Hill.

Nadler, E. B., 1959. Yielding, authoritarianism, and authoritarian ideology regarding groups. *Journal of Abnormal and Social Psychology* **58:** 408–410.

Naisbitt, John, 1982. *Megatrends: Ten new directions transforming our lives.* New York: Warner Books.

Newcomb, Theodore, 1943. *Personality and social change.* New York: Dryden.

———, 1963. Persistence and regression of changed attitudes: long-range studies. *Journal of Social Issues* **19:** 3–14.

Nicholas, John M., and Marsha Katz, 1985. Research methods and reporting practices in organization development: A review and some guidelines. *The Academy of Management Review* **10:** 737–749.

Nye, Robert, 1973. *Conflict among humans.* New York: Springer.

Ober, Nelson, and Fred E. Jandt, 1973. Students' self-concepts and evaluations of discussion instruction. *Speech Teacher* **22:** 64–66.

Ogden, Charles K., and I. A. Richards, 1946. *The meaning of meaning.* New York: Harcourt, Brace.

Organ, Dennis W., and Thomas Bateman, 1986. *Organizational behavior* (3rd ed.). Plano, Tex.: Business Publications, Inc.

Osborn, Alex, 1953. *Applied imagination: Principles and procedures of creative thinking.* New York: Scribner's.

Osborn, Susan M., and Gloria H. Harris, 1984. Using the small group for assertive training. In Robert S. Cathcart and Larry Samovar, *Small group communication: A reader* (4th ed.). Dubuque, Iowa: Wm. C. Brown.

Osgood, Charles, 1969. Calculated de-escalation as a strategy. In D. G. Pruitt and R. C. Synder (eds.), *Theory and research on the causes of war.* Englewood Cliffs, N.J.: Prentice-Hall, pp. 213–216.

Ouchi, William, 1981. *Theory Z: How American business can meet the Japanese challenge.* Reading, Mass.: Addison-Wesley.

Parkinson, C. Northcote, 1957. *Parkinson's law: And other studies in administration.* Boston: Houghton Mifflin.

Patton, Bobby, and Kim Giffin, 1973. *Problem-solving group interaction.* New York: Harper & Row.

———. and ———, 1981. *Interpersonal communication in action.* (3rd ed.). New York: Harper & Row.

Payne, Sam, David Summers, and Thomas Stewart, 1973. Value differences across three generations. *Sociometry* **36:** 20–30.

Penley, Larry E., and Brian Hawkins, 1985. Studying interpersonal communication in organizations: A leadership application. *Academy of Management Journal* **28:** 309–326.

Petelle, John, 1964. The role of conflict in discussion. *Speaker and Gavel* **2:** 24–28.

Pettinger, Robert, 1964. *The first five minutes.* Itasca, N.Y.: Peacock.

Pfeffer, Jeffrey, 1981. *Power in organizations.* Marshfield, Mass.: Pitman.

Pfeiffer, J. William, and John Jones, 1969. *Structured experiences for human relations training.* Iowa City: University Associates.

Phillips, J. D., 1948. Report on discussion 66. *Adult Education Journal* **7:** 181–182.

Popkey, Dan, 1986. NFL football sacks Monday meetings of Boise Council, *The Idaho Statesman,* March 1, p. 1.

Psychology Today, 1970. Del Mar, Calif.: CRM Publications.

Quinn, Robert, 1973. *Job satisfaction: Is there a trend?* Washington, D.C.: United States Department of Labor.

Rarick, David, Gary F. Soldow, and Ronald S. Geizer, 1976. Self-monitoring as a mediator of conformity. *Central States Speech Journal* **27:** 267–271.

Redding, W. C., 1972. *Communication within the organization: An interpretive review of theory and research.* New York: Industrial Communication Council.

Regula, C. Robert, and James Julian, 1973. The impact of quality and frequency of task contributions on perceived ability. *Journal of Social Psychology* **89:** 112–115.

Ringwald, Barbara, Richard Mann, Robert Rosenwein, and Wilbert McKeachie, 1971. Conflict and style in the college classroom: An intimate study. *Psychology Today,* February, pp. 45–47, 76–79.

Roberts, W. Rhys, 1941. Rhetoric. In Richard McKean (ed.). *The basic works of Aristotle.* New York: Random House, pp. 1318–1451.

Robinson, F. P., 1961. *Effective study.* New York: Harper & Row.

Roethlisberger, Fritz, and William Dickson, 1939. *Management and the worker.* Cambridge, Mass.: Harvard University Press.

Rogers, Carl R., and F. J. Roethlisberger, 1952. Barriers and gateways to communication. *Harvard Business Review* **30:** 48.

Rogers, Everett, and Dilip K. Bhowmik, 1971. Homophily-heterophily: Relational concepts for communication research. In Larry Barker and Robert Kibler (eds.), *Speech communication behavior: Perspectives and principles.* Englewood Cliffs, N.J.: Prentice-Hall, pp. 206–225.

———, and F. Floyd Shoemaker, 1971. *Communication of innovations* (2nd ed.). New York: Free Press.

Rokeach, Milton, 1948. Generalized mental rigidity as a factor in ethnocentrism. *Journal of Abnormal and Social Psychology* **43:** 259–278.

———, 1954. The nature and meaning of dogmatism. *Psychological Review* **61:** 194–204.

———, 1960. *The open and closed mind.* New York: Basic Books.

———, 1968. *Beliefs, attitudes, and values.* San Francisco: Jossey-Bass.

———, 1971. Long-range experimental modifications of values, attitudes, and behavior. In William A. Hunt (ed.), *Human behavior and its control.* Cambridge, Mass.: Schenkman, pp. 93–105.

———, 1973. *The nature of human values.* New York: Free Press.

Rosenfeld, Howard, 1965. Effect of approval-seeking induction on interpersonal proximity. *Psychological Reports* **17:** 120–122.

———, 1966. Instrumental affiliative functions of facial and gestural expressions. *Journal of Personality and Social Psychology* **4:** 65–72.

Rosenfeld, Lawrence B., and Gene D. Fowler, 1976. Personality, sex, and leadership style. *Communication Monographs* **43:** 320–324.

———, and Vickie Christie, 1974. Sex and persuasibility revisited. *Western Speech* **38**: 244–253.

———, and Kenneth Frandsen, 1972. The "other" speech student: An empirical analysis of some interpersonal relations orientations of the reticent student. *Speech Teacher* **21**: 296–302.

Ross, Edward, 1920. *The principles of sociology.* New York: Century.

Ross, Raymond, 1970. *Speech communication fundamentals and practice.* Englewood Cliffs, N.J.: Prentice-Hall.

Ruben, Brent, 1972. General system theory: an approach to human communication. In Richard Budd and Brent Ruben (eds.), *Approaches to human communication.* New York: Spartan, pp. 120–144.

———, and John Y. Kim (eds.), 1975. *General systems theory and human communication.* Rochelle Park, N.J.: Hayden.

Ruch, Richard S., 1972. An analysis of the Freudian slip and errors in speech communication. *Journal of Technical Writing and Communication* **2**: 343–352.

Ruch, Richard S., and Ronald Goodman, 1983. *Image at the top: Crisis and renaissance in corporate leadership.* New York: Free Press.

Runyan, Kenneth, 1973. Some interactions between personality variables and management styles. *Journal of Applied Psychology* **57**: 288–294.

Russo, N. F., 1967. Connotations of seating arrangements. *Cornell Journal of Social Relations* **2**: 37–44.

Sattler, William, and N. Edd Miller, 1968. *Discussion and conference.* Englewood Cliffs, N.J.: Prentice-Hall.

Schachter, Stanley, 1951. Deviation, rejection, and communication. *Journal of Abnormal and Social Psychology* **46**: 190–207.

———, Norris Ellertson, Dorothy McBride, and Doris Gregory, 1968. An experimental study of cohesiveness and productivity. In D. Cartwright and A. Zander (eds.), *Group dynamics* (3rd ed.). New York: Harper & Row, pp. 192–198.

Scheidel, Thomas, 1970. Sex and persuasibility. *Speech Monographs* **37**: 292–387.

Schein, Edgar, and Warren Bennis, 1965. *Personal and organizational change through group methods.* New York: Wiley.

Schelling, Thomas C., 1960. *The strategy of conflict.* Cambridge, Mass.: Harvard University Press.

Schneider, Frank W., and James G. Delaney, 1972. Effect of individual achievement motivation on group problem-solving efficiency. *Journal of Social Psychology* **86**: 291–298.

Schools reject longstanding medical oath, 1986. Associated Press, *The Idaho Statesman,* May 18.

Schutz, William C., 1958. *FIRO: A three-dimensional theory of interpersonal behavior.* New York: Holt, Rinehart and Winston.

———, 1967. *Joy: Expanding human awareness.* New York: Grove.

———, 1971. *Here comes everybody: Bodymind and encounter culture.* New York: Harper & Row.

Schweiger, David M., William R. Sandberg, and James W. Ragan, 1986. Group approaches for improving strategic decision making: A comparative analysis of dialectical inquiry, devil's advocacy and consensus. *Academy of Management Journal* **29**: 51–71.

Seeger, John A., 1983. No innate phases in group problem solving. *The Academy of Management Review* **8**: 683–689.

Seiler, John A., 1967. *Systems analysis in organizational behavior.* Homewood, Ill.: Irwin-Dorsey.

Sereno, Kenneth, and Edward Bodaken, 1975. *TRANS-PER: Understanding human communication.* Boston: Houghton Mifflin.

Shaw, Marjorie, 1932. A comparison of individuals and small groups in the rational solution of complex problems. *American Journal of Psychology* **44**: 491–504.

Shaw, Marvin E., 1964. Communication networks. In Leonard Berkowitz (ed.), *Advances in experimental social psychology* (Vol. 1). New York: Academic Press, pp. 111–147.

——, 1981. *Group dynamics: The psychology of small group behavior* (3rd ed.). New York: McGraw-Hill.

Sheldon, William, 1940. *The varieties of human physique.* New York: Harper & Row.

——, 1942. *The varieties of temperament.* New York: Harper & Row.

——, 1954. *Atlas of man: A guide for somatotyping the adult male of all ages.* New York: Harper & Row.

Sherif, Muzafer, 1963. *The psychology of social norms.* New York: Harper & Row.

——, Carolyn Sherif, and Roger Nebergall, 1965. *Attitude and attitude change: The social judgment-involvement approach.* Philadelphia: Saunders.

Shils, Edward, 1951. The study of the primary group. In Harold Lasswell and Daniel Lerner (eds.), *The policy science.* Stanford, Calif.: Stanford University Press, pp. 44–69.

Simmel, George, 1955. *Conflict.* Trans. K. H. Wolff. Glencoe, Ill.: Free Press.

Sims, Henry P., Jr., and James W. Dean, Jr., 1985. Beyond quality circles: Self-managing teams. *Personnel,* pp. 25–32.

Smircich, Linda, and Charles Stubbart, 1985. Strategic management in an enacted world. *The Academy of Management Review* **10**: 724–736.

Smith, David C., 1974. WAW adds its selections to '75 model name parade. *Ward's Auto World* **10**: 13.

——, 1975. The new small Seville: Cadillac's King-size gamble. *Ward's Auto World* **11**: 23–28.

——, 1985. Team Taurus: Ford's $3-billion mid-market plunge. *Ward's Auto World,* February, pp. 26–33.

Sommer, Robert, 1959. Studies in personal space. *Sociometry* **22**: 247–260.

——, 1965. Further studies of small group ecology. *Sociometry* **28**: 337–348.

——, 1969. *Personal space: The behavioral basis of design.* Englewood Cliffs, N.J.: Prentice-Hall.

South, E. B., 1927. Some psychological aspects of committee work. *Journal of Applied Psychology* **11**: 348–368, 437–464.

Stech, Ernest, and Sharon A. Ratliffe, 1985. *Effective group communication: How to get action by working in groups.* Lincolnwood, Ill.: National Text Book Company.

Stein, Carroll, 1973. Group grope: The latest development bromide. *Personnel Journal,* January, pp. 19–26.

Steiner, Ivan D., 1972. *Group process and productivity.* New York: Academic Press.

Steinmetz, Lawrence, 1969. *Managing the marginal and unsatisfactory performer.* Reading, Mass.: Addison-Wesley.

Steinzor, B., 1950. The spatial factor in face-to-face discussion groups. *Journal of Abnormal and Social Psychology* **45**: 552–555.

Stigler, G. J., 1974. Free riders and collective action: An appendix to theories of economic regulation. *Bell Journal of Economics and Management Science* **5**: 359–365.

Stogdill, Ralph, 1948. Personal factors associated with leadership. *Journal of Psychology* **25**: 35–71.

——, 1972. Group productivity. *Organizational behavior and human performance,* 8, pp. 26–43.

——, 1974. *Handbook of leadership: A survey of theory and research.* New York: Free Press.

Stoner, J. A. F., 1961. *Comparison of individual and group decisions involving risk.* Unpublished master's thesis. Massachusetts Institute of Technology, School of Industrial Management.

Streigel, Quincalee Brown, 1975. Self-reported behavioral and attitudinal changes by participation in a women's consciousness-raising group. Paper presented at the annual convention of the Central States Speech Association, April, Kansas City, Missouri.

Strodbeck, Fred, and L. H. Hook, 1961. The social dimensions of a twelve-man jury table.
Sociometry **24**: 397–415.

Strongman, K., and B. Champness, 1968. Dominance hierarchies and conflict in eye contact.
Acta Psychologica **28**: 376–386.

Symington, James W., 1971. *The stately game.* New York: Macmillan.

Tannenbaum, Robert, Irving Weschler, and Fred Massarik, 1961. *Leadership and organization:
a behavioral science approach.* New York: McGraw-Hill.

——, and Warren Schmidt, 1972. How to choose a leadership pattern. In Jay Lorsch and Paul
Lawrence (eds.), *Managing group and intergroup relations.* Homewood, Ill.: Irwin, pp. 188–
200.

Tavris, Carol, 1974. Women in China: They speak bitterness revolution. *Psychology Today,* May
7, pp. 43–49.

Teger, Allan I., and Dean G. Pruitt, 1970. Components of group risk taking. In R. Cathcart
and L. Samovar (eds.), *Small group communication: A reader.* Dubuque, Iowa: Wm. C.
Brown, pp. 72–81.

Terman, L., and C. Miles, 1936. *Sex and personality: Studies in masculinity and femininity.*
New York: McGraw-Hill.

Thayer, Lee, 1968. *Communication and communication systems.* Homewood, Ill.: Irwin.

Thelen, Herbert, and Watson Dickerman, 1949. Stereotypes and the growth of groups. *Educational Leadership* **6**: 309–316.

Thibaut, John W., and Harold H. Kelley, 1950. An experimental study of the cohesiveness of
underprivileged groups. *Human Relations* **3**: 251–278.

——, and ——, 1959. *The social psychology of groups.* New York: Wiley.

——, and ——, 1986. *The social psychology of groups* (2nd ed.). New Brunswick, N.J.: Transaction Books.

Thomas, Evan, 1986. Growing pains at 40. *Time,* May 19, pp. 22–41.

Thompson, J. D., 1967. *Organization in action.* New York: McGraw-Hill.

Tichy, Noel M., and Mary Anne Devanna, 1986. *The transformational leader.* New York: Wiley.

Time, January 19, 1976, pp. 55–56. Groupthink.

Time, July 23, 1973, pp. 31–32. The return of the gang.

Time, January 14, 1974, p. 58. The impresario of the brain.

Time, August 3, 1981, p. 32. The trust builder.

Thornton, G., 1944. The effect of wearing glasses upon judgments of personality traits of persons seen briefly. *Journal of Applied Psychology* **28**: 203–207.

Tillman, R., Jr., 1960. Problems in review: committees on trial. *Harvard Business Review* **47**:
162–172.

Tosi, Henry L., John R. Rizzo, and Stephen J. Carroll, 1986. *Managing organizational behavior.*
Marshfield, Mass.: Pitman.

Toulmin, Stephen, 1958. *The uses of argument.* Cambridge: At the University Press.

Triandis, Harry C., 1971. *Attitude and attitude change.* New York: Wiley.

Tubbs, Stewart L., 1976. The transactive nature of therapeutic communication. Paper presented at the annual convention of the Speech Communication Association, San Francisco, December.

——, 1985. Consulting teams: A methodology for teaching integrated management skills.
Organizational Behavior Teaching Review, Fall, pp. 52–57.

——, and John Baird, 1980. *Self-disclosure and interpersonal growth.* Columbus, Ohio: Special
Press.

———, and Robert M. Carter, 1977. *Shared experiences in human communication.* Rochelle Park, N.J.: Hayden.

———, and Sylvia Moss, 1974. *Human communication: An interpersonal perspective.* New York: Random House.

———, and Sylvia Moss, 1987. *Human communication: An interpersonal perspective.* (4th ed.) New York: Random House.

Tuckman, Bruce, 1965. Developmental sequence in small groups. *Psychological Bulletin* **63:** 384–399.

Tuddenham, R. D., 1961. The influence upon judgment of the apparent discrepancy between self and others. *Journal of Social Psychology* **53:** 69–79.

Underwood, W., 1965. Evaluation of laboratory method training. *Training Director's Journal* **5:** 34–40.

Unger, Mark, 1974. Unpublished behavioral science term paper. Flint, Mich.: General Motors Institute.

Valiquet, M. I., 1968. Individual change in a management development program. *Journal of Applied Behavioral Science* **4:** 313–326.

Vegetarian graduates get paper diplomas, 1986. Associated Press, *The Idaho Statesman,* May 10, p. 2.

Viscott, David, 1972. *The making of a psychiatrist.* Greenwich, Conn.: Fawcett.

Von Bertalonffy, Ludwig, 1968. *General system theory.* New York: George Braziller.

Wahlers, Kathy J., and Larry L. Barker, 1973. Bralessness and nonverbal communication. *Central States Speech Journal* **24:** 222–226.

Wallach, Michael A., Nathan Kagan, and Daryl J. Bem, 1962. Group influence on individual risk taking. *Journal of Abnormal and Social Psychology* **65:** 77.

Walker, E. L., and R. W. Heynes, 1967. *An anatomy for conformity.* Belmont, Calif.: Brooks/Cole–Wadsworth.

Walster, E., V. Aronson, D. Abrahams, and L. Rohmann, 1966. Importance of physical attractiveness in dating behavior. *Journal of Personality and Social Psychology* **4:** 508–516.

Warschaw, T., 1980. *Winning by negotiation.* New York: McGraw-Hill.

Watson, Kathleen M., 1982. An analysis of communication patterns: A method for discriminating leader and subordinate roles. *Academy of Management Journal* **25:** 107–120.

Watzlawick, Paul, Janet Beavin, and Donald Jackson, 1967. *Pragmatics of human communication.* New York: Norton.

Weaver, Richard, 1971. Sensitivity training and effective group discussion. *Speech Teacher* **20:** 203–207.

Weick, K. E., 1979. *The social psychology of organizing.* Reading, Mass.: Addison-Wesley.

Werther, William B., William A. Ruch, and Lynne McClure, 1986. *Productivity through people.* St. Paul, Minn.: West Publishing.

Whetten, David A., and Kim S. Cameron, 1984. *Developing management skills.* Glenview, Ill.: Scott, Foresman.

White, Ralph, and Ronald Lippitt, 1968. Leader behavior and member reaction in three social climates. In D. Cartwright and A. Zander (eds.), *Group dynamics* (3rd ed.). New York: Harper & Row, pp. 318–335.

Whyte, William F., 1943. *Street corner society.* Chicago: University of Chicago Press.

———, 1955. *Money and motivation.* New York: Harper, Chapter 10.

Widgery, Robin, 1974. Sex of receiver and physical attractiveness of source as determinants of initial credibility perception. *Western Speech* **38:** 13–17.

———, and Bruce Webster, 1969. The effects of physical attractiveness upon perceived initial credibility. *Michigan Speech Journal* **4:** 9–19.

———, and Stewart L. Tubbs, 1972. Machiavellianism and religiosity as determinants of attitude change in a counterattitudinal situation. Paper presented at the annual convention of the International Communication Association, April, Atlanta.

Wilmot, William, 1975. *Dyadic communication: A transactional perspective.* Reading, Mass.: Addison-Wesley.

Wilson, Paul, 1968. Perceptual distortion of height as a function of ascribed academic status. *Journal of Social Psychology* **74:** 97–102.

Wolfe, T., 1979. *The right stuff.* New York: Farrar, Straus & Giroux.

Wong, H., and W. Brown, 1923. Effects of surroundings upon mental work as measured by Yerkes' multiple choice method. *Journal of Comparative Psychology* **3:** 319–331.

Wood, Julia T., Gerald M. Phillips, and Douglas J. Pedersen, 1986. *Group discussion: A practical guide to participation and leadership.* New York: Harper & Row.

Yates, Douglas, 1985. *The politics of management.* San Francisco: Jossey-Bass.

Zajonc, Robert, 1966. *Social psychology: An experimental approach.* Belmont, Calif.: Brooks/Cole.

Zalenik, Abraham, and David Moment, 1964. *The dynamics of interpersonal behavior.* New York: Wiley.

Zander, Alvin, 1961. Resistance to change: Its analysis and prevention. In Warren Bennis, Kenneth Benne, and Robert Chin (eds.), *The planning of change.* New York: Holt, Rinehart and Winston, pp. 543–548.

Zimbardo, Philip, 1972. Pathology of imprisonment. *Society* **9:** 4–8.

INDEX

ABOUT THE AUTHOR

Stewart L. Tubbs is Dean of the College of Business and Professor of Management at Eastern Michigan University. He received his doctorate in Communication and Organizational Behavior from the University of Kansas. His master's degree in Communication and his bachelor's degree in Science are from Bowling Green State University. He has completed post-doctoral work in management at Michigan State University, the University of Michigan, and Harvard Business School.

Dr. Tubbs has also taught at General Motors Institute, and at Boise State University where he was Chairman of the Management Department and later Associate Dean of the College of Business.

He has been named an Outstanding Teacher three times, has consulted extensively for Fortune 500 companies, and is Chairman of the Organizational Communication division of the Academy of Management. Dr. Tubbs is the co-author, with Sylvia Moss, of *Interpersonal Communication* and *Human Communication*. He is also listed in *American Men and Women of Science, Contemporary Authors, Directory of American Scholars*, the *International Who's Who in Education*, and *Outstanding Young Men of America*.